# למען תספר

**A Journal of *Divrei Torah***
**in honor of Pesach 5782**

***Compiled by the Members of the***

***Bais Medrash of Ranchleigh***

A project of the
**Zichron Yaakov Eliyahu Fund**
of the Bais Medrash of Ranchleigh

6618 Deancroft Rd
Baltimore, MD 21209



**For your convenience, this *Kuntress* along with other Torah works and Shiurim associated with the Zichron Yaakov Eliyahu Fund are available online for free download at www.zichronyaakoveliyahu.org**

**We all know** that time seems to be rushing by us. The weeks, months and years seem to be fleeting, and as my mother often says, “the older you get, the faster it goes”! I think that one of the contributors to this phenomenon is that the moment the last flame flickers away on *Zos Chanukah,* Rabbi Naiman begins his efforts in bringing this *kuntress* to the *kehillah* in time for Pesach. It demonstrates the diligence and dedication that Rabbi Naiman invests in this project, which spices the Seder tables and Pesach season with illuminative *Divrei Torah.* I therefore feel most privileged to have been asked to sponsor the *kuntress* for this year.

In the spirit of *Lemaan tesapeir b'aznei binchah u'ven binchah,* I would like to dedicate the volume and learning to all our grandchildren that Hashem has blessed us with. May we all see *nachas* from all our children and grandchildren. I would also like to express appreciation to Rabbi Naiman for all he does for Klal Yisrael and the Ranchleigh community. Huge shoutout to my special *mechutanim,* Moshe and Lisa Rock, for the special love and attention they show to our children and grandchildren.

One of the questions on this *pasuk* of *lemaan tesapeir* is what is the significance of telling the Pesach narrative “in the ears” of our children? Will we be directing our words to another body part other than their ears?

Rav Avraham Schorr, *shlit"a,* relates in his Haggadah that one of the severe impacts and results of the *galus Mitzrayim* was losing our ability to hear deeply, to grasp, contemplate, reflect, and absorb messages. This was Moshe's challenge when he first came to *Bnei Yisrael* and told them the great news of their redemption — of becoming Hashem's people. Moshe was greatly disappointed. The nation was unable to hear the message *mi'kotzer ruach u'mei'avodah kashah.* They simply did not have the wherewithal to listen and absorb Torah. It was an *orlas ha'ozen,* a metaphysical covering of the ear. While the sound was heard, the message was lost and could not enter the heart.

Rav Schorr brings a *Chasam Sofer* that points out that the letters prior to the ones in the word אזן, *ears,* are מות, *death.* This clearly implies that an inability for the heart to comprehend the messages of *geulah,* Torah, and *mussar* are akin to a spiritual malaise. This is why the *Targum Onkelos* translates *shemiyah*/listening as "accepting and absorbing." This was the *galus* of Mitzrayim. And the *geulah* from this exile was the ability to hear, listen deeply, and absorb. The method of reliving our release from *galus Mitzrayim* is by us telling over and our children leaning over, listening and contemplating. This is the gift and responsibility of Seder night, as we gather our children and grandchildren, young and old, and celebrate our freedom by enriching them *b'aznei bincha* the eternal message of our people being passed from generation to generation.

May we all experience and feel and true *zman cheiruseinu* by being able to express the words, lessons, and deep meanings of the Haggadah to our receptive and listening children, and *iy"H,* soon merit to offer the *korban pesach* in Yerushalayim!

Moshe and Sara Lea Dear

# Preface

You hold in your hands our eleventh Pesach *kuntress,* the work of the members of our *chashuveh kehillah, bs"d.* To get a picture of what we have accomplished, take a look in this issue at the cumulative 10-year Table of Contents, created by R' Yehoshua Dixler. (All of our editions are available as a free-download at zichronyaakoveliyahu.org.)

We have hopefully emerged from the *mageifah* in which we were engulfed last year. But unfortunately, I am afraid that as a nation we have not emerged unscathed, besides the obvious losses, *r"l,* here, and in the entire Jewish world – including the yeshivah world.

Let me explain. The famous Mishnah at the end of *Sotah* presents various signs of the coming of Mashiach. Many of us have experienced some of the first signs mentioned there: חוּצְפָּא יִסְגֵּא, *chutzpah* will increase (no comment necessary), and יוֹקֶר יַאֲמִיר, costs will soar (remember the double-digit inflation in the 70's?). But later in the Mishnah we find: הָאֱמֶת תְּהֵא נֶעְדֶּרֶת, *truth will be absent.*

I think this is the stage that we now unfortunately witness. We all know, and even expect, that many men running for political office on either side of the aisle will do whatever they can to keep their jobs. If they will not succeed through their past performance, they will resort to lies, or what has now been termed "alternative truths." We have always known to take their statements with a grain of salt, the same way we react to someone trying to sell us the Brooklyn Bridge. What has changed as a result of the *mageifah* is that sources we would and should usually trust as conveying accurate information have become the very mouthpieces of the worst type of falsehood. It is so sad that our so-called *frum* magazines and blogs have spread falsehoods that have caused harm to many of our *mishpachos.*

Without getting into details that might be termed "political," I will just present one example. Until now, when we had a health issue, we knew that Hashem gave permission to a *rofei* to advise us, while recognizing that true *refuah* comes from Hashem. But somehow some of our *"frum"* advisors in the magazines and blogs have tried to sell us the *sheker* that we should accept *their* research when it comes to a *mageifah.* Our personal doctor is suddenly not *ne'eman* to tell us whether or not a certain type of *refuah* might be helpful to us. And when we read their "research," what do we find? One of our media advisors headlines that the government telling people to get a certain recommended *refuah* is like the Gestapo dispensing their "medicines." How can he profane the memory of our *Kedoshim*! Why isn't this "advisor" banned from any Jewish home? (I will repeat that there could be very legitimate reasons for someone's personal doctor to give specific advice to an individual; I am addressing the shrill words of some of our *"frum"* media advisors who claim to know more than our personal physicians.)

The *sheker* of these advisors, in addition to the other *shekarim* they promulgate, has *r"l* resulted in chasms in our society. People who used to be friends no longer want to associate with one another. At the Agudah Convention this year, HaRav Aharon Lopiansky, *shlit"a* explained the *matzav* in his usual perceptive manner. It used to be that we recognized that we were in *galus.* We would look at the two sides of the political spectrum and decide which was the better option for us as Torah Jews at that time. But when we become emotionally involved in one political side or the other, we are becoming part of the *galus,* rather than trying to escape its vicissitudes. And, yes, this emotional involvement has sadly led to *sinas chinam* among us. For example (my own), if someone prefers to daven at one shul because he likes the cholent, and someone else at another because of the *derashah,* they can still be close friends. But if they each become emotionally invested in their shul as being the only valid place to be a Torah Jew, they will not have any common ground. This is what has unfortunately occurred to some of us who have become emotionally involved in the politics of our host country in *galus.*

With the *sheker* of *galus* attacking us from all sides of the aisle, we must escape into the *emes* of our *Torah HaKedoshah.* We have once again collected beautiful thoughts from our Rabbeim, members, and friends that will help us connect with true reality. We have added a new genre of articles in our Memoriam section this year — the stories of two "ordinary" people from Europe who helped create our Torah community in Baltimore in very different ways. I hope this will be a catalyst for others to contribute stories of their ancestors in coming issues.

I will close with a thank you to the members of the *maareches* who were again indispensable in producing this work: R' Chaim Sugar, R' Moshe Rock, and R' Arkady Pogostkin. A very special thank you to Rabbi and Mrs. Moshe Dear, who once again dedicated our *Kuntress Lemaan Tesapeir.* And to clarify, R' Moshe contacted me before I even had a chance to ask him if he would be our dedicator. Also, thank you to R' Avi Dear for producing another beautiful cover despite his tremendously busy schedule. May the Torah learning the Dears have engendered be a *zechus* for their entire family.

A final thank you is due to my *eishess chayil,* the *Rebbetzin,* who once again allowed me to spend time away from my family duties to work on this *kuntress* and also offered her talents to enhance it, including her words that grace the pages that follow.

Each year I express the wish that we be *zocheh* to produce another *kuntress* next year, in Eretz Yisrael, with the coming of the *Mashiach.* We have produced another *kuntress,* but sadly we are still in *galus* as of this writing. May we be speedily redeemed with the *geulah sheleimah, bimheirah biyameinu, amen.*

Abba Zvi Naiman
Adar HaRishon 5782

## Words from the Rebbetzin: Redemption in the Winter[1]

It is freezing out, yet we read about the roots of Pesach. The world seems still – frozen in its tracks, but we read the *parshayos* of *geulah*. Why? What's going on? There must be a reason here; after all, the *parshayos* always coincide with the potential of that time of year. For example, we know that the *parshayos* of purification from *Vayikra* are *lained* as we prepare ourselves for *Kabbalos HaTorah* on Shavuos. So again, why read about Pesach in the winter?

The answer lies in that key term above – roots. These frozen weeks where we do not see any visible change in the realm of nature are the roots of the redemption; they are the most appropriate weeks for *geulah*. After all, The *Ribono Shel Olam* did not forget about us and pull us out of Mitzrayim at the last minute when He remembered us there at the 49th level of *tumah*; no, it was precisely the right moment. No. The Torah is not a history book reporting one-time events of the past but a guide for our lives filled with eternal relevance. Therefore, these are the weeks of *geulah* here and now. It behooves us to hear their messages, for the time to act is now. The time period redolent of *geulah* is these very weeks, the weeks of Shevat, when spring is actually sprouting under the frozen earth, as the works of the *Nesivos Shalom* explain.

First, we have to understand what *galus Mitzrayim* was. The slavery in Egypt was unique in our history: only in Mitzrayim were both our bodies and our souls enslaved. We are taught that this slavery was likened to "a calf in its mother's womb"; in other words, we were surrounded by idolatry and vice to the point that it was our "milk," our "air," our environment. In this environment the enslaver distances the Jew from Hashem. A Jew can withstand all trials, but to feel himself flung to the garbage heaps, rejected because he incorrectly surmises that he is no longer worthy of Hashem's care because he has sunk to the 49th level of immorality as a result of the tremendous struggle to feel Hashem's presence in the "womb" of Egypt – this is the worst pain. This distance is *galus*; *galus* is exile from Hashem. We will see later that this desire for closeness and pain about the distance is precisely the redeeming power of *galus*.

The key to redemption from this slavery is found in the commandment of remembering that Hashem took us out of Egypt in this *Parashas Bo*. First, let's consider what is to be learned from Moshe Rabbeinu as the paradigmatic redeemer. We all know that Moshe was the most humble person to have ever lived. *Nesivos Shalom* applies this trait to each of us as we struggle to climb out of our personal exile from the Ribono Shel Olam by saying that it is our humility that will be the key to *geulah*. As we recognize that we are like a small candle flame compared to a blazing torch, we will recognize our futility in contrast to Hashem's

---

[1] Reprinted with permission from WIT Baltimore.

power. And yet we are not to remain frozen in this knowledge, for Hashem wants us to know with absolute clearness of faith that we have the potential to connect to him in a way that can never be broken.

Our unbreakable covenant with Hashem is taught through these richly-detailed *parshayos* related in rich detail to demand their application to our lives. First, we learn an essential principle from the fact that Hashem declares us His "child, [his] firstborn son" when we are sunk in almost the lowest level of Egyptian depravity. Hashem saw us as worthwhile – but we did not – as Moshe's concern that the people would not believe he was sent to take them out reflects. Therefore, we are enjoined to believe in ourselves. In other words, the rope or lifeline, so to speak, to save ourselves from drowning in the delusions of feeling utter distance from Hashem is to believe in ourselves – to believe in us like Hashem has always believed in us.

These obstacles are presented to us in the *parsha* through the essential detail that Hashem himself took us out of Egypt through *makkas bechoros,* which took place in the middle of the night. This plague took place at the darkest time of night, which is also the time of night closest to dawn. It was exactly at this time that Hashem desired to show us and the Egyptians just who we were to Him because, as *Nesivos Shalom* explains, when a light is lit in the great darkness of struggle and pain, or from within the lethargy of superficiality, it has a great power, a tremendous spiritual power, that brings a person to a transformative stage of spiritual awareness and a nation to a transformative stage in history. We do not need to fear that great light to which we in comparison are but a dim flame, for, ironically, in focusing on Hashem's greatness and our weakness, our humility provides us a lasting reality.

So we see again that the **power** of Moshe Rabbeinu's humility appears to provide us with the prescription for *geulah.* The experience of Mitzrayim had dulled our spiritual dynamic, and it was only the restoration of this awareness that was needed for *Klal Yisrael* to be redeemed. In conclusion, in killing the power of *tumah* represented by the Egyptian firstborn – be that in the Egyptian people or that which we had imbibed in the Egyptian womb – we became Hashem's sanctified firstborn forever. And for us today, in knowing our potential and Hashem's unconditional love for us, we find our way to *geulah.*

This is a gift that, in these very weeks when we lain these *parshayos*, we can access for ourselves both personally and nationally. We are commanded to remember leaving Mitzrayim because we **can** leave Mitzrayim. We just have to remember who we are. We need to remember this in the dark times of night when we certainly yearn for the redemption as well as in the days when we seem satisfied with life. And in the commandment to remember that we must leave Egypt in the good times –the days – we find the last profound tool that the *Nesivos Shalom* hands to us to redeem ourselves, especially during these weeks.

We began with nature imagery: where is the redemption in the dead of winter? *Nesivos Shalom* answers with the image of "the seed of life." Imagine planting an apple seed. You will see it peek forth from the ground as a soft green shoot in the spring, but by that time the main work of growth is complete. Actually, it was in the winter that the apple seed you planted opened up under the earth slowly, so slowly that it almost disintegrated. Only when its two sides that had fallen open were almost to the point of separating did the tiny seed of life in the center take root and begin to grow upward. So too, only when we were almost at the 50th level of *tumah,* when we were at the darkest point of night, so to speak, were we near the dawn. No, Hashem had not forgotten us and then remembered us at the last minute before we drowned in the sewers of Mitzrayim: it was precisely the right time. Our matzos, described in this *parsha* as wrapped in our clothes on our heads because there was no time to bake them, were no accident. This is another aspect of the emunah that redeemed us and will redeem us: we need to know that Hashem makes no mistakes. Everything he does is at precisely the right time, for, as we said above, the flame lit from within the darkness has a unique, tremendous power to forge a new spiritual identity. Therefore, the *galus* – the time of challenge, winter, darkness – is precisely the soil to grow redemption, to "*mazmiach Yeshuah."* The *galus* is where the *geulah* takes root.

For the individual, *Nesivos Shalom* states clearly, the seed of life is the dissatisfaction with one's *galus* situation. When the days seem "good," we still need to remember we have to leave Mitzrayim. We can never be satisfied with the pareve, the superficial, or any other form of distance from Hashem. The register of frustration, longing, or unhappiness is the catalyst that pushes that tiny seed upward at the crucial moment to redeem us. In another sense, it is the seed itself. The challenge of *galus*, then, in order for it to "grow" *geulah,* is to resist its quality of dulling one's spiritual senses. This can only be accomplished through humility, by turning to the Ribono Shel Olam in tefillah from whatever place we find ourselves, knowing He is always there for us and loving us as his firstborn son.

I found all these points in an account that Ilene Bloch-Levy writes on aish.com in an article called "Coming Home from Gaza." Here she describes driving her soldier-son home as he returned from this recent war. He tells his mother:

Ima, I'm tired now, but I have to tell you how extraordinary this nation is. The children who wrote us, the people who sent their good wishes with their packages of food … the soldiers I served with, each caring deeply about the other one… But mostly, mostly, this was a war that was guided by the hand of Hashem. Every day we felt His presence – whether deciding to enter a building by smashing down the back wall rather than entering through the front door, only to discover a tunnel under a bed we had lifted where tens of Hamas terrorists were hiding in the hopes of kidnapping one of us, or dozens more stories.

I looked at this child's face and saw the extraordinary young man he had become. Filled with faith. Feeling a passion for those values that have held this nation together for thousands of years. And, his very presence. His very modesty. His deep-felt pride at being part of this nation. All of this wrapped around my heart and left me humbled.

Humbled and grateful.

And I will lift up my eyes unto the mountains, from where my strength will come.

We are living in times pregnant with the birth of *geulah.* These weeks, the Torah teaches us, are the weeks with the power to bring the *geulah.* Let's use the time wisely, with humility, gratitude, and compassion to pull ourselves out with the Ribono Shel Olam's presence guiding us; may we leave our personal stumbling blocks we have allowed to separate ourselves from our Creator, as at the same time, our nation rediscovers its potential.

The seed has been planted. It is the season of the *geulah, b'ezras Hashem.*

Rochel Naiman
Adar HaRishon 5782

# *Table of Contents*

## SECTION III *GEULAS MITZRAYIM* AND OTHER MIRACLES



## SECTION IV: THE SEDER

## SECTION V: *Kerias Yam Suf* through Shavuos



## SECTION VI: TEFILLAH



## SECTION VII: BAR MITZVAH *DIVREI TORAH*



## SECTION VIII: IN MEMORIAM

## CONSOLIDATED TABLE OF CONTENTS 5772-5781

Compiled by Yehoshua Dixler

## חלק ט: מדור לשון הקדש

# Crumbling Foundations [1]

## HaRav Aharon Lopiansky

*A building should ultimately be judged not by its height or dimensions, but by its structural integrity*

Over two millennia ago, a magnificent building stood on a mount in Judea. The building was impressive and splendid and admired by all.

All, that is, except for Chazal.

When Nevuchadnetzar destroyed the Beis HaMikdash and boasted that he had "bested" HaKadosh baruch Hu, a voice said in response, "You have ground into flour that which was already flour" (*Midrash Rabbah Shir Hashirim* 3:4). Meaning, the Beis HaMikdash was already rotten and destroyed from within because of our sins; all that Nevuchadnetzar accomplished was to bring this state of spiritual decay into plain view.

This is an incredible description of a state of affairs whose reality was so different from its appearance. *"Man sees with his eyes, while Hashem probes the heart"* (*I Shmuel* 12:7).

In the last few months, *Klal Yisrael* has been centrally involved in three devastating structural crashes: on Lag B'omer in Meron, on Shavuos in Karlin, and right before Shivah Asar B'Tammuz in Surfside. Each of the many resulting *petiros* is an enormous tragedy

---

[1] We introduce this year's edition of *Kuntress Lemaan Tesapeir* with the always-timely and profound words of HaRav Lopiansky, *shlit"a,* who has allowed us to convey his *daas Torah* regarding the events of the past year. Printed with permission by Mishpacha Magazine, www.mishpacha.com, where this was originally featured in Issue 869. 

beyond words. And the resulting horrific injuries and trauma are, of course, yet additional layers to the tragedies. This article intends to speak only to the experience of our *tzibbur's* tragedy – as *Klal Yisrael* – and not to the individuals who were, *Rachmana litzlan,* directly involved in the disasters.

We do not know the "why" of these tragedies, nor is that the salient point. Rather, we need to internalize the "what." That "what" is that no matter its appearance, a building should ultimately be judged not by its height or its dimensions, but by its structural integrity. For if a building is not sound, then not only is its height not impressive, but every additional story actually increases the danger of collapse, and the danger to its occupants.

The Mishnah (*Avos* 3:17) likens a person whose knowledge exceeds his deeds to a tree whose branches are more numerous than its roots. The *baalei mussar* explain that this does not mean merely that the roots cannot adequately support the tree. Rather, it means that the more branches there are, the more likely that the tree collapses! It is the lopsided ratio of branches to roots that causes disaster.

Eastern Europe in the 1800s looked religiously impressive. Mitzvah observance was the norm, communities obeyed their Rabbanim, *chassidish* courts were booming, Volozhin was an incredible makom Torah, and there were many "kloizen," small *batei medrash* where *talmidei chachamim* sat and learned Torah, without any formal yeshivah structure. A look at the face of it would bring a smile to any Torah Yid.

But there was a person who could see a bit closer "to the heart," and he was greatly troubled. Reb Yisrael Salanter sensed that the foundations of European Jewry had crumbled, with nothing done to shore them up.

Most Rabbanim of the era rebuked people for *aveiros* committed; Reb Yisrael, however, does not speak of specific *aveiros.* Instead, he bemoans a lack of tangible *yirah.* In his famous letter about Elul, he points out the lack of emotional awe, and he in fact dedicated his life to try and rectify that. He understood that a hollowness had gnawed its way into the heart of *Klal Yisrael,* and unless that bedrock of *yirah* was greatly reinforced, it would all come crashing down.

Many Rabbanim opposed him. They felt that an investment of time, money, and resources into reinforcing the foundations would come with the price of a shorter, less beautiful building. Reb Yisrael did not contest that argument per se, but he maintained his point: if you erect a tall building on foundations that can't support it, you're inviting destruction.

His point was not only about foundations. You can have a rock-hard foundation, but if you do not keep adding columns to provide additional foundation for each added floor, then you are simply moving the danger zone a bit higher up. This project, Reb Yisroel postulated, is the work of a lifetime.

Unfortunately, Reb Yisrael Salanter was proven right. He passed away in 1883. And by the time World War I was over, 35 years later, Europe's Torah Yiddishkeit had crumbled. Yes, the Haskalah was to blame, secular Zionism was to blame, Socialism was to blame, World War I was to blame.

But the Mishnah in *Avos* says otherwise. It says that if the roots are numerous enough, then all the winds cannot uproot the tree! If the tree was in fact uprooted, we need to ask ourselves why the roots weren't up to the task. We have little control over the "winds" that buffet us; but we do have the ability to strengthen the roots.

In the last half-century or so, HaKadosh baruch Hu has put up the edifice of the post-Holocaust Torah community with breakneck speed. When I was growing up in the '50s and '60s, the question was which Orthodox shul would be the next to go Conservative. In yeshivos the question was which kids would remain frum; the idea of a secular Jew becoming frum was almost unheard of. The number of people sitting in kollel in all of America back then could probably not fill the main beis medrash of a big yeshivah today.

And here we are. HaKadosh baruch Hu wrought a miracle; big people invested incredible *mesirus nefesh;* and we rub our eyes in astonishment.

But Rav Yochanan (*Gittin* 55b) admonishes us concerning the Churban: *"Fortunate is the person who is constantly apprehensive"* (*Mishlei* 28:14). He points out some seemingly "minor" events — cracks on the walls here and there — that were the beginning of the end.

When we look at the incredible amount of *lomdei Torah, kein yirbu,* and the magnificent *batei medrash* of today, we should be grateful to Hashem and feel admiration and appreciation of those who built Torah with such *mesirus nefesh.* But we should become apprehensive, as well. Here and there, there are cracks, unusual sounds, and tremors. Is that simply a flaking of paint? A creak of a well-worn – but structurally sound – floor? Or... is it something more troubling?

Several years ago, the Hebrew-language edition of Yated Neeman published excerpts of a conversation that had been conducted during Rav Shach's lifetime, in which he expressed this sense of foreboding:

*Russia once had a very strong Jewish community. There were strong lay leaders, schools, yeshivos. There were many talmidei chachamim and gedolim. Every shul had many shiurim in the morning and at night. You have no idea how a pre-World War I Jew looked, suffused with Torah and yiras Shamayim. What has happened? I am fearful... I remember sitting with my uncle Rav Isser Zalman, learning in a shtibel. I, on the second floor of a building. Jews, who until yesterday had prayed with us, had become our persecutors. They were there to persecute us for studying Torah. We had to jump from the second floor in order to escape.*

*Did you ever think, how did the Haskalah in Europe succeed in toppling so many households like a stack of cards? The Jews are such a stiff-necked people, yet they were devastated overnight! How did this happen?*

*I'll tell you. There were indeed Jewish homes with Judaism; but it was a Judaism of habit, practice by rote. Jews who observed the mitzvos, but without a soul!*

*Yiddishkeit is so beautiful, so rich. The life of an observant Jew is a life of song, a song that is both pleasant and uplifting.*

*And yet this had become a Judaism of rote, with no sense of being uplifted, no Divine spirit. And these houses collapsed overnight. And we must begin the slow and painful process of reconstruction.*

The more important question for us is, are we building our children with solidity? When we choose a yeshivah for our children, do we note only how "tall" they'll grow in this or that place, or do we take a deeper look at how solid a Torah persona and foundation they will form? There is an expression in Yiddish that describes this concept:

"*a geboyter bochur*" — literally, a "built-up young man." It describes someone who wasn't merely left to grow tall, but whose every floor was meticulously laid.

This is true not only of *yiras Hashem* and *ahavas Hashem* but of Torah learning itself. The crown of learning is the *lomdus.* At times, one feels that today's yeshivah bochur has a solid command of the "facts on the ground," and the *lomdus* is indeed the crown that rises atop his mastery of those facts. But sometimes a bochur will be very involved in *lomdus* even as his knowledge of the Gemara and Rishonim remains a bit vague. A learning experience of that nature may be very exciting and engrossing for the young man, but inevitably the hollowness gets to him, and the desire for learning evaporates.

When we speak of laying an appropriate foundation, we often make the common mistake of focusing on the young, cheder-age children. And sure enough these wonderful, angelic-looking children sing "Hashem is One" and recount beautiful *sippurei tzaddikim.* But the strongest bedrock cannot support tall buildings on its own, unless the foundation is extended through columns as the building is built up.

This means that at each stage of a person's development, one must keep extending the foundations in a way that is appropriate for that age and child. The mussar must engage, inspire, and enlighten each according to his age and temperament.

There are many different yeshivos and approaches. It is our responsibility as parents to find the yeshivah appropriate for building those structural columns within our children.

There is one more factor in any discussion of structural strength, and that is corrosion. No matter how well-structured the building, corrosion is a process that starts at the very first moment of its construction, and it does not stop until everything has disintegrated. Yochanan was a Kohen Gadol for 80 years — at which age he became a Tzidduki (*Berachos* 29a)!

How do we deal with corrosion? We can minimize it by building in areas not so susceptible to corrosion, and we can paint our structures and apply chemicals that will resist corrosion, but the process itself cannot be stopped. The only solution is to keep inserting new supports, knowing that the old ones will fade at some point. Similarly, Reb Yisrael Salanter did not aim his mussar only at yeshivah bochurim; he aimed it at fully grown talmidei chachamim and *yirei Shamayim*.

There are many different support systems for buildings. Each one is suitable for a different type of building, or a different environment; all are an equally valid way of accomplishing the same goal. Reb Yisrael had a very specific method to achieve "structural integrity." Different branches of the mussar movement interpreted it somewhat differently. Chassidus offered a multitude of approaches in order to achieve the same goal. All are equally valid and are suited for specific personalities. The only thing unpardonable is neglect and apathy.

For as the Navi warned us, *"Fortunate is the person who is ever apprehensive!"*

# Plumbing [in] the Depths of the Temple

## How They Cleaned the *Azarah* Floor on Erev Pesach[1]

Rabbi Yoav Elan

> *The procedure of the Korban Pesach was identical whether performed on a weekday or on Shabbos, except that [on Shabbos] the Kohanim would rinse the floor of the Azarah against the will of the Sages.*
>
> *Mishnah, Pesachim 64a*

### The Water System of the Beis HaMikdash

The Beis HaMikdash had a robust plumbing system that supplied water to many different locations throughout the complex. This water was used for a variety of purposes, including ritual purity, drinking, and washing. From the Talmudic sources and commentators, we can identify the following components of this system:

A. Mikveh in the Chamber of *Metzoraim* (*Tosefta Negaim* 8:9). A person who had contracted *tzaraas* would undergo a purification process that concluded in the Beis HaMikdash. At one point the *metzora* was required to immerse, and would do so in a mikveh built for this purpose within the Chamber of *Metzoraim* located in the northwestern corner of the *Ezras Nashim* [Women's Courtyard].

B. Well, or cistern, within the Chamber of the *Gooleh* (*Middos* 5:4). The Chamber of the *Gooleh* [Basin] was located in the northeastern

[1] Editor's note: This article is adapted from the author's blog post on this topic and from his book *The Original Second Temple* (Feldheim, 2020). For more information about the Beis HaMikdash and the book, please visit BeisHamikdashTopics.com.

corner of the *Azarah*. Inside this chamber was the opening to a cistern that provided clean drinking water for the needs of the Kohanim in the Beis HaMikdash.

C. Mikveh above the Chamber of Parvah (*Middos* 5:3). The Chamber of Parvah (named for the person who designed it), located in the southeastern corner of the *Azarah*, was where the Kohanim would tan the hides of the sacrificial animals. On the roof of the chamber was a mikveh used by the Kohen Gadol on Yom Kippur.

D. Channel of flowing water (*Middos* 3:2). Starting near the southwestern corner of the *Mizbei'ach* and running due south was a channel of flowing water in the floor of the *Azarah* called the *Amah* (since it was one *amah* wide). The water that flowed through the *Amah* was used for a variety of purposes, such as washing clothing, immersing vessels, and as a place to sweep hot coals that had spilled onto the floor. For safety purposes the *Amah* was normally kept covered but these covers could be removed as needed.

E. Mikveh above the Water Gate (*Yoma* 31a). One of the major gates on the southern side of the *Azarah* was the Water Gate. It took its name from the fact that on *Succos* the *nisuch hamayim* [water libation] was brought in through this gate. Above the gate was a mikveh used by the Kohen Gadol on Yom Kippur.

F. Pit for the *Kiyor* (*Yoma* 37a). The *Kiyor* was a copper vessel that held the water used by the Kohanim to sanctify their hands and feet in preparation for the *avodah*. For halachic reasons, the *Kiyor* was lowered into a pit of water each night and then raised out of the pit the next morning.

G. Place of Drainage Water (*Middos* 4:7). This was a large pool located on the southern side of the *Heichal* Building. Rainwater that drained off the roofs of the *Heichal* collected here.

H. Mikveh for the Kohanim located beneath the Beis HaMikdash (*Middos* 1:6). [Not shown since its exact location is unknown.] The Kohanim who had been sleeping in the *Beis HaMoked* [Hall of the Fire] would immerse here prior to beginning the *avodah* each morning. Additionally, should any Kohen sleeping in *Beis HaMoked* became *tamei* during the night he would go down to this mikveh and immerse. See diagram.

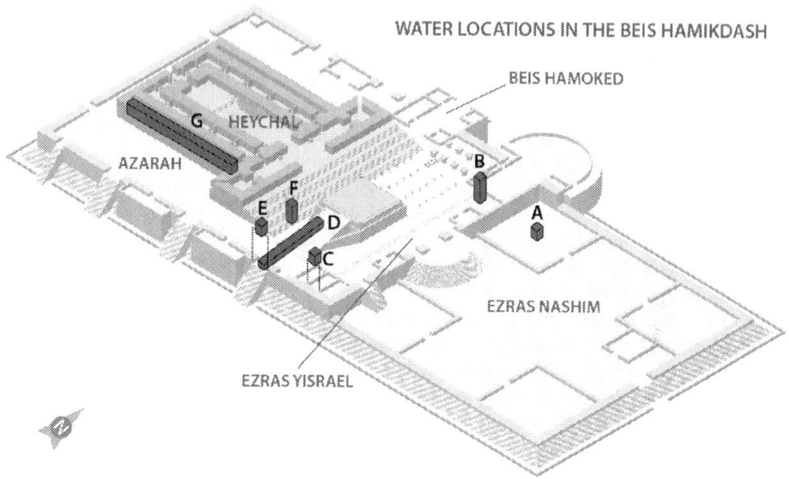


The sources further indicate that many of these locations all received their water from the same place:

• The mikveh above the Water Gate (*Yoma* 31a) as well as the mikveh above the Chamber of Parvah (*Meiri* ad loc.) were both filled from the Eitam Spring, a natural source of water located outside of Jerusalem.

• The channel of flowing water was also fed by the Eitam Spring (see *Tiferes Yisrael* to *Middos* 2:6 §75 and his *Beis HaMikdash Diagram* §33).

• The pit for the *Kiyor* was filled with water from a spring (*Rashi* to *Zevachim* 20a).

• The Place of Drainage Water was connected to the channel of water (*Chanukas Habayis*).

Based on this information we can conjecture that the water system may have worked as follows: Water from the Eitam Spring entered the *Har HaBayis* from the west and was directed beneath the *Kodesh HaKodashim* (see *Tiferes Yisrael* loc. cit.). From there it entered the Place of Drainage Water (G) and flowed east, through the *Kiyor* pit (F), into the channel of water (D) that began near the southwestern corner of the *Mizbei'ach*. This channel ran south, out the Water Gate, and near the gate some of the water was diverted up to the mikveh above the gate (E) as well as to the mikveh above the Chamber of Parvah (C). See diagram.

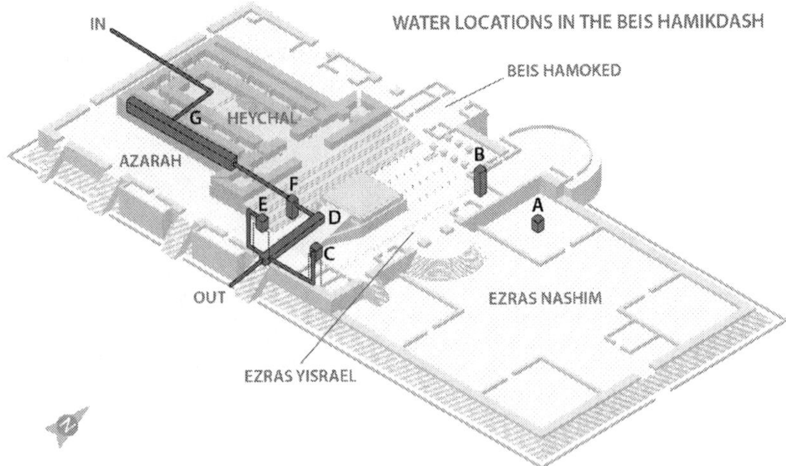


I have not seen any sources indicating that this water system also connected to the mikveh in the Chamber of *Metzoraim* or to the mikveh beneath the Beis HaMikdash used by the Kohanim, although it does seem logical to have all these mikvaos connected and fed by the same source. We do know that the well, or cistern, in the Chamber of the *Gooleh* was *not* connected to this water system since the water in that chamber was clean and sweet and more suitable for drinking, as opposed to the water found elsewhere in the Beis HaMikdash.

**The Eitam Spring and Siphons**

The water that fed the system described above came from a spring called Eitam located outside Jerusalem. This spring was at an elevation of approximately 23 *amos* above the floor of the *Azarah* and the water was directed through pipes that ran beneath the floor of the Beis HaMikdash and then up to the two elevated mikvaos using the concept of a siphon.

A siphon is used to move water against the pull of gravity, often for the purpose of transporting it over some barrier (such as a wall that cannot be breached). One end of a pipe is inserted into the water and the other end is placed on the other side of the barrier, arranged in such a manner that the open end of the pipe is lower than the end inside the water. Suction is temporarily applied to the open end of the pipe to start the flow of water. Once the water is moving through the pipe the suction can be removed, and — thanks to Hashem's beautiful system of fluid dynamics — the flow of water will continue up and over the barrier and out the lower end of the pipe with no further intervention.

Just as a siphon can move water up and over a barrier, it can also move water into, and then out of, a valley. When the water flows down and then up it is called an inverted siphon. See diagram.

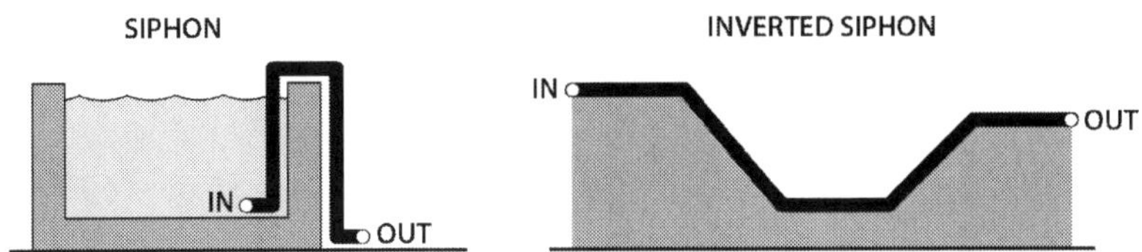


The Beis HaMikdash used an inverted siphon system. Aqueducts carried the water from the Eitam Spring to *Har Habayis* and from there it entered into a system of underground lead pipes and clay pipes mounted in niches along the walls. First the water traveled under the *Heichal* Building and *Azarah* floor and then it flowed up to the two elevated mikvaos above the Water Gate and Parvah Chamber. See diagram (only the Water Gate mikveh is shown in this diagram).

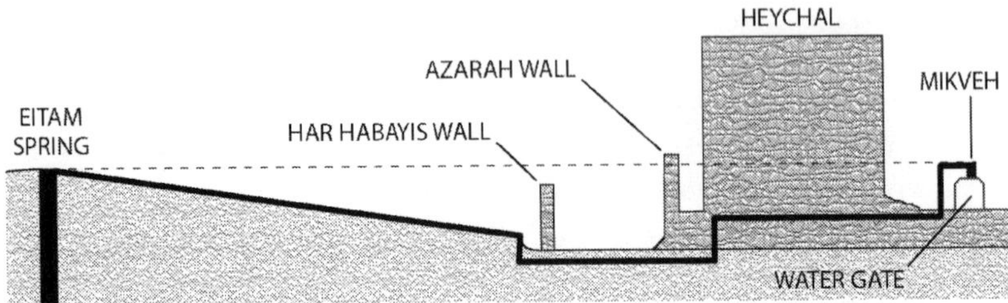


One difficulty with the system of pipes described above is that, in order to bring water up to the two elevated mikvaos, the entire system must be closed (that is, it must be completely sealed from the point where the water enters the pipe at the Eitam Spring until it exits the pipe into the mikvaos). Unfortunately, at every point along the way there were openings: The Place of Drainage Water needed to be open in order to receive the runoff from the *Heichal* Building roof; the *Kiyor* pit needed to be open so that the *Kiyor* could be lowered and raised; the channel of water needed to be open near the *Mizbei'ach* to allow the excess blood poured on the *Mizbei'ach* to drain into it. This difficulty may be resolved by assuming that the Beis HaMikdash had the means to close the entire system. [This could be accomplished by simply plugging the openings temporarily.] On the day before Yom Kippur (which is the only day of the year the two mikvaos were used) the Place of Drainage Water, *Kiyor* pit, and *Mizbei'ach* drains leading into the channel of water would be closed, allowing water to flow up against the pull of gravity into the mikvaos.

### Cleaning the *Azarah* Floor on Erev Pesach

On a daily basis, sacrificial blood entered the channel of water in the *Azarah* floor and was carried out of the Beis HaMikdash. On Erev

Pesach, however, the Kohanim would block the channel at the Water Gate and close the doors of all the other gates [at the beginning of each of the three shifts of people who came to slaughter their Pesach offerings], sealing the perimeter and causing the water to back up and flood the *Azarah*. Not only did this trap the water, but also the blood of the thousands of Pesach offerings slaughtered upon the floor, and the Gemara records that [by the end of each shift] the blood was knee-deep, forcing the Kohanim to walk upon platforms to keep from soiling the hems of their robes (*Pesachim* 65b). After all of the offerings had been completed [at the end of each shift] the Kohanim would remove the plug blocking the channel of water and the blood-water mixture would drain from the *Azarah*. [The *Ezras Yisrael* (the eastern portion of the *Azarah*) was 2.5 *amos* lower than the main *Azarah* and so any liquid that collected there would not be able to flow out via the channel of water. This area therefore required its own set of drains.]

The Mishnah cited at the beginning of this article states that the Kohanim rinsed the floor of the *Azarah* on Erev Pesach even when it occurred on Shabbos. The Sages maintain that rinsing the floor in this fashion is similar to *sweeping* a floor, an act that is prohibited on Shabbos, and for this reason did not approve of how the Kohanim cleaned the floor in the Beis HaMikdash (for further discussion and explanation of this dispute, see *Pesachim* 65a).

# Yishmael ben Pabi: A Kohen Gadol in the Second Beis HaMikdash

## Dani Zuckerbrod

Kohanim are required to offer the *korban pesach* each year. I thought it would be worthwhile to discuss what we know about various Kohanim Gedolim, particularly Yishmael ben Pabi.

When we think about the Kohanim Gedolim in the *Bayis Sheni,* many things come to mind. Corruption, bribery, Tziddukim and death in the *Kodesh HaKodashim* on Yom Kippur are in the forefront. Names of righteous Kohanim Gedolim like Shimon HaTzaddik, Yochanan Kohen Gadol, Yehoshua ben Gamla, and Matisyahu ben Yochanan Kohen Gadol also are in our first thoughts.

This unfortunate reality is confirmed by the Gemara (*Yoma* 9a, *Yerushalmi Yoma* 1:1, *Tosefta Yoma* 1:6): Originally, the Kohanim Gedolim would serve and their sons and grandsons would take over for them. The first Beis HaMikdash stood for 410 years and had 18 Kohanim Gedolim serve in it. The second Beis HaMikdash stood for 420 years and had over 300 Kohanim Gedolim serve there. Remove from this list Shimon HaTzaddik who served for 40 years (*Yoma* 39a), Yochanan Kohen Gadol who served for 80 years (*Berachos* 29a), Yishmael ben Pabi who served for 10 years, and some say R' Elazar ben Charsom who served for 11 years. If we add up the years of these Kohanim Gedolim, it comes out that the remaining Kohanim Gedolim served for less than a year on average [$420 - (40 + 80 + 10 + 11) = 279$ years for approximately 300 Kohanim Gedolim]. The reason for the high turnover is that the new Kohanim Gedolim would either bribe the government to be appointed to the position or kill the previous Kohen Gadol through *kishuf,* magic, to attain the title of Kohen Gadol on a very regular basis.

The *Tashbetz* (Vol. III, 37:1 and 135:12), however, comments that the Kohanim Gedolim in the second Beis HaMikdash were not the *reshaim* that everyone has made them out to be. The Gemara (*Yoma* 9a) calls them *reshaim* because they were not of the same caliber as those in the first Beis HaMikdash, since they did not follow the father-son progression. They did resort to paying for the position, but nonetheless were worthy of the post. He brings many examples of righteous Kohanim Gedolim from the *Bayis Sheni* mentioned in Chazal who are not listed in *Yoma.* If a Kohen Gadol was ever found to be an actual Tzidduki, he would be removed from his post immediately and dealt with right away (*Yoma* 19b, *Yerushalmi Yoma* 1:5). The Gemara (*Pesachim* 57b, *Kereisos* 28b) tells us of the *Azarah* crying over what was going on during the *Bayis Sheni.* The worst of those mentioned is the story of Yissachar from Kfar Barkai who would wear silk gloves when doing the *avodah* so that he wouldn't get his hands dirty. He prioritized his own *kavod* over the *kavod Shamayim* by doing the *avodah* with a *chatzitzah.* This is hardly the crime we would have thought enough to classify a Kohen Gadol as a *rasha.*

The *Tashbetz* continues that the worst sin that these Kohanim Gedolim committed was *sinas chinam* – by paying for their position and taking it from one another. Although this is not the way of a *tzaddik gamur*, it is in line with how *Klal Yisrael* acted in the time of the second Beis HaMikdash and hardly enough to call them *reshaim gemurim.* The reason why the Mishnah (*Avos* 5:5) tells us that certain miracles were missing in the second Beis HaMikdash was not due to the level of the Kohanim Gedolim; it was because the people would not rely on the miracles. They would always appoint a backup Kohen Gadol on Yom Kippur and take other precautionary measures. Since they were not willing to rely on the miracles of Beis HaMikdash, Hashem did not make the miracles happen.

Many of the other *meforshim* take this list of righteous Kohanim Gedolim to be very literal. If you are on the list, then you must have been a Kohen Gadol *tzaddik,* and if you are not on the list than you were not. This raises the question: who would we assume should be on the list, but is not; and on the flip side, who is on the list whom we would not expect? The *Maharsha* (*Pesachim* 57b) asks why Matisyahu ben Yochanan Kohen Gadol, through whom all of the miracles of Channukah occurred is not on this list. The *Dover Meisharim* (*Pesachim* 57a) answers that Matisyahu ben Yochanan Kohen Gadol was not himself a Kohen Gadol. His father Yochanan was the Kohen Gadol, and this is why he is not directly called Matisyahu Kohen Gadol in *Al Hanisim*. The Gemara (*Megillah* 11a) does refer to him as Matisyahu Kohen Gadol without his father's name, but there is dispute over the *girsa* there.[1]

Yehoshua ben Gamla was a Kohen Gadol, and is described by the Gemara (*Bava Basra* 21a) as "without him, Torah would have been forgotten from all of *Klal Yisrael*" because of the *chinuch* system he instituted. He is also mentioned in a positive light for beautifying the lots used on Yom Kippur by covering them in gold (*Yoma* 37a). Why was he left off the list of *tzaddikim gamurim* in the *Bayis Sheni*? The *Ben Yehoyada* (*Yoma* 9a) points out that although he was certainly a *tzaddik* and lived a long life, his tenure as Kohen Gadol was tainted. The Gemara (*Bava Basra* 21a) tells us that his wife, Miriam bas Baisus, paid a *tarkav* of *dinarim* to King Yannai to install her husband as Kohen Gadol. He was not aware of this and served completely *lishmah*, but his wife paid this bribe for the bragging rights of being the wife of the Kohen Gadol. This blemish prevented Yehoshua ben Gamla from being added to the list.[2]

---

[1] See *Chidushei Chasam Sofer Pesachim* 57b and *Yabia Omer* Vol. IIX *Orach Chaim* 57:3 for further discussion of this topic.

[2] See *Ritva* to *Bava Basra* 21a, *Yoma* 18a, and *Yevamos* 21a.

The list in *Yoma* contains two people we certainly expect, Shimon HaTzaddik and Yochanan Kohen Gadol. We are familiar with them and know that they were worthy Kohanim Gedolim. But who are R' Elazar ben Charsom and Yishmael ben Pabi? The same famous Gemara (*Yoma* 35b) that tells us that Hillel HaZakein obligates the poor to learn Torah —he was found learning Torah on the roof of the Beis Medrash and covered in snow — also tells us that R' Elazar ben Charsom obligates the rich to learn Torah. His father left him a tremendous amount of money, but he spent all of his time learning. So much so, that his servants once did not recognize him since he had nothing to do with his money. They tried to press him into public service, but let him off after he paid a large sum of money. Chazal held him in high esteem and it makes sense that he is on the list of righteous Kohanim Gedolim.

When I started looking into who Yishmael ben Pabi, I was shocked to find that he is mentioned a number of times across Chazal. I expected to find only one or two stories about him. By looking at the different *maamarei Chazal* we get a good picture of who he was.

The Gemara in *Yoma* (35b) tells us the halachah that under certain circumstances a Kohen may do the *avodah* wearing his own private clothing. Regularly, he would have to use the generally available *bigdei kehunah* from the Beis HaMikdash. This private clothing matched the regular *bigdei kehunah,* but was homemade and would be donated to the Beis HaMikdash when the Kohen used it. It was said about Yishmael ben Pabi that his mother made him a *kesones*, a tunic, worth 100 *maneh.* He wore it while performing the *avodah* and then donated it to the Beis HaMikdash. The *Ben Yehoyada* (*Yoma* 35b) points out that the fact Yishmael ben Pabi specifically wore a *kesones* made by his mother is very important. The Gemara in *Makkos* (11a) tells us that people who kill someone unintentionally are exiled to an *ir miklat*, city of refuge. They would be released from their exile upon the death of the Kohen Gadol. The mother of the Kohen Gadol would provide food and clothing for these people so that they should not *daven* for the death of the Kohen Gadol. The Gemara in *Zevachim* (88b) tells us that the *kesones* atones for murder like we find by Yosef HaTzaddik where the brothers dipped his *kesones* into blood (*Bereishis* 37:31). This is why the mother of the Kohen Gadol would make a *kesones* for her son to use in the Beis HaMikdash. The *zechus* of using this special *kesones* would protect *Klal Yisrael* and prevent accidental murders. This in turn would prevent the accidental murderers from being exiled to the *ir miklat* and ultimately prevent them from *davening* for the death of the Kohen Gadol.

The Gemara (*Yoma* 47a, *Yerushalmi Yoma* 1:1) tells us of another righteous Kohen Gadol named R' Yishmael ben Kimchis. The *Maharsha* comments that since R' Yishmael ben Kimchis is not on the list in *Yoma* 9b, but was clearly a *tzaddik,* he must be the same person as Yishmael ben Pabi. Pabi is his father's name and Kimchis is his mother's name. The Gemara in *Yoma* (47a) uses his mother's name because it is focusing on his mother's virtues when it comes to *tzenius*. The Gemara tells of a story where R' Yishmael ben Kimchis served on Yom Kippur and in the middle of the day he happened to be talking to an Arab in the market. Some spit from the Arab's mouth landed on the Kohen Gadol's clothing which made him *tamei* and unfit to finish the Yom Kippur *avodah*. They chose his brother Yesheivav to fill in for the rest of Yom Kippur. On that day his mother saw two of her sons serve as the Kohen Gadol. The Gemara continues that a similar story took place on another Yom Kippur when Yishmael was speaking with a gentile, and he became *tamei* from his spit. This time, his brother Yosef stepped in as the replacement Kohen Gadol. The Gemara concludes that Kimchis saw seven sons serve as Kohen Gadol because of her care in regards to the mitzvah of *tzenius*. In all of her days, the beams of her house never saw the locks of her hair nor the seams of her robe.[3]

*Avos DeRabbi Nassan* (35:5) says that there were ten miracles that happened in the Beis HaMikdash. One of them was that the Kohen Gadol never became *tamei* from *tumas keri* on Yom Kippur, with the exception of R' Yishmael ben Kimchis in the story above. R' Yehuda ben Klonymus of Spire, the rebbe of the *Rokeach* (*Erchei Tanaim V'Amoraim* Vol II, "Yishamel ben Kimchis"), points out that the simple reading of the *Baraisa* is that R' Yishmael ben Kimchis had a *keri* episode which made him *tamei*. However, when you look at the Chazal cited above, we see that although he did become *tamei tumas keri*, it was through a transmission from someone else. The wording used in the *Baraisa* is similar to the Gemara (*Rosh Hashana* 37a) where wheat became *tamei tumas keri,* and clearly the *tumah* was transmitted to the wheat through an external source.

R' Reuven Margaliyos (*Lachkor Sheimos Vekinuyim BeTalmud*, p. 46) points out that the typical reason for a Kohen Gadol replacement is the death of the Kohen Gadol. Why would it be praiseworthy for Kimchis to see all seven of her sons serve a Kohen Gadol; did they all die in her lifetime? It must have been that they did not replace each other due to death or other unfortunate circumstances. Rather some other factor like spit from a gentile making the Kohen Gadol *tamei* was the cause for the seven sons to serve as Kohanim Gedolim. Based on the different versions of the story brought throughout Chazal, we know five of the seven sons' names: Yishmael (*Yerushalmi Yoma* 1:1), Yesheivav (ibid.), Yosef (ibid.), Shimon (*Vayikra Rabbah* 20:11, *Pesikta D'Rav Kahana* §26) and Yehudah (ibid.).

---

[3] This story is brought in close to a dozen places in Chazal, each with a slight variation.

Why would R' Yishmael ben Kimchis be replaced by a new brother each time he became *tamei,* instead of being replaced by the same brother every time? R' Reuven Margaliyos answers that R' Yishmael ben Kimchis was nervous about losing his job as Kohen Gadol. According to *Tosafos* (*Nazir* 47a ד"ה וכן משיח), when a Kohen Gadol is elevated into his job based on *ribui begadim*, wearing the clothing of the Kohen Gadol, it is based on *chazakah*. Should a Kohen Gadol have to go into *galus* and someone else were to take his place for a few years, the *chazakah* would transfer to the new Kohen Gadol. If the original Kohen Gadol were released from his *galus* he would not be able to reassume his post for he had lost the *chazakah*. In the second Bais HaMikdash, all of the Kohanim Gedolim were inaugurated by donning the clothes since there was no *shemen hamishchah*. R' Yishmael ben Kimchis was nervous that if the same brother would fill in for him more than once, that brother would get the *chazakah* as Kohen Gadol, and R' Yishmael ben Kimchis would not be able to continue to serve after him. To prevent this from happening, every time he needed to get a replacement, he found someone who had never filled in as Kohen Gadol before.

R' Reuven Margaliyos also points out that the name Kimchis is not his mother's real name but rather a nickname. The Gemara (*Yoma* 47a, *Yerushalmi Yoma* 1:1) says that due to her excellent *tzenius* they would say about her כל קמחא קמחא, וקמחא דקמחית סולת, *All flour is flour, but he flour of Kimchis is fine flour*. I.e., although many women behave modestly in their homes, Kimchis's conduct was especially deserving (*Pnei Moshe*). Hence the name Kimchis, which is similar to *kemach,* flour. The Gemara continues (*Yoma* 47a, *Yerushalmi Yoma* 5:1), R' Yishmael ben Pabi was the physically largest Kohen Gadol who ever served in the Bais HaMikdash. When he poured the *ketores* out of the *kaf* on Yom Kippur it did not fill up his hands like it did for the other Kohanim Gedolim. There were three *kav* of coals and typically a Kohen Gadol could not fit more than three *kav* of *ketores* into his hands, making the proportion of *ketores* to coals almost equal. R' Yishmael ben Kimchis could fit four *kav* of *ketores* into his hands. The Gemara attributes his large size to either a special porridge that his mother fed him or to something special that happened when she conceived him.[4]

Chazal (*Pesachim* 57a, *Tosefta Menachos* 13:4) tell us that even though Yishmael ben Pabi was a *tzaddik*, not everyone in his family followed in his ways. They list off a number of Kohen families who acted improperly and said "Woe is to me because of the house of Yishmael ben Pabi, woe is to me because of their *egrofin* (lit. fists). They were Kohanim Gedolim and their children were *gizborin* (treasurers) in the Beis HaMikdash. Their sons-in-law were *amarkolin* (trustees) and their servants hit people with sticks." The Gemara (*Pesachim* 57a, *Kereisos* 28a) tells us a contrasting story that the *Azarah* gave out four cries. Two of the cries were related to bad things people were doing and two were cries for people who were doing the right things. The first two cries were for the children of Eli HaKohen who contaminated the *Heichal* with *tumah,* and Yissachar Ish Kfar Barkai who honors himself and profanes the *kodshei shamayim* (see *Tashbetz* above). The second two cries were for the gates to open and let enter Yishmael ben Pabi, the student of Pinchas, to let him serve, and Yochanan ben Narbai, the student of Pinkai, to enter to fill his stomach with the *korbanos* of Hashem.

Chazal begin with a negative story about Yishmael ben Pabi and his family, but then cite a positive story about him. *Rashi* and the other *meforshim* point out that Yishmael ben Pabi was a *tzaddik,* and even though his family did not follow in his ways, he was not led astray by them.

The *Yaavetz* (*Pesachim* 57a) based on the Gemara (*Chullin* 4b) asks how Yishmael ben Pabi's children and servants could be *reshaim*?

[4] See *Marah HaPanim* (*Yerushalmi Yoma* 5:1) who discusses whether the four *kav* fit into his two hands combined or even in one of his hands.

The Gemara derives from *Mishlei* (29:12) that if a ruler listens to the truth, all his servants are righteous. The Gemara (*Pesachim* 57a) is implying that Yishmael ben Pabi's servants were not righteous; they would hit people with sticks. He was clearly a *tzaddik* and according to the *drashah,* they should have followed in his ways. The *Yaavetz* answers that the children of Yishmael ben Pabi were not *reshaim;* rather they were *baalei zeroa v'koach*, strong men. We find the same word *egrofin* used by Chazal (*Sanhedrin* 21a, 49a) when describing the *bnei yefas toar* of *David HaMelech.* These 400 children would grow their hair in a *bloris* (style of *avodah zarah*) and sit in golden carriages in the front of *David HaMelech's* army. They are called *baalei egrofin b'koach chayil.* The word *egrofin* was not used in a negative connotation by the *bnei yifas toar,* but rather to say how impressive and strong they appeared. But the Gemara in *Pesachim* is saying "woe is me" in connection to the *egrofin* word! It must mean that they were passing judgement on the people themselves and not bringing their arguments to *Beis Din.*

The *Maharsha* (*Pesachim* 57a) understands the word *egrofin* differently. The Gemara in *Sotah* (41b) says מיום שגברה אגרופה של חנופה נתעוותו הדינין, *from the day the power of flattery prevailed the judges were perverted.* This story is in reference to *Agrippas HaMelech* (note the *shoresh* of אגרוף in his name אגריפס) where the judges changed their ruling to fit with the will of *Agrippas HaMelech.* The judges were flattering Agrippas by perverting the *din.* The family of Yishmael ben Pabi were *baalei gaivah*; they all held high office in the Beis HaMikdash. Yishmael was the Kohen Gadol, his sons were the *gizborin* (treasurers) and his sons-in-law were the *amarkolin*[5] (trustees). They did as they saw fit, flattering *reshaim* and having their servants hit people with sticks. The *Maharsha* points out that this is true only of Yishmael ben Pabi's

[5] See Mishnah *Shekalim* 5:2 and *Tosefta Shekalim* 2:15 for an explanation of what the *amarkolin* did in the Bais HaMikdash.

family, but not of him. We know from the other places in Chazal that he himself was a *tzaddik*.

The *Aruch LaNer* (*Kereisos* 28b) asks why the *Azarah* was crying out to open its doors for Yishmael ben Pabi as a *tzaddik* when there were likely plenty of other Kohanim Gedolim who were also *tzaddikim*? He answers that the *Azarah* specifically chose him, since his family was rotten but he was not affected by them. The *Chidushei Chasam Sofer* (*Pesachim* 57a) says that based on the explanation of the *Maharsha* it makes sense why the *Azarah* called Yishmael ben Pabi the *talmid* of Pinchas. Just like Pinchas would not flatter the *reshaim* around him and was willing to kill a *nasi* who was not following the Torah, so too Yishmael ben Pabi would not flatter those in his family and was not affected by them.

*Doros HaRishonim* (Vol. III pp 10-14) suggests that the *Baraisa* in *Pesachim* is referring to a later Kohen Gadol named Yishmael ben Pabi, a descendant of the Yishmael ben Pabi we have been talking about in all of the positive *divrei Chazal*. This is based on a story in Josephus (Antiquities Vol XX 8:8).

The Mishnah in *Parah* (3:2) lists all of the *paros adumos* in history. The first two *paros adumos* were brought by *Moshe Rabbeinu* and *Ezra HaSofer*. It then brings the Chachamim who say that there were seven *paros adumos* from *Ezra HaSofer* and on. The breakdown of who performed the *avodah* for them is as follows: Shimon HaTzaddik and Yochanan Kohen Gadol each did two (for a total of four), Eliyahu Einei ben Hakof, Chanamel HaMitzri, and Yishmael ben Pabi each did one (for a grand total of seven). The *Tashbetz* (ibid.) points out that we can see through this Mishnah how great Yishmael ben Pabi was. He is mentioned in the same exclusive list as *Moshe Rabbeinu* and *Ezra HaSofer*; he must have been quite the *tzaddik*!

The *Rosh* (*Peirush Mishnayos Parah* 3:7) says that the Tziddukim understand the *pasuk* of ואסף איש טהור (*Bamidbar* 19:9) to mean that the person doing the *avodah* of the *parah adumah* must be *tahor* from all *tumah*. The Chachamim understand it to mean *tahor* to eat *maaser*. This means that someone who was *tamei* and went to the *mikvah* (called a *tevul yom*) is allowed to perform the *avodah* of the *parah adumah* the same day he went to the *mikvah* (*Sifrei Chukas* 19:9, 19:18). The Chachamim eventually made a *takanah* to prevent people from following the Tziddukim. The *takanah* was that the Kohen who performed the *avodah* of the *parah adumah* must become *tamei* and go to the *mikvah* the day he performs the *avodah* of the *parah adumah*. This way he would be a *tevul yom* who is fit to serve only according to the Chachamim and unfit according to the Tziddukim. To stick to this *takanah* it was critical to do the *avodah* on the same day as going to the *mikvah* since once nightfall occurs, he has *herev shemesh* and becomes completely *tahor*. This would make him eligible to perform the *avodah* according to the Tziddukim.

The *Tosefta* (*Parah* 3:4), as understood by the *Rash*, tells a detailed story of Yishmael ben Pabi's *parah adumah* experience. Yishmael ben Pabi was actually involved in the *avodah* of two *paros adumos*. When preparing to serve on the first *parah adumah*, Yishmael ben Pabi had a conversation with the Chachamim about when to perform the *avodah*. He was pushing to do the *avodah* after nightfall or the next day after going to the *mikvah*. His reasoning was that for all other services in the Beis HaMikdash we define a minimum level of *taharah* the Kohen must be at to do the *avodah*. However, we always allow him to perform the *avodah* at a higher level of *taharah* and we do not force him to be at the minimum level. Why can't he also be at a higher level of *taharah* when performing the *avodah* of the *parah adumah*? The Chachamim responded that if they let him do the *avodah* this way he will cast a bad name on the *paros adumos* of the past and people will think they were invalid as they were done by a *tevul yom.* They decreed that his *parah adumah* water be poured out on this account. He later had another opportunity to do the *avodah* of *parah adumah* which he did in accordance with the *takanah* as a *tevul yom.*

There is an adjacent *Tosefta* (*Parah* 3:5) that has a similar story, but a completely different outcome, which attests to the respect with which the Chachamim held of Yishmael ben Pabi. There once was a Kohen Gadol who secretly was a Tzidduki. He had the opportunity to do the *avodah* of the *parah adumah* and was planning to do it not as a *tevul yom* but rather as a *meurav shemesh* (after sunset the day he went to the *mikvah*) in accordance with the opinion of the Tziddukim. Rabban Yochanan ben Zakkai found out and confronted the Tzidduki in the middle of the *avodah.* He performed *semichah* on the head of the Kohen Gadol to make him *tamei* again and force him to go to the *mikvah.* This would return him to the state of *tevul yom* so that he could perform the *avodah* in the proper way. He then struck him in the ear, causing a blemish (the *meforshim* debate who struck whom) and the Tzidduki said "ben Zakkai, I will get you". Rabban Yochanan ben Zakkai responded "When you get a chance!" Within three days the Tzidduki died, and his father visited Rabban Yochanan ben Zakkai. The father said that his son's "sun had set" (play on words, *herev shemesh*) and he never had a chance to get you.

In the second *Tosefta*, the Tzidduki Kohen Gadol tried to do the same thing that Yishmael ben Pabi wanted to do, perform the *avodah* of the *parah adumah* not as a *tvul yom.* In the case of Yishmael ben Pabi there was a debate and ultimately Yishmael ben Pabi submitted to the Chachamim and the *mei chatas* was poured out. In the case of the Tzidduki there was a physical fight which ultimately ended in the death of the Tzidduki. If the *Chachamim* had even a suspicion of Yishmael ben Pabi being a Tzidduki, the story would have played out differently.

The *Chazon Ish* (*Parah* 6:14) points out the Yishmael ben Pabi must have been mistaken on why the Kohen Gadol was required to do the *avodah* as a *tevul yom* (to avoid giving credence to the understanding of the Tziddukim). If he knew it was a special *takanah,* he wouldn't have tried to go against it. Yishmael ben Pabi himself was a *tzaddik* and in some places he is referred to Rebbi Yishmael ben Pabi which implies he had *semichah*.

R' Yehuda ben Klonymus of Spire (*Erchei Tanaim V'Amoraim* Vol. I, "Yehoshua ben Gamla") says that Yishmael ben Pabi knew the reason of the *takanah* to perform the *avodah* of the *parah adumah* as a *tevul yom.* Even so, he still wanted to do it after sunset when he transitioned to the status of *meurav shemesh*. The Gemara in *Chagigah* (22a) says that we have certain leniencies in *tumah* and *taharah* out of a fear that if we did not allow them, everyone would build their own *bamah* and bring their own *parah adumah*. Yishmael ben Pabi was telling the Chachamim this same concern. Even though we specifically burn the *parah adumah* when the Kohen is a *tevul yom,* it would still be valid if it was done after nightfall when he is even more *tahor*. If we burn the *parah adumah* then, it will also make the Tziddukim happy and stop them from trying to make their own *parah adumah*. The Chachamim were not willing to give in to this compromise and poured out the Yishmael ben Pabi's *mei chatas*. The second *parah adumah* that Yishmael ben Pabi burnt was done in accordance with the *takanah* and the Chachamim were happy with it.

The second *Tosefta* about Rabban Yochanan ben Zakkai is used as a proof in a *machlokes* between *Rashi* and *Tosafos* as to whether Rabban Yochanan ben Zakkai was a Kohen, and if he served as the Kohen Gadol in the second Beis HaMikdash. There is a story in Chazal (*Sifrei Bamidbar* 19:2, *Tosefta Parah* 4:4) where the students of Rabban Yochanan ben Zakkai asked him what kind of clothes the Kohen wore when he burnt the *parah adumah*. Rabban Yochanan ben Zakkai said he wore gold vestments. The students responded that previously Rabban Yochanan ben Zakkai had taught them it was done with white vestments. Rabban Yochanan ben Zakkai responded that we can learn a major lesson from this. "If something which I did with my own hands and saw with my own eyes (burnt a *parah adumah*) I cannot remember, then that which I hear with my ears (Torah) can be forgotten and must be reviewed." Some say the story took place with Hillel HaZakein and the part about "doing it with my own hands" has to be removed.

*Rashi* (*Shabbos* 34a ד"ה טורמוסי) says that we see from the *Sifrei* and *Tosefta* that Rabban Yochanan ben Zakkai was a Kohen Gadol in the second Beis HaMikdash. *Tosafos* (*Menachos* 21b ד"ה שהכהנים) says that a Gemara in *Menachos* clearly excludes Rabban Yochanan ben Zakkai from the Kohanim and not only was he not a Kohen Gadol but wasn't a Kohen at all. The *maamar Chazal* about the clothing the Kohen wore when burning the *parah adumah* is not a proof, since we can either say he presided over it (the story with the Tzidduki and the *parah adumah*) and did not perform it himself or we can go with the second opinion that it was Hillel HaZakein who said it.

The *Yaavetz* (*hagahos* to *Menachos* 21b, *Lechem Shamayim Parah* 3:8) brings the Mishnah (*Parah* 3:2) that tells us who made each *parah adumah,* and Rabban Yochanan ben Zakkai is not on the list. The last one was brought by Yishmael ben Pabi and he lived much earlier than Rabban Yochanan ben Zakkai. We know this because the Gemara (*Pesachim* 57a) that tells us about the evil things Yishmael ben Pabi's family did was said over by Abba Shaul ben Botnis. We know from the Gemara in *Shabbos* (157a) that Abba Shaul ben Botnis was a contemporary of the father of R' Tzadok. From the Gemara in *Gittin* (56a) about the destruction of the Beis HaMikdash we know that R' Tzadok was an old man during the *churban* which occurred during the prime years of Rabban Yochanan ben Zakkai. The Gemara in *Rosh Hashana* (31b) tells us that Rabban Yochanan ben Zakkai was the *nasi* for the 40 years before the *churban Bayis Sheni* and his tenure extended after the *churban* as well.

The *Sefer HaYuchsin* (Vol. I, "Chanina ben Dosa") and *Shalsheles HaKabalah* both say that Yishmael ben Pabi and Chanamel HaMitzri brought *paros adumos* during the lifetime of Rabban Yochanan ben Zakkai. As we have just proved, Yishmael ben Pabi lived long before Rabban Yochanan ben Zakkai, so this is a mistake. The *parah adumah* spoken about in the *Tosefta* with the Tzidduki was not counted in the Mishnah because it was not successfully completed, just like Yishmael ben Pabi's first *parah adumah.* Once it was determined that the Kohen Gadol was a Tzidduki, it was terminated. An alternative would be if Chanamel HaMitzri, who is mentioned in the Mishnah as bringing a *parah adumah*, and by the *Sefer HaYuchsin,* was the Tzidduki Kohen Gadol in our *Tosefta.* The Mishnah's list of all the *paros adumos* was simply not in order. Chanamel HaMitzri is not mentioned in the list in *Yoma* (9a) of righteous Kohanim Gedolim, so even though he brought a *parah adumah* he must not have been a true *tzaddik.*

The Gemara in *Sotah* (49a) tells of how when different people died, certain things or character traits ceased from being in this world. It says that when Yishmael ben Pabi died, the *ziv haKehunah*, glory of the priesthood, ceased from being in this world. *Rashi* tells us that he was a *chacham* and *ashir* and many Kohanim ate at his table. The Gemara is clearly telling us that Yishmael ben Pabi was the last Kohen to epitomize the great traits of a Kohen Gadol in the *Bayis Sheni*.

We can now return to our original question of who Yishmael ben Pabi is and why he is on the short list of Kohanim Gedolim *tzaddikim* in the *Bayis Sheni*. He was a respected Kohen Gadol, a *tzaddik,* and a *talmid chacham*. He wore a *kesones* made by his mother to save *Klal Yisrael* from accidental murder. He was the same person as R' Yishmael ben Kimchis, which meant his mother was the epitome of *tzenius*. He was a very large man, and he was replaced by all of his six brothers on different Yomei Kippur to perform the *avodah*. His family was prestigious and held many high positions in the Beis HaMikdash, but they abused their power and did not follow in his righteous ways. He was involved with two of the rare occasions that a *parah adumah* was prepared in the Beis HaMikdash, one of which was successfully completed. He lived at least three generations before the *churban Bayis Sheni* and may have had *semichah*.

# *Taanis Bechorim* – Not so Fast

## Dr. Barry Reiner [1]

It is a widespread practice in *Klal Yisrael* for *bechorim,* the firstborns, to attend a *siyum* on Erev Pesach in order to avoid fasting on that very day, which is designated as *Taanis Bechorim*, Fast of the Firstborn. Indeed, I recall attending *siyumim* with my father, *a"h,* from the time I was very little. Reasons given for avoiding this fast include the strenuous work that must be done on Erev Pesach, the potential health consequences of eating marror on an empty stomach (*Aruch HaShulchan* 470:3) and the need to be in optimal condition for the multiple mitzvos of the Seder (*Mishnah Berurah* 470:2). It is most unusual and enigmatic to have a fast day on the books and yet go out of our way to avoid fasting.

What is the origin of this fast and what is its Halachic status? What is the underlying reason for this fast?

In *Meseches Sofrim* (21:3) it is stated: אין מתענין עד שיעבור ניסן אלא הבכורות שמתענין בערב הפסח והצנועין בשביל המצה כדי שיכנסו בה בתאוה, *There is no fasting until Nisan has passed. The only exception is [the fast of] the firstborn who fast on the eve of Passover. The very pious also fast on that day on account of the unleavened bread, in order that they shall eat with great appetite.*

*Tosafos* in *Pesachim* (108a ד"ה רב ששת) cite the *Meseches Sofrim* there as the source for the *custom* of firstborns fasting on Erev Pesach: והבכורות נהגו להתענות ערב פסח דקתני במסכת סופרים שאין מתענין בניסן אלא הבכורות בערב הפסח.

[1] With thanks to Rav Daniel Goldberg, Associate Rabbi, Cong. Ahavath Torah, Englewood, NJ, who delivered a most enjoyable and stimulating *shiur* on this topic, Pesach 5781, for his assistance.

The *Yerushalmi Pesachim* (82a) cites a *machlokes* between Amoraim regarding any individual eating on Erev Pesach, whether matzah alone is prohibited or all foods. A proof is brought from the Tanna, Rebbi, who fasted on Erev Pesach, but the Gemara refutes that premise suggesting that this involved special circumstances; and the true reason that Rebbi fasted was that he was a *bechor.* R' Mana then states that R' Yonah, his father, did, in fact, eat on Erev Pesach despite being a *bechor.* The *Yerushalmi* concludes that Rebbi fasted not because he was a *bechor,* but because he was an *istenis,* a delicate individual, who would not be able to tolerate the eating involved in the mitzvos of Pesach night had he eaten during the day.

It appears then, that Rebbi had a different reason altogether, other than being a *bechor,* for fasting on Erev Pesach. On the other hand, if there was no basis whatsoever for a *bechor* to fast, it could be expected that the *Yerushalmi* would have specifically stated that a *bechor* was prohibited from doing so, like any other day in Nissan. We can therefore understand the *Yerushalmi* as concluding that while there is not a requirement for a *bechor* to fast (indeed, the *Yerushalmi* specifies that R' Yonah, a *bechor*, did not fast), the notion of such a fast was recognized.

The *Rosh* (*Pesachim* 10:19), based on these sources, supports the *minhag* of firstborns fasting on Erev Pesach. *Tosafos,* cited earlier, also refer to the fast in terms of *minhag.*

In contrast to the *Rosh*, the *Maharil* (cited in the *Mishnah Berurah*) states that *Taanis Bechorim* is considered to be a *taanis tzibur,* a communal fast.

This brings with it a whole host of considerations regarding a *taanis tzibur* applying to a segment of the population, such as whether the prayer service would be modified (i.e., *Keriyas HaTorah, Aneinu*) if the *shaliach tzibur* was a *bechor* who chose to fast, or if the Minyan was composed exclusively of *bechorim*. The *Maharil,* consistent with this position, also held that if one did not fast, a make-up (*tashlumin*) fast is required.

If the fast is a *minhag,* we can certainly understand the blanket lenient dispensation to avoid fasting. If the fast is accorded the status of a *taanis tzibur,* this is less likely to be the case.

In stark contrast, the *Pe'er Yitzchak* (25:4) writes that certain Hasidic leaders who were *bechorim* did not fast on Erev Pesach. The basis for this, explains the *Pe'er Yitzchak,* is that the *Meseches Sofrim* as we have it has an errant version and the word מתענין, fasting, should, in fact, be מתענגין, celebrating.[2]

The widely understood reason for the Fast of the Firstborns is given by the *Tur* (*Orach Chaim* §470), that the firstborns were miraculously spared during the tenth plague. The obvious question on this, asked by many, is that most commemorations of miracles are in the form of celebration and feast, not a fast. Why then, would a miracle on behalf of the firstborns be commemorated by fasting?

Several reasons are given (see *Mishnah Berurah, Dirshu* Ed. 470:1), including *Chasam Sofer*, that the fasting is commemorative of the fasting that the *bechorim* did in supplication that they be spared while the Egyptian firstborns were destroyed. This is similar to the fast that precedes Purim commemorating the three days of fasting per Esther's request. Additionally, the firstborns fasted because the miracle performed on their behalf consumed the *zechuyos* they had accumulated.

---

[2] Of course, this is difficult to understand in the context of the aforementioned sources. In fact, the Munkatcher Rebbe (*Divrei Torah Chamishaah,* end of §9; see also his *Nimukei Orach Chaim* 470:1) had great objections to this work, stating that with this approach one could violate all of the mitzvos of the Torah, saying that they are just printers' mistakes.

R' Shlomo Zalman Auerbach, in *Halichos Shlomo,* questions the entire notion that *bechorim* fast זכר לנס, in commemoration of the miracle. In addition to the question regarding the atypical nature of fasting as opposed to celebration and feast, he raises the following objections:

1. If the fast was in commemoration of the firstborns being miraculously spared during the tenth plague, this occurred on the night of Pesach, not Erev Pesach; and if the fast was being pushed earlier, it should have been pushed to the thirteenth of Nissan (the day before Erev Pesach).
2. The fast should apply to all the descendants of the firstborns, regardless of order of birth, who were actually impacted by the miracle. That I am a *bechor* in the present day is of no relevance.
3. The fast should apply to males and females, as well as heads of households, as they were included in the tenth plague. (Of note, there are minority opinions that do include them in the "requirement" to fast.)

For these reasons, R' Auerbach concludes that there is an entirely different reason for the Fast of the Firstborn. In the aftermath of the miracle, the firstborns were sanctified and the responsibility and privilege for the *avodah* was bestowed upon them. This was subsequently confiscated from them due to their participation in the sin of the Golden Calf and bestowed upon the Leviim, who did not participate in that sin. Every Erev Pesach, at the very time that the firstborns were sanctified, it is a mark of shame that they are not participating in the *avodah,* including the preparation of the *korban pesach.* R' Auerbach cites the *Ohr HaChaim HaKadosh* (*Bereishis* 49:28) that at the time of the *geulah shleimah,* the final redemption, the *bechorim* will participate in the Avodah alongside the Kohanim.

**Additional "fast for thought" – *Taanis Bechorim* or *Bechoros*?**
I personally have always referred to the Fast of the Firstborns as *Taanis Bechoros,* despite the obvious grammatical difficulty that *bechor* is masculine. The title of the *siman* in *Shulchan Aruch* refers to it this way, as well: שהבכורות מתענין בערב פסח . ובו ג סעיפים. Similarly, *Meseches Sofrim*, *Tosafos* in *Pesachim,* the *Rosh* (all cited above) all use the form בכורות. The *Maharil* (quoted in *Mishnah Berurah,* cited above), though, refers to the fast as תענית בכורים. A recent encyclopedic *sefer* on the topic is also entitled תענית בכורים. If the term *bechorim* is grammatically correct, why do we find references to the first born fasting as *bechoros*?

Perhaps we can say that in a grammatic parallel, the tenth plague is almost universally referred to as *Makkas Bechoros,* the Plague of the Firstborn. (see *Rashi, Berachos* 9a for an exception). Although this too demands an explanation, it might be because of our familiarity with the term *Makkas Bechoros* that we have adopted the term *Taanis Bechoros.* It should further be noted that the title of the *Mesechta* relating to the sanctity of first-born animals is *Meseches Bechoros.*

One answer that I saw was that there is a general preference in Aramaic towards the suffix וֹת – as opposed to ים. Another suggested that as the spellings are the same, בכורים, *bechorim* could be confused with *bikkurim.*[3]

Perhaps the topic for the *Kuntress* article next year, *bs"d.*

May we be *zocheh* to experience that *geulah*, *bimheirah biyameinu!*

[3] Torah Discussion Forum, *Kollel Iyun HaDaf* of Yerushalayim, *Berachos* 9a, with thanks to Rabbi Binyamin Marwick for assistance.

# Selling Chametz to a Gentile Before Pesach

## R' Eliezer Shames

There is a Biblical prohibition for a Jew to own or possess chametz on Pesach. The obvious way to avoid transgressing this prohibition is to destroy all chametz from one's house before Pesach. Since this can be costly, many people sell their chametz to a gentile for the duration of Pesach and then buy it back from them after Pesach. In this way, the chametz is not owned or possessed by a Jew on Pesach.

I have heard different iterations of the same question many times: Is this sale to the gentile just gaming the system? After all, we know that we will buy back the chametz after Pesach. In fact, even before Pesach begins, we know what time the chametz will be bought back when Pesach is over!

I think we can break up this question into two:

Question 1: Since everyone knows that the Jew will buy the chametz back after Pesach, this will lead people to believe that the sale is a joke and not an actual sale, which means there was not proper intent for the sale. I believe this is a valid question only if at least one of the parties has in mind that the sale is a joke (lacking proper intent for the sale). But if all the parties have in mind that the sale is real, even though the parties know that the Jew will buy back the chametz after Pesach, it should be a *bona fide* sale.

Question 2: Is selling the chametz to a gentile bypassing a mitzvah? That is, while selling the chametz before Pesach will prevent one from violating the negative mitzvah of owning or possessing chametz, it also prevents one from fulfilling the positive mitzvah of *tashbisu* (*Bo* 12:15, positive mitzvah §156 according to the *Rambam*) to destroy chametz in one's possession prior to Pesach.

To strengthen the question, the Mishnah in *Maaser Sheni* (4:4) explains how one can create a system to prevent one from being obligated in the mitzvah to pay the added fifth (*Bechukosai* 27:31) for redeeming one's own *maaser sheni* (part of the 128th positive mitzvah according to the *Rambam*). The Mishnah explains that one can give the money to his adult children to redeem the produce on a coin of equal value that will remove the sanctification of the produce, and then the coin must be used for limited purchases. Since the mitzvah of adding a fifth when redeeming *maaser sheni* applies only to one's own *maaser sheni*, having an adult child redeem the father's *maaser sheni* avoids paying the added fifth because the child is redeeming someone else's (the father's) *maaser sheni.*

Rabbi Yaakov Lorberbaum (1760-1832), in his *sefer Kehillas Yaakov,* explains, based on the *Yerushalmi* in *Maaser Sheni,* that because the *pasuk* of *maaser sheni* states that fulfilling *maaser sheni* is a "blessing" (*Re'eh* 14:29), one has permission to bypass the positive mitzvah of paying the extra fifth. But such permission is not given for any other positive mitzvah that does not have the word "blessing." Therefore, it should be prohibited to sell chametz to a gentile because one cannot fulfill the mitzvah of *tashbisu* on the chametz that was sold.

Rabbi Hershel Schachter, in his *sefer Be'ikvei HaTzon* (p. 75), writes that there is no minimum requirement for a positive mitzvah where no minimum requirement was stated. When one sells the overwhelming majority of his chametz, so long as he can destroy some chametz before Pesach, one can fulfill the mitzvah of *tashbisu.* This is under the assumption that destroying, for example, one morsel of chametz[1] is the same as destroying 100 morsels of chametz in fulfilling the positive mitzvah of *tashbisu.* This justifies the practice of selling the chametz to the gentile prior to Pesach, for most

[1] I do not mean for the word "morsel" to imply that this is the minimum requirement to fulfill *tashbisu*, I am just using it by way of example.

people have the custom to burn the ten pieces of bread from *bedikas chametz* on Erev Pesach.

The purpose of this article is not intended as practical halachic guidance. In fact, by way of demonstration of the varying opinions in this matter, Rabbi Yosef Dov Soloveitchik (as quoted in *Be'ikvei HaTzon*), instructed his students not to sell plain chametz (that is, chametz *not* mixed with non-chametz) to a gentile. Rabbi Soloveitchik's reason was that since plain chametz according to all opinions is Biblically prohibited on Pesach, one should hold like those Acharonim (not mentioned in this article) who maintain one should try to fulfill positive mitzvos to the maximum extent (not like Rabbi Hershel Schachter's explanation). However, when chametz *is* mixed with non-chametz, there is an opinion that holds that it is not Biblically prohibited on Pesach (that is the opinion of the *Rabbeinu Tam*) and therefore one can be lenient and avoid doing the positive mitzvah of *tashibisu* on a Rabbinic prohibition.[2]

[2] I don't know if Rabbi Soloveitchik would agree with Rabbi Hershel Schachter's opinion for mixed chametz or would allow the students to sell the chametz and avoid the positive mitzvah of *tashbisu* altogether.

# The *Shechinah* at Yaakov's Bedside

## Rabbi Paysach Diskind [1]

The Midrash in our *Parashas Vayechi* shares the following story. As the *Shevatim* surrounded Yaakov's bed before his leaving this world, Yaakov wanted to reveal the time when they would reach their destiny; the coming of Mashiach. To appreciate the scene, we must recognize that with Yaakov on his bed surrounded by the twelve *Shevatim*, he was carrying the *Shechinah,* the Presence of Hashem, similar to the Mishkan surrounded by the twelve tribes in the desert. As he lay there with the *Shechinah* upon him, he intended to reveal the ultimate time of Mashiach. However, the moment before he was to reveal it, the *Shechinah* suddenly left him.

With the departure of the *Shechinah,* Yaakov assumed that perhaps one of his children was not completely dedicated to Hashem. He therefore asked them, "Is there anyone here who is not entirely committed to Hashem?" And they responded in unison, *"Shema Yisrael Hashem Elokeinu Hashem Echad."* They meant to say, "Just as you are completely with Hashem, so are we all together in complete dedication to Him."

To gain a fuller appreciation of this Midrash, I wish to share the *Chasam Sofer's* insight to the *Shema.*

The four-letter Name of Hashem, which is the Name that we are not allowed to pronounce, carries two essential meanings. The first meaning is that Hashem transcends time; He existed before the creation of time, He exists within the frame of time, and He will exist after time expires. The second meaning is that He is the source of all

[1] To subscribe to Rabbi Diskind's weekly *dvar Torah,* please contact him at paysach@achim.org.

existence. It therefore follows that He is the only true existence; everything else exists only after He created it and nothing created Him.

The very name of Hashem therefore indicates that He is One and there can be none other. Hence, the *Chasam Sofer* asks what is the intent of the verse "Hashem is our G-d, Hashem is One." Why the redundancy? His very Name already indicates that He is One.

He answers that the second reference, that Hashem is One, is not intended to identify Hashem as being One. Rather, it is for us to articulate that in our life, in our ambitions, in our drives and goals He is One and there is none other. The verse therefore reads "*Shema Yisrael,* Hashem Who is our G-d, He is the only destination of all of our dreams and aspirations."

In this light we can appreciate why this verse represents the Jew's acceptance of the yoke of Hashem's sovereignty. With this statement the Jew proclaims that there is nothing in his life that does not move him in the direction of serving Hashem.

R' Yitzchak Aizik Chaver draws the parallel of the human body with its soul to the Jewish people with Hashem. The healthy body is one in which all the organs serve the greater body. The only way the soul can function as the life force is when all the body parts are completely dedicated to serving the larger body and its soul. The moment one of the organs chooses to follow its own path and its own interests to the exclusion of the body, the entire body will weaken and the soul will depart. So it is with the Jewish people. *Am Yisrael* is our body, Hashem is our soul, and every member of our people serves as a unique organ. We are the body of humanity who contain Hashem in this world. However, we can contain His Presence only when all the organs are completely dedicated to serving the larger nation and our Soul.

We can now appreciate why with the departure of the *Shechinah* from Yaakov he suspected that the dedication to Hashem was diminished. In their response with the *Shema* they answered with unequivocal clarity that they all accepted upon themselves the complete yoke of Hashem's sovereignty.

As heirs to this great legacy, we can remember this scene twice daily when we recite the *Shema* and bring the *Shechinah* into our lives.

# What *Moshe Rabbeinu* Saw [1]

## Ari Weiss

The *pasuk* in *Shemos* 2:11 says: *And he (Moshe) went to his brothers and looked upon their burdens...*

*Rashi* explains that Moshe "set his eyes and heart to feel pain for them." The *Gur Aryeh* points out an obvious question: Hadn't Moshe already seen his brethren toiling at labor, since he was a grown man at this point? The *pasuk*, *Rashi* tells us, must therefore be alluding to a deeper understanding of the situation than a mere visual observation; rather a deliberate effort by Moshe to comprehend and feel the agony of his fellow Jews.

*Moshe Rabbeinu* witnessed hundreds of thousands of Jews being tortured and subjected to back-breaking labor. Surely the facts registered in Moshe's mind. But it was not until Moshe looked again, not just to *see*, but to *feel* their suffering, that the Torah records him actually seeing their plight. Is it possible that a *tzadik* of Moshe's stature could overlook the details of the bondage?

Incredible as it may seem, man can look, and not clearly see; he can hear, yet not fully understand. Even *Moshe Rabbeinu*, the greatest prophet who ever lived, on some infinitesimal level, didn't completely feel the tragedy until he made an additional, intensive effort to totally empathize with their pain.

We should not trust our own senses nor our own sensitivities to receive an accurate picture of our fellow man's plight. Many of our brothers and sisters stagger under heavy burdens in life. People have emotional, financial, and social needs that cry out for help; but we

[1] Adapted from the talks of Rabbi Henach Leibowitz.

sometimes walk right by them and never hear that cry, unless we try to feel their pain. If *Moshe Rabbeinu* needed a special effort to gain a deeper understanding of the suffering of his brethren, and to respond properly, how much more should we be aware and sensitive by expending an extra measure of concern to properly feel the plight of our fellow Jews.

# A Burning Opportunity

## Rabbi Yehuda Menchel

It should be abundantly clear to everyone that the world we currently live in continues to descend into darkness and palpable uncertainty. Our only truly effective response as *bnei* and *bnos Torah* is to find strength in the *Torah HaKedoshah* and press ahead; looking for ways to increase *kevod Shamayim.* Below is another possible pathway to earn our much-needed *hatzlachah* and *rachamei Shamayim.*

שמות ב, י - וַיִּגְדַּל מֹשֶׁה וַיֵּצֵא אֶל אֶחָיו וַיַּרְא בְּסִבְלֹתָם
*And Moshe grew and he went out and he saw their suffering*
רש"י - וירא בסבלותם. נתן עיניו ולבו להיות מיצר עליהם
*He put his eyes and heart to be in pain on them*
שמות ב, כה - וַיַּרְא אֱלֹהִים אֶת בְּנֵי יִשְׂרָאֵל וַיֵּדַע אֱלֹהִים
*And Hashem saw Bnei Yisroel and Hashem knew*
רש"י - וידע אלהים. נתן עליהם לב ולא העלים עיניו:
*He put His heart on them and did not hide His eyes*
שמות ג, ו' - וַיַּסְתֵּר מֹשֶׁה פָּנָיו כִּי יָרֵא מֵהַבִּיט אֶל הָאֱלֹהִים
*And Moshe hid his face because he was afraid to look at Hashem*
בעל הטורים - ב' במסורה הכא ואידך ויסתר עמל מעיני. שאילו היה מביט בזיו השכינה בתוך הסנה והיה מבקש רחמים על ישראל לא היו גולים יותר כי הסנה הוא סימן עמו אנכי בצרה
*The word vayasteir is found twice, here and in Iyov, to teach us that if Moshe would have looked at the Shechinah in the sneh, and he would have asked for mercy for Bnei Yisroel then they would not have been exiled any longer because the sneh is a sign of "I (Hashem) am with him in pain."*

The Torah tells us that Moshe saw the suffering of *Klal Yisrael. Rashi* explains that he made himself understand and feel their pain. Later the Torah describes Hashem seeing *Bnei Yisrael* and again *Rashi* explains that Hashem made Himself feel their agony. Hashem then appears to Moshe in the *sneh,* a small shrub. Moshe hides his face, in direct contradistinction to his looking at *Klal Yisrael's* pain; he does not look at the *Shechinah's* pain symbolized in the *sneh.* The *Baal HaTurim* tells us that if Moshe had looked and *davened*, then *Klal Yisrael* would have been immediately freed from any further *galus*. What an incredibly powerful opportunity! But the question that begs to be asked is what was so significant here? What are we missing?

Conceivably, we can understand this by connecting with a famous idea from R' Chaim Volozhiner. In his sefer, *Nefesh HaChaim*, he writes that the most powerful *tefillah* a suffering person can *daven* is when he communicates to Hashem that while his own suffering is difficult, he recognizes that since Hashem loves him, Hashem is also hurting. He will then cry out "Please Hashem, I don't want You to suffer, remove my pain so You will not be in pain." It is difficult for us to look outside of ourselves when we are miserable, frightened and seemingly adrift in a raging storm we cannot control. To think of Hashem and take the perspective that Hashem's pain is more important than our own discomfort and *daven* for mercy to alleviate Hashem's pain is a very selfless *tefillah* of astonishing proportions.

Perhaps this is what the *Baal HaTurim* is referring to. Hashem appeared to Moshe in a small shrub, to convey that the *Shechinah* is in *tzar* pain/anguish. When hearing this reality, one must be or should be completely overwhelmed with wonder that the majestic, all-powerful Creator of the world is hurting, that His children are suffering so much. Can we even begin to comprehend what a *tefillah* would mean here? "Hashem, redeem Your nation and erase all the tears from all Your children because we can't bear to focus our hearts and see You in such pain!"

Moshe tried and succeeded being *noseh ohl im chavaro* and feeling *Klal Yisrael's* brutal suffering; but from Hashem's suffering, Moshe hid his face, he did not dare to attempt to be *noseh ohl* in Hashem's suffering because he thought: how can a human being look at such a thing.

Let us take a lesson from here that whenever we *daven*, we should try and take a few minutes to recognize the pain, the *tsaar,* of our *chaver*, our neighbor, our friend and realize Hashem is in *tsaar,* in suffering as well. Imagine if we could find it in ourselves to *daven* that Hashem should remove our *chaver's* suffering and *yesurim* so Hashem should not suffer. The ramifications could be instant and global in ways we could not imagine.

# The Matter Has Become Known

## Rabbi Avraham Bukspan [1]

וַיְהִי בַּיָּמִים הָהֵם וַיִּגְדַּל מֹשֶׁה וַיֵּצֵא אֶל אֶחָיו וַיַּרְא בְּסִבְלֹתָם וַיַּרְא אִישׁ מִצְרִי מַכֶּה אִישׁ עִבְרִי מֵאֶחָיו: ויפן כה וכה וירא כי אין איש ויך את המצרי ויטמנהו בחול: וַיִּפֶן כֹּה וָכֹה וַיַּרְא כִּי אֵין אִישׁ וַיַּךְ אֶת הַמִּצְרִי וַיִּטְמְנֵהוּ בַּחוֹל: וַיֵּצֵא בַּיּוֹם הַשֵּׁנִי וְהִנֵּה שְׁנֵי אֲנָשִׁים עִבְרִים נִצִּים וַיֹּאמֶר לָרָשָׁע לָמָּה תַכֶּה רֵעֶךָ: וַיֹּאמֶר מִי שָׂמְךָ לְאִישׁ שַׂר וְשֹׁפֵט עָלֵינוּ הַלְהָרְגֵנִי אַתָּה אֹמֵר כַּאֲשֶׁר הָרַגְתָּ אֶת הַמִּצְרִי וַיִּירָא מֹשֶׁה וַיֹּאמַר אָכֵן נוֹדַע הַדָּבָר:

*It happened in those days that Moshe grew up and went out to his brothers and saw their burdens; and he saw an Egyptian man striking a Hebrew man, of his brothers. He turned this way and that and saw that there was no man, so he struck down the Egyptian and hid him in the sand. He went out the next day and behold, two Hebrew men were fighting. He said to the wicked one, "Why would you strike your fellow?" He replied, "Who made you a man, a ruler, and a judge over us? Are you saying that you are going to kill me, as you killed the Egyptian?" Moshe was frightened and he thought, "Indeed, the matter has become known"* (*Shemos* 2:11-14).

The simple meaning of Moshe's statement, "Indeed, the matter has become known," is that now he realized that his treasonous conduct of the day before was in fact seen and would soon be reported to the authorities.

*Rashi* (citing *Shemos Rabbah* 1:30) tells us the deeper meaning of Moshe's words. Until now, he had wondered why *Bnei Yisrael* deserved to endure the oppressing servitude of Egypt, more than any other nation. However, now that he saw that Jews were informing on one another, he understood that they deserved the intense suffering they were being forced to undergo.

---

[1] Rabbi Bukspan has recently published the second edition of his *sefer, Classics and Beyond,* Parsha Pearls from Classic Commentators to Modern Times. It is available at the distributor, Feldheim.com, and *sefarim* stores.

In his *sefer Yabia Omer,* Rav Yehudah Leib Grubart expounds on this. The Torah writes that the day before, just prior to killing the Egyptian, "he turned this way and that and saw that there was no man." Rav Grubart explains that Moshe looked back and forth, to see if any of the victim's fellow slaves would intervene and come to his rescue. Unfortunately, Moshe saw "that there was no man," that the Jews were unable to stand up in their own defense and that he alone would have to intervene. Moshe presumed that the years of brutal oppression had beaten down *Bnei Yisrael* to the point where they had become disheartened and demoralized, unable to stand up for themselves.

Yet this assessment was challenged the next day, when he saw two Jewish men fighting. He saw that they still had reserves of spirit, and that they were able to stand up and defend their personal interests. Far from being broken with no strength, as he had assumed the day before, the people possessed a zealous and violent rage, but only in defense of grievances against one another. This answered Moshe's question regarding the reason for their servitude. He sadly realized that they were not worthy of redemption, as they showed strength when protecting their own interests, but not the interests of others.

The *Ksav Sofer* uses this to explain why Pharaoh felt the need to enslave *Bnei Yisrael*, why he was so worried that *Bnei Yisrael* would join the Egyptians' enemies and chase them out of their own land (1:10). When bringing *bikkurim,* we state (*Devarim* 26:6), *Vayarei'u osanu haMitzrim.* The word וירעו has the word רע, *evil,* at its root, meaning that the Egyptians mistreated us. The *Ksav Sofer,* however, has a different interpretation of the word: The Egyptians viewed us as רע, *evil*; we were a people who could not be trusted to remain loyal to the country. For their self-preservation, they felt compelled to enslave us.

The question is: Why? What gave Pharaoh the notion that his loyal and honored guests would turn against their accommodating hosts and benefactors?

When Moshe saw how one brother could turn on another, and also that they were willing to inform on Moshe himself, he understood. If brother can turn against brother, then what's to stop them from treating the Egyptians with any less disdain? What's more, they had no respect for their own elders and instead felt the need to bring their cases and complaints before the king. The Egyptians had reason to fear; if one can harm a brother and not properly honor his own leaders, he can certainly harm another.

The *Kli Yakar* brings proof of *Bnei Yisrael*'s tendency toward conflict and how it brought about their undoing from elsewhere in the *parashah*. When Hashem first appeared to Moshe, it was from a burning bush (3:2): *Vayeira malach Hashem eilav be'labas eish mi'toch hasneh vayar ve'hinei hasneh bo'er ba'eish ve'hasneh einenu ukal*, An angel of Hashem appeared to him in a flame of fire from within the thornbush. He saw and behold, the bush was burning in the fire but the bush was not consumed.

*Rashi* tells us that Hashem appeared to Moshe in a fire within a thornbush and not any other tree, to convey the idea of (*Tehillim* 91:15): *Imo Anochi be'tzarah,* I am with him in distress. However, according to the *Kli Yakar,* the burning thornbush represents the noisy infighting, which sounds like the crackling thorns inside a fire. Furthermore, the fire appeared *mi'toch hasneh,* from within the thornbush, to symbolize that our prickly and contentious nature, like that of the thornbush, was the trigger that ignited the flames of our current suffering. Similarly, the *pasuk* says, *Ve'hinei hasneh bo'eir ba'eish,* Behold, the bush was burning in the fire, instead of saying that the fire was burning in the bush. Again, the implication is that the fire came from within the thornbush, that it was the cause of the fire, and not that the fire was the cause of the bush burning.

*Bnei Yisrael*'s abrasive behavior toward one another was the cause of our unusual suffering, more than any other nation.
Normally, an oppressed and enslaved population finds comfort and succor from one another. When the overlords dominate, we must band together to survive. I help you and you help me, and somehow we will see it through. But when our old nemeses of *sinah* and *kinah* are still to be found, we only exacerbate our suffering.

The saddest thing, the *pasuk* concludes, is that although the *Yidden* were burning in a fire of their own making, they were not yet ready to do what it took to change. The suffering from the oppressive Egyptians – which may have been the result of their own contempt for one another – should have caused them to put aside their differences and destroy the "thorns" that plagued them, just as the fiery flames should have consumed the bush. Yet, *hasneh einenu ukal*, the bush was not consumed; the fighting endured, as the Jews refused to give in and make peace. Although the conflict caused so much pain and so much harm, the people were not wise enough to end it.

So often, people "set fire" to their lives through senseless bickering and fighting, refusing to allow the "thorns" to be consumed. They will not relent, give in, back down, and move forward, despite the havoc the conflict is causing. The *Kli Yakar's* image of the burning thornbush should serve as a reminder to put an end to conflict – before the "fire" overwhelms.

The Midrash (*Shemos Rabbah* 2:5) relates that a gentile asked Rabbi Yehoshua ben Karchah: Why did Hashem reveal Himself to Moshe from within a thornbush, a low and insignificant bush? Rabbi Yehoshua answered that this is to teach us that there is no place uninhabited by the *Shechinah,* even a thornbush.

Two questions present themselves. First, if no place is without the *Shechinah,* why do we have a mitzvah to build the Mishkan, a place in which to house the *Shechinah*? Second, why is this the message given to Moshe specifically at this point, when he was charged with his mission to go save the Jews?

The *Maharal* (*Gevuros Hashem* §23) has a different, more positive, way of explaining the symbolism of the thornbush, which will also answer these questions. The Maharal explains that Rabbi Yehoshua ben Karchah was not saying that the Shechinah is in every place. Rather, it can reside in every place, however lowly that may be. Were Hashem to have revealed Himself in a tall sycamore tree, one may have thought that only great people are capable of perceiving the *Shechinah* and connecting to Hashem. But that is not so.

Until this point, Moshe felt that *Bnei Yisrael* were unworthy of being saved; he had seen their conduct the day he was forced to flee. In addition, the Jews had descended to the forty-ninth level of impurity. Who's to say that people so spiritually low could connect to the Divine and be rehabilitated?

Hence, Moshe was shown the *Shechinah* from within the *sneh,* a lowly bush, to allude that no matter how low as a person or a people have fallen, the *Shechinah* can still grace that place. No one is beyond hope; no one is beyond the elevation that connection to the *Shechinah* can bring. *Bnei Yisrael* may have been as low as the thornbush, but they could still rise to the forty-ninth level of holiness and receive the Torah.

When it comes to a relationship with Hashem and beholding the *Shechinah,* the past is not nearly as significant as the future. As long as the lowly bush is willing to strive and grow into a tree, Hashem is prepared to grace His *Shechinah* upon it.

# The Making of a *Manhig*

## Rabbi Avraham Bukspan [1]

וַיְהִי בַּיָּמִים הָהֵם וַיִּגְדַּל מֹשֶׁה וַיֵּצֵא אֶל אֶחָיו וַיַּרְא בְּסִבְלֹתָם וַיַּרְא אִישׁ מִצְרִי מַכֶּה אִישׁ עִבְרִי מֵאֶחָיו.

*It happened in those days that Moshe grew up and went out to his brothers and saw their burdens; and he saw an Egyptian man striking a Hebrew man, of his brothers* (*Shemos* 2:11).

The Torah mentions only a few short details about the life of Moshe before he was chosen to lead the Jews out of Egypt and through the *midbar*. Yet each vignette describes his care for others, clarifying just why he was chosen as *Klal Yisrael's* leader.

On the *pasuk* cited above, *Rashi* points out that the previous *pasuk* already informed us that Moshe grew up. As such, the words in this *pasuk* are not referring to growing in age, but in position, stature, and authority; for Pharaoh appointed Moshe over his household. Yet despite the fact that he was raised in the royal palace and was recently chosen to be in charge of the palace, Moshe went out to his brothers and saw their burdens. *Rashi* tells us that this means that he directed his eyes and his heart to be distressed over their predicament.

The Midrash (*Shemos Rabbah* 1:27) describes how Moshe put aside his own rank and responsibilities and offered his shoulder to his brothers to help with their burdens. Rav Yerucham Levovitz (*Daas Chochmah U'Mussar* §11) elaborates: Moshe went out to see the suffering firsthand and ingrain it in himself, to make it his own. Moshe was not so much assisting the downtrodden slaves – how

[1] Rabbi Bukspan has recently published the second edition of his *sefer, Classics and Beyond,* Parsha Pearls from Classic Commentators to Modern Times. It is available at the distributor, Feldheim.com, and *sefarim* stores.

much can one person to do for each and every one? – as trying to experience what they were experiencing. He wanted to understand just what they were going through and to really feel their pain.

The *pesukim* continue (2:12 through 3:1), informing us how Moshe saw an Egyptian striking a Hebrew man, and how he quickly killed the Egyptian to save the Jew. The next day, Moshe saw two Jews quarreling and censured them for fighting with each other. Unhappy that Moshe was meddling in their affairs, these two Jews told Pharaoh about Moshe's murderous act the day before, and Moshe was put on death row and forced to flee the country – all because he interceded to help a coreligionist. After fleeing to Midian and finding himself at the local well, Moshe saw the daughters of Yisro being harassed and again intervened, rescuing them and watering their flocks. As a result, he became the husband of one of these girls, Tzipporah, and the shepherd of the sheep belonging to her father.

The Midrash (*Shemos Rabbah* 2:2) inserts an important detail regarding Moshe's conduct as a shepherd. One day, as Moshe was looking after Yisro's sheep, one of the sheep ran away. Moshe ran after it until the lamb reached a small, shaded place. From a short distance, Moshe watched as the lamb found a pool of water and bent down to drink. He went over to the lamb and said with compassion, "I didn't know you ran away because you were thirsty. You must be so tired!" With that, he put the lamb on his shoulders and carried it all the way back to rejoin the flock. Hashem saw this and declared, "Since you take care of the sheep of human beings with such amazing mercy, I swear that you will become the shepherd of My sheep, *Klal Yisrael*." Soon after, Hashem spoke to Moshe and appointed him the leader of the Jews.

The common denominator of all these events – saving a fellow Jew from an Egyptian or from another Jew, saving girls from harassment, showing compassion to an animal – is Moshe's empathy, coupled with a willingness to do something to improve the state of affairs. All these acts speak of a person with an incredible feeling and concern for the needs of others, who truly shares their anguish and distress. Such a person is worthy of becoming a leader, for only one completely devoted to others can be trusted to rule over them.

As the Midrash (*Shemos Rabbah* 2:3) states, Hashem does not put a person in a position of greatness until he has been tested with small things. For this reason, both *David HaMelech* and *Moshe Rabbeinu* first served as shepherds, where they demonstrated their unbridled concern for others' needs, even the small ones, and thus earned the right to serve the Jewish nation as its leaders. As Rav Simchah Zissel, the Alter of Kelm, explains (*Ohr Rashaz, Shemos* §190), the Torah detailed the history of Moshe to show that it was because of the *middah* of being *nosei be'ol* (carrying another's burden) that he was chosen as our nation's leader.

The Alter points out how the extent of Moshe's sense of caring can be seen from the progression it took. When assisting his fellow brothers with their burdens, Moshe was showing his compassion to an entire group of people. His next action, though, demonstrated the importance he placed upon the individual, as well, as he saved just one person from being killed by an Egyptian. The following scene also involved him saving an individual, this time from being hit not by an Egyptian but by a fellow Jew. Yet this kind of behavior did not happen only in his country of his birthplace, but also in Midian, where he himself was a fugitive who was running away for his life; there and then, he was willing to save a group of non-Jewish girls and even willing to give their sheep to drink. As described by Rav Simchah Zissel, the greatness of Moshe's compassion was always on the rise.

Rav Yitzchak Goldwasser (*Tzerufah Imrascha, Parashas Shemos* 3:1) elaborates, explaining that the sequence in the Torah indicates how Moshe's *middos* advanced and improved with each act. In general, the more prestigious the recipient, the easier it is to do an act of kindness. Hence, as the level of the object of the kindness descended, the level of the giver of the kindness – Moshe – ascended. First, says Rav Goldwasser, he saved the precious *neshamah* of a holy Jew, allowing the person to live and continue serving Hashem. He then became involved in order to save a Jew from physical pain. After, he showed his concern for non-Jewish girls, from *Bnei Noach*. Finally, mercy on animals. In Rav Goldwasser's words, this act was the most beloved: "*Acharon acharon chaviv* – The final is the dearest."

Rav Goldwasser then adds that perhaps this is teaching us a lesson in our *avodas Hashem*. It is impossible to jump levels; one must start at the right point. If a person begins his growth by demonstrating mercy for animals, he may end up losing sight of what is truly important in the world, and may end up fulfilling the words of "*Zovchei adam agalim yishakun* — Those who slaughter man shall kiss the calves" (*Hoshea* 13:2). Rav Goldwasser makes mention of how the accursed German soldiers brutally beat the Jews while acting kind and loving to their dogs.

The Midrash (*Shemos Rabbah* 1:27) mentioned above also demonstrates how Moshe made a determined effort to develop this sensitivity of being *nosei be'ol*. When Hashem first appeared to Moshe from the burning bush, the verse says (*Shemos* 3:4), "Hashem saw that he turned aside to see, and G-d called out to him from amid the bush, and said, 'Moshe, Moshe,' and he replied, 'Here I am!' " The basic meaning of the first part of the verse is that Hashem saw that Moshe turned to take a look at the burning bush, which was aflame but was not being consumed by the fire, and then He called to him. But the Midrash explains that Hashem saw that Moshe worked on himself and his *middos*, purposely turning aside from all of his duties in the palace of the king to look into the suffering of his brothers. For that very reason, Hashem called to him and made him the leader.

Even more, Rav Simchah Zissel (*Chochmah U'Mussar* §99) teaches that in the merit of Moshe's being *nosei be'ol* and, as *Rashi* explained earlier, directing his eyes and his heart to be distressed over them, Hashem also directed His heart upon the Jews and did not hide His eyes from them (*Shemos* 2:25, *Rashi*).

This trait of Moshe's was already apparent when he was an infant. Earlier in the *parashah* (2:6), we read, *Vatiftach vatireihu es hayeled ve'hinei naar bocheh vatachmol alav vatomer mi'yaldei ha'Ivrim zeh, She opened it and saw him, the boy, and behold, a youth was crying; she took pity on him and said, "This is one of the Hebrew children."* When Pharaoh's daughter opened the basket that held Moshe, *Rashi* tells us that she noticed that a youth – not an infant – was crying, as his voice was like that of a *naar.* In response, she did not say, "This is a Hebrew child," but a lengthier phrase: "This is one of the Hebrew children."

Rav Meir Shapiro (*Imrei Daas, Parashas Shemos* 2:6) explains that an infant instinctively cries when in need. Babies are completely self-absorbed, focusing solely on their own comfort. A *naar,* however, an older boy, can look outside himself and see the distress of another. The tears he cries are not necessarily for himself but may very well be for others.

It made sense, Rav Shapiro says, that the infant inside the floating basket was crying because of his personal distress; he was, after all, in mortal danger. However, *Bas Pharaoh* noticed that even once the basket was out of the water and she had opened it, he was still crying.

At that point, she realized that the child was not crying because of his own hurt and pain, but due to the pain and suffering of his nation. That was when she concluded that this was no selfish infant crying, but a *naar,* who was thinking of others. Although miraculously saved from his own danger and distress, the child inside was consumed with thoughts of the other children who were being killed or were being thrown in the river. So she stated, *Mi'yaldei ha'Ivrim zeh,* that the child was crying for the suffering of all the other *yaldei ha'Ivrim,* all the other Hebrew children.

Even in his infancy, Moshe already displayed concern for others and cried for their suffering.

In fact, Pharaoh himself was keenly aware of the concept that only a person who is *nosei be'ol im chaveiro* (carrying the burden along with his friend) is worthy of being a leader. It is for this reason, explains Rav Yonasan Eibeshitz (*Tiferes Yehonasan, Parashas Va'eira* 6:14), that he did not enslave *shevet Levi*. Pharaoh knew, through witchcraft, that the eventual redeemer of *Klal Yisrael* would come from the tribe of Levi. Certain that only one who has suffered along with others can step up and become their leader, Pharaoh made sure to exempt *shevet Levi* from slavery so that the redeemer would not have a chance to develop the trait of being *nosei be'ol.* But Moshe involved himself in the work on his own, and so he was worthy of redeeming *Bnei Yisrael.*

Based on these words of the *Tiferes Yehonasan,* Rav Baruch Sorotzkin (*HaBinah VeHaBerachah, Parashas Shemos* 2:3) writes that this is the reason Moshe was placed in the water where so many other baby boys had been drowned. Although he could have been saved in any number of ways, he needed to share the painful experience of those mercilessly killed right there in the water. In this way, though Moshe was part of *shevet Levi* and not included in the servitude, he would still suffer along with his brothers and thus be able to serve as their redeemer.

Levi, the patriarch of the *shevet* and forebear of Moshe, already took steps years before the *galus* of Mitzrayim to ensure that his children would always feel the suffering of their brothers. The *Shelah HaKadosh* (*Derech Chaim Tochechos Mussar, Parashas Va'eira*) explains that this is why Levi gave his sons names reminiscent of the Yidden's suffering: The name Gershon (גרשון) is derived from the root of *geirim* (גרים), that the Jews were strangers in a strange land; Kehas (קהת) comes from the word meaning blunt, as the Jews' teeth were blunt from all their suffering and subjugation; and Merari (מררי) has the root of bitterness, as the Egyptians embittered the lives of *Bnei Yisrael*. That is why the Torah explicitly states (*Shemos* 6:16): "These are the names of the sons of Levi," as we can learn a lesson from their names, to participate in the pain and sorrow of the *tzibbur*, even if we ourselves are untouched.[2]

From such a home and such an upbringing can develop a *Moshe Rabbeinu*.

---

[2] See *Mikeitz,* True Empathy, *Mishpatim,* Sanctifying our Sanctuaries, and *Tazria, Tochachah* on Target, on this topic.

# Miracles and Hashem's Mercy

**Rabbi Moshe Grossman**

In the beginning of *Parshas Va'eira* (*Shemos* 6:3), Hashem tells Moshe, "I appeared to Avraham, to Yitzchak, and to Yaakov as *Keil Shakai* (often translated as G-d Almighty), but by My name, Hashem (the Tetragrammaton), I was not known to them." There is much discussion in the commentaries as to the meaning of this *pasuk*. Probably the most obvious question regarding this *pasuk* is that in *Sefer Bereishis* (15:7, 27:7, and 28:13) Hashem had indeed revealed Himself to the *Avos* by His name, Hashem. Why does this *pasuk* state that they did not know Him by that name?

The *Ramban* discusses this *pasuk* in great detail. I think that we can answer this question based on some of the ideas that he presents.

The *Ramban* first cites the *Ibn Ezra*, who clarifies the difference between Hashem's acting with strict justice and His acting with mercy. The *Ibn Ezra* begins by explaining what is meant by Hashem's acting with strict justice and then describes His relationship with the *Avos*. Hashem rewarded the *Avos* with wealth, success, and happiness through strict justice. All the largesse that He bestowed upon them was in accordance with normal, natural workings of the material world. He used the natural system that He had created to provide for them and to protect them. All that He did for them was done through the normal workings of the world and appeared as normal outcomes through cause and effect, always in accordance with the laws of nature. Now, however, Hashem informs Moshe that He will deal with their descendants with His attribute of Mercy. He will save them, guide them, and help them mercifully, even employing means that change the natural order.

The *Ramban* (*Shemos* 6:2) expands on the *Ibn Ezra*'s comments and explains that Hashem is revealing to Moshe that there will now be a change in how He is manifest in the world and in how He relates to the Jewish people. Hashem dealt with the *Avos* through His *Midas HaDin*, His Attribute of Divine Justice. Hashem did treat them with special care and protection and did bestow great reward commensurate with their magnificent and extraordinary efforts in serving Him. However, all of the reward and care came to them only through what appeared to be the natural course of events, as the *Ibn Ezra* stated. Hashem will now conduct His relationship with their descendants through His Attribute of Mercy, that is, by His great Name, the Tetragrammaton. The Jewish people will form His nation when they accept the Torah, which was given by His great name. What does all this mean?

We can understand the *Ramban*'s comments based on the explanation of the full implication of the Tetragrammaton found in the *Sefer Nefesh HaChaim* [2:2]. Hashem is referred to by many names in the Torah. However, unlike the Tetragrammaton, the other names describe Hashem's specific activities and actions in the world as they are. The Tetragrammaton describes how He relates to His entire creation, in general. That is, it describes His overall conduct towards the world, which is through His Attribute of Mercy. Hashem created and now maintains the world to bestow His goodness on humans to the greatest degree possible. This is an act of pure kindness. Furthermore, all that He does for us is done with kindness and compassion for our ultimate good. The *Ramban* is telling us that now He is about to show how much He cares for the Jewish people even if they do not deserve it. From now on, Hashem will demonstrate the degree to which He cares for the Jewish people by showing them that, in His mercy He will even upend the natural order in order to save them, to teach them that He holds absolute control over the world.

The significance of the amazing extent of Hashem's mercy is immense. Hashem gave humans free will so that they must choose good or evil. It is absolutely vital for Hashem's plan that we perfect ourselves and thereby acquire the goodness that He wants to bestow on us rather than accepting it as a gift, since only then it is truly ours. If we were to see Hashem regularly performing open miracles, especially if these miracles alter the natural order, His involvement in the world would be apparent, and we would lose our free will. Therefore, His hand in the world must be hidden. It is up to us to discover Him. However, in order to forge the Jewish people into His nation, Hashem performed open miracles in Mitzrayim to ingrain in the Jewish consciousness His involvement and control of the world and to shower them with mercy to convince us of His caring for us.

Recounting the Exodus every year reinforces our awareness of Hashem's special relationship with His nation and strengthens our dedication to Him. We need this annual spiritual injection grow further in Torah and deepen our relationship with Hashem.

# Thoughts about the *Makkos*

## Chaim Sugar

The *pasuk* in *Shemos* 8:17 tells us that Hashem is going to send the wild animals and the land that they are on. The *Chanukas HaTorah* questions what it means when it refers to sending land against the Mitzrim; how do you send land? He provides a very novel explanation.

*Rashi* explains that this *makkah* included all the animals. The *Chanukas HaTorah* questions how this is possible since the *Rash* in *Meseches Kelayim* refers to an animal that is called a *Yidoni*. This animal is tied to the ground by a cord connected to its body. If the cord is cut, the *Yidoni* dies.

This explains the *pasuk*. The only way this animal could have been part of this m*akkah* is if it, and the ground that it is attached to, both were sent to Mitzrayim.

The *pasuk* in *Shemos* 9:29, tells us that Moshe told Pharaoh he will need to leave the city in order to be able to *daven* for him. The *Chanukas HaTorah* asks why only after this *makkah* did Moshe need to leave the city to *daven*. Explains the *Chanukas HaTorah:* normally sheep are kept outside of the city. The Egyptians worshiped sheep. The prior *makkah* was the *makkah* of *barad*. The righteous Egyptians brought their sheep into the city to protect them from *barad*. Since the Egyptian *avodah zarah* was now in the city, Moshe had to leave the city to be able to *daven*.

The Midrash in *Shemos* 14:1 writes that all the *malachim* agreed with Hashem when He told them about the *makkah* of *choshech.* The Medrash gives two reasons explaining the need for this *makkah.* One was to allow the *Bnei Yisrael* to go to the Mitzrim's houses to see where their valuable property was kept. The second reason was to keep hidden the fact that many of the *Bnei Yisrael* were going to die during this time.

The *Chanukas HaTorah* points out that the Midrash listed the reasons out of order; first it should have given the reasons for the *choshech* and then talked about all the *malachim* agreeing.

The answer he gives is again extremely clever. We know the halachah is if all of a Beis Din agree on a guilty verdict, the defendant is set free. This is if the whole Beis Din give the same reason for the guilty verdict. If different reasons are given, the verdict of guilty remains. Now that the *malachim* all agreed that the *makkah* of *choshech* was appropriate, why is this not a case of the full Beis Din all agreeing? This is why the Midrash lists the two reasons for the verdict, and therefore even if the full court agrees on a guilty verdict, the verdict stands.

In the first two *pesukim* in *Shemos* 11 Hashem tells Moshe that Pharaoh would chase out the *Bnei Yisrael* and that Moshe should convince them to "borrow" the Mitzrim's valuables. The *Chanukas HaTorah* sees a definite connection between these two *pesukim.*

The halachah is that if a worker quits the job before the proper time, he is at a disadvantage. On the other hand, if the owner forces the worker to leave the job before the proper time, the boss is at a disadvantage. The *Bnei Yisrael* were supposed to work for 400 years. They left Mitzrayim after 210 years. The Mitzrim wanted the *Bnei*

*Yisrael* to give back all that they took when they left because they did not finish the job. But now that it was Pharaoh, the boss, who made the worker leave early, the worker had the upper hand and therefore the *Bnei Yisrael* were not obligated to return what they took with them when they left.

In *Shemos* 10: 8-9, we are told of a brief conversation between Pharaoh, and Moshe and Aaron. Pharaoh asks which of the *Bnei Yisrael* should be allowed to leave Mitzrayim to bring a *korban* to Hashem. Moshe answers that "our young and old will be leaving." The *Baal HaTurim* explains the conversation as follows.

Pharaoh is saying to Moshe, why do you need all of the people to leave Mitzrayim? Do you want them all to enter Eretz Yisrael? All will not enter; they will die in the desert. Only Calev and Yehoshua will survive. And the words in *pasuk* 8, where Pharaoh asks *mi v'mi ha'holchim,* is the *gematria* of *Calev v'ben Nun.*

Moshe's response is "our young and old." Meaning those under twenty and those over 60 will not die in the desert and they will enter Eretz Yisrael.

The *Shach* in his *derashos* on the Haggadah (in a *sefer* called *Derushim Yekarim*, available on hebrewbooks.org or at Beigeleisen) has a number of interesting comments/questions about *Dayeinu.*

He points out that normally, this style of narrative would start with the greatest achievement and each step would go down a level. It should say "If not this great achievement, then even a lesser one

would be enough." Then it would continue to an even lower level. In our *Dayeinu*, however, it is the opposite; we start from a lower level and continue to move to higher levels.
He also questions why the author specifically chose these 15 events and no other miracles experienced while leaving Egypt. There is no mention of the pillars of light and fire, the well the accompanied them, the battle with Amalek, etc. He, of course, gives elaborate answers to these and the many other questions he poses, but space limitations do not allow for them to be detailed here. Maybe next year.

But let's begin with one issue. We say that had Hashem brought us "close" (*karov*) to *Har Sinai* and not given us the Torah, that would be sufficient. How could that be? The whole purpose of the world's existence is for us to get the Torah.

Could it be that the word *karov* used here does not mean "close" but actually "a relative?" Meaning, at *Har Sinai* is where He showed we are all related, we all have the same *yichus;* I too am a nephew or cousin of this *gadol* or that *gadol.* We are all related from the day of *Har Sinai.*[1]

[1] Editor's note: See the *Ramchal* in *Daas Tevunos* (§158, p. 171) for his approach to this question.

# Two Types of Blood

## Rabbi Yitzchak Friedman

וָאֶעֱבֹר עָלַיִךְ וָאֶרְאֵךְ מִתְבּוֹסֶסֶת בְּדָמָיִךְ וָאֹמַר לָךְ בְּדָמַיִךְ חֲיִי וָאֹמַר לָךְ בְּדָמַיִךְ חֲיִי (יחזקאל טז, ו), *I passed over you and saw you downtrodden in your blood, and I said to you, "Through your blood shall you live!" and I said to you, "Through your blood shall you live!"*

Our Rabbis (see *Mechilta*) point out that for Jews to have merited the Egyptian exodus, they needed to provide two types of blood. One would be the blood of the *korban pesach* and the other, the blood of male circumcision. Is there a deep connection between these two acts?

The Gemara in *Taanis* (27a) says:

אלו הן מעמדות (ופרש"י לעיל כ"ו.: המתענין מתפללין בעריהם שיתקבל ברצון קרבן אחיהם). ומה טעם תיקנו מעמדות, לפי שנאמר "צו את בני ישראל ואמרת אליהם את קרבני לחמי לאשי", והיאך קרבנו של אדם קרב והוא אינו עומד על גביו. התקינו נביאים הראשונים עשרים וארבעה משמרות, על כל משמר ומשמר היה מעמד בירושלים של כהנים ושל לוים ושל ישראלים. הגיע זמן משמר לעלות, כהנים ולוים עולין לירושלים.

The *tamid* offering was brought twice a day as part of the Temple service. It was a communal offering but was brought by the Kohanim alone. However, a group of Yisraelim would travel to Yerushalayim to represent the Jews on whose behalf the offering was brought. They would camp in Yerushalayim to oversee that the offering was indeed favorable to the Almighty. After all, the Torah uses the individual possessive in describing the communal Tamid offering, "את קרבני".

פסח וקדשים. ופ' רש"י הבעלים נצטוו דכתיב "וסמך ידו ושחט" (פסחים ז:)

An individual's *korban* requires that the owner himself do at least the *semichah* (the pressing of one's hands on the offering to prepare it for the Altar) by himself. If a communal offering is described in individual possessive terms, how much more so an individual's own offering must be brought by the individual themselves.

However, with the *korban pesach,* this would create a logistical nightmare. The Gemara there states:

דתניא רבי יונתן אומר, מנין שכל ישראל כולן יוצאים בפסח אחד, שנא' "ושחטו אותו כל קהל עדת ישראל בין הערבים", וכי כל הקהל כולם שוחטים, והלא אינו שוחט אלא אחד, אלא מכאן שכל ישראל יוצאים בפסח אחד.

It would create an impossible state of affairs had every Jew been required to enter the Temple courtyard on the afternoon before Pesach. The Torah provides a solution for this issue, *shechitah* through agency. The Gemara continues to say that all individual offerings, as well, can be brought through agency.

Similarly, the *Shulchan Aruch* (*Yoreh Deah,* 265:9) regarding the mitzvah of *bris milah*: אבי הבן עומד על המוהל להודיעו שהוא שלוחו, *the father of the son stands by the mohel to let him know that he is his agent.*

A *milah* can be performed by another Jew, the *mohel,* on behalf of the father. However, here it is necessary that the father be present to notify the *mohel* that he is acting as the father's agent. I assume that this necessity is to dispel any notion that the father does not agree to circumcise his son. At that point, any *mohel* can step forward and perform the *bris.* Although the *pesach* and *tamid* offerings have the same need for agency, practically speaking all the owners of the offering could not crowd into the Temple courtyard.

However, the *Beur HaGra* on the *Shulchan Aruch* (§40) cites the aforementioned Gemara in Taanis 27a, concerning the *maamodos*. He posits that just like the *tamid* offering needs the representatives of the Jewish people to be proximate at the time that it is offered, so too the father of the young son needs to be proximate. Though this comparison is already made by the *Tur* (loc. cit.), the *Gra* expresses the point by saying, שהמילה דוגמת קרבן, *circumcision is akin to an offering*. He marshals a proof to this comparison from a Midrash (*Vayikra Rabbah* 27:10).

The Midrash writes that just as an animal may not be brought as an offering before it passes through a Shabbos (an offering is invalidated if it is an animal younger than eight days old), so too a child must pass through a Shabbos before it can be circumcised on the eighth day. But what is the underlying connection between these two mitzvos?

The Midrash is connecting the two by saying that to achieve a higher status, the object of the mitzvah needs to encounter Shabbos. With that hint, perhaps, we can say as follows: Shabbos is on the seventh day of the week. In Jewish numerology, seven represents the natural order that was created in seven days. Shabbos is the highest value or number in that order. Shabbos gives meaning to the six-day work week. It symbolizes that all that we do in the natural world is meaningful when it is done in the service of Hashem. It also serves to give meaning and purpose to the subsequent work week.

The number eight represents an ascent above the constraints of natural order, the metaphysical. *Milah* is the rejection of the physical impulse to use the body to follow animalistic drives. It enables the Jew to realize his physicality only in the spiritual realm of marriage.

A *korban* also is the way a Jew reaches beyond the confines of this world and achieves closeness to Hashem. The word קרבן, *korban,* has the same root as the Hebrew word, קרוב, *karov* or close. A practical manifestation of this principle is the *halachic* insistence that a Jew pray facing towards the Holy of Holies. This is because from that location, prayers ascend to the Heavenly throne. The source for this halachah is probably the fact that absent a Temple where one could bring a offering to bond with Hashem, our prayers serve that function of getting close to Hashem.

However, the message in the law of the eight-day requirement is that to aspire to transcend the temporal, one has to first go through a Shabbos. One must first make sure that his daily life is led in an elevated fashion. One must be Shabbos-like, the whole week.

If the previous explanation is true, the *Gra z"l* can be understood in this light. *Milah* is like a *korban* in the sense that it is an attempt to live a transcendent life of connection to Hashem, and not to be ruled by one's natural impulses. At the naissance of the Jewish people, they were asked for a *korban pesach* and to circumcise themselves. This was an object lesson of what Hashem told Avraham, that the Jewish people would be beyond the control of astrological force of the *mazalos*. Hence, they needed both of these mitzvos to put them on their course of livingלמעלה מן הטבע, *elevated beyond physical nature.*

# Why a Donkey?

## Baruch Raczkowski

The first *perek* of *Bechoros* deals with the mitzvah of *peter chamor,* the commandment to redeem one's firstborn donkey. This is a unique mitzvah in the Torah in that a donkey, a non-kosher animal, is given a special sanctity of needing to be redeemed. The Gemara (5b) asks why we redeem a donkey, and not a camel or a horse. It answers that the donkey is given this special sanctity because it helped the Jewish people carry out all the riches from Mitzrayim. The Gemara describes that each Jew left with ninety Libyan donkeys filled with gold and silver. Many Rishonim and Acharonim talk about this Gemara. I heard a deeper explanation of this Gemara from Rabbi Sholom Rosner who explained it using the *Meshech Chochmah.*

The *Meshech Chochmah*[1] suggests a novel approach. He cites the *Yerushalmi* stating that the price for the *pidyon* of a human *bechor* is based on Rachel's firstborn son, Yosef, being sold for 20 *kesef,* or five *shekalim.* The implication of this *Yerushalmi* is that this mitzvah is a penalty for the sale of Yosef. But if the reason we redeem the firstborn is because of what the *shevatim* did to Yosef, why do the Leviim not have to also redeem their children? The money should definitely not be given to any descendants of Levi; it should be given to Yosef's descendants. Furthermore, why does the tribe of Yosef have to perform this mitzvah at all?

In order to answer these questions, the *Meshech Chochmah* explores the reason why we need to redeem every firstborn in commemoration of the events that happened long ago. One of the most prominent aspects of *makkas bechoros* is the clarity that Divine providence is constantly running the world. If there is constant

---

[1] As quoted by Rabbi Sholom Rosner.

Divine providence, then even when a person goes through a difficult time, we know that Hashem orchestrated that as well. These are not separate events, but all pre-planned as part of the Divine will for the destiny of *Am Yisrael* and the world. For this reason, when commemorating this *makkah* by performing the mitzvah of redeeming the firstborn, we also find references to the beginning of the process that started our servitude. When a person performs this mitzvah, he will realize that all the suffering and salvations (on both personal and national level) are part of the Divine will which will result in the ultimate redemption. The price for redeeming a firstborn son is set to remind a person that the same Divine providence that took us out of Egypt with open miracles was the exact same Divine providence that was behind Yosef being sold to Mitzrayim. All done with *hashgachah pratis.*

Then why was the donkey singled out for this special status? The *Meshech Chochmah* explains that the donkey was how the *shevatim* first traveled down to Egypt because of famine, which seems to be a random event in history. In his notes on the bottom of the *Meshech Chochmah,* Rabbi Kuppermen notes that the Torah mentions the donkey numerous times in *Parashas Miketz.* However, in *Parashas Vayigash,* when Yaakov left for Egypt to see his son Yosef, the Torah no longer mentions donkeys. A lot of times we see things happen in life that really do not seem to relate to each other. A person might think that it was good luck or bad luck, but the events are not connected. However, when we look back, we see that really these events were connected and that ultimately it was for our good. Hashem is always preparing every event in the world. Starting with Yosef being sold and the brothers going down to Mitzrayim on donkeys to buy food in a famine, all the events were orchestrated by Hashem's *hashgachah pratis* like a chain that led to the exit from Egypt.

The redemption of the firstborn donkey reminds us that from the time we went down to Egypt to the time that we left Mitzrayim was all *hashgachah pratis.* At the same time that Hashem promised Avraham that He would bring us to a strange land where the Jewish people would become a great nation, there was also a promise that He would bring the Jewish nation out with great miracles. At the very beginning all the plans were there: how the Jewish people would come to Mitzrayim, the suffering in Mitzrayim, and the salvation. Those who saw the final redemption understood that everything that happened was *hashgachah pratis.*

This could be a deeper understanding of the Gemara mentioned earlier. By being a part of both the beginning and the end of the story of Mitzrayim, the donkey symbolizes that the entire story was with the exact same level of Divine providence. The same Hashem who used donkeys to bring the Jewish nation down to Mitzrayim was the same Hashem who sent *Bnei Yisrael* out with the spoils of Mitzrayim on donkeys.

Rabbi Shalom Rosner quotes the following question from Rabbi Lau: Why are the stanzas of *Chad Gadya* separated? The entire story seems to be one chain of cause and effect leading to Hashem slaughtering the *malach hamaves.* If so, only the last part, with the complete story, should be sung, not all the stanzas separately, adding only one piece at a time. The Haggadah *Shiras Miriam,* written by Rabbi Yosef Zvi Rimon, discusses the lessons of *Chad Gadya.* He writes that there are times when all we see is the world in upheaval. When the world is in chaos, it is very difficult to feel a guiding hand coordinating events behind the scenes. Sometimes we are able to get a glimpse of a piece of the story, but more often than not we do not understand at all. We sing the story of *Chad Gadya* the way we experience it. When we perform the mitzvah of *pidyon haben,* the mitzvah will help us internalize this idea – that there is a master plan that connects all of history even if we only see pieces. When we get to the last stanza, it will become clear that everything is in its proper place.

Hashem promised Avraham that He would bring us into a land where we would be strangers, and that we would become slaves, but He would take us out as a great nation. Hashem's promises are never broken; they are guaranteed even though nobody knows the details. He brought the *shevatim* on donkeys with no food to Mitzrayim and brought the Jewish nation out with 90 donkeys each laden with gold and silver.

Hashem took us out of Jerusalem; He will most certainly bring us back to Jerusalem with *nissim* and *niflaos* greater than what was seen in Egypt. And the different events that take place is a chain which will ultimately lead Mashiach to come very soon in our time.

# *Mitocham* [1]

## Moshe Rock

In the history of the world, there has never been a greater example of a weak and captive people being rescued and redeemed in miraculous fashion from the grip of a stronger and overly oppressive nation than the story of *Yetzias Mitzrayim. Rashi* tells us (*Shemos* 18:19) that the Egyptians "locked" their land to the point that even a single stray servant was unable to slip away undetected. The Egyptian sorcerers, the most powerful in the entire world, even cast a spell around the borders of Egypt, denying anyone the right to leave (*Ibn Ezra*); yet in the blink of an eye, well over a million men, women, and children just walked right out!

The *Ben Ish Chai,* Chacham Yosef Chaim *z"l,* writes that this allusion is found in the word מתוכם, *mitocham,* meaning "from their midst." It begins with an open *mem,* מ, and ends with a closed *mem,* ם, to symbolize that when *Bnei Yisrael* came into the land of Mitzrayim, it was open to them. Later, however, when they wanted to leave, it was closed off. Thus, the greatness of *Yetzias Mitzrayim* lies in the *pasuk* that states, "*V'hotzeisi es Yisrael mitocham,* I will take out *Bnei Yisrael* from their midst" (*Shemos* 7:5). The word מתוכם can be divided to convey מתוך ם, *mitoch mem.* That is, Hashem will take out *Bnei Yisrael* from (מתוך) the confines (ם) of Egypt. Hashem redeemed his Chosen Nation amid miracles and wonders even from the constricted borders of the land of Mitzrayim.[2]

---

[1] Printed with permission from Rabbi Hoffman, author of *Torah Tavlin* on the Haggadah.

[2] Someone pointed out further that the word מצרים itself begins with an open *mem* and ends with a closed *mem.* It is easier to enter, but the exit is closed.

I heard another explanation of the term *mitocham,* which fits with the *remez* of the *Ben Ish Chai.* In the other places in the *Parshah,* Hashem says that he will take the Jewish people out of "Mitzrayim." Why does He say here that He will take them out *mitocham,* from their midst?

The answer in short is that it is easier to take the Jews out of Mitzrayim than to take Mitzrayim out of the Jews. In other words, Hashem could certainly take the physical bodies of the Jews out of Mitzrayim. But they would still act like Egyptian slaves. Hashem was promising that He would take the entire Egyptian culture out of the Jewish people's consciousness. That is, He was going to take the Jews out of "the midst" of Mitzrayim, i.e., out of the Egyptian's way of life.

# Ben Amram

## Rabbi Yehoshua Silverberg

In the special *Haftarah* we read on Shabbos *Erev Rosh Chodesh* we find a curious conversation between *Shaul HaMelech* and his son Yehonasan. Although they are both discussing the same person, they continually refer to him by different names. Shaul only uses the name *"Ben Yishai"* whereas Yehonasan always calls him by his name "Dovid."

*Rashi* in *Tehillim* (§4) explains that the idea of not calling someone by their own name is a form of disgracing that person, as if they have no name. We find a similar idea in *Parshas Shelach*, after the *Meraglim* return and begin delivering their report to discourage the *B'nei Yisrael* from continuing to Eretz Yisrael. The *pasuk* says that Calev quieted down the mob by directing their attention toward *Moshe Rabbeinu*. As *Rashi* explains, Calev called out "Is this the only thing that *'Ben Amram'* has done for us?", indicating that Calev planned on adding additional derogatory information about *Moshe Rabbeinu* which the crowd was eager to hear.

After *Klal Yisrael* left Mitzrayim and traveled to Succos, Hashem told *Moshe Rabbeinu* to turn back towards Mitzrayim, tricking Pharaoh into thinking that the Jews were lost in the desert. The *pasuk* states ויעשו כן, that the Jews did so, and *Rashi* explains that the Torah is praising the Jews, for they did not say "How can we approach our pursuers, we must flee!" Rather they said, "We only have the words of *Ben Amram."* This language, which *Rashi* quotes from the *Mechilta*, seems out of place. Here we find the Jews blindly following *Moshe Rabbeinu's* directive even though it would seem a bit risky. Why do they use the usually derogatory name of *Ben Amram*?

This is especially difficult in light of the words of the *Baal HaTurim* in *Parshas Masei*. The Torah there refers to this encampment with the word וישב, *it dwelled,* using a singular form. The *Baal HaTurim* explains that this reflects their unanimous desire to follow *Moshe Rabbeinu's* command. This magnifies the question: At this point, as *Klal Yisrael* demonstrated such a dedication to the words of *Moshe Rabbeinu*, why would they not call him in the most respectful way?[1]

In the ninth *perek* of *Hilchos Melochim*, the *Rambam* lists the development of the mitzvos. *Adam HaRishon* received six mitzvos, *Noach* was given the seventh mitzvah of אבר מן החי, the *Avos* added additional mitzvos, and in *Mitzrayim,* Amram was commanded in additional mitzvos until *Moshe Rabbeinu* came, through whom the Torah was completed. There is no clear source for the words of the *Rambam* that Amram was commanded in additional *mitzvos*, (see *Kesef Mishneh*), and various sources are suggested by the *Meforshim.*

The Gemara in *Sotah* (12a) relates that after Pharaoh decreed that all male babies must be thrown into the Nile, Amram divorced his wife Yocheved, and all of the Jews followed and divorced their wives. Miriam complained to her father that his decree (to divorce) was more severe than Pharaoh's for three reasons: (1) Pharaoh decreed only on the males, but your decree of divorce is even on female babies; (2) Pharaoh*'s* decree only affects *Olam HaZeh*, whereas your decree is even in regard to *Olam HaBah*; (3) Fulfillment of Pharaoh's decree is in doubt, but your decree will definitely be fulfilled.

The *Maharatz Chayes* cites this Gemara as the source for the *Rambam* in the beginning of *Hilchos Ishus.* The *Rambam* explains

[1] See also the *Sfas Emes* (5638) that the *amud haanan* did not lead the way to guide them in this instance; rather, Hashem wanted the Jews to trust in *Moshe Rabbeinu.*

there that before *Matan Torah* marriage was not based on any *kinyan*; rather, if they both wanted to get married, they would simply begin living as husband and wife. Similarly, if they chose to dissolve the relationship, no formal act of *geirushin* was required, since there was no *kiddushin.* So why does the Gemara state that Amram did a *geirushin* and *a maaseh likuchin* when he divorced his wife and remarried her? It must be that these are the mitzvos that Amram was commanded in Mitzrayim.

The obvious difficulty with this *pshat* is that of all the 613 mitzvos, the *Rambam* explicitly states that the mitzvos of *kiddushin* and *geirushin* were given at *Matan Torah.* Certainly, it is not simple to say that they were given earlier, in Mitzrayim.

In addition, it does not seem to be a strong proof that they were commanded already, for we find many times that the Jews kept the mitzvos even before they were commanded. We even find specifically regarding this mitzvah of *kiddushin* that this mitzvah was kept earlier, as *Rashi* quotes in *Parshas Vayechi* that Yosef showed *Yaakov Avinu* his *shtar eirusin.*

A slightly different source for the *Rambam*, also based on this Gemara, is printed in the name of *R' Chaim.* The mitzvah that was given to Amram was the mitzvah of *chuppah*, as the *Gemara* states that הושיבה באפריון, referring to the mitzvah of *chuppah.* The advantage of this *pshat* is that we don't find any source of this mitzvah before Amram; However, the other question asked previously would still be difficult, as the fact that the mitzvah was performed is not necessarily proof that the Jews were commanded. In any event, the *Rambam* says that Amram was commanded in מצוות יתירות, multiple mitzvos.

In the *Sefer Chidushei Ben Aryeh,* we find another possible explanation. One of Miriam's claims against Amram was that his decree will definitely be fulfilled, but the fulfillment of Pharaoh*'s* decree is in doubt. The *Chidushei Ben Aryeh* notes that even before *Matan Torah* the Jews were obligated in the mitzvah of לא תסור, to fulfill the decrees of the *Chachamim*. For this reason, it was certain that Amram's decree would be fulfilled, for the Jews had an obligation to listen to Amram, as it says in the Gemara in *Sotah* that *Amram* was the *Gadol HaDor*.

My dear cousin, R' Gedalya Hoffnung of B'nei Brak, suggested that according to this we can provide an answer to our original question. Why did the Jews here refer to *Moshe Rabbeinu* as *Ben Amram*, a seemingly derogatory name? The answer is that the name was not derogatory; rather, it was a reference to the reason it was absolutely required to listen to *Moshe Rabbeinu*. *Moshe Rabbeinu* is indeed *Ben Amram*, the son of Amram, who was *mekabel* the *mitzvah* of listening to the Gedolim. Certainly, we must listen to his own son's decrees!

I would like to add one more *pshat* in the *Rambam* in *Hilchos Melachim*. The *Meshech Chochmah* in *Parshas Shemos* offers another suggestion. The *pasuk* says: אנכי אלקי אביך אלקי אברהם אלקי יצחק ואלקי יעקב. When speaking to Moshe, Hashem is putting Moshe's father Amram together with the *Avos*. How did Amram make this list? The *Meshech Chochmah* says that this is the source for the *Rambam* that Amram was part of the *Mesores HaTorah*, the transmission of Torah, and received additional mitzvos in Mitzrayim.

According to this *pshat,* the *Rambam* is very exact. The *Rambam* there lists the specific mitzvah which each of the *Avos* were commanded. But in regard to Amram the *Rambam* does not specify, saying *only that in Mitzrayim, Amram was commanded in "additional mitzvos."* According to the *Meshech Chochmah*, the reason for this is because the *Rambam* did not have a source as to which mitzvos Amram was commanded, just a proof that he was one of the *Mekablei HaTorah*.

# *Yeshuos Hashem,* Large and Small

## Jeffrey Silverberg

The wonders of Hashem are without limit. The goodness that He bestows upon the world is unimaginable. As we celebrate Pesach, we relive and re-experience two of the greatest expressions of Hashem's might and love for His people, the *geulah* of *Yetzias Mitzrayim* and *Kerias Yam Suf,* and we begin to count toward the greatest manifestation of Hashem's Kingship, the revelation of His Glory at *Har Sinai* and *Matan Torah.*

Stunning in their power, sweeping in their beauty, *Yetzias Mitzrayim* and *Kerias Yam Suf* were unprecedented events that upended the natural order of the world and shouted a powerful message that reverberated through the universe and continue to echo through the generations.

As we reflect on the magnificent, large-scale miracles that forged our nation and continue to bind each of us in a powerful, personal relationship with Hashem centuries later, we also recognize the smaller-scale, personal miracles that Hashem performs for each individual. Hashem watches over every individual every moment, every second; and there are seemingly small, but actually momentous moments of rescue and salvation, every day. Let me tell you about one such event.

I was born and raised in Charleston, West Virginia, a small, but surprisingly cosmopolitan town, with a population of about 70,000; and a Jewish community of about 1,500 people. Although only a handful of people were truly observant, almost everyone in the Jewish community was very committed to the Bnai Jacob synagogue, and day to day activities frequently centered around the shul. There was no day school, but boys went to *cheder* for four years, girls for two. There was an active Sunday school, very competitive boys' and girls' basketball teams in the city Church League, and many social programs for adults. There were morning and evening *minyanim* and the congregants kept count and took great pride in the *minyan* "streak." (A hot breakfast every morning played no small part in that endeavor).

Bar mitzvah boys were expected to learn and lead the Shabbos morning *davening,* both *Shacharis* and *Musaf.* The shul owned a full set of *Nevi'im* in *klaf* and almost everyone read his *haftarah* from the *klaf.* The RCA De Sola Pool *siddur* was on the shelves, and the *bimah* was properly situated in the middle of the shul, although the pews around the *bimah* were populated with mixed seating.

Paul Reiss, *a'h* was our cantor, as well as a Hebrew School teacher and the leader of the youth program. Cantor Reiss thought it important that the children of the shul be exposed to Orthodoxy, and Bnai Jacob became affiliated with Yeshiva University Shabbatons, and later, when it came into existence, NCSY.

Unfortunately, Cantor Reiss passed away suddenly when I was in the tenth grade. The shul, perhaps because of the shortcoming of mixed seating, was unable to secure a new *chazan.* But no problem! Since the boys were taught and became somewhat fluent in leading the services on Shabbos morning, a rotation was set up. You would get a postcard that you were leading one of the services on a particular week, and you would show up and lead that service. Again, there was pride in the shul and the services, and it was rare for a boy not to change his plans (not every boy went to shul every Saturday morning) and not show up to help. At that point in my life, it would have taken me fifteen or twenty minutes of breaking my teeth to say a weekday *shemoneh esrei,* but I knew Shabbos morning davening, beginning from *shochein ad,* practically by heart.

I had a friend named Joel Zacks who was a year older than I and was on his way toward observance due to NCSY. (He has now been sitting and learning in Jerusalem for many years). We both attended George Washington High School and Joel was in the United Nations Club. The yearly mock Security Council meeting was approaching, and Joel was busy in the school library for weeks. GW was going to be Israel at the meeting and the protocol was for each "country" to give its opening statement in its native language. Joel was occupied with his Hebrew-English dictionary for quite a while.

But there was a problem. The Security Council was set to meet on a Saturday morning, and it was just about at this time that my friend reached the point in his progress towards observance that he just could not get in a car and drive or be driven on Shabbos to attend and deliver his remarks. So, hey Jeff, buddy, would you mind doing me a favor, even though you are not in the UN club, and read the speech for me? Since it was not my turn to lead the *davening* at shul, I agreed.

The fateful morning arrived. Every high school in the Charleston School District sent a delegation to Stonewall Jackson High School (since merged into Capitol High). There must have been close to 300 people in a very large, very well-lit auditorium, as the mock Secretary General called the mock Security Council to order.

Shortly, the Speaker called upon the distinguished representative of the State of Israel to deliver his opening remarks. I stepped to the lectern, looked around the room, and pulled the folded speech from my inside jacket pocket.

I opened it.

For the first time.

The speech was not typed, it was not printed neatly, it was scribbled in a sort of *Rashi* script that, no disrespect intended, closely resembled chicken scratch. I had no chance. I had 300 people looking at me. I had some sense that in some very small way I was representing the Jewish people and the State of Israel. And I had no chance.

And then Hashem saved me. He saved me from personal embarrassment. He saved me from shaming my high school, its UN Club, and my friend, who had counted on me (even though it was *he* who did not type the speech). And in some way, He saved me from reflecting poorly on my people and the State of Israel.

It would not be at all accurate to say I thought of it. It just came into my head.

*"Mechalkail chaim bechesed,"* I found myself saying. *"Mechayei meisim b'rachamim rabim,"* I said with conviction. *"Someich noflim vrofei cholim"* I shouted, ***"UMATIR ASSURIM,"*** I thundered!

And I basically recited most of *Musaf.*

I looked around the auditorium, nodded respectfully, and went back to my seat.

One lady, a Gentile lady who lived some distance from Charleston and would not have had occasion to be in a synagogue, told me afterwards that something about my speech sounded familiar. She was the only one.

I did not tell Joel what happened for many years.

Hashem surely saved me that morning. It was not as dramatic as *Kerias Yam Suf.* But it was cut from the same cloth.

Let us appreciate all of the *yeshuos Hashem,* large and small, whether personal or national, whether we are aware of them or unaware, for they surely happen every day, morning, noon, and night.

# The "Miracle" of an NDE

## Yirmiyahu Lauer [1]

Probably one of the most famous questions in discussing the momentous miraculous events which happened during *Yetzias Mitzrayim* is "where are all the open miracles today?" Here we are at this pivotal time of the year when our ancestors experienced such monumental supernatural events. Why don't we see any open miracles today? Why is it seemingly so different today?

A common assumption is that if only Hashem would perform some open miracles today, the clarity would remove all doubt, since we now would see the hand of Hashem with our own eyes. Wouldn't life be so much better and so much easier if only Hashem would just repeat what He did in the past? Is it even fair that Jews during the time of the Torah had such a tangible, open realization of Hashem's reality and His *hashgachah* and today we have none of that? Why shouldn't we experience this same manifestation of Hashem? Can our *emunah* be really judged at the same level as those who experienced such miraculous events? At first glance, it seems like they had it so much easier since Hashem made it so much clearer for them.

The answer frequently given for this fundamental question is that the premise of the question is not true. Who says there are no miracles today? Of course there are! There are indeed a plethora of miracles happening every second. From the birth of a child to the sun rising in the morning, we see miracles through every aspect of our lives. Therefore, it doesn't seem like this problem is a problem at all.

---

[1] Yirmiyahu Lauer is a respiratory therapist who has researched the phenomenon of NDE's for many years. He shares his findings with us.

However, as true as this is, it does not quite answer the question. Sure, the fact that we are breathing, walking, talking, and thinking is nothing short of a miracle, but the question wasn't why don't miracles happen today. The question was why don't miracles like those of *Yetzias Mitzrayim* happen today. Why don't we see open miracles that defy nature? Where are all the seas splitting and the Prophets resurrecting children?

Yes, the miracles we see today are theoretically miracles, too; but we don't see them as such because we are used to them. We are used to seeing the sun rise in the morning and even seeing a baby born, so we don't consider these as "real" miracles. The impact these everyday happenings have on our *emunah* and ultimately how they inspire us to do what's right is minimal at best. The assumption is that to be sufficiently inspired and truly want to become a changed person we need to see a phenomenon we don't expect. All miracles we experience today we fully expect.

Therefore, we are back to the original question which we haven't answered. Why don't we see open miracles today and how is it fair that *Klal Yisroel* during *Yetzias Mitzrayim* saw miracles and we don't?

I'd like to suggest that not only do we see miracles today, we have been documenting these miracles for many decades and have probably been experiencing them for centuries. Supernatural miracles are constantly occurring which are on par with the Biblical miracles we so wish we would see today.[2]

So what are these miracles? They are known as Near Death Experiences (NDEs). Most people have heard of this; many know of

---

[2] See the famous *Ramban* at the end of *Bo,* who says that from the open miracles we can learn that Hashem is always directing the world in a miraculous way, even if we do not immediately recognize it.

someone who has experienced; and a few may have experienced it personally. It's estimated over nine million people alive today have been through an NDE. I would like to show why I believe NDEs are Hashem's way of giving us a small glimpse of the truth and giving us a chance to be inspired just like they were in Mitzrayim so long ago. There is so much evidence associated with this phenomenon, that I am convinced that it has to be true and the skeptics who deny it really have no alternative explanation.

What exactly is an NDE? An NDE is defined as an "out of body" experience of someone who is clinically dead or facing impending death. These experiences vary, but the typical features are a perception of seeing and hearing apart from the physical body, passing into or through a tunnel, encountering a mystical light, intense and generally positive emotions, a review of part or all of one's prior life experiences, encountering deceased loved ones, and a choice to return to their earthly life.

The common fallacious argument against NDEs being miracles is that they are just illusions, with our brains playing tricks on us. These are all just very sophisticated dreams of preconceived ideas we have been taught are supposed to happen. Let's go through eight irrefutable facts about NDEs and see how they prove this experience is actually Hashem revealing Himself and helping us see Him with some modern-day supernatural miracles that defy natural or scientific explanations.

<u>Evidence #1: Lucid, organized experiences while unconscious, comatose, or clinically dead</u> – Near-death experiences occur at a time when the person is so physically compromised that they are typically unconscious, comatose, or clinically dead. Considering NDEs from both a medical perspective and logically, it should not be possible for unconscious people to report highly lucid experiences that are clear and logically structured.

A common rationalization of these experiences is to associate them with dreaming. The claim is that these are nothing more than very vivid dreams. The problem is that 75% of those surveyed claimed that their NDE was with more consciousness and alertness than they normally have even while awake.

Evidence #2: Seeing ongoing events from a location apart from the physical body while unconscious (out-of-body experience) – A common characteristic of near-death experiences is an out-of-body experience (OBE) which is an apparent separation of consciousness from the body. About 45% of near-death survivors report OBEs that involve seeing and often hearing ongoing earthly events from a perspective that is apart, and usually above their physical bodies. Following cardiac arrest, NDErs may see, and later accurately describe, their own resuscitation.

The high percentage of accurate out-of-body observations during near-death experiences does not seem explainable by any possible physical brain function. This is corroborated by OBEs during NDEs that include accurate observations made while those experiencing them were verifiably clinically comatose. Further corroboration comes from the many NDEs that have been reported with accurate OBE observations of events occurring far from the person's body, and beyond any possible physical sensory awareness. Moreover, NDE accounts have been reported with OBEs that accurately described events completely unexpected by the NDErs. This further argues against NDEs being a result of illusory memories originating from what the individuals might have expected during a close brush with death.

Evidence #3 Near-death experiences with vision in the blind and supernormal vision – There have been a few case reports of near-death experiences in the blind. One investigation included 14 blind or substantially visually impaired individuals who had NDEs or out-of-body experiences. During their experience, they described vision. They had never seen anything in their entire lives, but somehow, they were able to describe what it meant to have vision. They were able to describe highly visual content consistent with typical NDEs. This is impossible to explain rationally.

<u>Evidence #4 Near-death experiences that occur while under general anesthesia</u> – Under adequate general anesthesia it should not be possible to form lucid organized memories. Prior studies using EEG and functional imaging of the brains of patients under general anesthesia provide substantial evidence that the anesthetized brain should be unable to produce lucid memories.

<u>Evidence #5 Near-death experiences and life reviews</u> – Some NDEs include a review of part or all of one's prior life. This NDE element is called a life review. NDErs typically describe their life review from a third-person perspective. The life review may include awareness of what others were feeling and thinking at the time earlier in their life when they interacted with them. This previously unknown awareness of what other people were feeling or thinking is often surprising and unexpected to the NDErs.

Life reviews may include long-forgotten details of their earlier life that the NDErs later confirm really happened. If NDEs were unreal experiences, it would be expected that there would be significant error in life reviews and possibly hallucinatory features. The consistent accuracy of life reviews, including the awareness of long-forgotten events and awareness of the thoughts and feelings of others from past interactions, further suggests the reality of NDEs.

<u>Evidence #6 Encountering deceased loved ones in near-death experiences</u> – Near-death survivors may describe encounters with familiar people who are now deceased. In dreams or hallucinations when familiar persons are present, they are much more likely to be

living and from recent memory. This is in sharp contrast to near-death experiences where familiar persons encountered are almost always deceased. Cases have been reported by NDErs of seeing a person who they thought was living, but in fact had recently died. These cases illustrate that NDEs cannot be explained by the experiencer's expectation of what would happen during a life-threatening event. Further evidence that NDEs are not a result of expectation comes from a study done where in one-third of the cases the encountered deceased person had a poor or distant relationship with the NDEr, or was someone who had died before the NDEr was born.

Evidence #7 Near-death experiences of young children – Investigations of NDEs in very young children is important because at an early age they are less likely to have established religious beliefs, cultural understandings about death, or even an awareness of what death is. Very young children would be very unlikely to have heard about near-death experiences or understand them and would not have any preconceived idea of what is expected.

A survey was done with children 5 years old and below as well as children above the age of 5 and the study found that the content of NDEs in children age five and younger was the same as the content of NDEs in older children and adults.

Evidence #8 Cross-cultural study of near-death experiences – Over 500 NDEs in foreign languages have been shared over the years. Both the non-English and English versions of the NDEs are strikingly similar. If near-death experiences were considerably influenced by pre-existing religious and cultural beliefs, it would be expected that there would be significant differences in the content of NDEs from different cultures around the world.

There are many more fascinating facts regarding NDEs, but the point is that Hashem reveals Himself in every generation, including now.

Miracles are in fact part of the reality of our everyday life. We are commanded to have *emunah* and *bitachon* with or without any type of supernatural event. However, Hashem gives us that little push and little nudge to help us in our trek to understand and believe and to make it just a bit easier.

The obvious question after all this is what ever happened to that little thing called *bechirah*? If Hashem is doing these miracles for us and is seemingly making it that much easier for us to have *emunah* and know the truth, how can we have appropriate *bechirah*? Will we really have any choice if the hand of Hashem is so tangible and clear in our lives as we see from NDEs?

The answer is that although our *bechirah* might have been slightly reduced due to Hashem's intervention in our lives, this is completely necessary. A certain degree of transparency simply gives us the opportunity to make an informed decision. However, as we see from the multitude of those who rationalize NDEs, there is no standing in the way of someone who is determined to believe what he wants to believe despite Hashem's miraculous intervention.

We also see this countless times throughout our history. When Chiel, the good friend of Achaz, started rebuilding Yericho 500 years after Yehoshua's curse, forbidding anyone to rebuild it, was given, he didn't hesitate. The threat of the death of the children of the one who rebuilds Yericho did not stop Chiel. In fact, even after his first son died and it was so obvious the curse was happening, he kept rebuilding. He was in complete denial despite the clarity of the situation. Then his next son died, but he just kept on building, too stubborn to face reality.

It really doesn't matter how many miraculous events we have in our life. If we are determined to do the wrong thing, we will. The fact that Hashem gives us a little help does not mean we lose our *bechirah*. Our *bechirah* is completely intact. However, we need to take advantage of these clear signs that Hashem is sending our way. We need to utilize them to build our *emunah* and increase our realization that Hashem is in charge and the Torah which we learn today with its ultimate reward and punishment are real and oh so beautiful. The *yetzer hara* inside all of us will work hard to try and convince us that no matter what we experience, it's just a mirage and there's always a reasonable explanation.

Hashem gave us this gift called NDE and we need to study it, understand it, and be inspired by it. It's undeniable evidence that there's so much more than meets the eye.

# Insights on the Haggadah from *Avudraham* [1]

## Yehoshua Dixler

הָא לַחְמָא עַנְיָא דִּי אֲכָלוּ אַבְהָתָנָא בְּאַרְעָא דְמִצְרָיִם.

Q – Why does the Haggadah describe matzah as the bread "our forefathers ate *in* Egypt," when, in fact, the matzah is eaten because the dough did not have time to rise when they were *leaving* Egypt?

A – R. Yehosaph HaAzuvi describes that when Ben Ezra was held captive in India (Hodu), he was fed only matzah because it does not digest as quickly as regular bread, requiring a minimal amount to keep one alive. The Haggadah is referring to how the Egyptians fed matzah to the Jews for the same reason. Additionally, eating matzah for the first time at the Seder is similar to the first night after a wedding. Just like before the wedding the chassan and kallah cannot live with each other, so too the matzah may not be eaten in anticipation of Pesach. And just like seven blessings are required under the chuppah before the couple can live together, so too we can only eat the matzah after seven blessings at the Seder. These are: blessing on wine (*hagafen*) during kiddush, kiddush, *shehechiayanu,* blessing on *karpas* (*haadomah*), blessing on wine after Haggadah, and two blessings on matzah (*hamotzi* and *al achilas matzah*).

עֲבָדִים הָיִינוּ לְפַרְעֹה בְּמִצְרָיִם, וַיּוֹצִיאֵנוּ ה' אֱלֹהֵינוּ מִשָּׁם בְּיָד חֲזָקָה וּבִזְרֹעַ נְטוּיָה. וְאִלּוּ לֹא הוֹצִיא הַקָּדוֹשׁ בָּרוּךְ הוּא אֶת אֲבוֹתֵינוּ מִמִּצְרָיִם, הֲרֵי אָנוּ וּבָנֵינוּ וּבְנֵי בָנֵינוּ מְשֻׁעְבָּדִים הָיִינוּ *לְפַרְעֹה* בְּמִצְרָיִם.

[1] R' Dovid Avudraham was a Rishon who lived in Spain during the 14th century. Well-known for his commentary on the siddur, he also authored a lesser-known commentary on the Haggadah. I hope you enjoy these extracts from *Avudraham's* Haggadah commentary as much as I do. I will comment on some of his *chidushim* in footnotes.

This is the answer to the questions of *Mah Nishtanah.* We eat matzah and marror tonight as our forefathers ate as slaves to Pharaoh in Mitzrayim.[2]

If Hashem would have found that the Jews in Egypt did not deserve to be taken out, due to the *reshaim* and *eirev rav* among them, then certainly the generation today, who are *reshaim*, would have no merit to leave Egypt. However, today Egypt is not ruled by a Pharaoh; it is therefore no longer possible to enslave us to Pharaoh in Egypt. Consequently, the word "Pharaoh" in the phrase "We would be slaves to Pharaoh in Egypt" should be removed.

אָמַר רַבִּי אֶלְעָזָר בֶּן־עֲזַרְיָה הֲרֵי אֲנִי כְּבֶן שִׁבְעִים שָׁנָה.

R. Elazar was 13 years old when he was appointed *Nasi.* After his appointment, his beard miraculously grew 13 rows of white hair, making him appear an elder of 70, so that he would be given the proper respect by other scholars.[3]

בָּרוּךְ הַמָּקוֹם, בָּרוּךְ הוּא, בָּרוּךְ שֶׁנָּתַן תּוֹרָה לְעַמּוֹ יִשְׂרָאֵל, בָּרוּךְ הוּא.

Hashem is called *HaMakom,* "the place," because He is the place (i.e., creator and supporter) of the world; the world is not "the place" of Hashem. *Makom* (מקום) has the same numeric value (186) as the four-letter name of Hashem (הוי"ה) using the calculation: 10 times *yud* (100), 5 times *hei* (25), 6 times *vav* (36), 5 times *hei* (25) = 186.[4]

---

[2] Author's note: In contrast, *Maharal* (*Gevuras Hashem* §51) strongly rejects commentators who connect matzah to servitude.

[3] Author's note: In contrast, *Berachos* (28a) records R. Elazar as 18 years old with 18 rows of white hair.

[4] Author's note: Hashem is described here specifically as *HaMakom* to show that His absolute control of world events, including the Exodus, is sourced in His creation and on-going support of the world.

וְהִיא שֶׁעָמְדָה לַאֲבוֹתֵינוּ וְלָנוּ. שֶׁלֹּא אֶחָד בִּלְבָד עָמַד עָלֵינוּ לְכַלּוֹתֵנוּ.

To demonstrate His *hashgachah,* "oversight," over the Jewish people, in every generation, Hashem enables enemies to rise against us and then saves us.[5]

וְעָבַרְתִּי בְאֶרֶץ מִצְרַיִם בַּלַּיְלָה הַזֶּה – אֲנִי וְלֹא מַלְאָךְ; וְהִכֵּיתִי כָל בְּכוֹר בְּאֶרֶץ־מִצְרַיִם. אֲנִי וְלֹא שָׂרָף; וּבְכָל־אֱלֹהֵי מִצְרַיִם אֶעֱשֶׂה שְׁפָטִים. אֲנִי וְלֹא הַשָּׁלִיחַ; אֲנִי ה'. אֲנִי הוּא וְלֹא אַחֵר.

Q – How can the Haggadah write that Hashem alone killed the first-born when the Torah writes, "I will not allow the destroyer to enter your houses" (*Shemos* 12:23), implying there is a "destroyer" killing the firstborn, not Hashem. A – Hashem is described as the "destroyer," as He is the One killing the first-born that night. The verse is interpreted as if it said, "I will not allow the *destruction* to enter your houses."[6]

רַבִּי יְהוּדָה הָיָה נוֹתֵן בָּהֶם סִמָּנִים: דְּצַ"ךְ עַדַ"שׁ בְּאַחַ"ב.

Q – What does R. Yehudah's sign add to our understanding of the *makkos*? A – The sign provides three insights:

1) He is dividing the *makkos* into categories: those affecting the land, those affecting temporal beings (*mikrim*) upon the land, and those affecting the sky.

2) To confirm the order of the *makkos* in the Torah is the correct chronological order, which is not always the case.

3) The first three were executed through Aharon, the next three by Moshe, and the last four by Hashem.

---

[5] Author's note: Without Hashem's help, our enemies would have the capability to harm us. These painful reminders, necessary in our current state of exile, will no longer occur once Hashem brings Mashiach and rebuilds the Beis HaMikdash.

[6] Author's note: See my article in the BMR 5780 Kuntress titled "Plague of the Firstborn: Who Did It and Why?" for alternative answers to this question.

אִלּוּ הוֹצִיאָנוּ מִמִּצְרַיִם וְלֹא עָשָׂה בָהֶם שְׁפָטִים, דַּיֵּנוּ.
אִלּוּ הָרַג אֶת־בְּכוֹרֵיהֶם וְלֹא נָתַן לָנוּ אֶת־מָמוֹנָם, דַּיֵּנוּ.

Q – How can we say it would have been sufficient if Hashem did not punish the Egyptians or did not provide us wealth when leaving Egypt? We know both of these were promised to Avraham and must occur! A – Instead of punishing all Egyptians, Hashem could have punished just some of them. Instead of giving us both the booty when we left Egypt and the booty of the Red Sea, Hashem could have given us just one.

אִלּוּ קֵרְבָנוּ לִפְנֵי הַר סִינַי, וְלֹא נַתַן לָנוּ אֶת־הַתּוֹרָה, דַּיֵּנוּ.

Instead of Hashem telling us the Ten Commandments Himself, He could have given them to Moshe to then tell us, as He did for the rest of the Torah. Or, instead of giving us all 613 mitzvos, He could have given us only some of them, as we find Hashem giving just a few mitzvos to Noach and Avraham. Alternately, being at Sinai expunged the spiritual filth (*zuhama*) we inherited from Adam and Chavah's sin with the snake.[7]

לְפִיכָךְ אֲנַחְנוּ חַיָּבִים לְהוֹדוֹת, לְהַלֵּל, לְשַׁבֵּחַ, לְפָאֵר, לְרוֹמֵם, לְהַדֵּר, וּלְקַלֵּס.

The Haggadah was only a retelling of events, but now we break out in song which requires wine. Seven forms of praise are listed corresponding to the seven levels of *Shamayim*, heaven.[8]

הַלְלוּיָהּ הַלְלוּ עַבְדֵי ה', הַלְלוּ אֶת־שֵׁם ה'.

There are five words in Hallel with an extra letter *yud*: לְהוֹשִׁיבִי ,מוֹשִׁיבִי ,מְקִימִי ,הַמַּשְׁפִּילִי ,הַמַּגְבִּיהִי. The numerical value of five *yuds* is hinting to the 50 *makkos* executed on the Egyptians by the Red Sea.[9]

---

[7] Author's note: *Avudraham* understands *Dayeinu* as suggesting every item could actually have been done in a different way. Incredibly, this includes even the Torah's 613 mitzvos!

[8] Author's note: Our Haggados add two more,"לְבָרֵךְ, לְעַלֵּה" for a total of nine.

זֵכֶר לְמִקְדָּשׁ כְּהִלֵּל. כֵּן עָשָׂה הִלֵּל בִּזְמַן שֶׁבֵּית הַמִּקְדָּשׁ הָיָה קַיָּם. הָיָה כּוֹרֵךְ מַצָּה וּמָרוֹר וְאוֹכֵל בְּיַחַד, לְקַיֵּם מַה שֶּׁנֶּאֱמַר: עַל מַצּוֹת וּמְרוֹרִים יֹאכְלֻהוּ.
We imitate Hillel's practice in the Beis HaMikdash by wrapping the matzah in the *chazeres* "lettuce" used as marror, dipping both together into the *charoses* and eating the sandwich while leaning (quoting *the Rambam* and *Rosh*).[10]

The proliferation of Haggados through the generations until today is astounding. While each new Haggadah enhances our understanding of this important night, we should not overlook the many interesting insights available to us in Haggados written by the Rishonim hundreds of years ago. ۵

[9] Author's note: While the second paragraph of Hallel, "When the *Bnei Yisroel* left Egypt", is obviously associated with the Seder, the first doesn't mention Egypt or Exodus. This hint connects it to the theme of the Seder.

[10] Author's note: Per *Avudraham*, the Hillel sandwich is matzah wrapped with marror on the *outside*. With marror on the outside, it's then sensible to dip the *entire* sandwich into charoses. In contrast, our custom is to first dip the marror in charoses and then place the marror *inside* two pieces of matzah.

# The Quest for Truth

## Avi Dear

מִתְּחִלָּה עוֹבְדֵי עֲבוֹדָה זָרָה הָיוּ אֲבוֹתֵינוּ, וְעַכְשָׁו קֵרְבָנוּ הַמָּקוֹם לַעֲבוֹדָתוֹ,
*At first, our forefathers were idol worshipers, and now Hashem has brought us close to His service.*

The *Som Derech* asks, what does the *Baal Hagadah* gain from this statement? Why is this part of the Haggadah? [I assume his question is operating under the opinion that עבדים היינו is the מתחיל בגנות.]

Additionally, regarding Yisro, the Torah refers to him as כהן מדין חותן משה, *The Kohen of Midyan, the father-in-law of Moshe* (*Shemos* 18:1) Why would the Torah describe Yisro with two completely opposite traits? One a praise, one an apparent insult?

The answer, the *Som Derech* explains, is that the *Baal Haggadah* and the Torah are teaching us the greatness and value of ביקוש האמת, *searching for the truth.* Both descriptors were in fact praises of Yisro. The fact that he was the Kohen of Midyan and was constantly trying different practices and religions to finally and eventually find *Yiddishkeit* is a most valuable trait. Searching for truth. The entire process was a path and vessel to reach the ultimate *emes*. Avraham as well searched for *emes* until he found it; this is a beautiful praise, something worthy and special to mention here at the Seder.

Interestingly, the *Som Derech* continues and asks, why didn't the Torah mention the story of Ur Kasdim, where Avraham was saved from the fire? He says, it is because the people in Ur Kasdim never reached the *emes*! The Torah is *kulo emes*, only *emes,* and won't have any *sheker*. They did not search out *emes* to say, "Wow! Avraham must be on to something here! Why is he alive? What is he doing differently? Maybe we should reconsider our lifestyle!"

Contrast this with Mitzrayim. The Torah details the magicians in Mitzrayim trying to mimic the different plagues. But why?! Weren't they *sheker*?

The *Som Derech* explains that since they eventually reached the point of realizing and saying, אצבע אלוקים הוא, *this was all the finger of Hashem*, the entire process turned into a quest for the truth! The Torah therefore chose to detail the entire story of the Mitzrim because they eventually reached *emes,* which retroactively made the entire process *emes*, a quest for truth.

The *Som Derech* continues: גם הכשלון הוא מכלל דרך הלימוד, *the struggles and difficulties are included in the process of learning.*

I believe this explains the value in "toiling in Torah" the *yegiyah*: the effort itself has value, and is, in fact, the goal! As long as you are on the path, then everything to get there is the goal. As long as you are on the proper *derech* and aimed at the *emes,* you are doing the right thing. Why doesn't the Gemara just skip to the end of the *shakla v'tarya*? Why does the Gemara detail the entire process of questioning different *sugyos* or *shitos*? Just tell us what to do! What's the bottom line?! I think the answer is the same: As long as we are on a path to *emes*, the process itself is *emes* and Torah.

But why tonight? Why is now the time to teach us this lesson of the value of searching for *emes*? Seder night is a night of *chinuch.* It is the quintessential time and place for *chinuch* to happen. It is, in a sense, seen as a source for how we should be *mechaneich* our children. And a hugely important point to teach our children is the value of the process. The value of effort. It is not the grade received; what is important is the work you put in to get there. Because as we see: work itself is the goal. We have to teach ourselves and our children that the work and effort has value. Our goal is not even to reach *emes*, our goal is to be on a constant quest for *emes.*

Carol Dweck famously discusses the difference between having a growth mindset and having a fixed mindset. Having a growth mindset means that you believe that intelligence can be developed. This individual values the process, the challenge. If I don't know something, then I can learn it. I know HOW to learn, if I don't know something yet. I can figure it out. Having a fixed mindset means you believe that your intelligence is fixed. This individual sees themselves as not able to change or develop. I either know something or I don't. I either have the answer or I don't have the answer, but I can't figure it out if I don't already know it. This differentiation has been studied and points to dramatic differences in growth and achievement across numerous areas between people with these two different mindsets.

Tonight is the night to turn to our kids and to speak to ourselves and say, "you see Yisro? You see Avraham? The Torah is proud of them for constantly trying to find Hashem, to find the *emes*! The Torah is NOT only proud that they found the *emes*; the Torah is proud of everything they did to get there! Hashem loves that they worked so hard to get there! Hashem loves when you work hard! Hashem loves when you try and you try to write that *aleph* but it's still crooked. Hashem loves when you try to read a *patach* but it comes out a *kamatz*. Because Hashem loves when you TRY. Hashem loves when you stay up late to try to memorize Mishnayos. And you still can't. Hashem loves it. Because Hashem wants you to try. It's more important to Hashem that you TRY and not even that you have it memorized!"

And when we try and put in the effort, and when we spend our night learning about this, עכשיו קרבנו המקום לעבודתו. R' Elimelech Biderman explains that this can and should also be taken 100% literally, RIGHT NOW during the Seder, Hashem will reach out and bring us closer to Him and to his *avodah*. ♁

# Teaching the Four Sons: The ABC of Jewish Education

## Moshe Arie Michelsohn

Rabbi Samson Raphael Hirsch's essay, "The Four Sons," presents a fascinating understanding of the archetypes represented by the *chacham*, *rasha*, *tam*, and *she'eino yodeia lish'ol*, providing not only deep insight into the Haggadah, but also a foundational framework for Jewish education that is as timely and meaningful today as ever.

### The Youngest Child

Rav Hirsch begins with the *she'eino yodeia lish'ol*, the youngest child at the table, who does not yet know how to ask questions. The Haggadah instructs us to 'open him up' (*at p'tach lo*) to our joyful experience of performance of *mitzvos* – "and you shall tell your son on that day [*bayom ha'hu*], for the sake of this [*baavur zeh*] – the performance of *mitzvos* –that G-d acted on my behalf when I went out of Egypt!" (*Exodus* 13:8). Rabbi Hirsch expounds:

> Lead your child to the table set with matzah and bitter herbs—Do not begin your educating work with discourses and sermons about religion. You do not win your child by speeches and preaching. Let your child *see you* in happily devoted *fulfillment* of the G-dly commandments.

While your youngest child sees you actively engaged and joyfully devoted to the fulfillment of the mitzvos of matzah and maror, it is precisely in this context that you explain to him that it is *only* for the fulfillment of the mitzvos—*ba'avur zeh*—that G-d acted on our behalf when we went out of Egypt. It was not because of our prowess or military might, not because of our treasures or wealth, nor because of our erudition in the arts and sciences. The Egyptians possessed all of these while we had none of them. The only thing we had, and still have today, is our simple devotion to the fulfillment of G-d's commandments – they are the reason for our very being, and it is through their fulfillment that we – each and every one of us – experience true happiness. We must all see ourselves as if we went out of Egypt: The Angel of Death passed over *my* house solely in order that *I* may fulfill the commandments. G-d acted for *me* and took *me* out of Egypt for this reason alone. The mitzvos "are the language in which my G-d and I speak to each other," states Rav Hirsch. This is as true for me today as it was for my forefathers in Egypt:

> Do not celebrate with him the remembrance of an old story of bygone times. Let what the father experienced be your experience. Let what the fathers bequeathed be to you as certain as if you personally had witnessed it… Then your child will receive the legacy of Redemption and the legacy of the consecration of his life in equally vigorous terms.

Judaism, Rav Hirsch emphasizes, is a religion of *naaseh v'nishma*—first we do, and then we listen; this is the way we communicate with *Hashem*. "Throughout Judaism, and therefore also in Jewish education, *naaseh* must come before *nishma*." Moreover, "G-d expects this *chinuch*, this initiation of our youth into Judaism, to come from the father. Every father is capable of it, and where the father neglects it, it can scarcely be compensated for by anyone or anything else." There are no surrogates for providing such *chinuch* as "even the best teachers and schools cannot replace the table at which your child sees you perform the precepts of your G-d with joyful earnestness." The joy of being an *eved Hashem* begins at the Seder table with matzah and maror right in front of us, as we acknowledge with joy and gladness that it is only for the sake of our doing these mitzvos that Hashem took us out of Egypt in the first place.

Demonstrating our simple devotion to performance of Hashem's mitzvos *b'simchah* is how we must begin to educate Jewish children.

**The Lad**

As our children start to mature and speak on their own, they begin to ask questions—particularly the question, "Why?"—which should very much be encouraged. Thus, when the lad, the *tam*, asks you, "What is this?" Rav Hirsch notes that when the *tam* asks, "What is this?" this lad means to ask the following: "I see and feel the joy you experience in doing *mitzvos*, but why do we specifically do *these* mitzvos? What is their deeper meaning? Why does Hashem 'designate just these acts as the sign of our worship, our devotion, and our obedience?' " And to this question the Haggadah instructs us to answer as follows: "With a mighty hand has G-d led us out of Egypt from the house of bondage (*B'chozek yad hotzianu Hashem mi-Mitzrayim*)!"

According to Rav Hirsch, the father would teach his son, saying, "Do you know why we have matzah and maror on our table before us on Pesach night? Because they remind us of the most fundamental principle of the universe: That Hashem is in charge of everything. Everything in the universe is nothing short of miraculous. We may not think about the fact that Hashem controls everything when we see the laws of nature operating the same way each and every day—so Hashem performed miracles for us in Egypt, He performed signs and miracles and passed over our houses and slew the firstborn of every Egyptian, in order to indelibly mark upon our consciousness that the laws of nature "have their Lord and Master Who established them, and Who remains their Lord and Master after He established them." It was to impress upon us the miraculous nature of the universe that Hashem took us out of Egypt *b'chozek yad*, with a mighty, miraculous, outstretched hand. By the natural order of this world, we had gone to ruin in slavery and misery in Egypt. As Rav Hirsch so powerfully describes, "There, proud concepts of man's moral freedom—the freedom that makes him in a small way resemble G-d—lay buried in nature deification, in the madness of the caste system. There, the Egyptians tried to transform us into a house of slaves, a pariah caste. Serfdom was to be ours from the cradle." By the natural order of the world, we were destined for an eternal abyss.

In delivering us from the doom of eternal subjugation to natural forces, Hashem "commanded us to perform such deeds which would make us resolutely aware of the Redemption from Egypt." We remember and experience *b'chozek yad* when we see the matzah and maror before us on the Seder table. Rav Hirsch continues:

> With chametz and matzah you demonstrate each year the thoroughly G-dly character of your origin. Thereby, however, you do not celebrate the mere memory of an event belonging to the past. In this G-dliness of your origin is rooted the dependence upon G-d of your whole present existence, with all its vicissitudes, in every moment of your life. Because your freedom is entirely G-d's work, therefore your soul and body, which have become free, belong to G-d. He acquired you when He delivered you. Every thought of your mind, every beat of your heart, every act of your hand is *His own.*

So too with *mitzvos* more generally. We remember and experience *b'chozek yad* when we place our *tefillin* on our hands and between our eyes and recite the verses that recall our miraculous exodus from Egypt. We remember and experience *b'chozek yad* when we redeem our firstborn children to the kohen. The *mitzvos* we perform are our daily reminders that *b'chozek yad* Hashem took us out of Egypt; that the entire universe is miraculous, that our very existence as *ovdei Hashem* is, itself, a miracle.

**A Fork in the Road**

As our children grow into young adulthood, we are hopeful that the lessons we taught them through joyful demonstration of *naaseh v'nishma* have had the desired impact, but the Haggadah recognizes that this is not always the case. The Haggadah informs us how we should continue to educate our Jewish children as they grow up, whether they have maintained the path of *Yiddishkeit* (the wise son), or not (the scornful son).

**The Wise Son**

The wise son has recognized Hashem as his G-d and is familiar with the mitzvos from daily practice. He understands the *eidos*, the *chukim*, and the *mishpatim* are derived from the Torah but also appreciates it "is not only Scripture, the Book, it is the Tradition of the father" to which the son must turn for answers to spiritual questions. So, the wise son asks his father, "What are these signs and testimonies and laws that G-d, our Father, has commanded you?" The wise son thirsts for detailed knowledge of all of the mitzvos. But notably, Rav Hirsch observes, citing the *Mechilta*, his question does not include mention of the laws of Pesach nor of the commemoration of *Yetzias Mitzrayim*, at all!

And so, the wise son's education is surely not yet complete. The Haggadah, accordingly, instructs us to answer the wise son thus: "According to the laws of Pesach, we do not eat dessert after finishing the meat of the *korban pesach*." Rabbi Hirsch explains:

> Do not sit down at the feet of your father and your teachers as long as you do not stand with them on one and the same soil, the soil of the foundation that was laid with *Yetzias Mitzrayim*. Leave the great volumes unopened if you do not from the outset bring with you the basic sense in which their contents should be studied and can be comprehended.

The exodus from Egypt, in its miraculous glory, "is the prerequisite for *limud Torah.*" It is the root of *naaseh v'nishma. Yetzias Mitzrayim,* Rav Hirsch explains, "transformed our whole existence and raised us up on the 'Eagle's wings of G-d' to an entirely different level of perception." It is this experience that we must savor on the *Seder* night, and so the taste of *Yetziyas Mitzrayim* must remain on our lips and not be washed away by any form of dessert. *B'chozek yad* Hashem took us out of Egypt, to be His *avadim.* To be truly wise, we must always have this basic fact at the forefront of our minds. Our learning must always keep alive this fundamental tenet and memorial of *naaseh v'nishma* by which we act each day as *ovdei Hashem.*

**The Scornful Son**

The Haggadah additionally contemplates those times Rav Hirsch describes vividly as "when the father seats himself with joyful earnestness at the Seder, but the 'progressive' son passes by the table with derisive mockery, and interjects the heartbreaking taunt: "What does this Service mean to you (*Ma ha'avodah hazos lachem*)?" In other words, this child asks, "Why do we bother with this nonsense every year?"

Rav Hirsch asks, "What should be said to the members of this fallen generation who, in their apostasy, fancy themselves to be the 'progressives,' and deride the loyal elders as 'backward'?" And to this he answers: "*To them nothing should be said*!" And indeed, Rav Hirsch points out the answer the Haggadah gives—"*ba'avur zeh asa Hashem li b'tzaisi mi'Mitzrayim*" is precisely the same answer that is given to the youngest child, the *she'eino yodea lish'ol.* This is because there is nothing to say to someone who has no desire to listen to you. The scornful son does not expect instruction from you; he has "'advanced' so far beyond you" in his own eyes that it is he who wants to instruct you. "Do not expect that your words, or the most brilliant arguments in defense of your ancient Divine Law, can cause their hearts to return."

The best one can do, as a mindful Jewish parent under such circumstances is, as it were, to return to basics—the "Jewish ABC" as Rav Hirsch calls it: Just as for your youngest children, show your scornful son the joy you experience in doing the mitzvos, and remind him that it is only for the sake of doing mitzvos that Hashem took us out of Egypt. Let him sense from you that by not accepting this fact it is just as if he had left himself in Egypt to succumb to the natural order of things and live a life subject to the whims of men. The return of the scornful son to the path of Torah is only in the hands of Hashem:

> Only experience can bring them back, the experience of the hollowness, the nothingness, the bleakness and emptiness of all those delusions into whose arms they have thoughtlessly thrown themselves. One day those hearts will once more be filled with yearning for the happiness of possessing the ancient Truth which was thrown away. One day these words will be put in their mouth: "I would fain return to G-d, to my ancient loyalty; because I was happier then than now!" (Hosea 2:9).

Those who are fortunate enough to learn their Jewish ABC's when they are young, those who inculcate the miracle of *Yetzias Mitzrayim* into their lives as young children, are fortunate indeed. Those who are unable to do so have it much harder later in life, for such individuals must then first experience the vapidity of a universe devoid of miracles, devoid of mitzvos, devoid of Hashem's presence, until, with Hashem's help, they learn of their own accord to yearn for the happiness of living a life of Torah, and are able to return home.

As one who has personally experienced the vapidity of a life without spiritual connection, I can attest to the deep truth of Rav Hirsch's words. May we be *zocheh* to educate our children to love and appreciate the miracle of *Yetzias Mitzrayim* and to live a life of doing mitzvos in the service of Hashem.

# *Motzi Matzah* vs. the *Afikoman*

## Roman Kimelfeld

Rabbi Shimon Eider writes in his *Halachos of Pesach* (Feldheim, 1998 edition, p. 241) that according to most Poskim eating the *afikoman* is a Rabbinic requirement (*Mishnah Berurah* 486:1), whereas according to some Poskim it is a Biblical obligation. He further states that according to some Poskim, eating the *afikoman* represents the main fulfilment of the obligation to eat matzah (this view is mentioned in *Shaar HaTziyun* 477:4, which cites *Rashi* and the *Rashbam* on *Pesachim* 119b). In this article, I will discuss this opinion of *Rashi* and the *Rashbam*.

At first glance, this view of *Rashi* and *Rashbam*, that eating the *afikoman* represents the main fulfilment of the mitzvah of eating matzah, appears to be difficult to understand. We make the *berachah* "*Al Achilas Matzah*" before we eat the first piece of matzah (at *Motzi Matzah*), and then we proceed to eat matzah with great enthusiasm. As we do it, we feel that we are fulfilling the mitzvah. On the other hand, *Rashi* and the *Rashbam* state explicitly that this matzah: "*eina l'shem chovah,*" does not represent fulfillment of the obligation. Their view feels unsettling.

The *Aruch HaShulchan* (477:2) points out another difficulty with the aforementioned language of *Rashi*. First, *Rashi* says: "One has to eat matzah at the end of *seudah* to remember (*zecher*) the matzah that was eaten with *korban pesach.*" The *Aruch HaShulchan* adds that when *Rashi* says that one eats the *afikoman* "to remember," it sounds like we are dealing with a Rabbinic mitzvah. However, shortly afterwards, *Rashi* says that the *afikoman* is eaten "*l'shem chovas matzah,*" for the sake of the obligation of matzah. This makes it sound like it is a Biblical mitzvah, and consequently the main fulfilment of the mitzvah of eating matzah. Thus, *Rashi* appears to say that eating the *afikoman* is both a Rabbinic and Biblical obligation.

A concept in the *Tos. Bikkurim* (§651, printed at the end of *Aruch LaNer*) might help us understand the opinion of *Rashi* and the *Rashbam.* He discusses a case of a person who has a kosher esrog that is not *mehudar,* but he expects to get a *mehudar* esrog in the afternoon. Should this person make a *berachah* on his non-*mehudar* (but kosher) esrog in the morning, and recite *Hallel* with the *arba minim* together with the congregation, or should he delay taking the *arba minim* until he receives this *mehudar* esrog in the afternoon?

The *Tos. Bikkurim* concludes that this individual should make a *berachah* on his non-*mehudar* esrog in the morning; and recite *Hallel* with the congregation, using his non-*mehudar arba minim.* Later in the afternoon, when he gets the *mehudar* esrog, he should then take this *mehudar* esrog (with the remainder of *arba minim*), and he will be considered as having fulfilled the mitzvah of *arba minim* with *hiddur.* Thus, it is possible to fulfil the *hidur* even after being *yotzei* with a non-*mehudar* esrog. This is so because, as *Tos. Bikkurim* explains, the mitzvah is not considered to be completed until it is fulfilled in the *mehudar* fashion (based on *Tosafos* in *Sukkah* 39a ד"ה עובר לעשייתן). As long as the *zman* for the mitzvah has not expired, there is an opportunity to perform the mitzvah again with *hiddur.*

Thus, a person can be *yotzei* with the mitzvah in a *mehudar* fashion, even after he was initially *yotzei* with the same mitzvah in a *non-mehudar* fashion. Apparently, once the person eventually performs the mitzvah with *hidur*, the *mehudar* act becomes the ultimate completion of the mitzvah, whereas the previous, non-*mehudar* act is now viewed as merely the beginning of the mitzvah.

Perhaps, with this concept of the *Tos. Bikkurim*, we can resolve the difficulties with the aforementioned *Rashi* and *Rashbam.* When

*Rashi* says that one needs to eat the *afikoman* at the end of the meal to remember the matzah that was eaten with *korban pesach*, he indeed means that the person who ate matzah for *Motzi Matzah* has now only a Rabbinic obligation to eat the *afikoman.* This is because this person already fulfilled his Torah obligation at *Motzi Matzah*, so at this point he only has a Rabbinical obligation to remember the matzah which was eaten with *korban pesach.* In other words, when *Rashi* seems to say that eating the *afikoman* is only a Rabbinic obligation, this is when we evaluate the person's obligation *before* he eats the *afikoman.*

However, *after* this person has eaten the *afikoman,* thus fulfilling the *hidur* of remembering the matzah eaten with *korban pesach*, the *afikoman* now becomes the most *mehudar kezais* of matzah eaten at the Seder. As such, it is now considered to be the completion of the Biblical mitzvah of eating matzah, whereas the matzah eaten during *Motzi Matzah* is now considered to be merely the beginning.

Therefore, when *Rashi* and the *Rashbam* say that the matzah eaten during *Motzi Matzah* does not represent fulfilment of the obligation, i.e., "*eina l'shem chovah,*" perhaps they mean that it is not viewed as the ultimate fulfillment of the mitzvah, but only as the beginning of the mitzvah, because the *afikoman* became the ultimate fulfilment of the mitzvah. But, if one never ate an *afikoman,* then *Motzi Matzah* would have been his fulfillment of the Biblical mitzvah.

In summary, based on the approach of the *Tos. Bikkurim*, it appears that even according to *Rashi* and the *Rashbam* one initially fulfills a Biblical mitzvah of eating matzah when he eats the first *kezais* of matzah during *Motzi Matzah.* However, later, when one eats the *afikoman,* it then becomes the ultimate fulfilment of the Biblical mitzvah, which results in the matzah of *Motzi Matzah* now being viewed as merely the beginning of the mitzvah.

# The Promise of the *Arizal*

## Jeffrey Silverberg

Mitzvos form the fabric of our lives and the focal point of our existence. But what drives a Jew to dedicate his life to fulfilling the mitzvos? There exists a curious tension between the conflicting motivations of a Jew in keeping the mitzvos of Hashem. Are there reasons for Hashem's commands, and if so, are we to observe them as rational actions with beneficial results? Or are the mitzvos to be fulfilled simply as the commandments of the King, with no rational reason given or needed?

The *Rambam* famously writes that although we blow the shofar on Rosh Hashanah solely because Hashem commanded that we blow it on that day, there is a hint of a reason for this commandment, as the shofar is a powerful tool that arouses the people from their slumber and inspires them to do *teshuvah*. This suggests that there is room for both motivations in our mitzvah observance. Above all, we are enjoined to keep the mitzvos, all of the mitzvos, because Hashem commanded us to keep them. But there is room, and indeed there is an additional obligation to be mindful of the rational reasons for the mitzvos when they exist and to incorporate the lessons that Hashem wishes us to learn from the mitzvos into our beings.

There is a well-known and astounding promise from the *Arizal*, brought in the *Be'er Heteiv* (447:1). He assures us that if a person is extremely careful about chametz one hundred percent of the time during the entire seven days of Pesach as commanded in the Torah and does not consume even a crumb of chametz over the entire holiday, he or she will be assured of not sinning during the entire year.

But think for a moment and an obvious question arises.

Rabbi Yaakov Frand, *shlit"a,* in a shiur last year, asked that if the promise of the *Arizal* is true, how could the Jewish people have committed the sin of the Golden Calf? The Torah testifies that the Jewish people kept the first Pesach perfectly. The Torah tells us *ki lo chametz,* that there was no chametz, that the Jewish people did not eat even a morsel of chametz during Pesach that year. And yet, they perpetrated a grievous sin in the history of our people! How can this be, given this promise?

There is a simple answer to this question. The Gemara in *Pesachim* (96b) asserts that the prohibition against chametz that first year was only for one day. Now, the promise of the *Arizal* specifies that the Jew be free of chametz for all seven Biblical days of the festival. Only a sustained effort for a full week will protect a person from sin. But if the Jewish people in Mitzrayim had to refrain from chametz only one day that year, it would presumably follow that the promise could not have come into effect.[1]

We can explain this further: The *Kaf HaChaim* (447:2) cites the source for the *Arizal's* dictum from the *Zohar,* which says that someone who is careful to refrain from chametz will be protected from his *yetzer hara*; therefore, if someone is careful to refrain from *chametz* during Pesach, Hashem will reward him with help against his *yetzer hara* the rest of the year. Adding to this idea, the *Ramchal*

---

[1] It is interesting to note that although the *Be'er Heitev* presents this famous quote of the *Arizal,* it is not found in any of his writings. However, a similar concept is found among his disciples, including *Mishnas Chasidim* (*Meseches Nissan,* 3:4, as cited by *Kaf HaChaim* 447:2); but he states only that one who refrains from chametz properly will "give his soul great help for the entire year;" he does state there is a *guarantee* not to sin. R' Pinchas of Koretz (*Imrei Pinchas* §252) was therefore objected to the *Be'er Heitev* writing that the person will be "assured" of not sinning because it is not possible to *assure* a person with freewill that he will not sin. This would be an additional answer to the question about the sin with the Golden Calf. The *Arizal* did not say it was "guaranteed," only that Hashem would help such a person. However, many other *sefarim* do accept the version of *Be'er Heitev.*

writes (in the chapter about Seder Night in his *Maamar HaChochmah,* p. 162 in "The Elucidated Maamarei HaRamchal") that by eating matzah during the seven days of Pesach, which is food solely associated with the *yetzer tov* without any *yetzer hara* whatsoever, one will be prepared for holiness the entire year. Based on the *Zohar* and the *Ramchal,* we can understand why only a sustained, seven-day abstinence from *yetzer hara* food will protect one from sinning with his *yetzer hara* the rest of the year.[2]

Although this successfully answers the question, Rabbi Frand, took this opportunity to bring a fascinating explanation of another difference between the Pesach of the *Yetzias Mitzrayim* and the Pesach we celebrate nowadays, which could also explain why even if the Jewish people had refrained from chametz in Mitzrayim for a full seven days they would not have been protected from sin that year.[3]

Rabbi Frand first cited two other commentators (besides the *Kaf HaChaim* cited above) as a source of the *Arizal's* statement. The *Chida* (*Dvash LePi* מערכת ח' אות ח"י) brings as a source the *pasuk* (*Shemos* 12:17) ושמרתם את המצות, *you shall guard the matzos.* The words "matzos" and "mitzvos" are spelled exactly the same, and the *Chida* extrapolates that if one is perfectly careful about guarding the matzos from becoming chametz, he will be guarded from sin when performing the other mitzvos. The *Panim Yafos* learns from the

---

[2] Before we move on, we should mention that these words of the *Arizal* are the subject of much discussion in the *sefarim.* One famous question, cited by the *Shoel U'Meshiv* (*Tinyana,* 3:11), was posed two hundred years ago by "the *Rabbanis, Tzadeikas Maras* Sarah Rivka Rochel Leah, who composed many *techinos* in the *Korban HaMinchah Sidder.*" She was the wife of R' Shabsi, the *Av Beis Din* of Krasna.

[3] We should note here that one of the Kamarna Rebbes (cited in *Shnei HaMeoros*) answered this question with the Gemara in *Avodah Zarah* (4b), that the *Bnei Yisrael* sinned with the Golden Calf only to teach the value of *teshuvah* to future generations. For otherwise, their carefulness in refraining from chametz would have protected them from that sin.

*pasuk* (*Shemos* 13:10) ושמרת את החקה הזאת למועדה מימים ימימה, *you shall guard this law, from year to year.* If you guard this mitzvah of eating matzah and not eating chametz one year, you will be guarded until the next year from sin. Note that both of these sources mention the mitzvah of eating matzos in addition to refraining from eating chametz, which fits with the *Ramchal* cited above.

Rabbi Frand next examined a unique facet of *Pesach Mitzrayim*, the very first Pesach which took place in Egypt. The *pasuk* instructed that the first *korban Pesach* should be eaten *bechipazon,* in a rush as quickly as possible. They were to eat it hurriedly, as if they were in a tearing rush to catch a train. This requirement was only for the first Pesach in Egypt and does not apply to our observance of Pesach during the millennia that have followed.

Two questions arise. Firstly, the *pasuk* connects the requirement of *bechipazon* to *Pesach hu Lashem,* eat hurriedly because it is a Pesach to Hashem? What does this mean? What is the connection? The rush to eat the *korban pesach* is not intrinsic to the mitzvah, as we know because it was only done that first year. So what is the Torah showing us by making this connection? Secondly, and more importantly, the bringing of the *korban pesach* was the very first mitzvah performed by the Jewish people as a nation. Why would Hashem want us to do this mitzvah as fast as possible? Why would Hashem want us to do *any* mitzvah in as big a hurry as possible? This is not how one is to fulfill the commandments of Hashem! We need to study the mitzvah, examine it, prepare for it, discuss it with others, relish it! We need to savor the mitzvah, enjoy it, and love and appreciate the opportunity to serve our Creator.

No less than the *Mesilas Yesharim* emphasizes that we are to do mitzvos slowly, that we are to enjoy them and bask in them. We surely wish to fulfill commandments as soon as opportunities arise, demonstrating our zerizus and zeal to do mitzvos. But we are not to then rush through the actual performance of mitzvos. We are not to appear as someone who simply wishes to put down a load as quickly as he can!

Simply put, rushing through a mitzvah is the polar opposite of the optimal mitzvah performance. So why did Hashem require it for the first Pesach?

The *Amudei Ohr,* one of the Gedolim of Lithiuania, offers an explanation. The underlying goal of our lives should be to become closer and closer to the *Ribono shel Olam,* to achieve a *kurvah*, an attachment to Hashem. Our blueprint for achieving this closeness is the Torah, and the mitzvos are the path that leads to this *deveikus.* When a person is engaged in doing a mitzvah, serving Hashem with his body, mind, and heart, he is automatically becoming closer to Hashem. The more effort and understanding and love that he expends in performance of the mitzvah, the more he accomplishes in strengthening his *kurvah.*

*Chazal* teach that one moment of *teshuvah* and *maasim tovim,* repentance and good deeds, is better than *Olam HaBa,* the state of having *kurvah* with Hashem. Performing mitzvos is the *vehicle* to achieve this, the single best way to get closer to Hashem. Every moment in which a person is engaged in these activities brings him closer to Hashem and nothing is better than that.

The Gemara in *Succah* teaches us that Hashem desires this closeness and promises to reciprocate. Says the Gemara, if you come to My house, I will come to your house, Hashem tells us. If you don't come to My house, I will not come to your house. Doing mitzvos in the best way possible earns a Jew an invitation to be a guest in Hashem's house, and perhaps even better, the opportunity to host Hashem, as He visits our homes. We will be welcome in Hashem's home and He will be pleased to visit ours. What could be better than having

Hashem as an honored guest, Who feels comfortable in your living room? This closeness with Hashem is the goal of *kiyum hamitzvos,* and *kiyum hamitzvos* is the easiest way to reach this goal.

Asks the *Amudei Ohr,* did the *korban pesach* of *Pesach Mitzrayim* not have a much different purpose? Was the purpose of this mitzvah to become closer to Hashem? Did the Jewish people want to have Hashem in their homes at that most significant moment in history, the night of *makkas bechoros?* Would it have been beneficial to be in close proximity to the *Ribono shel Olam* during the plague of the killing of the first born, a night in which there was not one Egyptian family without a corpse in its home?

No! This first *korban pesach* was different from all other *korbanos pesach* that would come after. The blood of the sacrifice was applied to the doorposts and lintels of the Jewish homes, not so that our mitzvah observance would draw Hashem closer, but *to keep Him away!* The goal was to make sure that He skipped over our homes as He visited this final plague on Mitzrayim.

Explains the *Amudei Ohr*, what is a surefire method to keep Hashem from visiting your home, to make sure that He does not feel welcome and come close, but instead stays far away? Do mitzvos as fast as possible. Do them without taking the time to savor them. Do them pro forma, in a tremendous hurry, as if you simply want to do them and be done with them. That behavior will make sure that Hashem keeps His distance.

With this, the *Amudei Ohr* answers the questions asked earlier. What is the connection of *v'achaltem oso bechipazon* to *Pesach hu Lashem?* Why eat the *korban* quickly? Because we **wanted** *Pesach hu Lashem,* the skipping over of Hashem! We wanted Hashem to skip over our homes! And the way to make that happen is to do the mitzvah hurriedly, as fast as possible, in what would otherwise be a far less than desirable way to fulfill Hashem's command. *That* was what the Jews did by design, to keep Hashem away from them that first Pesach night.

With this, Rabbi Frand suggested another possible reason why the Jewish people's refraining from eating chametz that year did not prevent the sin of Golden Calf. Perhaps refraining from eating chametz protects one from the *yetzer hara* only when he is keeping mitzvos in a way that draws him closer to Hashem. But refraining from chametz as they did in Mitzrayim, in order for Hashem to skip over their houses, will not result in Hashem wanting to protect them from sin the rest of the year even though they were properly fulfilling the mitzvah. Therefore, while the hurriedness of the first *korban pesach* was necessary, it did not result in the closeness with Hashem that guarantees against sin.

Every Jew has many mitzvos to savor and relish during the preparation for and observance of Pesach. If the Jew guards the sheaves, grinds the wheat, kneads and bakes the dough before it becomes chametz, prepares the maror, finds new insights into the Haggadah, sits at the Seder table with reverence, love, awe and gratefulness to Hashem, works hard to teach his children the *emunah* in Hashem that has its source on *Leil Pesach*, and eats and drinks the required amounts of matzah and wine with joy, he will become close with Hashem, he will be a guest in the home of Hashem and Hashem will grace his home with His holy presence. He will be as a son who serves his father with no thought to rationale or reward, yet the closeness to Hashem that his actions engender is the ultimate reward.

We spoke above how a person should fulfill the mitzvos with the goal of having *deveikus* with Hashem in *Olam HaBa*. However, there seems to be a conflicting motivation for mitzvah observance. Near the beginning of *Pirkei Avos*, Antignos Ish Socho instructs us to serve Hashem not as a servant who wishes to acquire reward from his Master, but as a servant who is not looking for a reward. This dichotomy is amplified when considering the distinction between serving Hashem as His son or, in contrast, as His servant. A loving child will constantly be on the lookout, eager to please his parents in any way possible, and is amply rewarded by the opportunity to serve his parent. A servant does what he is commanded to do in order to earn his reward and then goes back to his own business. It would certainly seem that achieving reward, including the ultimate award of *Olam HaBa*, should not be the goal of a Jew in keeping mitzvos. He may trust that great reward will assuredly await him, but he should serve Hashem without regard to the reward.

But not so fast. Our *mora d'asra,* Rabbi Naiman, *shlita,* has mentioned in his shiurim many times that his rebbe, the Rosh HaYeshiva, HaRav Shmuel Yaakov Weinberg, *z"l,* taught that a person's goal *should* be to achieve the *deveikus* of *Olam HaBa.* After all, Hashem created the world because He wanted to bestow His goodness on His creations. The ultimate good is to achieve the eternal paradise of *deveikus* to Hashem, basking in the glow and warmth of His *Shechinah.* Therefore, by striving to keep mitvzos to reach this level, we are fulfilling the ultimate will of Hashem just as we should. The Rosh HaYeshivah used the *mashal* of a father who promises his child ice cream if he performs a certain chore. When the child's goal in his work is to receive the ice cream, is it because he relishes the sweet taste of the ice cream or because he will be excited to see the expression of happiness on his father's face. Antignos Ish Socho is teaching that we should be performing the mitzvos because we want to feel good from the pleasure we receive. We should be doing them because we want to give Hashem the opportunity to do His will, which is to bestow His goodness upon us.

When mitzvos are done with great haste, just to be *yotzei,* we will not achieve the same level of *deveikus* with Hashem as when we are doing them in order to fulfill His will.

# Matzah for All:
# The *Sugya* and Saga of Oat Matzos[1]

## Rabbi Moshe Tzvi Schuchman

**Five Grains: Four Plus Oats**

Producing matzah fit for the mitzvah entails baking dough that is made from any of the Five Grains: wheat, barley, spelt, rye or oats (Mishnah *Pesachim* 2:5).[2] However, *Rama* (453:1) records that the *minhag* is ideally to make matzah only from wheat. Reasons for the *minhag* are that wheat is generally more enjoyable and thereby a "*hiddur mitzvah*" (*Mishnah Berurah* from *Chok Yaakov*), or because the structure of a wheat kernel is hardier than the other grains, thus prolonging the time it takes to become chametz (*Tiferes Yisroel, Pesachim* 2:5).[3]

---

[1] Much has been written about the relatively recent innovation of matzah made from oats. The value of publishing another treatment of the topic is to provide current information and to maintain an awareness that oat matzos are not simply another (albeit more expensive) variety available to consumers. Rather, they are a niche product intended for a specific demographic group. To a lesser extent, some of the issues may apply to spelt matzos as well.

[2] Other halachos affected by being classified among the Five Grains are: the ability to become chametz, *hafroshas challah*, *brochah rishonah* and *acharonah*, *chodosh*, and *bikkurim*.

[3] Another connection between wheat and matzah is found in *Rama* (475:7) who describes a now-defunct custom to bake matzah in a way that is reminiscent of *lachmei todah*, which were baked from wheat. On the level of *machshavah*, a linkage between wheat and matzah can be developed following the position of R' Yehuda (*Brachos* 40a) that the *Eitz HaDaas* was wheat and eating matzah is, on some level, a rectification of that primordial sin.

Almost sixty years ago, there was a challenge to identifying *shiboles shu'al* (שִׁבֹּלֶת שׁוּעָל), the last of the Five Grains, as oats.[4] Nonetheless, the consensus of *Poskim* has been that oats are properly on the list.[5] Our *mesorah* follows the earliest *Chachmei Ashkenaz*, Rabbeinu Gershom and *Rashi* (*Pesachim* 35a, *Menachos* 70a), who translate *shiboles shu'al* as *avoine* (אביינ"א), which means oats in French and other Romance languages.

Inside the hull of a grain kernel are three sections: bran (thin outer layer), germ (small, nutrient-rich part), and endosperm (bulk of the kernel, source of white flour). The endosperm contains gluten, a

---

[4] Professor Yehudah Felix (d. 5765/2005), whose works on flora and fauna in the Mishnah were respected by *Gedolei Yisroel*, objected to identifying *shiboles shu'al* as oats, primarily on grounds that the historical agricultural record indicates oats (and rye) were not cultivated in the region of Eretz Yisroel during times of Chazal. Therefore, he gave weight to another identification offered by the *Aruch*, also a Rishon, as more authentic. (Similarly, he argued that תמכא in the Mishnah cannot be *chrein*, horseradish, since that too did not exist in Mishnaic Eretz Yisroel.) See article by Rav Shmuel Meir Katz, Chaver Beis Din for Kof-K Kosher Supervision, in Kof-K's journal *Food For Thought*, Pesach 5773.

[5] Rav Shlomo Zalman Auerbach (*Halichos Shlomo*, Pesach, chap. 9, note 326) concerning both oats and *chrein*, emphasizes that our *masorah* is the final determinant for halachic application. Many cite Rav Elyashiv and Rav Moshe Feinstein as also being adamant in this regard. Likewise, Rav Yoshe Ber Soloveitchik (*Nefesh Harav* p.53, *MiPeninei Harav* p. 69) was steadfast in his family's understanding of the position articulated by his great-grandfather, the *Beis HaLevi*, that establishing the identity of a species for mitzvah fulfillment (e.g. the Five Grains for matzoh, *chilazon* for producing *techeiles*) can only be accomplished through *masorah* and not reconstituted by scientific methods. See also *Masorah* Journal, vol. 13; *Torah, Chazal and Science*, by Rav Moshe Meiselman, p.156.

Interestingly, Rav Sternbuch, in *Teshuvos v'Hanhagos* I:302, countenances the possibility that the status of oats among the Five Grains is a *safek*. However, in V:130, published 17 years later, he discounts the notion entirely. It seems that the record of *Poskim* who were initially *choshesh* for Prof. Felix's assertion, *lechumrah*, before later dismissing it, has been redacted from the literature.

water-insoluble protein, which performs a dual role. When a kernel germinates for further reproduction, gluten nourishes the growing stalk; when a kernel is ground into flour and made into dough, gluten (the Latin word for glue) provides a sticky and elastic texture which prevents carbon dioxide gasses emitted by fermenting grain sugars from escaping. This allows dough to rise and gives bread its fluffy texture.

Among the Five Grains, oats are an outlier since, unlike the other four, oats do not contain gluten[6]. In place of gluten, oats have a different water-insoluble protein called avenin. Compared to wheat flour where gluten comprises up to 85% of protein content, the concentration of avenin in oat flour is only about 15%.[7] Therefore, when dough made from oat flour is left to ferment there is little to trap gas bubbles inside, resulting in bread that is much denser and crumblier than bread made from the other grains. Evidently, our *mesorah* regards this weakened and more subtle form of leavening by oats as sufficient to be considered chametz. This is in contrast to other types of flour, such as rice or corn, which when mixed with water reach a state of *sirchon*, spoilage, but never become chametz (*Pesachim* 35a).[8]

**Celiac Disease and Gluten**

Celiac disease, where the lining of the small intestine is damaged and prevents the body from absorbing vital nutrients, was first described 1,900 years ago by the Greek physician Aretaeus. It was linked with

---

[6] While oats do not naturally contain gluten, they are often tainted with gluten due to cross-contamination from other grains during growing and processing.

[7] https://www.ncbi.nlm.nih.gov/pmc/articles/PMC5635790/

[8] See *Torah, Chazal and Science* which notes the confidence *Chazal* had to state definitively that only the Five Grains become chametz. They were unequivocal that another grain fitting this description could never be discovered in the future.

grain consumption during World War II by a Dutch pediatrician who observed how symptoms were relieved when sufferers avoided products made with wheat flour. In the 1950s, gluten specifically was identified as the component which triggers adverse effects.[9] Further studies concluded that celiac is a hereditary autoimmune disorder, where gluten provokes the immune system to attack the person's own body.[10]

About 1% of the population, on average, is affected by celiac disease, with a higher-than-average prevalence among Jews.[11] The condition may progress to the point where even trace amounts of gluten can be dangerous. Research is still ongoing into whether Non-Celiac Gluten Sensitivity exists, inducing symptoms even in people without genetic markers. Those who feel their digestive health is impacted by gluten try to maintain intake levels below certain thresholds but do not take measures to avoid it entirely.

**Spiritual Gain vs. Physical Pain**

How does this impact the mitzvah of matzah? Standard *shmurah* matzos today are produced from a wheat variety called 'soft red winter'.[12] 'Hard' and 'soft' refer to kernel texture and reflect gluten content. Hard wheat contains more gluten than soft wheat, making it ideal for breads and pastries. Soft wheat is better for crumbly items like pretzels, crackers, and matzah. (In actual practice, manufacturers

---

[9] Wheat gluten is composed of gliadin and glutenin proteins in approximately equal proportion. The amino acid sequences within the gliadin proteins are responsible for the celiac reaction, https://en.wikipedia.org/wiki/Gliadin.

[10] Celiac, an immune disorder, is not the same as wheat allergy, where the body produces antibodies to fight proteins in wheat. People with wheat allergy may consume other grains, even those with gluten.

[11] https://celiac.org/main/wp-content/uploads/2016/06/ethnicitymanuscriptproofs.pdf

[12] Winter wheat is planted in fall and harvested in late spring / early summer, thereby avoiding the prohibition of *chodosh*.

use wheat blends to ensure uniform results.) Even though soft wheat has a lower gluten level, someone with actual celiac disease may still find it difficult to tolerate.

Generally, whenever there is a chance of dangerous consequences to one's vital health, he is exempt from mitzvah obligations - אֲנוּס רַחֲמָנָא פַּטְרֵיהּ. Performing a positive mitzvah in a way that poses risk to life is actually an *aveirah*, a transgression. Maharam Shick (O.Ch. 260) rules that one who chooses to perform the mitzvah and endanger himself has no license to make a *berachah*. However, when doing a *mitzvah* would only cause discomfort or temporary illness without long-term repercussions, the halachah is less defined.

Regarding the requirement to drink four cups of wine at the Seder, *Shulchan Aruch* (472:10) states: מי שאינו שותה יין מפני שמזיקו או שונאו צריך לדחוק עצמו ולשתות לקיים מצות ארבעה כוסות, *One who does not drink wine because it harms him or because he dislikes it must push himself and drink it to fulfill the mitzvah of daled kosos.*

The source for this ruling is the Talmud (*Bavli*, *Nedarim* 49a; *Yerushalmi*, *Pesachim* 10:1) which cites Amoraim who would drink wine at the Seder even though it caused them headaches for months afterwards. *Poskim* (see *Mishnah Berurah* and *Kaf HaChaim*) note that one must exert himself only if he will still be able to function, albeit with discomfort. However, if he will be rendered immobile, i.e., confined to bed, then there is no obligation for one to drink wine.[13]

---

[13] When these *halachos* were formulated, grape juice was not available during Pesach. In the Talmud, grape juice appears in the context of squeezing grapes and drinking it immediately thereafter (*Bava Basra* 97b). Before the advent of refrigeration and pasteurization, grapes (fruits or their juice) – which are harvested in fall – would spoil long before spring, unless fermented and preserved as wine. *Poskim* permit using grape juice for *daled kosos* when necessary. However, fulfilling the *derech cheirus* component of the mitzvah requires some alcoholic content. One can minimize the amount

*Kaf HaChaim* extends this halachic distinction to eating matzah as well. Someone who will experience discomfort must still eat the minimal amount for *motzi matzah* and *afikoman*, but someone who will become immobilized is exempt.

*Mishnah Berurah*, on the other hand, appears to disagree with this extension. He too distinguishes between discomfort and immobilization with regard to *daled kosos*. But in *Shaar HaTziyon* he adds that the reason for the exemption when becoming bedridden is the requirement to drink wine at the Seder "*derech cheirus*", in a matter of freedom, which is contravened when it causes severe illness. This implies that other *mitzvos* without the limitation of *derech cheirus*, e.g., matzah, must be performed even to the point of illness – provided there is no reason to suspect any danger to life.

Indeed, the position of *Maharam Schick* (ibid.) is that one must eat matzah (and maror) even if it may cause illness, as long as there is no chance of risk to life.[14] He does not make this point, but it's reasonable to assume that even *Maharam Schick* agrees there is no obligation to perform a mitzvah if it will result in lifelong bodily malfunction. The prooftext for this halachah is from Amoraim becoming ill after drinking wine for a few months, but not indefinitely.

Later *Poskim* explain the *Mishnah Berurah* as agreeing with *Kaf HaChaim*, that one is not obligated to become severely ill, even temporarily, for a mitzvah. Why then does he mention the reason of

---

of wine to drink by: 1) only drinking a majority of the *revi'is/kos*, and not the whole cup, 2) diluting the wine. Rav Moshe Heinemann holds that the resultant mixture should contain at least 4% alcohol. Therefore, wine which has 12% alcohol content can be diluted to 1/3 wine and 2/3 water. See STAR-K's annual Pesach Directory for further details.

[14] Maharm Schick writes the halachah of *daled kosos* applies "*kol shekain*" (כל שכן) to matzah and marror. Matzah is understood since it's a *mitzvah d'oraisa*. Why there is a *kol shekain* to marror is unclear.

*derech cheirus* which is unique to *daled kosos*, implying that other mitzvos do not share this exemption? Various approaches are offered:

1) *Daled kosos* is in a category of mitzvos established for *pirsum haNeis*, publicizing the miracle (along with reading Megillas Esther on Purim and lighting the menorah on Chanukah). These mitzvos, although Rabbinic, require one to stretch himself beyond normal halachic limits.[15] For example, while one usually does not need to spend more than one-fifth of his assets to perform a mitzvah, for mitzvos involving *pirsum haNeis* one must sell all his possessions. Therefore, it's conceivable that *daled kosos* is stricter than other mitzvos in this aspect too, obligating one to undertake a chance of becoming bedridden or contracting long-term illness (that is not life-threatening) for the sake of the mitzvah. However, since that would not be considered drinking *derech cheirus*, there is no such obligation.[16]

2) Even though one is not obligated to become bedridden for the sake of a positive mitzvah, one who extends himself to that degree has nevertheless fulfilled it. An exception is *daled kosos*, since drinking *derech cheirus* is essential to the mitzvah. If drinking wine causes severe illness (as opposed to annoying pain, like a hangover) that's not *derech cheirus*, and no mitzvah has been performed.[17]

**Oat Matzah: The Solution**

For many years, sufferers of celiac disease confronted these issues when it came to the mitzvah of matzah on Pesach. They would evaluate if ingesting matzah would merely cause discomfort or more

---

[15] See Beis Medrash of Ranchleigh, *Kuntress Lemaan Tesapier* Pesach 5781, page 199.

[16] See Rav Tzvi Pesach Frank, *Mikraei Kodesh*, Pesach II, *siman* 163; *Shu"t Minchas Asher* III, *simanim* 42-43.

[17] See *Teshuvos v'Hanhagos* I:302

serious symptoms and seek halachic guidance accordingly. More often than not, they devoutly relied on the dictum of שׁוֹמֵר מִצְוָה לֹא יֵדַע דָּבָר רָע (קהלת ח, ה) – one who obeys mitzvos will not confront danger.[18] "Is there another option?" is a question that was left unasked.

Almost forty years ago, in the mid-80s, Rabbi Ephraim Kestenbaum, a chemist in Golders Green, London, was prompted by his young daughter who was diagnosed with celiac disease, to capitalize on the inclusion of oats in the list of Five Grains and solve the dilemma, creating gluten-free oat matzah. After much experimentation and perseverance working with the gluten-less crumbly dough[19], his endeavor yielded a product that has become popular among the community of celiac sufferers. Other bakeries have since followed suit.

For reasons we shall see, these matzos are not for everyone. People who suspect they have gluten intolerance but not celiac, or who have a mild wheat allergy, should ideally consume a minimal *shiur* of wheat matzah. If necessary, they can eat only a bite for *motzi matzah* and save the requisite *kezayis* for *afikoman*.[20] Alternatively, they may use *shmurah* matzah made from spelt. Gluten found in spelt is a

---

[18] *Teshuvos v'Hanhagos, ibid.*

[19] At least in the beginning, oat matzos were not folded over on a stick and placed inside the oven the same way as ordinary wheat matzos, since they would break apart. Instead, they were placed on a sheet and maneuvered onto the oven floor. Lakewood Matzah Bakery (email communication) says they use a stick for oat matzos, except that some crumble before reaching the oven (which doesn't happen with wheat matzos) and are discarded. Once left to bake in the oven they stay together well enough to be flipped.

[20] *Minchas Asher* III *siman* 43, explains that someone who limits matzah consumption at the Seder to just one *k'zayis* has eaten his *afikoman*, after which nothing else may be eaten. Therefore, it should be saved for the end. Additionally, eating the *k'zayis* after partaking from the *seudah* fulfills the enhanced mitzvah of eating *al hasovah*, to do the mitzvah while already partially satiated.

more fragile variety than the gluten in wheat and is more water-soluble. Furthermore, spelt has higher fiber content than wheat, aiding its digestion.

**Oat Matzah: Challenges**

We have long-established traditions, evolved over thousands of years, in making matzah from wheat. Granted, the matzah we eat today is not identical to what was consumed centuries ago.[21] But the methods of working with wheat flour are familiar, built upon ample precedent in the realms of both halachic theory and practice, minor discrepancies between communities notwithstanding. With respect to other grains, there is no such strong basis; oat flour, in particular, poses special challenges.

After stalks are removed during harvest, the remaining whole oats consist of a protective hull, which goes for animal feed, and an inner groat, which is processed into human food. Oat groats contain a unique concentration of enzymes and lipids which become decompartmentalized during milling. Their interaction starts a reaction that eventually leads to a rancid aroma and a bitter taste in a matter of days. Shelf-stable oats are produced industrially by deactivating the enzymes in a process called kilning. This involves a long vertical cylinder where live steam is injected to raise the temperature of the groats, followed by radiant heat which evaporates excess moisture. Only then are the oats milled to various specifications.

The regular kilning process is not an option for Pesach as steam will cause the oats to become chametz. Consequently, a different technique had to be developed specifically for producing oat matzah.

---

[21] Our matzah today is much thinner and more rigid than what our ancestors used. See *Shu"t Minchas Asher* III, *siman* 64; *Hakirah* Journal vol. 17, "The Thick and Thin of the History of Matzah", by Ari Z Zivitofsky and Ari Greenspan.

Rav Osher Westheim, Dayan of the Manchester Beis Din (*niftar* at the beginning of the COVID-19 epidemic) was involved with the kashrus of oat matzah from the very beginning. In 5744/1984 he consulted with Rav Chanoch Dov Padwa of London (author of *Cheshev HaEifod*) to allow heating the groats with dry air blown through the cylinder. Rav Betzalel Rakow in Gateshead was also part of the discussion. The following year, Rav Yitzchak Yaakov Weiss (author of *Minchas Yitzchak*), previously the chief Dayan in Manchester until 5730/1970 when he assumed the helm of the Eidah HaCharedis in Yerushalayim, published a *teshuvah* prohibiting oat matzos. After Rav Westheim met with Rav Weiss and discussed the matter, the latter agreed to allow oat matzos for *cholim* (sick people) only, provided it was made in small batches and for personal use, not commercially.

Among the concerns is that the Five Grains are divided into different categories, both for the purposes of *kilayim* - the prohibition of planting seeds of disparate species in proximity to one another (Mishnah *Kilayim* 1:1), and for *challah* - determining which mixtures combine to form a dough large enough that obligates separation of *challah* (Mishnah *Challah* 4:2). Oats are considered a close relative of barley but not of wheat. Halachah regards barley as more susceptible to becoming chametz than wheat (*Pesachim* 40a, *Shulchan Aruch* 453:5) and oats should be treated with the same stringency. As such, the usual time allowance for wheat dough before it enters the oven (known colloquially as “18 minutes”) would not apply and a shorter time window is needed.

Additionally, the nature and consistency of oat flour necessitates making oat matzos thicker than the acceptable norm today. This raises the possibility that perhaps the inside of the matzah is not baked thoroughly enough to remove concerns of being chametz.[22]

---

[22] This concern is not exclusive to oat matzos. For economic reasons, commercial matzah bakeries keep their ovens very hot, well over 1,000°F.

### *Mei Peiros*

A decade later, in 5755/1995, additional halachic issues regarding oat matzos that Rav Westheim and his colleagues encountered were posed to Rav Shmuel HaLevi Wosner in Bnei Brak (author of *Shevet HaLevi*; also, grandfather of Rav Westheim's son-in-law).

One question concerned the considerable amount of *zeiyah*, moist vapor, emitted by the groats while they are heated by the stream of forced hot air. Although the groats themselves emerge completely dry, perhaps we should be concerned that some of the moisture is absorbed by kernels in the chamber before steam escapes through vents. This moisture has the status of *mei peiros* (literally, fruit juice). Even according to the opinion that *mei peiros* does not cause grain to become chametz, nevertheless, when water is added the grain becomes chametz very quickly. (*Shulchan Aruch* 462:1-2). *Bei'ur Halachah* (beginning of *siman* 462) cites different viewpoints about our case where *mei peiros* is first absorbed in grain and completely dried, and only subsequently is water introduced. He rules that in a *sha'as hadchak*, extenuating circumstance, when there is no other reasonable alternative, there is grounds to rule leniently. Can this leniency, issued in reaction to a rare, unexpected situation, be utilized to permit making such matzos on a regular basis?

---

This enables matzos to be baked quickly, about 12 seconds per matzah, increasing the amount produced per shift. Rav Yosef Eliyahu Henkin (5641/1881-5733/1973; sefer *Lev Ivra*, p.40; *Teshuvos Ivra* p.20) cautioned that this results in a downside that the outer surfaces are baked (קרימת פנים), while the inner layer is still raw (חוטי בצק נמשכין ממנו). When Rav Heinemann supervises matzah baking, every single matzah is checked for this concern. A few minutes after being taken out of the oven, after it cools down a bit, a matzah should be hard and dry enough to "snap" when broken. Matzos still pliable at this stage are deemed '*vasser matzos*' - too soft - and are rejected for STAR-K (although the bakery's own *hashgochah* may accept them). Later, after the matzos are boxed, is too late to check, since everything will harden by then. This problem is more likely in matzos that are rolled too thick. Some *chaburos* insist on the oven temperature being lowered to obviate this problem.

**What is Matzah: Arrested Chametz or Avoided?**

Rav Westheim posed a second question to the *Shevet HaLevi* that he says was mentioned initially in discussions with his colleague and was raised again by a prominent American rabbi who felt it was a serious challenge to the production of oat matzah. We know this rabbi to be none other than Rav Moshe Heinemann, Kashrus Administrator of STAR-K Certification, and *Mara D'Asra* of Agudath Israel of Baltimore.

The question stems from the fact that applying heat to deactivate the enzymes in the oats not only prevents them from becoming rancid but also prevents them from becoming chametz! The Gemara (*Pesachim* end of 39b, see *Rashi*) indicates, followed by the *Rambam* (*Chametz U'Matzah* 3:3) that fully roasted grain kernels (*kilayos,* קְלָיוֹת) can no longer become chametz when mixed with water. Although we may not rely on this leniency practically, lest the kernels are not fully roasted, the fact remains.

What problem does this present? To the contrary, shouldn't removing the possibility of becoming chametz be an advantage when making matzah and not a detriment?

The Scriptural source in the Gemara (*Pesachim* 35a) for only the Five Grains being eligible for matzah is based on a hekeish, a juxtaposition between two parts of a pasuk: לֹא־תֹאכַל עָלָיו חָמֵץ, שִׁבְעַת יָמִים תֹּאכַל־עָלָיו מַצּוֹת לֶחֶם עֹנִי וגו' (פרשת ראה טז:ג), *Do not eat with it chametz; for seven days you shall eat with it matzah,* etc. This establishes a relationship between chametz and matzah, which is formulated as: דְּבָרִים הַבָּאִים לִידֵי חִימּוּץ אָדָם יוֹצֵא בָּהֶן יְדֵי חוֹבָתוֹ בְּמַצָּה, יָצְאוּ אֵלּוּ שֶׁאֵין בָּאִין לִידֵי חִימּוּץ, אֶלָּא לִידֵי סִירְחוֹן, *Items which become chametz (i.e., the Five Grains, when dough is left to rise) one may use to fulfill his obligation of matzah, excluding these (other grains) that cannot become chametz, only sirchon (spoilage).* The precise meaning of the phrase "items which become chametz" is a matter of dispute among the major Rishonim.

The *Rambam* (*Chametz U'Matzah* 6:5) writes that matzah kneaded from a mixture of flour and fruit juice (מי פירות) is eligible for the mitzvah.[23] Earlier (5:2), he writes that dough kneaded with fruit juice without any water whatsoever cannot become chametz.

Combining these two rulings together, *Rambam's* position emerges that the requirement to use "items which become chametz" for matzah production does not mean it's necessary for this specific batch of dough to become chametz were it left to rise. If so, he would not allow using *mei peiros* for the mitzvah. Rather, Chazal were expressing the uniqueness of the Five Grains. Since they alone can become chametz when mixed with water and left to rise, only they are qualified for making matzah.

Accordingly, the *Rambam* should allow using roasted kernels from the Five Grains to make matzah, even though mixing them with water will not produce chametz.[24]

The *Maggid Mishnah* (6:5) quotes an unnamed Rishon ("ואמנם ראיתי מי שכתב") who disagrees with the Rambam and holds that one does

[23] Rabbeinu Tam concurs with the *Rambam*, but *Rashi* (*Pesachim* 35a) and *Raavad* (*Hasagos* 5:2) disagree and hold that dough made with *mei peiros* will become *chametz nukshah* if left to rise. There is no *kareis* for this type of chametz, only a לא תעשה or perhaps an איסור דרבנן. Rama (462:3) rules to follow *Rashi* and *Raavad*, except for *cholim* who may rely on the majority view.

[24] This conclusion in the *Rambam's shitah* is assumed by the *Chayei Odom*, cited below. Rav Heinemann, however, maintains that even the *Rambam* might disallow *kilayos*. He only permitted regular grains with fruit juice since they would become chametz if kneaded with water. However, when gluten proteins are deactivated by heat, that changes the nature of the grain to the extent that even the *Rambam* would possibly agree it can't be used. See the discussion about deglutenized wheat below.

not discharge his obligation by eating matzah from dough that was kneaded with fruit juice only. At least some water must be added in the mixture. *Maggid Mishnah* endorses this position as correct.

The source for this viewpoint is the *Ramban* (who preceded him as Torah leader in the Girona region of Spain by about a century). In *Milchemes HaShem* to *Pesachim* 10b (pages of the Rif) *Ramban* elaborates: 1) the relationship between chametz and matzah established by the *hekeish* requires that this specific dough must be an "item which can become chametz"; 2) the requirement for *shemirah* (guarding) of matzah (וּשְׁמַרְתֶּם אֶת־הַמַּצּוֹת – פרשת בא יב:ז) during production entails watching over the dough from becoming chametz during kneading. Dough that only contains fruit juice fails this requirement of being watched since it can never become chametz.

According to the *Ramban*, placing the dough into the oven must be the act which arrests the chametz process. Actively stopping the fermentation is mandated by the *mitzvah* of *shemirah*. It follows, therefore, that dough made with roasted kernels cannot be made into matzah since no *shemirah* from chametz involved in its production.

Whom do the *Poskim* follow? *Pri Megadim* (*Mishbetzos* 461:2) and *Shulchan Aruch HaRav* (462:1) both rule in accordance with *Ramban, lechumrah*. *Chayei Adam* in *Nishmas Adam* (*Hilchos Pesach, Sh'ailah* 15) deals with a question similar to ours, about wheat that was harvested for matzah while the stalks were still moist.[25] To inhibit mold growth during storage, the stalks were then dried in an oven – like *kilayos*. Are these kernels still fit for matzah? After a lengthy and exhaustive review of all the sources, he

[25] Great care is taken when harvesting wheat for matzah that the kernels should not be moist. Harvesting takes place in the afternoon after all dew has evaporated. A sample is tested (by taste and in the lab) to confirm that moisture content is approximately 14% or below.

concludes that the *Rambam's* lenient opinion can be relied upon *bsha'as hadchak*, when there is no other alternative.

As with the question of *mei peiros*, can this ruling of the *Chayei Adam*, issued for a fluke, unanticipated case, provide basis for an ongoing system to bake matzah on behalf of celiac sufferers? Perhaps we must take the *Ramban* into account?

**Outcomes for Oat Matzah**

From the above discussion we see that the unique challenges of oat matzah production can be categorized into two types of difficulties (besides what is typically encountered with wheat matzah production): one, avoiding possibility of chametz; two, producing matzah suitable for fulfilling the mitzvah at the Seder. As can be expected, various Poskim adopt different postures in their halachic judgements.

*Shevet HaLevi*'s response to Rav Westheim was that the *Chayei Adam*'s leniency to rely on the *Rambam* applies here and the heated groats may be used to fulfill the mitzvah. This is especially so since it's not certain that these enzyme-deactivated groats truly attain the status of *kilayos*. To minimize the *chashash* of chametz, he concurred with the recommendation of Rav Westheim and other English Rabbonim that batch sizes be limited and production hastened so that dough will reach the oven more quickly than in traditional wheat matzah production. However, because not all halachic doubts were resolved in this uncharted enterprise, he ruled that someone using oat matzah for the mitzvah should not make his own *berachah*. Instead, he should listen to *berachah* of *al achilas matzah* made by someone using standard matzah and be *yotzei* through *shomei'ah k'oneh*.

Rav Sternbuch (*Teshuvos v'Hanhagos* V:130) does not express any such hesitation about making one's own *berachah* on the mitzvah at the Seder. He is more concerned about the possible chametz issue. Therefore, he recommends that oat matzah kneaded with just water should be reserved for the obligatory mitzvah. During the rest of Pesach, oat matzos kneaded with 100% fruit juice and no water should be consumed. Packaging should contain a prominent mark noting that these matzos are exclusively for *cholim*.

Rav Elayshiv is quoted as allowing celiac sufferers to eat regular oat matzah made with water for the entire Yom Tov. However, for the Seder, they should make an effort to eat a *kezayis* of wheat matzah, if possible (*Mishnah Berurah*, *Dirshu* ed., *siman* 453, note 3).

**Deglutenized Wheat**

Regular wheat bread typically has a gluten level of 75,000 ppm (parts per million). American labeling laws allow products with a gluten level below 20 ppm to be advertised as gluten-free. Just as a *hechsher* attests to a product's kosher status, there are certifications that verify a product's gluten-free status.

Currently, there is active scientific research developing technology to produce a genetically modified wheat plant with very low gluten (gliadin) content, below the threshold where it would have a deleterious effect on people with celiac disease.[26] Previously, Italian researchers worked on reducing the gluten content in wheat through a form of hydrolysis (which breaks compounds into its component parts) using lacto-fermentation with specific lacto-bacilli and fungi.[27]

Possibly, even the *Rambam,* who allows using dough mixed with fruit juice for the mitzvah even though that dough will never become chametz, would agree that deglutenized wheat is invalid for the

---

[26] https://www.ncbi.nlm.nih.gov/pmc/articles/PMC6470674/

[27] https://www.ncbi.nlm.nih.gov/pmc/articles/PMC1932817/, and https://www.sciencedaily.com/releases/2011/01/110119120406.htm

mitzvah. A basic characteristic of wheat, as defined by Chazal, is its ability to ferment and become chametz. Removing gluten could effectively render the resultant wheat a different sort of species, no longer one of the Five Grains.[28] Both Rav Wosner and Rav Elyashiv are reported as saying that matzah made with deglutenized wheat should not be used for the mitzvah.[29]

In recent years, items made with gluten-free wheat starch have become available. This starch is derived through a simple process of washing out the water-soluble starch from wheat dough or processed endosperm and then evaporating the water until a fine powdery starch is left. Because the gluten proteins have been removed (the result contains less than 5 ppm gluten), wheat starch does not lend any elasticity to dough and is primarily used as a thickener.[30] Despite the presence of a wheat component, the *berachah* on such products made with this starch is *shehakol* and cannot be used as an ingredient in matzah.

**Improvements and Developments**

Over the past forty years oat matzah bakeries have continually improved and developed their production methods. Consequently, it is feasible that circumstances changed sufficiently so that the *piskei halachah* quoted above may not necessarily apply to the products commonly used today.

---

[28] See above, note #24, that Rav Heinemann holds roasted and deglutenized kernels are the same in this regard. However, see *Tosafos*, *Yevamos* 44a, ד"ה כל שאינו, who differentiate between intrinsic status and an impediment.

[29] See sources in *Piskei Teshuvos*, *siman* 453 note 8, and *Dirshu Mishnah Berurah*, *siman* 453 note 5; also *Ashrei Ho'Ish*, *Hilchos Pesach*. The effect this advancement has on all the halachos outlined above in note 2 requires further exploration.

[30] https://www.schaer.com/en-us/a/gluten-free-wheat-starch

One change took place in advance of Pesach 5773, when it was reported that the temperature and duration for heating groats used in Kestenbaum matzos was reduced from 350°F for 35 minutes – which generated the question of *kilayos* – to 270°F for 11 minutes. Moreover, dough that was subsequently made from these oats was allegedly tested and found that when left unbaked it germinated and became chametz. Based on this information, Rav Heinemann withdrew his primary objection to using these matzos for the mitzvah at the Seder (for people with no other option).

A more significant change has taken place in recent years.[31] As of this writing (for Pesach 5782), oat matzah bakeries no longer heat the groats prior to milling, thus solving the problem of *kilayos*. Instead, they endeavor to mitigate the bitter taste by baking the oat flour into matzah soon after milling. The (broader) food industry considers the impact of the enzymatic reaction to be minimal within the first seven days. Most bakeries can accomplish this time frame, particularly for their hand matzah product.[32]

Despite this effort, consumers still detect some bitterness in oat matzos not found in regular matzos. The degree of adverse taste depends on a few factors, including the brand,[33] how long after

---

[31] Material contained from here until the end of this section is gleaned from communications (email and phone) with dedicated and knowledgeable senior management at Lakewood Matzah Bakery and Tiv Hashibolet in Eretz Yisroel. Their passion to help all segments of Klal Yisroel fulfill the mitzvah is apparent, far surpassing business considerations. Any misrepresentation of facts is solely the shortcoming of the author. I am indebted to Rabbi Yosef Moshe Naiman for connecting me with Rabbi Yehoshua Perlman of Tiv Hashibolet.

[32] For machine matzah production, this time frame is harder to control if the bakery does not have its own manufacturing equipment and ships their oat flour to an outside manufacturing facility.

[33] This article does not address the complications faced by matzah bakeries in sourcing gluten-free oat fields, which impacts the final product.

milling they were baked, how long the matzos were exposed to air after being removed from sealed plastic packaging, and the sensitivity of a person's taste buds.

Like wheat, the milling of oats is carefully controlled to prevent any heat build-up caused by grinding friction. But unlike wheat, oats have significantly higher fat content and produce an oily residue during grinding which is an impediment to producing clean, workable flour. Out of necessity, matzah bakeries have had to innovate proprietary systems designed specifically for oat matzah flour.[34]

Now that the issue of eligibility for the mitzvah at the Seder has been resolved, the issue of chametz is left to be addressed. We saw that some earlier Poskim, most notably the *Minchas Yitzchak* and *Shevet HaLevi*, felt that oats are similar to barley and the time allowance for the dough prior to baking should be considerably less that what is accepted for regular wheat dough ("18 minutes"). On a practical level, it appears that bakeries do not heed this concern. An argument to the contrary is advanced, since the chametz process in dough is a function of its gluten component, oats that don't contain gluten should take longer than wheat to become chametz. Empirical observation seems to support this notion.[35]

---

[34] On the subject of using machines for milling matzah flour, see *Kovetz Halachos* (Piskei Rav Shmuel Kamenetsky) who explains why it has the exact same level of *hiddur* as flour made in a hand (or bicycle) grinder.

[35] Taking this logic a step further, one can conceivably present an argument that the classic "18 minutes" no longer applies to today's varieties of genetically modified wheat. Industrially produced wheat ubiquitous today contains much higher gluten levels than historic, natural varieties. Because of economic factors, what is referred to as "heritage" or "heirloom" wheat has fallen into general disuse, except by people who value it for health advantages. (In fact, some attribute increased gluten sensitivity in recent decades to the modification of wheat.) If chametz is a function of gluten, then our wheat dough should become chametz quicker than in the past.

The concern about the thickness of oat matzos is dealt with differently by various bakeries. Lacking gluten, oat flour dough crumbles easily and is exceedingly difficult to handle with. Efficiencies in place for producing wheat matzos don't work for oat matzos. Regular handmade wheat matzah has up to six people working the dough before it reaches the oven.[36] Oat dough is very fragile and cannot withstand the intensity of this process, which is designed to make a matzah as thin as possible without ripping. For oat matzah, often just a single person handles the dough all the way through. Even with this delicate touch, significant amounts of oat dough break apart during rolling and large quantities are discarded at the end of each production run. To keep the operation viable and meet production demands, many bakeries must roll their oat dough thicker than wheat.

Tiv Hashibolet takes a slightly different route. Their goal is to produce a matzah that closely resembles wheat matzah so that nobody sitting at a Seder – particularly children – should feel they are using an 'inferior' product because of their health condition. Achieving comparable thinness adds additional inefficiency into an already arduous process. Starting off with a very wet dough helps keep the brittle mixture somewhat pliable, however, a lot of the moisture is absorbed into paper which covers the wooden tables and poles[37] (for traditional reasons, they don't use metal). They accept

[36] Stations in a commercial hand-matzah bakery, after initial mixing and kneading of water and flour are: kneader, '*finner*", slicer, roller, '*gomeir'*, transfer by pole, '*reddler'*, transfer by pole, baker.

[37] In the beginning, oat matzos were not folded over on a stick to be inserted in the oven like ordinary wheat matzos since they would break apart. Instead, they were placed on a sheet and maneuvered onto the oven floor. Today, oat matzos are folded on a stick, with the expectation that many will crumble and fall to the floor before reaching the oven (something which does not happen with wheat matzos). Once left to bake in the oven they stay together well enough to be flipped.

the increased yield loss as a trade-off in their quest for thin(ner) oat matzos.

Even Tiv Hashibolet has not succeeded in making oat matzos the same size (diameter) as regular wheat matzos. Their attempt at making large, thin oat matzos resulted in numerous broken matzos with a very small number of *shleimos* usable for *lechem mishneh.* However, in keeping with their mission, they strive for maximum tastiness by sifting the oat flour many times over, much more than necessary, in order to produce a 'clean' result. This too has repercussions and can result in a 50% loss from the starting stock.[38]
On one hand, bakeries strive for the highest standard of kashrus they can achieve on a commercial scale. On the other hand, they recognize the need to produce as many matzos as feasible so that consumers seeking gluten-free matzos can have them. Unfortunately, there are many uninformed people who unknowingly purchase gluten-free "matzah" that is actually made with potato starch – certainly not one of the five grains! Manufacturers have gotten better with their labeling, calling those items "Matzah Style." But the high cost of oat matzos, which can be triple the cost of its wheat matzah equivalent, dissuades some consumers from purchasing what they need.[39]

To meet this demand, Tiv Hashiboles, for example, has two tiers of product. The vaunted *Badatz Eidah HaCharedis* approves their "*Chaburah* 18 minute" oat matzah productions. Although the *Badatz*

---

[38] Tiv Hashibolet says it takes them up to four days of baking to produce what other bakeries produce in just one day!

[39] The high cost should be understandable given the difficulty in producing oat matzos and the attendant yield losses. In addition, unpredictable factors such as weather – temperature and humidity – play a role in whether a day's oat matzah production will be successful or a loss. While atmospheric conditions are a factor in any baking operations, it usually affects the ingredient proportions. With oat matzah, the wrong weather, on rare occasion, can make baking impossible for the day.

has been reluctant to authorize their trademark flowery symbol to be printed on oat matzah packaging – in deference to the *Minchas Yitzchak*, their past leader, who did not sanction oat matzos – their name appears along with a prominent disclaimer that the product is not for general use, only for people sensitive to gluten. A less costly variety bears the *hechsher* of *Rabbanut Yerushalayim Mehadrin*, also with a disclaimer. This product is made with the same attention and care, but the production goes a few minutes longer between total clean-outs.[40]

**Chametz and the Existential Enemy**

This fundamental dispute between the *Rambam* and *Ramban* about the relationship between chametz and matzah provides a portal into the message of the mitzvah.

The *Radvaz* (prolific leader of 16th century Egyptian Jewry) in a *teshuvah* (977) investigates the Torah's seeming hyper-sensitivity toward chametz on Pesach. Not only does eating chametz incur a harsh punishment, *kareis*, the prohibition carries other exceptional stringencies, on both the Torah and Rabbinic levels. Namely, the injunction against chametz includes both eating and deriving benefit; even a speck of chametz that becomes mixed with food on Pesach prohibits the mixture since chametz is not nullified (אָסוּר בְּמַשֶׁהוּ); the obligation to search for chametz and rid it from one's possession goes well beyond any other *issurim* – even for *avodah zarah* this isn't required!

The *Radvaz* concludes from these halachos that while all mitzvos convey an underlying lesson and message, when it comes to chametz on Pesach the straightforward *peshat* is its symbolism. Chazal teach

---

[40] See the article by Rabbi Tzvi Rosen, *Machine Matzos: Timing is Everything!*, in the Spring 2009 edition of Kashrus Kurrents. https://www.star-k.org/articles/articles/seasonal/342/machine-matzos/

that chametz represents the *yetzer hara*[41], the insidious inclination that infiltrates our consciousness and lures us to pursue a spiritually harmful path. Just as a bit of sourdough starter (שְׂאוֹר שֶׁבָּעִיסָּה – *Berachos* 17a) is all it takes to catalyze a modest combination of flour and water causing it to expand and rise beyond proportion, or one minuscule cell can metastasize, רַחֲמָנָא לִצְלַן, into a devastating force, so too once the *yetzer hara* gains a foothold, no matter how small, it can grow, at first slowly then rapidly, eventually overwhelming our moral sense and judgement. Only by eradicating the *yetzer hara* totally and eliminating its influence is one able to burst the overblown fantasies it projects and gain the clarity needed for his life mission.

All year we contend with the *yetzer hara*. A perpetual tug-of-war, it pulls us downwards as we strive to ascend higher, or at least maintain traction. On Pesach, the holiday of freedom, in our quest to break free and soar to attain the lofty spiritual heights afforded by the Yom Tov, we are enjoined to eradicate the representation of the *yetzer hara*.

Matzah, the antipode of chametz, symbolizes redemption from the shackles of body and mind. The *hekeish* between matzah and chametz shows they are not disparate entities. Rather, one is the outcome of the other. Matzah is a product that results from the abnegation of chametz.

The *Rambam's* approach is that matzah mays be produced from grain that could conceivably become chametz, even though this specific dough would never reach that point. This demonstrates that direct confrontation is not necessary to vanquish the *yetzer hara*. Success is achievable by recognizing the existence of evil and

---

41 זוה"ק (ח"א רכו:) - וְאִקְרוּן חָמֵץ, יֵצֶר הָרָע; רבינו בחיי (פרשת ויקרא ב:י) - והשאור והדבש הן הן יצר הרע עצמו, כמו שאמרו רז"ל לענין חמץ ומצה בפסח צריך אדם לפנות לבבו מיצר הרע; ע"ע רמ"א בס' תורת העולה

acknowledging its latent destructive forces and taking a path that circumvents danger.

*Adam HaRishon* was initially charged with this task. *Midrash Koheles Rabbah* (7:13)[42] describes how *HaKadosh baruch Hu* placed him in Gan Eden and took him around to every tree in the Garden saying, "See My handiwork, how beautiful and praiseworthy it is. All that I created is for your benefit. Take care not to ruin it and destroy My world, etc."

*Adam* understood the ruination and destruction that could be wrought by following the *yetzer hara*. Choosing to engage only with good would have been an accomplishment worthy of ushering in the epoch of eternal *geulah*. Just like grain is eligible for matzah through its potential for becoming chametz, man's redemption is possible through the potential to encounter evil, with no need for direct engagement.

The *Ramban* has a different conception. He requires active suppression of the formation of chametz in order to produce matzah. Overcoming the *yetzer hara* involves confronting it directly. In this realm, one must struggle to remain in control without succumbing to its alluring temptations. Constant *shemirah* is required to stay on guard and not be left vulnerable. *Geulah* arrives when the evil force is exposed and neutralized.

After *Adam* and *Chavah* partook from the *Eitz HaDaas* and the serpent injected its venom into mankind,[43] the battle ground shifted from evil lurking along the periphery, which can be avoided, and became an internal clash where the *yetzer hara* is invariably engaged. Hashem told Kayin: הֲלוֹא אִם־תֵּיטִיב שְׂאֵת וְאִם לֹא תֵיטִיב לַפֶּתַח

[42] Cited in *Mesilas Yesharim*, chap. 1

[43] See *Shabbos* 146a; *Beis HaLevi, Parshas Bereishis,* ד"ה הן האדם

חַטָּאת רֹבֵץ וְאֵלֶיךָ תְּשׁוּקָתוֹ וְאַתָּה תִּמְשָׁל־בּוֹ (בראשית ד, ז) ... *if you do not improve, sin crouches at the door; Its urge is directed toward you, yet you can master it.*

The allure of *cheit* is ever-present; either we control it, or it controls us. The Gemara (*Sukkah* 52) describes how in the future, when Hashem will slaughter the *yetzer hara*, both tzaddikim and *rashaim* will cry. Tzaddikim will be overwhelmed as it will appear they resisted a force as formidable as a mountain, while *rashaim* will feel deep sorrow for not resisting a force no stronger than a strand of hair. The *Beis HaLevi* (*Parshas Bereishis*) asks, which depiction is correct? Is the *yetzer hara* powerful like a mountain, or weak like a piece of hair?

Adapting his explanation to our premise, the answer is that both are true, depending on the mode of interaction. A tzaddik takes precautions, at times extreme, to avoid direct engagement. Despite not experiencing it up close, he is fully aware of the danger and does everything in his power to steer clear of the *yetzer hara*. He's not interested in becoming entangled with such a force. In the future, when he realizes how indominable the *yetzer hara* really was, he will be astonished and wonder how he successfully avoided an encounter with the looming mountain dominating the landscape.

A *rasha* is not willing to take any evasive measures. Besides not wanting to be bothered by inconvenience or hardship, he enjoys the pleasure of dabbling in the illicit, temporal pleasures offered. He too knows there are red lines that should not be crossed, but his overblown confidence deludes him into thinking he can pull away at any time. After getting too close to the edge he allows himself to fall off. Each time the cliff gets higher; eventually he falls into an interminable abyss. In the future, when he confronts the reality of a fatal spiritual injury, he will be dismayed to see how easy it would have been to take a step back and remain on firm footing, as simple as controlling a strand of hair. But at the time, in the heat of the moment that he allowed himself to enter, he wasn't interested.

The truth is more complex. Most people are an admixture of conflicting views and experiences, at the same time. A *cheit* such as eating *treif* food, for example, can remain in the realm of potential for one's entire life no matter how hungry he gets, while confronting the spiritual pitfalls of other sorts of pernicious activities, subtle or otherwise, can present a real and prolonged struggle.

*Mishlei* teaches (20:18): מַחֲשָׁבוֹת בְּעֵצָה תִכּוֹן וּבְתַחְבֻּלוֹת עֲשֵׂה מִלְחָמָה, *Plans with proper advisement will be firm; and with strategies wage war.* The Vilna Gaon explains the second part of this *pasuk* as referring to the war with the *yetzer hara*. Seeking advice from others is helpful, perhaps essential, but is not enough. Success in battle comes from formulating strategies and approaches by the only one who really understands the theater of operations – the person himself. Sometimes he'll need evasive techniques, other times the courage to fight. With persistence, the list of attractions requiring direct attack will wane as merely eluding them will be sufficient.

*Yehi Ratzon*, may we utilize our available resources to merit a complete fulfillment of the mitzvah of matzah, and succeed in eradicating chametz from our homes and hearts.

# Outsmarting Hashem: *Kerias Yam Suf* and *Shidduchim*

## Moshe Kravetz

Having been blessed by *HaKadosh baruch Hu* to marry off two children this past year, I would like to share with you this *vort* that may change the way we sometimes try to outwit and outsmart the *Shidduch* System.

We know the famous Gemara, which states (*Sotah* 2a): Rabbah bar bar Chana said in the name of R' Yochanan: It is as difficult to match a couple together as was the splitting of the Red Sea. But many ask what the comparison of marriage is to the splitting of the *Yam Suf.*

Pharaoh said (*Shemos* 1:10): הָבָה נִתְחַכְּמָה לוֹ, *Come, let us outsmart it, lest it become numerous, and it may be that if a war will occur, it, too, may join our enemies, and wage war against us and go up from the land.* Pharaoh's plan was to "outsmart Hashem" and harm the *Yidden* in a manner that he would not get punished *middah keneged middah.* For the Gemara teaches us (*Sotah* 11a): Pharaoh was saying: Come, let us deal wisely with Hashem. His advisors asked, "With what form of death shall we judge and decree upon them? If we shall judge them with fire, perhaps we will be punished measure for measure by fire, as it is written, *For behold, the Lord will come in fire* (*Yeshayah* 66:15)... Similarly, we cannot judge them with the sword, as it is written in the next *pasuk*: *And by His sword with all flesh.* Rather, let us come and judge them with water, by drowning the Jewish babies. Hashem will not punish us with water, for the Holy One, blessed be He, already took an oath that He will not bring a flood upon the world, as it is stated, *For this is as the waters of*

*Noach unto Me; for as I have sworn that the waters of Noach should no more go over the earth* (*Yeshayah* 54:9).

The Gemara comments: And Pharaoh's advisors did not know that Hashem will not bring a flood upon all the world, but He may bring destruction by water upon one nation. Alternatively, there is an additional way to punish the Egyptians with water: Hashem will not bring a flood upon them, but they may come and fall into water, and so it says, *The sea returned to its strength when the morning appeared; and the Egyptians fled toward it; and Hashem overthrew the Egyptians in the midst of the sea* (*Exodus* 14:27), indicating that the Egyptians fell into the water.

From the above Gemara we see that as hard as Pharaoh and his advisors were trying to outsmart Hashem and escape punishment through water, ironically Hashem planned and outsmarted them. Not only did the Mitzrim meet their end through water, but Hashem used the same water to bring about the salvation of the Bnei Yisrael with *Kerias Yam Suf*!

The same can be said of our *Shidduch* System. Hashem already has planned who we are supposed to marry; however, we sometimes put up obstacles and conditions, and Hashem has to "outsmart" us in order to bring the *shidduch* to fruition.

For example, we have criteria for the perfect *shidduch*, and will not even consider anything different. We are often judgmental when we hear about the shul the family *davens* in; the camp, Yeshivah, or seminary the boy or girl attended; or if they did not learn in Eretz Yisrael; without further checking into the quality of the people themselves. We often nix a recommendation so as not to travel; or sometimes we say, "I will never live in a certain city, so why look into it?"

Let me give some personal examples of how Hashem outsmarted us, without elaborating too much due to space constraints (but feel free to speak to me for the full details on the amazing *hashgachah pratis*). My daughter was ideally looking for a learner/earner and given her personality and demeanor thought an "out-of-towner" would be best suited for her. Ironically our *machatanim* would never consider an "out-of-towner," as there were enough local girls, so why should he travel? Plus, my son-in-law was learning at BMG at the time, so we would not have looked into it normally, as we could not pledge support. Be that is it may, my son-in-law made all the trips to Baltimore during their dating and engagement (as my daughter did not drive highways), and they are now actually happily married living in Lakewood, where she never thought she would live. Hashem orchestrated ways and outsmarted them to bring the *shidduch* to fruition.

One of my other daughter's friends taunted her that if she does not go to seminary in Eretz Yisroel she will never get a normal quality *shidduch*. Hashem outsmarted them, as she did not go to any seminary and was one of the first in the class to get married to a boy precisely "custom-tailored" for her. Ironically, she is also living in New York after always claiming that she would *never* live there. Hashem again orchestrated ways and outsmarted them.

We often think that we can outsmart Hashem with our actions when we are looking for the "perfect *shidduch*." Ironically Hashem has to come and outsmart us to overcome all our obstacles and criteria just like He did for Pharaoh. We can then realize that Hashem "split the sea" to bring about the *shidduch*. We have to proclaim that this came about from Hashem!

# Pirkei Avos: A Mishnah Out of Place

## Yehoshua Dixler

יְהוּדָה בֶן תֵּימָא אוֹמֵר, הֱוֵי עַז כַּנָּמֵר, וְקַל כַּנֶּשֶׁר, וְרָץ כַּצְּבִי, וְגִבּוֹר כָּאֲרִי, לַעֲשׂוֹת רְצוֹן אָבִיךָ שֶׁבַּשָּׁמָיִם. הוּא הָיָה אוֹמֵר, עַז פָּנִים לְגֵיהִנֹּם, וּבֹשֶׁת פָּנִים לְגַן עֵדֶן.

Towards the end of *Perek* 5 in *Pirkei Avos* (5:23), Yehudah ben Teima exhorts us to be "bold like a leopard..." His lesson, that we should be bold to perform mitzvos even in the face of embarrassment, fits well with the spirit of *Pirkei Avos*. However, the Mishnah ends with this statement: יְהִי רָצוֹן מִלְּפָנֶיךָ יְיָ אֱלֹהֵינוּ שֶׁתִּבְנֶה **עִירְךָ** בִּמְהֵרָה בְיָמֵינוּ וְתֵן חֶלְקֵנוּ בְתוֹרָתֶךָ, *It should be Your will... to rebuild Your city quickly in our days and give us our portion in Your Torah."*

While it is always good to pray for the holy city and Torah, it appears extremely out of place in this Mishnah. The *Yachin* commentary (loc. cit.) writes, "This prayer we do not find in all the order of the Mishnah, only here, and it's a wonder!" *Chasdei Avos* (p. 200) exclaims, "This is a great wonder! Every person is astounded by this..."

How does this prayer connect to the lessons of the Mishnah? The answer to this question, and its possible connection to other places with a similar prayer (e.g., *Shemoneh Esrei, Shabbos* candle lighting), are provided in this article.

*Bartenura* and the *Rambam* (ibid.) both address the question by connecting the prayer to the phrase in the prior sentence, "The bashful are for Gan Eden." Just as Hashem gave the attribute of bashfulness to us, so too he should rebuild the city etc. However, this approach is tenuous. The prayer could be associated with any good behavior, so why did the Tanna pick this one?

Several commentaries answer the question in context of an analysis of the entire Mishnah. At the start of the Mishnah, R. Yehudah praises the bold, yet at the end he says, "The bold-faced are for Gehinnom." Boldness can be used for the good, but a person can easily fall into abuse and use it for bad. Through praying for Mashiach, we are asking for the removal of this risk (*Maharal* in *Derech Chaim* on the Mishnah). Under the renewed influence of both the Beis HaMikdash, serving as the life-giving force to the world, and the Torah, which epitomizes the intellect of the world, people will become respectful of mitzvos and there will be no need for boldness. Additionally, in the future there will be no need for boldness to learn Torah as the "World will be filled with knowledge of Hashem as the water covers the sea." (*Tos. R. Akiva Eiger* quoting *Radak*).

*Chasdei Avos* (p. 200) connects the prayer to the prior statements. Boldness of *kedushah*, holiness, is absolutely necessary to reach the higher spiritual levels, through which we will merit the rebuilding of the holy city and, from there, to reach to the level of Torah and *tefillah* represented by the four-letter name of Hashem. Similarly, we pray to use boldness only for the good and not to acquire boldness under the influence of the Satan (*Yachin* on the Mishnah).

*Chidushei Toros U'Derashos* (p. 335-339), a collection of Torah from the first Satmar Rav, notes that we often need to leverage behaviors, like boldness, that appear to be the opposite of proper Torah behavior. For us, the challenge is to determine when boldness is warranted. For example, embracing boldness serves us well when it enables us to observe Torah in the face of scoffers, but at other times we should conduct ourselves with humility. This explains how R. Yehudah can say to both emulate the leopard in boldness and yet "a bold face goes to Gehinnom"; it all depends on the circumstances. Although boldness is often necessary today to face the chutzpah present in the last days before Mashiach, knowing how and when to use it appropriately is a great challenge. Hence, we pray for Hashem to rebuild the holy city, which will usher in a time when boldness will be unnecessary. The last phrase asks for "Our portion in Your Torah" since Mashiach will come only after each person completes his service of Hashem in this world, including the revelation of our unique portions (e.g., *chidushim*) in Torah.

Another approach considers whether this prayer belongs in the Mishnah at all! This prayer does not appear in some versions of the Mishnah (e.g., *Rabbeinu Yonah's* commentary on *Pirkei Avos*) indicating it is not an essential part of the work. According to *Gra z"l* (last Mishnah of *Perek* 5), the prayer should not have been placed together with R. Yehudah's lesson; rather, its proper place is at the end the *Perek* 5. Since *Perek* 6 is a Baraisa added later, this prayer at the end of *Perek* 5 acts as the closure for the entire tractate, similar to how other tractates ends with a piece of *aggadah*.

The fifth *Perek* is rather unique compared to the first four *Perakim* of *Pirkei Avos*. Whereas all the Mishnahs in the prior four *Perakim* are attributed to someone by name, those in the fifth are not. This *Perek* begins with lists of ten things, then seven things, then four things, finally progressing to lists starting with "all." R. Yehudah ben Teima is the first Tanna mentioned by name and that is not until Mishnah 23! *Meiri* (*Beis HaBechirah*, Avos, 5:23), suggests based on manuscripts that all Mishnahs through the end of *Perek* 5 were later additions, leaving this Mishnah, with its prayer to rebuild Yerushalayim, as a fitting end for the *Meseches Avos*.

***Shemoneh Esrei***

יְהִי רָצוֹן מִלְּפָנֶיךָ יְהֹוָה אֱלֹהֵינוּ וֵאלֹהֵי אֲבוֹתֵינוּ שֶׁיִּבָּנֶה **בֵּית הַמִּקְדָּשׁ** בִּמְהֵרָה בְיָמֵינוּ וְתֵן חֶלְקֵנוּ בְּתוֹרָתֶךָ: וְשָׁם נַעֲבָדְךָ בְּיִרְאָה כִּימֵי עוֹלָם וּכְשָׁנִים קַדְמוֹנִיּוֹת: וְעָרְבָה לַיהֹוָה מִנְחַת יְהוּדָה וִירוּשָׁלָיִם כִּימֵי עוֹלָם וּכְשָׁנִים קַדְמוֹנִיּוֹת

A version of this Mishnah's prayer is found at the conclusion of every *Shemoneh Esrei*. Although it's not mentioned by *Avudraham*,

*Tur,* or *Beis Yosef*, the *Rama* (*Shulchan Aruch*, 123:1) states that it is our *minhag* to say this. Our daily prayers, explains R' Eliyahu Munk, are only a substitute for the Temple sacrifices. We continually pray for the return of the Temple when we can serve Hashem to the utmost (*Olam HaTefillos*, p. 168). The two verses that follow this prayer, quoted from *Malachi,* fit in nicely with this theme: "We will serve You there with fear as in days of old..."

The prayer after *Shemoneh Esrei* appears similar to the Mishnah prayer, but is, in fact, very different. Not only is it longer, but we are also asking for different things. While in *Pirkei Avos* we ask to rebuild "Your city," ostensibly Yerushalayim, in *Shemoneh Esrei* we pray for rebuilding of the Beis HaMikdash.

Specific words were authored to serve the purpose of each prayer. We say "Torah comes from Zion and the word of Hashem from Yerushalayim." There is strong connection between Hashem and the holy city when it comes to Torah. Thus, the request to rebuild "Your city" followed by the entreaty for Hashem "to give our portion in Your Torah" is appropriate in the context of Torah learning, such as the Mishnah. However, in *Shemoneh Esrei,* which corresponds to the offerings, we specifically pray for the rebuilding of the Beis HaMikdash instead of Yerushalayim. [1]

**Challah, Shabbos Lights and Mikvah**

A variant of this prayer is also said after women perform any of their three special mitzvos: separating challah, lighting Shabbos candles, and immersing in the mikvah. The chosen prayer matches that said for *Shemoneh Esrei* asking for the rebuilding of the Beis HaMikdash. Why is that prayer appropriate for these mitzvos?

---

[1] Editor's note: We add to this prayer that we should be given our portion in Torah. Everyone has a unique portion of Torah that should be his specialty. This will not be clearly known until the Beis HaMikdash is rebuilt.

עַל שָׁלֹשׁ עֲבֵירוֹת נָשִׁים מֵתוֹת בְּשָׁעַת לֵידָתָן: עַל שֶׁאֵינָן זְהִירוֹת בְּנִדָּה, בַּחַלָּה, וּבְהַדְלָקַת הַנֵּר.

The Mishnah in *Shabbos* (2:6) records that laxity in these three special mitzvos can result in a woman dying in childbirth. Why are these three mitzvos so important to women? *Ben Yehoyada* (*Shabbos* 32a) explains that the impurity injected by the snake at the time of the Adam and Chavah's sin causes women to become impure through *niddah. Midrash Tanchuma* (58:1) explains that Chavah, through the sin of the *eitz hadaas,* caused spiritual damage to Adam, who is called the challah of the world, and dimmed Adam's spiritual light. This sin would affected not only Adam, but also future generations. To repair these damages, women are given primary responsibility for the mitzvos of Shabbos lights and challah along with the removal of impurity by immersion in the mikvah. The world will remain in spiritual disrepair when women are not careful to fulfill these mitzvos properly. During childbirth, a situation of great danger, proper observance of these important mitzvos protects a woman, while non-observance can result in death.

When Mashiach arrives and the Beis HaMikdash is rebuilt, the repair for the sin of *eitz hadaas* will occur, returning us to a level of Adam and Chavah before the sin. When women keep these three special mitzvos, they are helping to repair the world and bring Mashiach. Women say this extra prayer for the Beis HaMikdash to be rebuilt in hope that they too will experience the time when the world no longer suffers from the defects Chavah introduced through her sin. May this day come soon!

# Shavuos: The *Shirah* of the Children

## וְעַתָּה בָּנִים שִׁירוּ לַמֶּלֶךְ

## Rabbi Yitzchak Szyf

Someone *davening* with a *machzor* over Shavuos would notice some familiar words right after "*Kadosh Kadosh Kadosh*" in the middle of *Birkos Kerias Shema*: וְעַתָּה בָּנִים שִׁירוּ לַמֶּלֶךְ

Famous for its modern Chassidic tune, the *piyut* of וְעַתָּה בָּנִים שִׁירוּ לַמֶּלֶךְ fills this prominent slot in the Shavuos *machzor* – literally after the *kedushah* of the angels – on both days of Shavuos. Composed by the great rabbi and liturgical composer R' Shimon Bar Yitzkhak of Mainz, Germany (950-1020), it was commonly said in many, if not most, of the Nusach Ashkenaz shuls in Europe before the war and is still printed in most modern *machzorim*. It is recited today only in a handful of shuls, among them K'hal Adas Yeshurun ("Breuer's") in Washington Heights, NY. Its message, however, remains as relevant as ever.

By now, it is likely that many of you are singing or humming the joyous modern tune of וְעַתָּה בָּנִים to yourselves. Yes, the words of the popular song are two beautiful lines taken directly from our *piyut*, but they are actually not even consecutive lines. As you can see in the ArtScroll Hebrew-English *machzor* on page 188, the full *piyut* has five stanzas, each composed of four lines. The lines commonly sung in the modern tune are the first line of the first stanza and the first line of the third stanza. But the entirety of this relatively short *piyut* deserves our attention.

This article aims to shed light on the key role that וְעַתָּה בָּנִים plays within the Shavuos *davening*, which will hopefully allow us to better understand the overall theme of the Yom Tov.

But first, some interesting tidbits on וְעַתָּה בָּנִים:

**1-** The *piyut* takes the form of an "*ofan*" (a *piyut* said right after "*Kadosh Kadosh Kadosh*" and before "*ve-ha'ofanim*") and can be found in just about all traditional Ashkenazi *machzorim* for Shavuos.

**2-** It is one of the only *piyutim* that appears in the *machzor* for *both* days of Shavuos. Even *Akdamus* does not receive this honor.

**3-** It forms part of the liturgy of both Minhag Polin (Eastern European custom) and Minhag Ashkenaz (Western European custom). As such, while it is recited almost exclusively today at shuls that follow German customs, it is just as much a part of the heritage of Ashkenazi Jews of Polish or other Eastern European countries as it is of German Jews.

**4-** It was considered such a great *piyut* that even the Vilna Gaon (Gra) added it to the list of *piyutim* that he recited on Shavuos after *Hallel*. Generally, the Gra recited many of the *piyutim* of *Chazaras Hashatz* (after *Chazaras Hashatz*, or after *Hallel* on Yom Tov), but not many of those that were composed for the blessings of Shema. וְעַתָּה בָּנִים was an exception. In the first of only two *simanim* on *Hilchos Shavuos* in *Maaseh Rav* (§195), it mentions that "*Ve-ata banim shiru lamelech* is recited with *kol zimra* (chant) verse by verse (i.e., responsively)."

I would like to address the following questions:

1- What is the connection between the *piyut* and the holiday of Shavuos?

2- Why does it begin with the words "*Ve-ata*" (and now) if it's a stand-alone *piyut*?

3- Why is it placed in the *machzor* in a way that breaks up our description of the "Song of the Angels" (*Kadosh Kadosh*

*Kadosh* followed by *Baruch Kevod*) with a "Song of the Children"?

In doing so, let us take a step back to better understand the background of Shavuos and its connection to *Matan Torah*.

**Background to the Yom Tov of Shavuos – A Time of Partnership**
According to the Torah, Shavuos is an agricultural holiday. Rabbinic tradition, of course, also connects it to *Matan Torah*. This is based on *pesukim* in *Parashas Yisro*, which indicate that *Matan Torah* happened in the early days of the third month, Sivan, and very possibly on the day of Shavuos. But basic math – coupled with certain historical assumptions mentioned in the Gemara – relegates *Matan Torah* to the *51st* day of the Omer, which is the *second* day of Shavuos in the diaspora. Simply put, the Gemara (*Shabbos* 86a and 87b) concludes that *Yetzias Mitzrayim* occurred on a Thursday (and by extension the first night of the Omer began on Thursday night) and *Matan Torah* happened on *Shabbos*.[1] If the first night of the Omer is a Thursday night, the 50th night would also be a Thursday night, and the 50th day would have to be a Friday. Since *Matan Torah* happened on *Shabbos* (and within the early days of Sivan), it means that it must have happened on the 51st day of the Omer but not on Shavuos itself (the 50th day, which was a Friday).

---

[1] These days are also clearly listed in Seder Olam Rabbah 5:2. While there is a suggestion in the Gemara that they left Egypt on Friday rather than Thursday, which would solve the problem of the Torah being given on the 51st day of the Omer, *Machatzis Hashekel* explains that we don't follow that opinion since it would invalidate the *Tosafos*, which describes the miracle of *Shabbos Hagadol*. Specifically, it would mean that the tenth of Nissan (the day on which we were commanded to take the *Korban Pesach* and tie it to the beds) would have been on Sunday, rather than *Shabbos*. That in turn would invalidate the explanation in *Tosafos* that the miracle related to the process of taking the *Korban Pesach* (when the Egyptians who worshipped the lamb saw what we did and did not protest) happened on *Shabbos Hagadol*.

While it is possible that *Matan Torah* still happened on today's *calendar* date of Shavuos, the 6th of Sivan,[2] that is not technically the day of Shavuos. Furthermore, according to R' Yose in the Gemara,[3] which is viewed by many as the accepted opinion, the Torah was not even given on today's calendar date of Shavuos but rather on the *seventh* of Sivan. *Moshe Rabbeinu "Hosif Yom Echad Meda'ato"* – added an additional day to the preparatory days of his own volition.[4] In other words, the Torah was *meant* to be given on the sixth of Sivan, which was the 50th day of the Omer (Shavuos) but Moshe asked to push it off one more day to the seventh of Sivan, which was the 51st day of the Omer (*Shabbos*).

If so, it makes sense that the text of the Torah doesn't connect the holiday to *Matan Torah,* since the Torah *wasn't* given on that day; it was given a day later. But the Oral Torah does strongly connect the holiday with *Matan Torah.* If so, what are we celebrating on 6 Sivan/50 Omer if we are to hold that the Torah was given on 7 Sivan/51 Omer?

---

[2] Since there wasn't a set calendar yet at that time, and Nissan and Iyar could have been either 29 or 30 days, the 51st day of the Omer on which the Torah was given could have aligned with either the sixth or seventh day of Sivan. So, in theory, it could have still fallen on the same calendar date that we celebrate today.

[3] *Shabbos* 87, and also quoted in *Rashi* to *Shemos* 19:15

[4] While this is often viewed as the accepted opinion (and is used in *Yoreh Deah* as a basis by which to calculate "*onos*"), *the Magen Avraham* (Orach Chaim 492) is bothered by the fact that we call the sixth of Sivan *Zman Matan Toraseinu*, and concludes that this opinion of seventh of Sivan may just be used as a *chumrah* for calculating *onos*, since our practice shows that the Torah was given on the sixth of Sivan. Nevertheless, the issue regarding the 51st of the Omer is a bigger deal, and *the Magen Avraham* suggests that maybe this could be a proof for R' Yose's *Hosif Yom Echad Meda'ato*, though we would still have the problem that we say *Zman Matan Toraseinu* on the day before *Matan Torah*. He then considers the idea of the Torah being given a day later as a nod to *Yom Tov Sheini*, a topic we will soon discuss.

*Nitei Gavriel,* in his introduction to Shavuos, explains that we are celebrating our *partnership* in Torah. This is the day when Moshe asked to add an extra day and Hashem agreed. And it's the day when Hashem made it clear that we too have a role in shaping the scope of observance of Torah. That's why it is called *Matan Toras**einu*** (the day of giving of ***our*** Torah); it is when the Torah became *ours* and we became partners in its understanding.

**An insight into Yom Tov *Sheini* of Shavuos**

Interestingly, *Rema MiPano* (Italy, 1548 – 1620) points out that the Torah was given specifically in the diaspora on the 51st day of the Omer, which was *Yom Tov Sheini* and specifically on the day that Moshe "added" to show that Hashem Himself was celebrating on *Yom Tov Sheini*, after Moshe added a day of his own volition.[5] So too, on every *Yom Tov Sheini*, Hashem treats it as *His* Yom Tov. Torah is a partnership and Hashem takes into account our role in establishing the holidays in general (based on the sanctification of the month) or even in adding a second day in the diaspora.

Nevertheless, we still celebrate the holiday on the 50th day of the Omer (and in Israel only on that day) since that is the most important day. It is the day on which Hashem *agreed* with Moshe's (and our) partnership in Torah. This is when the partnership began.

The Gemara (*Shabbos* 88b, 89a) describes how the angels were not happy that the Torah was taken "down" to the people. Moshe had to argue that the Torah *cannot* be relevant to angels since it is focused on elevating the physical aspects of the world and humanity, which angels have nothing to do with. *Nitei Gavriel* explains that the angels must have been particularly upset about this new *partnership* that became clear on the 50th day of the Omer. Angels just follow orders blindly and they didn't like the idea that we can influence Torah, as

[5] The text of the Rema MiPano can be found at the end of this article.

Moshe did on the 6th of Sivan when he added an extra day "*mi-da'ato*" (of his own volition).

**וְעַתָּה בָּנִים שִׁירוּ לַמֶּלֶךְ – It is us, not just the angels, who will say Shirah**

I believe that this background can now help us understand the role of וְעַתָּה בָּנִים שִׁירוּ לַמֶּלֶךְ. More than other time of the year, on Shavuos, we need to make the point that the Torah belongs here in the physical world. It is, ironically, the only holiday that the Gemara (*Pesachim* 68b) concludes should be celebrated as "*kulu lachem,*" all for you (i.e., with more focus on physical enjoyment such as good food). As discussed above, Hashem expects a true *partnership* with us in Torah and it is humans, not angels, who can provide it.

Right after we describe the *kedushah* of the angels, *"Kadosh, Kadosh, Kadosh,"* on Shavuos, we cannot stop there without adding our two cents. On Shavuos, we are focused on the fact that we are *greater* than the angels; we are part of a true *partnership* with Hashem. The *piyut* of וְעַתָּה בָּנִים שִׁירוּ לַמֶּלֶךְ (literally, "and now, children, sing unto the King") interjects our typical (and daily) description of the angel's *kedushah* to make this point, and talks about the *shirah* of the *banim*. In other words, it is basically saying, "put that on hold, angels, now is the time for the children to sing!"

The *piyut* consists of five stanzas, each comprising four lines. It begins with the famous words: וְעַתָּה בָּנִים שִׁירוּ לַמֶּלֶךְ בְּתִפְאֶרֶת מְפוֹאַר, *And now, children, sing unto the King Who is glorified with splendor.*[6]

The first two words: "and now" are likely a follow up to the previous words in the *davening*: "*Kadosh Kadosh Kadosh*". They are basically saying the following: "And now" we will pause from our regular

[6] All *piyut* translations are taken from the ArtScroll Shavuos *machzor*

programming (the song of the angels) and sing *our* song, the song of the *banim*, the Children of Israel.

The *piyut* concludes with an incredible "punchline" that has not merited to be part of the popular song: אַחַר שְׁתֵּי תֵבוֹת מַזְכִּירִים שֵׁם קָדְשׁוֹ \ לְהוֹדִיעַ לַכֹּל כִּי הֵם זֶרַע קְדוֹשׁוֹ, *After two words they mention His Holy Name, to inform all that they are His holy offspring.*

Here, we are directly making the point that we have a right to interrupt the angels' song to sing ours on the morning of Shavuos. After all, we are *greater* than the angels since we mention Hashem's name after two "words."

What words are we referring to? The *piyut* is alluding to a discussion in the Gemara (*Chullin* 91b), about how the angels need three *teivos* (words) to sanctify Hashem's name while we only need two. In their key prayer, they say "*Kadosh Kadosh Kadosh,*" and only then "Hashem." In our key prayer, we say "*Shema Yisrael,*" consisting of just two *teivos*, and then "Hashem". This can be understood as "proof" that we are a step above the angels!

This concept of our superiority over angels is a key theme in the most famous *piyut* of Shavuos, *Akdamus*. Notably, after describing the greatness of the angels in depth, *Akdamus* includes the following line: עֲדַב יְקָר אַחְסַנְתֵּהּ חֲבִיבִין דִּבְקַבְעָתָא / עֲבִידָא לֵהּ חֲטִיבָא בְּדְנַח וּשְׁקַעְתָּא , *But the portion of His precious inheritance is better, for with regularity. They make Him their sole desire, at sunrise and sunset.* Based on the same Gemara described above (*Chullin* 91b), this line is referring to the fact that we daven more regularly than the angels and say Shema twice daily, in the "morning and the evening."

I believe the focus in *Akdamus* on our "regularity" and on serving Hashem at "sunrise and sunset" highlights the fact that we bring Torah into the physical world in a regular and consistent way, unlike the angels who say their praise at their specific allotted moment and then remain uninvolved. The *piyut* of וְעַתָּה בָּנִים plays a similar role as *Akdamus* in describing our remarkable status above the angels, but at a much earlier – and arguably more critical – point in the davening as far as angels are concerned.

Particularly on Shavuos, a holiday focused on pointing out the Torah's place among *Bnei Yisrael* (the "*banim*") in the physical world, the great *paytan* Shimon Bar Yitzchak of Mainz felt compelled to remind us of *our* song that we must offer Hashem. The song signifies our ability to be true partners in Torah – emulating Moshe's role on the day of Shavuos prior to *Matan Torah* – a role that only humans, not angels can achieve. This message, perhaps intentionally, is given to us at the height of our Yom Tov *tefillos* while our minds are on the angels. On Shavuos, there is lots of talk about angels – especially within *Akdamus* and in Yechezkel's vision of the Divine Chariot within the Haftarah—but ultimately, the angels take a back seat. The Torah is ours and the most important song is the song that we will be singing to our King.

To conclude, we reprint the *Rema Mipano*, followed by the *piyyut* on the next page:

**הרמע מפאנו** (עשרה מאמרות מאמר חקור דין ב טו): עוד טעמו וראו דבדידן תליא מלתא לחייב אותנו על הזהירות והזהירות במצות כפי כחנו והיינו חלקנו בתורתך כי אמנם חג ה' לנו ביום מתן תורתנו מקרא קדש לסוף חמשים יום אחר הפסח ופסח מצרים בחמשי בשבת היה ולכוליה עלמא בשבת ניתנה תורה שהוא לסוף נ"א יום והיא גופא קשיא. **אלא ודאי כיון שמתן תורה היה בחוץ לארץ ה' חפץ למען צדקו ליתן חלקנו בתורתו שכן הסכימה דעת עליון לחוג בעצמו ובכבודו ביום טוב של גליות שהוסיף משה מדעתו כדברי רבי יוסי** כי שם ערבים עליו דברי דודים המה היוצרים עת לעשות לה' לפיכך הפרו תורתו כתלונות הנביא ישעיהו לבד בך נזכיר שמך שדרשה בר יוחאי על הסוד הזה **ומשום הא לא אישתמיט קרא בשום דוכתא למימר שחג השבועות הוא יום מתן תורה ואין צורך למה שנתחבטו בו האחרונים** ואם מעקרא הוראת שעה היתה מן השמים כדברי סתם תנא בברייתא שם בפרק רבי עקיבא אשרי האב שמקלסין אותו כמדבר על אוזן שומעת ברוך שבחר בהם ובמשנתם.

ועתה בנים שירו למלך בתפארת
מפואר. ברקמי שיר מעטף ומעטר ומתואר.
בהוד והדר ושבח מבאר. בעטרת גאות
וכתר נורא יתפאר:

שמעו לי מללו. עזוז נורא פלאי גדלו.
ששמו ערב לו. וזכרו נעים להללו. והיכלו
נחמד לו. וכבודו נהדר לו. והודו נאר
לו. ומשרתיו מנעימים לו:

ואשרי עבדיו המשמיעים בקול שבחו.
כי ערבים לפניו ומקבלים נכחו. שמעיאל
השר משמיעם בכחו. לשתק המון מעלה
ברון בני אורחו:

דרכי וחובי תרת קדשה למקרה
אוירים. המשגב ומכתר בכתרי כתרים.
פאר מלכים תהלה לברורים. מפחדו יחילו
איתנים וצורים:

ישמרו נכספים בחצרות מעט מקדשו.
בפחד ויראה להעריצו ולהקדישו: חזן אחר
שתי תיבות מזכירים שם קדשו. להודיע
לכל כי הם זרע קדושו:

**A Word about this Copy of the *Piyut***

This image above was taken from the popular Hungarian Machzor set: Mákzór Imádságos Könyv, printed in Budapest in the late 1800s and early 1900s. With its clear layout and Hungarian translation to all of the *tefillos* and *piyutim,* this set was likely the "ArtScroll of Hungary." Most notably, all of the *piyutim* are printed in large letters (nothing is in the back) and fully integrated into the *tefillos.* The Machzor also includes a *tefillah* for Franz Joseph I in both Hebrew and Hungarian.[7]

I picked up this set in Oradea, (Transylvania) Romania where I was the rabbi in 2006-2007. There were, literally, thousands of volumes scattered in all of the different shuls that I visited throughout Romania, which shows how common (and necessary) it was for everyone to own a Machzor for the *Shalosh Regalim.* The community in Transylvania, Romania speaks Hungarian (as well as Romanian), and when I was there in 2007, there were still survivors who grew up in Transylvania before the war. I had the opportunity to serve as their *Baal Tefillah* on Yom Tov and was glad when they insisted that I recite many of the *piyutim* as printed in these Machzorim.

Unfortunately, these survivors have since passed away. A small community remains (and I visited a few years ago) but these *minhagim* of the past are no longer followed, and there is no longer a regular minyan. Hopefully, this article (and others that I hope to share on *piyutim*) will help keep these beautiful parts of our tradition alive.

[7] The Machzor:

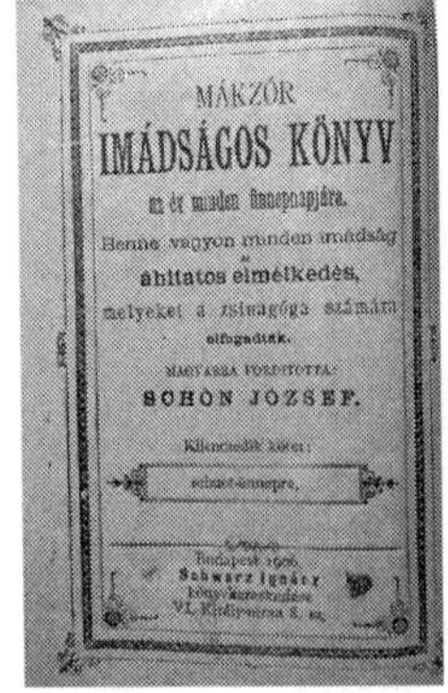
MÁKZÓR
IMÁDSÁGOS KÖNYV
Henne vagyon minden imádság
áhitatos elmélkedés,
SCHÖN JÓZSEF.
Schwarz Ignácz

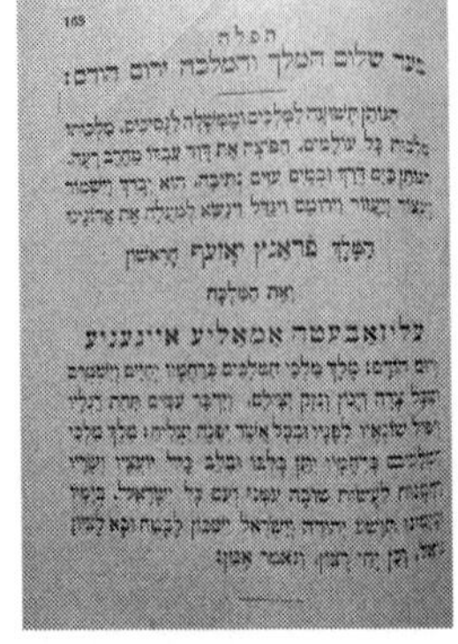
תפלה
הקיסר פראנץ יאזעף הראשון
ואת המלכה
עליזאבעטה אמאליע איינעניע

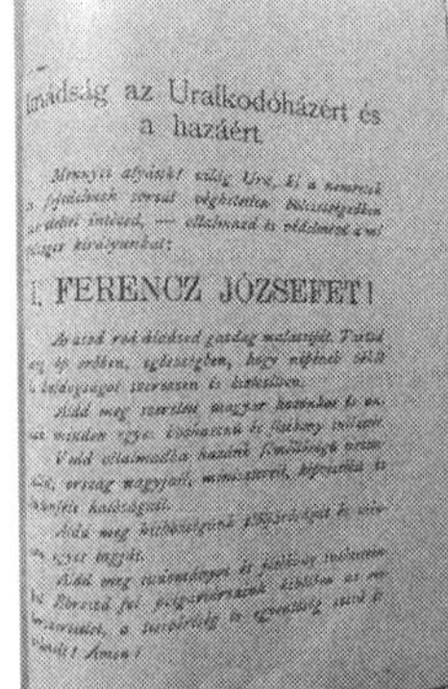
Imádság az Uralkodóházért és a hazáért
I. FERENCZ JÓZSEFET!

# Knock three times...[1]

## Dr. Eliyahu Eliezer Singman

In *Sanhedrin* (99b), we learn about Timna, the woman who bore Amalek, the archenemy of our people, to Yaakov's nephew Eliphaz. Notably, Eliphaz was the *bechor* of Eisav (*I Divrei HaYamim* 1:35) by his wife Adah (*Bereishis* 36:4). Timna wanted to become a *giyores,* so she approached Avraham, Yitzchak, and Yaakov. But she was refused all three times. She then volunteered to become a concubine to Eliphaz because she felt it was better to be a maidservant to someone in Yaakov's family than a princess in a gentile nation. Notably, Timna was a sister of Lotan, the *bechor* and chieftain of Seir the Chorite; the Chorite nation intermarried with the family of Eisav and were ultimately ruled by them. The Gemara explains that Timna was rejected by the *Avos* because she was a *mamzeres,* born from the adulterous union of Eliphaz and the wife of Seir.

The Gemara says that the result of the refusal of the *Avos* to accept Timna led to the birth of Amalek. Timna had *yiras shemayim,* but she was also *chutzpadik*. The *Avos* perceived that a significant part of Timna's motivation to convert was self-aggrandizement; they were proven correct when Timna demonstrated a willingness to settle by joining Eisav's family. Rabbi Meir Zvi Bergman *shlit"a* (son in law of Rabbi Elazar Menachem Man Shach *z"l*) questions why the *Avos* did not try to guide Timna to improve her *middos* and thereby ultimately accept her conversion? His answer is that Timna's lack of humility was too entrenched to allow her to incorporate the Torah's teachings.

[1] Inspired by R' Elya Caplan's *shiur* on *Perek Cheilek,* based on the *shiurim* of HaRav Moshe Shapira *z"l.*

If so, what did the *Avos* do so wrong that they could be faulted for the birth of Amalek? His descendants certainly proved to be the most *chutzpadik* nation in the world when they attacked the Jews after the miracles at the *Yam Suf* while all the other nations were awed into submission! Furthermore, *chutzpah* is considered a very difficult trait to conquer, precisely because it is the trait that fights self-improvement and *teshuvah.* A perfect example of the danger of this trait is provided in *Sanhedrin* (102a). Yeravam is one of the three kings whom the Mishnah says has no share in *Olam HaBa.* The Ribono Shel Olam himself offered Yeravam the opportunity to walk with Him and *David HaMelech* in Gan Eden! Yeravam asked "who's going to be at the head," and when Hashem told him *David HaMelech* will lead, Yeravam refused.

Clearly, *chutzpah* can cost someone their *Olam HaBa.* And so, perhaps the *Avos* perceived that it would be worse for Timna to be a *giyores* with no *Olam HaBa* than a *chutzpadik* gentile who displayed some *yiras shamayim.* Returning to our question of why the *Avos* were considered responsible for the birth of Amalek, I can only wonder whether the *Avos* were expected to try to bring Timna close before refusing her; i.e., one should always have the left (weaker) hand push away and the right (stronger) hand ***draw closer*"** (*Sotah* 47a and *Sanhedrin* 107b).

It is enlightening to compare Timna to another woman who wanted to become a Jew. Like Timna, Rus was also a princess (of Moav). Rus and her sister Orpah married the sons of Elimelech and Naomi, who had left Eretz Yisrael and settled in Moav because of a famine. Rus married into a prestigious and wealthy family, but then her husband and father-in-law died. Naomi, Rus's mother-in-law, urged Rus and Orpah to return to their royal lives, yet Rus insisted upon staying with Naomi, who was now poor and bereaved, and indicated a willingness to share Naomi's poverty and widowhood. Like Timna,

Rus demonstrated her desire to become a *giyores three* separate times when she said to Naomi:

1. "With you shall we return to your people."
2. "Where you go, I will go. Where you lodge, I will lodge. Your people are my people and your G-d is my G-d."
3. "Where you die, I will die, and there I will be buried. Thus, may G-d do to me, and more, for death will separate me from you."

In these statements, *Chazal* tell us that Rus was not only replying to Naomi's attempts to dissuade her from converting, but also demonstrating her sincerity (see *Me'am Loez, Megillas Rus*).

Statement 1: Rus said, "**we** will ***return.***" Although Rus had never been to Eretz Yisrael, her love of the land was so strong that, for her, going there was as if she were returning home.

Statement 2: When Rus said "where you go, I will go," she meant that even if Naomi would not let Rus accompany her, they would go to the same place (Eretz Yisrael) because they have the same goals. This also meant that she would not travel more than halachically permitted on Shabbos. When Rus said "where you lodge, I will lodge." she was accepting the Torah code of morality, including the laws of *yichud, mezuzah,* and *tznius*. When she said "your people are my people," she was accepting the Torah precepts between man and his fellow. When she said "your G-d is my G-d" she was accepting the Torah precepts between man and G-d and disavowing idolatry.

Statement 3: When Rus said "where you die, I will die," she declared that she understood the likelihood that no man in Eretz Yisrael would be willing to marry her and she was prepared to live and die alone with Naomi and also be buried next to Naomi rather than a husband. This was also a prayer that she be buried in Eretz Yisrael. Furthermore, she expressed acceptance of the four types of capital punishment for certain transgressions. Finally, Rus expressing that "death will separate" her from Naomi meant that she believed in both the resurrection of the dead and the eternal reward of *Olam HaBa*, where the righteous are uniquely rewarded.

Naomi tried to dissuade Rus *three* times, and all *three* times Rus proved that she was sincere. As we know, Rus eventually married Boaz and became the great-grandmother of *David HaMelech* and thereby the matriarch of the line of *Mashiach*. It is interesting to note that Rus's descendants are destined to meet Timna's descendants; *Mashiach* will be a future Jewish king in full control of all of Eretz Yisrael and will have a mitzvah to eradicate Amalek (soon in our times!).

Let us consider yet another *ger* among our ancestors: Onkelos. He was the nephew of the Roman emperor Hadrian (others opine that he was the nephew of the emperor Titus) and translated the Torah into Aramaic, to replace the lost translation originally created by *Ezra HaSofer*.

*Three* times did he ask whether he should become a *ger*, albeit via a novel medium (*Gittin* 57a): Onkelos bar Kalonikos, the son of Titus's sister, wanted to convert to Judaism. He went and raised Titus from the grave through necromancy, and said to him: Who is most important in that world where you are now? Titus said to him: The Jewish people. Onkelos asked him: Should I then attach myself to them here in this world? Titus said to him: Their commandments are numerous, and you will not be able to fulfill them. It is best that you do as follows: Go out and battle against them in this world, and you will become the chief, as it is written: "Her adversaries have become the chief" (*Eichah* 1:5), which means: Anyone who distresses Israel will become the chief.

Onkelos then went and raised Bilam from the grave through necromancy. He said to him: Who is most important in that world where you are now? Balaam said to him: The Jewish people. Onkelos asked him: Should I then attach myself to them here in this world? Balaam said to him: You shall not seek their peace or their welfare all the days (see *Deuteronomy* 23:7).

Onkelos then went and raised a sinner of Israel from the grave through necromancy. Onkelos said to him: Who is most important in that world where you are now? The sinner said to him: The Jewish people. Onkelos asked him: Should I then attach myself to them in this world? The sinner said to him: Their welfare you shall seek, their misfortune you shall not seek, for anyone who touches them is regarded as if he were touching the apple of his eye (see *Zechariah* 2:12).

Onkelos was a disciple of Rabbi Eliezer ben Hyrkanos and Rabbi Yehoshua ben Chananya, the great Tannaim who were disciples of Rabbi Yochanan ben Zakkai. I am guessing that he likely did not have much pushback with regard to his conversion from his teachers. On the other hand, he certainly had plenty from gentiles, both dead (see above) and alive. In *Avodah Zarah* (11a) we read: (Upon learning of Onkelos' conversion to Judaism) the Roman emperor sent a troop of Roman soldiers after him to seize Onkelos and bring him to the emperor. Onkelos drew them toward him with verses that he cited and learned with them, and they converted. The emperor then sent another troop of Roman soldiers after him, telling them: Do not say anything to him, so that he cannot convince you with his arguments. The troops followed this instruction and took Onkelos with them. When they were walking, Onkelos said to the troop of soldiers: I will say a mere statement to you: A minor official holds a torch before a high official, the high official holds a torch for a duke, a duke for the governor, and the governor for the ruler. Does the ruler hold a torch before the common people? The soldiers said to

Onkelos: No. Onkelos said to them: Yet the Holy One, Blessed be He, holds a torch before the Jewish people, as it is written: "And the Lord went before them by day in a pillar of cloud, to lead them the way, and by night in a pillar of fire, to give them light" (*Shemos* 13:21). They all converted. The emperor then sent yet another troop of soldiers, to capture Onkelos, and said to them: Do not converse with him at all. The troops followed this instruction and took Onkelos with them. While they were walking, Onkelos saw a *mezuza* that was placed on the doorway. He placed his hand upon it and said to the soldiers: What is this? They said to him: You tell us. Onkelos said to them: The standard practice throughout the world is that a king of flesh and blood sits inside his palace, and his servants stand guard, protecting him outside; but with regard to the Holy One, Blessed is He, His servants, the Jewish people, sit inside their homes and He guards over them outside. As it is stated: *The Lord shall guard your going out and your coming in, from now and forever* (*Tehillim* 121:8). Upon hearing this, those soldiers also converted to Judaism. After that, the emperor sent no more soldiers after him.

In my opinion, it is fascinating that Onkelos not only approached the subject of converting three times *but was also approached three times* by men who might reasonably be considered prospective converts (even if they themselves did not know it at the time!). This latter episode seems to have a striking parallel in *Navi.*

In *I Shmuel* (19:18-19), we learn that on one of the multiple occasions that David fled from Shaul, he escaped to the protection of Shmuel, who was located at Nayos in Ramah. It then says (19:20-23): *Shaul sent messengers to seize David. They saw a band of prophets prophesying, with Shmuel standing by as their leader; and the spirit of G-d came upon Shaul's messengers, and they too began to speak in prophesy. When Shaul was told about this, he sent other messengers; but they too spoke in ecstasy. Shaul sent a third group of messengers; and they also spoke in prophesy.*

Both the Roman emperor and Shaul had similar intent when they sent men three times to capture their respective victims. And each time, the band of men rose in spiritual stature. The denouement is diametrically different, however. *Shmuel* (19:23-24) continues: *So, he (i.e., Shaul) himself went to Ramah. When he came to the great cistern at Sechoh, he asked, "Where are Shmuel and David?" and was told that they were at Naioth in Ramah. He was on his way there, to Naioth in Ramah, when the spirit of G-d came upon him too; and he walked on, speaking in prophesy, until he reached Naioth in Ramah. Then he too stripped off his (royal) garments and he too spoke in prophesy before Shmuel.*

Whereas the Roman emperor abandoned his attempted capture of Onkelos after *three* failed attempts, Shaul himself went to find David after his *three* efforts (one could hardly call Shaul's efforts failures when his messengers became *Neviim*!). Both the Roman emperor and Shaul knew what happened to the messengers they sent, and they both must also have known that they themselves might experience similar changes. As we noted above, the nations (Amalek, Rome, Bilam) already made it clear that they prefer greatness in *Olam HaZeh* to that of *Olam HaBa*; the Roman emperor clearly decided to avoid risking losing his worldview by seeking Onkelos personally. On the other hand, even a sinner of Israel knew the value of *Olam HaBa* when counseling Onkelos. If a sinner of Israel can be so much greater spiritually than an emperor of Rome, then how much greater must a king of Eretz Yisrael be than a gentile king? Answer: "...higher than any of the people..." (*I Shmuel* 9:2).

# Capital Punishment in Judaism

## Chapter Four – Objectives [1]

**Rabbi Shmuel Chaim Naiman**

*Over the past several years, I've been working on a book about Judaism's death penalty. It is an exciting, ongoing, journey, full of surprises and challenges. Over the last three years I have shared in this journal abridged drafts of the first three drafts, which outlined the three basic doctrines which guide the Torah's death penalty: Discretion, Rescue, and Love. At the end of last year's excerpt, we pondered the inherent contradiction in this system, wondering how to reconcile the harsh judgment with all the discretion, reluctance to punish, and love. In this year's essay, we'll discuss one of the three general objectives for capital punishment. This will lay the groundwork for understanding the Chazon Ish's brilliant answer to our dilemma, which I hope to present and analyze next year.*

Most of the time, the Oral Torah functions as an elucidation of the Written Torah, clarifying the word of God. In this role, it operates as an accessory, possessing no noticeable independent form. However, in its original, archetypical state – how it was taught to Moses during his forty-day sojourn on Mount Sinai – this Torah, too, had its own distinct form. At the core of this biblical study guide lies a catalogue of 613 commandments, each one rooted in its own biblical verse. It was through this list that the Oral Torah molded the Pentateuch into a clear code of statutes (as I described at length in the Introduction).

Nonetheless, from its very first formal codification, the Mishnah, or Oral Torah, has repeatedly shed its initial form in favor of various other configurations, mostly man-made and artificial. With a few

[1] Editor's note: This is part of a work geared to the wider Jewish public. We have therefore not edited it to conform with our "*Kuntress Style Sheet.*"

exceptions, most of our numerous codes of Jewish law are not composed of 613 chapters, one for each commandment. Rather, the human intellect's preference for structured, thematic arrangements has always taken precedence over the sentimental benefit of the original sprawling, shapeless list. And that's the way it should be. This Torah's primary location is in the minds and hearts of human beings, so it must be transmitted with human methods of study and retention of information.

Yet all this does not render the original form irrelevant, an unwieldy index long replaced by more coherent systems. To resolve many questions of Jewish law, it is necessary to know whether a certain statute is a "counted" commandment, a corollary deduced through biblical exegesis, or a later Rabbinical institution. Furthermore, it is sometimes imperative to place a certain instruction in its original context in order to fully grasp the Torah's underlying message. Is this commanded action or prohibition a basic principle, or a method to achieve another ideal? And when several actions fall under one general rubric, does each one hold its own independent meaning, or are they all components of a common objective?

Let's ponder capital punishment. Should it be entered in the directory of biblical commandments as a direct expression of God's will for man? If so, how many times? I can think of at least three possibilities: an entry for every infraction punishable by death, four general entries for each method of execution, or maybe even a single comprehensive commandment. On the other hand, maybe the death penalty is merely His delegated response to infractions of other laws, and therefore was already included in whatever prohibition was transgressed. Alternatively, it can be viewed as a detail of the commandment to install a court system (Deuteronomy 16:18). Answering these questions will be the first step in ascertaining the *objective* of the Torah law's death penalty.

Yet this will prove to be a daunting task. While the Oral Torah's contents survive intact, the original record of the 613 commandments has long gone missing; we possess no authentic tradition as to which laws ought to be counted. But don't worry, all is not lost. Throughout the Middle Ages, several attempts were made to reconstitute the list, each one maintaining that the others left out some "counted" commandments and included some "non-countable" ones. Tremendous effort was invested in this project by many of the era's greatest scholars, resulting in several instrumental works covering all the underlying principles of Judaism.

We will listen closely to three diverging opinions on how – or if – to "count" capital punishment, each one pointing us towards a different objective. Upon close examination, we will see strong proofs for each viewpoint, suggesting that all three principles are equally authentic, and the dispute merely revolves around which is the most essential and defining. This type of thing happens quite often in such situations.

**Law and Order**

In his *Book of Commandments,* Maimonides makes his case clear. Each method of biblical punishment or atonement – monetary fines, sacrificial offerings, death – calls for a different action, and ought to be reckoned as a separate commandment. Therefore, four methods of execution equal four "counted" ways of fulfilling God's will.[i]

Sometime in the following century in his critical glosses on Maimonides' work, Nachmanides (1194-1270) took issue with this basic approach. If you view each sort of punishment as an individual directive, why not go a step further and count every crime that's eligible for the death penalty? What connects the stoning of an idol-worshipper with that of a Sabbath-desecrator, the strangling of a false prophet with that of an adulterer?

To prove his point, Nachmanides references how Maimonides himself counted each commandment separately to rest on the many festivals interspersed throughout the Jewish calendar – even though their laws are exactly identical. How are the various reasons to stone different than the various reasons to rest?

Therefore, Nachmanides posits that the entire death penalty program should be based on a certain verse which suggests a unifying principle behind every form of death. (Unlike holidays, where each one is observed to commemorate another event.) We'll get back to his view later; for now, let's attempt to resolve Maimonides' opinion.[ii]

It seems to me that Maimonides combined all offenses receiving the same sentence because *each punishment advances another dimension of the death penalty's objective*. To understand this, let's turn to what he wrote elsewhere about the Torah's philosophy concerning punishments in general.

Were sinners and attackers to go unpunished, *damages will never be removed from society, and those who consider wrongdoing won't be prevented.* This is unlike the lunacy of those who think that abandoning the laws of punishment expresses mercy towards people, for in reality that demonstrates outright cruelty *and the eradication of law and order.* True compassion is that which God has commanded (Deuteronomy 16:18), "You shall install judges and policemen in all of your cities."[iii]

The severity of each punishment and the intensity of its pain, continues Maimonides, were determined by evaluating each crime for four criteria: its destructive effect, availability, level of temptation, and ability to conceal. An easily accessible sin will require a stricter punishment to prevent than one which is harder to transgress; a very enticing action can only be forestalled by the fear of an especially painful consequence. And so on.[iv]

In a word, *deterrence.* The primary purpose of punitive measures is to dissuade prospective felons from committing sinful acts; a convict's execution serves only as a means to the end of ensuring a just and righteous society. And death alone, determined the Torah, will not suffice to discourage crime. An effective system of deterrence includes a graded scale of painful executions, each punishment proportionate to the corresponding wrongdoing.

This is why, I believe, Maimonides counted each method of execution as its own separate commandment: every method represents another dimension of God's compassion for His society, guaranteeing our continued spiritual, emotional, and physical prosperity. True, Maimonides would counter to Nachmanides, the *actual* destructive force of Sabbath-desecration is unrelated to that of idol worship, but the objective of their common punishment is the same: to *prevent* all potential crimes deterrable by this punishment. When counting holiday injunctions, we discern *each day* by the unique event being commemorated; regarding punishments, however, we focus on how the deterrent effect of *each method* of punishment serves the entire Jewish people – not just the specific idol worshipper or Sabbath-desecrator.

It might have been plausible to wind up our study of capital punishment's objectives and then head straight for the political conditions required for its implementation. All that's necessary is to conveniently export the practices of stoning, burning, beheading, and strangling to an era in which spiritual crimes were experienced by society as more destructive than any crimes we know of today. This could conceivably call for a level of deterrence unimaginable in our less ideology-based societies. In addition, perhaps the intangible nature of spiritual crimes creates a level of temptation that requires more deterrence than ones that also threaten physical life.

We'd then remain with some quaint moral lessons from the three doctrines of discretion, rescue, and love – plus a healthy dose of humility from our inability to understand today the immense damage inflicted by the Torah's capital sins. Capital punishment wouldn't be terribly relevant to me, but I might be able live with its morality – as long as it remains purely theoretical.

Yet we can do much better than such a simplistic cop-out. And we must, even if only to understand the theocratic society of old.

**Less than Once in Seventy Years**

Deterrence is a term commonly referred to in the contemporary capital punishment debate. Some experts swear that only a robust death penalty program can reduce violent crime rates, while others claim that the latest studies show that such the death penalty has no statistical effect. Does Judaism profess to own the facts on that hot controversy? I don't think so. Let's think through the mechanics of deterrence.

How do punishments work to prevent crime? It's very simple--- fear. When threatened with a painful *reaction*, I won't commit the *action*. People don't like suffering; they want to live out their natural lives happily. When a threat of miserable consequences hangs over a certain deed, we refrain from that deed.

But for deterrence to work, the threat must be credible. For decades, MAD (Mutually Assured Destruction) strategy protected humanity from a nuclear holocaust; neither the United States nor the Soviet Union was willing to initiate collective suicide. This only succeeded because both sides' missiles were locked and loaded; if either arsenal were down for maintenance, its deterrent effect would be immediately lost. And here lies the problem with a superficial understanding of the Torah law's deterrence system.

In earlier chapters, we saw how an extensive set of restrictions and procedures evolved from Torah law's intense respect and desire for human life. Capital jurists must meet fantastically strict expectations. The presiding judge can unilaterally dismiss all charges. Admissible evidence is limited to the direct observation of two witnesses, who are then subjected to a ruthless examination in court. The criminal must be threatened immediately prior to committing the sin and then openly accept the warning. The slightest judicial evaluation is strictly forbidden. Countless trial procedures focus on rescuing the defendant; guilt-seeking jurists are hampered at every turn. Even after the night-long vigil in search of merits, a conviction is handed down only with a majority of two or more. Finally, there is the exhaustive appeals process. And that's just a brief overview.

How easy it is to avoid accountability; how incredibly difficult to kill anyone with the vaguest desire to live. If the objective of the Torah's death penalty is deterrence of crime through fear of punishment, it doesn't seem awfully effective.

In such a judicial system, actual executions ought to be exceedingly rare. And they were, reports the Mishnah. Not just as a lucky side effect, but by careful design.

A Sanhedrin that executes once every seven years is [derisively] referred to as a destructive tribunal. According to Rabbi Eliezer the son of Azaria, even if they execute every seventy years. Rabbi Akiva and Rabbi Tarfon said, "Had we been around in the days of capital trials – no one would ever have been killed!"[2] Rabbi Shimon the son

[2] The Talmud shares their prospective strategy. For example, in murder trials they'd ask the witness if they conducted a complete post-mortem of the victim to determine that he didn't already have a mortal wound.

of Gamliel responded, "If so, you would have increased the number of murderers [for no one will be afraid of the courts[v].]"[vi]

All scholars agree that executions are to be avoided; opinions diverge only on the extent. The most extreme stance, suggesting a virtual moratorium, was rejected by Rabbi Shimon as undermining the deterrent effect. (By the way, we see here a clear Mishnaic source for Maimonides' view on the death penalty's objective as a deterrent.) But are the other opinions that much better? How many crimes will be prevented by a death penalty that's implemented once in a lifetime? Rabbi Yehudah Loew (c.1512-1609) saw significance in the frequencies provided by the two views that allow, at least, infrequent executions. In Jewish law, seven years is viewed as a full cycle of time, so if a court kills every seven years, it has normalized something supposed to be only a secondary action occasionally forced upon them. And seventy years is a standard lifetime in Torah sources: executing every lifetime, believed Rabbi Eliezer, also shows some regularity.[vii]

Of course, even more troublesome is the view of the esteemed Rabbis Akiva and Tarfon. What can they possibly respond to their colleague's charge that acquitting all murderers will cause countless future victims to die? Why would the Torah institute a harsh and extensive penal code, if it was never meant to be applied?

---

(According to Jewish law, someone who murders a dying person cannot be executed.) If they can somehow reply in the affirmative, they'd only press further: "How can you know for certain there was no previous incision in the exact place he was struck down?" Now, it's very hard to square such extreme vetting with other known principles of Jewish law, such as the power of the statistical majority to establish legal reality. Therefore, many early commentators suggested that the rabbis never intended to disqualify any witnesses that could not answer all of these impossible questions. Rather, they would keep on questioning until the two witnesses *contradict* each other.

All of these formidable problems point to a more nuanced understanding of deterrence.

*To be continued....*

[i] Maimonides *SH"M Shoresh 14* pp. 193, *M"T* 14:1-2

[ii] Nachmanides to *SH"M* ibid pp. 200

[iii] Maimonides *M"N* 3:35

[iv] Maimonides ibid 3:41

[v] Rashi (to Mishnah in next note)

[vi] Mishnah and Talmud *Makkos* 7a

[vii] Lowe, R' Yehudah *Be'er HaGolah* pp. 27

# The Cups in the Sinks

## Rabbi Abba Zvi Naiman

Sometimes stories take on a life of their own, even when they travel far beyond their original context. One that comes to mind is the story of how someone went to the Steipler *z"l* to request a *berachah* for his daughter who was having trouble finding a *shidduch.* The Steipler replied to him that her trouble stemmed from the family's lack of appreciation to Hashem for her birth. The man went home and made a *kiddush* for her that week, whereupon she subsequently became a *kallah* soon after. When this story made its rounds, the whole world started making *kiddushin* as a *segulah* for their daughters in *shidduchim,* unaware that the Steipler had directed his statement to this particular person because he recognized that his *hakaras hatov* was lacking.

A similar example is the story about the *chesed* of a *yeshivah bachur* who makes sure to fill up all the *negel vasser* cups with warm water and leave them in the sink for the *bachurim* to use. I don't know the context of this story, but I do know that it has led to some people unceremoniously leaving washing cups in sinks in shuls around the world without realizing that according to most Poskim there is no *halachic* requirement to even use a cup before *davening.* I would like to devote a few lines for us to understand the relevant *halachos.*

We will begin with a review of the two possible reasons to wash one's hands: (1) because they have a *ruach raah* on them; or (2) because they are not clean.

(1) We are familiar with the rules of *ruach raah* from waking up in the morning. Each hand should be washed entirely up to the wrist, or at least to the ends of his fingers.[1] And each hand needs to be washed

---

[1] *Mishnah Berurah* 4:38

alternating between them three times. If no water is available, there is no other way to remove this *ruach raah.*

But there are activities other than sleeping that can cause *ruach raah.* These include going out of a bathroom or a *mikvah*, even though one did not use it;. cutting one's nails or hair; going to a cemetery or funeral; and marital relations. In these cases, too water is needed to remove the *ruach raah.* And it should also be done as soon as possible so as not to be affected by this *ruach raah* (*Mishnah Berurah* 4:38). However, it is not necessary to wash three times to remove it, although some Poskim rule stringently in the latter two cases to require three washings on each hand (ibid. 4:39).[2]

(2) If someone is washing because his hands became dirty, he needs to wash only the part that became unclean (ibid. 4:38). And if no water is available, he may clean them by rubbing the dirty part on a cloth or anything else that can clean it (see below). Since this is only a cleanliness issue, the speed in which it should be done depends on the person's own feeling about being dirty.

The Gemara in *Berachos* (15a) learns from a *pasuk* in *Tehillim* 26:6), אֶרְחַץ בְּנִקָּיוֹן כַּפָּי וַאֲסֹבְבָה אֶת-מִזְבַּחֲךָ ה', *I wash in cleanliness my hands and circle around Your altar, Hashem,* that when one washes his hands before he prays it is like he built a *mizbei'ach* and brought a *korban* on it. The Gemara concludes that since the *pasuk* stresses, בְּנִקָּיוֹן, *in cleanliness,* if no water is available, one may clean his hands by rubbing them either with earth, or with pebbles, or with chips of wood. And based on the above, the commentators explain that this is effective only to clean one's hands from dirt before *davening,* but it does not remove *ruach raah* when this is needed.

[2] He also cites a view that someone walking out of a bathroom needs to wash three times, but notes that the *Magen Avraham* refutes this view. Moreover, there is a debate among the Poskim whether our bathrooms with modern plumbing have *ruach raah* at all.

There are four possibilities we have to examine when discussing washing before davening:

- If someone wakes up from a night's sleep, he certainly has to wash his hands three times – i.e., *negel vasser* – with a *berachah* of *al netilas yadayim* before *davening.* If there is no water available, he has to travel up to 18 minutes to find water. If there is none available within this distance, he should wipe his hands on something that will clean them,[3] which will be sufficient for *davening* even though it does not remove the *ruach raah.* In this case, the *Shulchan Aruch* rules that the *berachah* should be *al nekias yadayim* (*M.B.* 4:22).[4]
- If he already washed *negel vasser,* but touched something unclean or went to the bathroom, he also has to travel up to 18 minutes to find water (*M.B.* 92:15 and 92:26).[5] If by doing so, he will miss *davening* with a minyan, he should wipe his hands on something that will clean them (*M.B.* 92:20).[6]
- If he has no reason to think his hands are unclean (*stam yadayim*), he does not have to travel for water if it is unavailable where he is. Instead, he should wipe his hands on something that will clean them (*M.B.* 92:15 and 92:26).
- Even if he knows with certainty that his hands are clean, he should still wash them when water is available; but there is

[3] This cleaning includes the entire back and front of the hand since it is taking the place of washing with water (*M.B.* 4:57).

[4] The *Mishnah Berurah* (4:58) notes that some Poskim say that the *berachah* remains *al netilas yadayim,* but concludes that all of the Acharonim did not veer from the *psak* of the *Shulchan Aruch.*

[5] Even though going into a bathroom creates a *ruach raah* (see above), there is no requirement to travel more than the 18 minutes for water.

[6] This presumably applies to the first case, as well, where the person has just woken up without washing *neger vasser.*

certainly no need to travel for water (*M.B.* 233:20 and *Beur Halachah* there).[7]

For Shacharis we can assume that since one washed *negel vasser* when he woke up to remove the *ruach raah,* this washing will help for *davening* unless there was a long lapse of time between the washing and *Shacharis.* In this latter case, he should wash with water even if he does not know that they became unclean because of the possibility that he did touch something unclean. If no water is available, he should wipe them with something that would cleanse them (*M.B.* 92:26).

When it comes time to *daven* Minchah or Maariv, he certainly cannot rely upon his morning *negel vasser.* He must therefore wash his hands with water, and if no water is available, he is obligated to travel for 18 minutes to find water as long as this will not cause him to miss the proper time for *davening* or a minyan. This is true only if knows his hands are unclean. If he has no reason to think they touched something unclean – *stam yadayim* – he may wipe them with something that would cleanse them if there is no water available (see above). If he is davening Minchah and Maariv together, he does not have to wash his hands for Maariv if he already washed them for Minchah and did not divert his attention from them, i.e., *hesech hadaas* (*M.B.* 233:16). The same is true if he washed before *davening,* but learned in between (ibid. 233:18)

You will notice that no one said anything about how the washing before *davening* should be performed where he has already washed *negel vasser* in the morning. There certainly does not seem to be any reason to wash three times, when we are not dealing with the *ruach raah* of waking up from overnight sleep. All we have seen is that

[7] The *Beur Halachah* entertains the possibility that if he knows that his hands are clean there is no obligation to wash before *davening.* But he concludes by citing Poskim who clearly say that washing is nevertheless needed.

water is required in cases where there is a certainty that one's hands are unclean and preferred in cases where one has no reason to think he touched something unclean. The *Ketzos HaShulchan* (12:3, quoting the *Baal HaTanya's Siddur*) writes explicitly that if someone needs to wash again for *davening* because he had *hesech hadaas* after washing *negel vasser* in the morning, he does not need to use a utensil,[8] does not need a human to pour the water, and does not need any of the other requirements for the water before washing to eat.

There is, however, the entirely different approach of *Gra z"l.*[9] In his view, in dispute with the *Shulchan Aruch,* the primary institution of *netilas yadayim* was made for *davening.* One is therefore obligated to wash before every *tefillah* of the day with a utensil, and make the *berachah* of *al netilas yadayim* each time.

In conclusion, for most people, there is no need to use a cup to wash before *davening.* It is only those who follow the *Gra z"l* and make a *berachah* before each *tefillah* who would need to use a cup. We can therefore assume that the story about the *bachur* who filled all the sinks with cups of warm water was in a yeshivah that followed the *psak* of the *Gra.*[10] It should not be used as example for what to do in shuls that do not follow this view.[11] ۵

---

[8] This is also the view of the *Elyah Rabbah* among other Poskim.

[9] See *Maaseh Rav HaShalem* §3, with note 2.

[10] Or possibly they followed the stringent opinion, refuted by the *Magen Avraham,* that requires a full washing for leaving a bathroom, assuming that our bathrooms necessitate any washing at all. And it should be noted that *Yesod VeShoresh HaAvodah* (*Shaar* II, end of Chapter 1) concludes from the *Zohar* that one should wash three times with a utensil to rid oneself of the *ruach raah* of a bathroom.

[11] It was noted by R' Roman Kimelfeld that there is a case where it is worthwhile to have cups available at washing stations (but no reason to leave them in the sinks, of course). That is, in cases where davening begins early and the *mispallelim* washed *negel vasser* before *olas hashachar.* In this case, the *Rama* (4:14) writes that one should wash again, although without making a *berachah.*

# Gift Intention

## Nechemia Gelberman

Question: Someone handed a Bar Mitzvah *bachur* an envelope and said "I didn't know which *sefer* would interest you, so I am giving you money and you choose the *sefarim* you want." Does the Bar Mitzvah *bachur* have to buy *sefarim* with that money, or can he use it for something else?

Answer: The *Sefer Chasidim* writes that if someone sends food to another person and specifies that it is for Shabbos, then he is not allowed to eat it on a weekday. We presume that when someone clearly says that he wants his gift to be used for *kvod Shabbos,* it is a condition that he wants kept, and it is therefore *assur* to go against his express wishes.

There is a *machlokes* between Tannaim whether a person who utilizes an object for a purpose other than what the owner wanted is considered a *ganav.* There is a Gemara in *Bava Metzia* that asks: if someone collected money for poor people to use for the Purim *seudah,* may the recipients use it for something else? R' Meir holds that they may use it only for the Purim *seudah,* but R' Shimon Ben Gamliel argues that they may use it for other things. The *Tur paskens* in accordance with R' Meir, but the *Shulchan Aruch paskens* in accordance with R' Shimon Ben Gamliel.

The *Mishnah Berurah* writes that the *Sefer Chassidim's* ruling regarding Shabbos food is dependent on how we rule regarding the money for Purim. Therefore, the *Tur* would rule that it may not be eaten during the week, and the *Shulchan Aruch* would rule that it may. The *Shulchan Aruch HaRav* writes that the *Sefer Chassidim* did not rule that it is *assur* to eat food sent for Shabbos during the week, but rather that it is a *middos chassidus* (a good thing) not to do so.

The *Chavos Ya'ir* writes, however, that even R' Shimon Ben Gamliel agrees that one should not use the Purim *seudah* money for anything else. The disagreement is whether or not it is *geneivah* to use it for something else. In other cases of the Gemara, where an *ani* (poor person) is given money to buy one type of clothing and he wants to use it for another type, he may do so even *lechatchila* because there is no reason to believe that the giver insisted that it be used for that specific thing. The *Chavos Ya'ir* therefore rules in accordance with the *Sefer Chassidim* that food sent *lich'vod* Shabbos may not be eaten during the week, because we assume that the sender wanted it to be used for the mitzvah of *kvod* Shabbos.

The *Chavos Ya'ir* wonders what the halachah would be if a wealthy person pledged to send money for Kiddush wine each Erev Shabbos to a relative who is a *Talmid Chacham*, but this relative prefers to buy wine for Kiddush with his own money (because in a perfect world, one should buy mitzvah items himself rather than use something for free). Is he allowed to use the money he received from the wealthy relative for Shabbos food other than wine? The *Chavos Ya'ir* writes that according to the *Tur,* he may not use the money for any other purpose because Kiddush is a mitzvah *d'Oraisa* while other Shabbos foods are only *d'Rabanan,* and it is possible that this rich relative earmarked his money only for the *d'Oraisa.* According to the *Shulchan Aruch*, however, he would be permitted to use the money for other purposes.

The *Chavos Ya'ir* concludes by saying that even according to the more *machmir* opinions, if someone sent money to a *Talmid Chacham* and said, "Use it to buy wine or fish for Shabbos or Yom Tov," in order to give the gift graciously without making the recipient feel bad, there is no reason to believe that he wants this money to be used only for Shabbos food, and the recipient may use it for other purchases.

Now back to our case, when people give money as a Bar Mitzvah gift, they are generally not specifically earmarking their money for *sefarim.* "Buy *sefarim* with it" is a common thing someone may say when giving money as a Bar Mitzvah present to make it sound gracious. The giver knows it's likely that the Bar Mitzvah *bachur* may forget and use the money for something else; and if he really wanted it to be used for *sefarim,* he would have bought *sefarim* and actually given it to the *bachur* or given him a gift certificate to a *sefarim* store. Since we can assume that the statement "Buy *sefarim* with it" was not deliberate, the bar mitzvah *bachur* may use the money for other things.

If there is a reason to believe that the giver was deliberate in earmarking the money, like if he specifically named a *sefer* he would like the *bachur* to buy and especially if he said "I will share the *zechus* of your learning from the *sefarim,*" the bar mitzvah boy must use the money for *sefarim* according to the *Chavos Ya'ir.*

The bottom line is, if you give cash to a bar mitzvah *bachur* as a present, he is free to spend it however he wants.

# Kiddush Hashem

## Duvy Kaplan [1]

While *parshas Va'eira* does not have any direct *mitzvos*, it **does** have some important lessons that we can learn and apply in our daily lives.

For example, we learn a fundamental lesson from the action of the frogs. The *pasuk* says (7:28): וְשָׁרַץ הַיְאֹר צְפַרְדְּעִים וְעָלוּ וּבָאוּ בְּבֵיתֶךָ וּבַחֲדַר מִשְׁכָּבְךָ וְעַל מִטָּתֶךָ וּבְבֵית עֲבָדֶיךָ וּבְעַמֶּךָ וּבְתַנּוּרֶיךָ וּבְמִשְׁאֲרוֹתֶיךָ, *The Nile will swarm with frogs, and they will go up and come into your house and into your bedroom and upon your bed and into the house of your servants and into your people, and "into your ovens" and into your kneading bowls.*

The Torah teaches us that the frogs swarmed the whole land of Mitzrayim, and *even jumped into the burning ovens.* The Gemara in *Pesachim* (53b) tells us a story about three great men: Chananyah, Mishael, and Azariah, who lived in *Bavel* during the time of Nevuchadnetzar. Nevuchadnetzar made a statue of himself and made a decree that everyone must bow down to it or be thrown into a fire. While many Jews did bow down to this statue, Chananyah, Mishael, and Azariah refused. They thought that if the frogs, who did not have a *chiyuv* in the *mitzvah* of *Kiddush Hashem*, were willing to jump into the burning ovens, *kal vechomer*, they, as *Yidden*, who do have a *chiyuv* in the mitzvah of *Kiddush Hashem*, should be willing to sacrifice their lives and **not** bow down to the statue.

*Darchei Mussar* points out that Chananyah, Mishael, and Azariah's reasoning for their actions was based on their understanding that the frogs were *not* commanded to jump into the burning ovens.

[1] Adapted from my Bar Mitzvah *Pshetl.*

However, based on the *pasuk* I just quoted, *Hashem* tells Moshe that the frogs *will* go into the ovens. *Darchei Mussar* answers that while there was such a commandment for the frogs, still, the frogs were *not* restricted to go only into the ovens, but rather they had a choice to go into people's homes and bedrooms. Nonetheless, many frogs still chose to sacrifice their lives to make sure that Hashem's commandment was fully executed. Therefore, Chananyah, Mishael, and Azariah's reasoning still stands: if the frogs chose to jump into the fire, even more so, the Jews must be willing to give up their lives *al Kiddush Hashem*.

While sacrificing one's life is the ultimate fulfillment of this mitzvah, *Kiddush Hashem* can be performed in a variety of ways in our everyday lives. Anything that causes others to increase their admiration of Hashem and His people is *Kiddush Hashem*. As *frum* Jews, our actions are a constant representation of Hashem and His Torah; and therefore, we have to be cognizant of our behavior amongst our family, friends, and strangers – Jews and non-Jews alike.

While discussing the mitzvah of *Kiddush Hashem*, the Gemara in *Yoma* (86a) states: שֶׁיְּהֵא שֵׁם שָׁמַיִם מִתְאַהֵב עַל יָדְךָ, *Make the name of Hashem beloved through you.* This means that through our actions, be it speech or physical acts, we are instructed to bring the people we encounter to an appreciation and closeness to Hashem.

There is another important lesson that we learn in this *parshah*: Hashem commands Moshe to go to Pharoah and ask him to free the Jewish people. However, even before Moshe sets out to complete this command, Hashem tells him that Pharoah will refuse his request.

The *pesukim* sayy (7:2–4): וְאַהֲרֹן אָחִיךָ יְדַבֵּר אֶל פַּרְעֹה וְשִׁלַּח אֶת בְּנֵי יִשְׂרָאֵל מֵאַרְצוֹ, *Aharon your brother shall speak to Pharaoh that he should let the Bnei Yisroel out of his land.*

וַאֲנִי אַקְשֶׁה אֶת לֵב פַּרְעֹה וְהִרְבֵּיתִי אֶת אֹתֹתַי וְאֶת מוֹפְתַי בְּאֶרֶץ מִצְרָיִם, *But I will harden Pharaoh's heart, and I will increase My signs and My wonders in the land of Egypt.*
וְלֹא יִשְׁמַע אֲלֵכֶם פַּרְעֹה, *But Pharaoh will not listen to you...*

There is an obvious question here: if Pharaoh was *not* going to listen to Moshe anyway, why was it necessary for Moshe to go and speak to him in the first place?! Moshe could have said to Hashem that it is really pointless for him to do this; it would be a waste of time and very humiliating for him. But, as we see from the *pesukim* that follow, Moshe accepts this mission and goes to Pharaoh. As we see later on, there *was* a reason for what at that time seemed to be a pointless task: for every refusal by Pharaoh to let the *Bnei Yisroel* go, Hashem punished the Mitzrim with a *makkah*. The *Navi Yeshayhah* writes (19:22): וְנָגַף ה' אֶת מִצְרַיִם נָגֹף וְרָפוֹא, *Hashem struck Mitzrayim with a blow and a cure*. And the *Zohar Hakodesh* explains that this means, "a blow for Mitzrim and a cure for *Bnei Yisroel*."

We see from here that, even though, we may not always understand the purpose for every mitzvah, we must trust in Hashem and do it anyway because everything happens for a reason. We learn a very important lesson from the actions of Chananyah, Mishael, and Azariah, to stand up for what is right no matter how difficult it may be to do the *ratzon Hashem*. ♔

# Two *Dinim* in the *Daled Kosos* [1]

## Yerucham Rappaport

*Tosafos* in *Pesachim* (99b) holds that *me'iker hadin,* the *baal habayis* can be *motzi* everyone at the Seder with his *daled kosos,* just like regular kiddush on *Shabbos* where the *baal habayis* makes kiddush and is *motzi* everyone who hears the kiddush with the *din* of *shomei'a k'oneh,* which means that the one who listens is as if he said the words.

The *Rambam* (*Hil. Chametz U'Matzah* 7:7), disputes *Tosafos* and says that one cannot *be yotzei* with someone else's *daled kosos*. Every single person, including men and women, must drink all *daled kosos* by themselves.

What is the explanation of the *machlokes*?

The Brisker Rav famously explains this *machlokes* by stating that there are two separate *dinim* in the mitzvah of *daled kosos*. The first *din* is similar to regular kiddush on *Shabbos*. Just like regular kiddush, the *ikkur* is the *amirah* of kiddush, and the requirement to say it on a cup of wine is merely to enhance the *amirah;* here too, the first *din* of the *daled kosos* is the *amirah,* to express four separate *shevachos*: (1) kiddush, (2) Hagadah, (3) *birkas hamazon,* and (4) Hallel. The *din* to say it on a cup of wine is only technical and secondary because of *ein omrim shirah elah al hayayin.* The second din of *daled kosos,* says the Brisker Rav, is to actually drink four cups of wine because of the feeling of *cheirus* that it brings to a person when he drinks wine.

---

[1] Bar Mitzvah *pshetel* (*Vayikra* 5781)

A simple *nafka mina* is that if someone drinks the wine without saying anything, they would appear to be *mekayeim* the second *din,* the *shetiah* part of the mitzvah, but not the *amirah* part of the mitzvah. Conversely, if someone said the required *amirah* on the *daled kosos* but did not drink, he might fulfill the *amirah al hakos,* but not the *shetiah* part.

Based on this *chakirah,* the Brisker Rav beautifully explains the *machlokes Rambam* and *Tosafos. Tosafos,* who hold that the *baal habayis* can be *motzi* everyone holds that the entire mitzvah of *daled kosos* is only one thing – the *amirah al hakos.* Since the *ikkur* is *amirah,* then for anyone who listens to the *amirah,* it is as if they said it themselves because of the *din* of *shomei'a ke'oneh.* The *Chazon Ish* adds that even according to *Tosafos*, everyone who listens to the *baal habayis* gets the enhanced *amirah* because it is as if everyone listening said the four *shevachos* while holding a *kos* in their hand.

The *Rambam,* however, states his *din* of the *daled kosos* right after the halachah that every single person has a *chiyuv* to feel in his bones that he was freed from being an *eved.* The *Rambam* says *lefichach*, therefore, every person needs to recline in a way of freedom, and everyone needs to drink the four cups of wine since the *daled kosos* are supposed to cause a person to actually feel freedom. Says the Brisker Rav, the *Rambam* holds that in addition to the *din amirah* on the *kosos,* there is a separate *din* to actually drink four cups of wine. One without the other is not enough. The *shetiah din* is a mitzvah *shebigufo*, which is impossible to be *motzi* another person. Just like you cannot be *motzi* someone else with lulav and esrog or sitting in the sukkah, you cannot be *motzi* someone else with drinking four cups of wine. Each person needs to drink the four cups themselves to be *mekayim* this aspect of the mitzvah of *daled kosos*.

These two separate *dinim* can explain why *Rashi* brings two separate *mekoros* for the *daled kosos*. One is the four *leshonos* of *geulah,* which seemingly implies that one should feel four feelings of *cheirus.* This is the *din shetiah.* The other *mekor* is the three cups in Pharaoh's dream plus *birkas hamazon,* which seems to be the *mekor* for the din *amirah* on four cups of wine.

There are at least four other *nafka minos* that will depend on these two separate *dinim* in the mitzvah of *arba kosos*:

(1) How much of the *kos* does one need to drink? If the *ikkur* is *amirah* like regular Shabbos kiddush, then all you should be required to drink is *melo lugmov,* a cheekful, just like regular kiddush. The *Rambam,* however, holds that unlike regular kiddush, one must drink *rov kos* of each of the four *kosos.* Why? Because the *Rambam* holds *lishitaso,* that the second *din* of *daled kosos* is to feel cheirus from *drinking* the wine – which requires *rov kos.*

(2) If someone uses *chamar medinah* instead of wine, are they *yotzei* the *daled kosos*? According to the *Rambam,* the answer is no, because the second *din* of *daled kosos,* of *shetiah,* is *davkah* to drink wine that brings about the feeling of freedom. According to *Tosafos*, it should be no different than *Shabbos* kiddush which is acceptable with *chamar medinah.*

(3) Similarly, the Gemara says *shasan chai*, meaning if someone drinks the *daled kosos* undiluted, *yedai arba kosos yoytzei, yidei cheirus lo yatzah.* According to the Brisker Rav, the Gemara is understandable. One who drinks undiluted wine is not <u>*yotzei*</u> the *din* of drinking wine to feel *cheirus* because the feeling of *cheirus* only comes from diluted wine, which has optimal taste. One will, however, still be *yotzei* the *amirah* aspect of the *daled kosos* just like one is *yotzei* kiddush on *Shabbos* with undiluted wine. (*Tosafos* has a different explanation of the Gemara).

(4) If someone drinks all four cups in a row, are they *yotzei* the mitzvah? They would appear to be *yotzei* the *din* of drinking four cups of wine, but not the *din* of *amirah al hakos.* In fact, the *Rambam*'s *lashon* in Halacha 9 is "If you drank all four cups in a row, you are *yotzei* the *din cheirus* but not the *din daled kosos.*"

No matter how you learn, however, the *daled kosos* have a *din* of *pirsumei nisa,* which is why women are obligated in the *daled kosos* even though it is a *mitzvas asei shehazman gerama.* They are still obligated because they were part of the *neis,* just like Megillah on Purim and menorah on Chanukah. This *din* of *pirsumei nisa* is also the reason why just like *ner Chanukah*, an *ani* is *chayav* in the mitzvah no matter how poor; the public soup kitchen, *tamchuy,* is required to provide the *ani* with four cups of wine.

*Lichora,* the *pirsum hanes* is related to the first part of the *din arba kosos,* the *amirah,* because drinking is a personal act. *Amirah* is the *pirsum hanes.*

If so, even according to the *Rambam*, if women are only *chayav* because of *pirsum hanes,* they should be able to be *mekayem* all *dinim* of the *daled kosos* by listening to someone else. Why do women need to drink? A possible answer can be that *af heim hayu beneis* requires them to also feel the *cheirus* by drinking (even if there is no aspect of *pirsum hanes* in the drinking).

One question which needs a *hesber* on *Tosafos* is that if according to *Tosafos* the wine is simply a *memeilah din,* meaning only secondary and technical, because the *ikkur* is the *amirah* (for *pirsum hanes*), then why is the *din daled kosos* from the *tamchui* applicable? The *tamchui* does not supply kiddush for *Shabbos,* so why would the *daled kosos* be different? Why is Pesach any different that the *tzibbur* is *mechuyav* to support an *ani* and see to it that he has four cups of wine? Everyone holds of this *din*; it is a *befeirush* Mishnah?

The answer could be that even according to *Tosafos*, it is possible that in a certain way the *daled kosos* is different than a regular kiddush on *Shabbos*. It is possible that for the *daled kosos*, the *amirah al hakos* needs to be a different *amirah* than a regular *Shabbos amirah.* The *daled kosos amirah* requires an *amirah davka "al hayayin"* because wine represents *cheirus* which is part of the *pirsum hanes.* A regular *amirah* is not enough. It needs to be an *amirah al kos yayin.* There still might be no separate *din* to drink the wine and feel *cheirus,* but you might still need wine to be *mekayem* the *amirah* part of the mitzvah. Just like *ner Chanukah*, the *ikkur* is to say the *berachos* and for a menorah to be lit in the house; here too, the *din* is *amirah* in front of four cups of wine. On *Shabbos*, the *ikkur* is *amirah*, and the *din al hakos* is merely ancillary. For Pesach, the *al hakos* is an *ikkur* part of the *amirah* requirement. So, the *din tamchui* is relevant because it is part of the *din pirsum haneis* even if *Tosafos* does not hold of the separate *din* to drink and feel *cheirus* from the drinking.

# *Sheratzim*

## Yitzchak Solomon[1]

One of my father's Rebbeim in Yerushalayim wrote the following on *Parashas Shemini* last year at the beginning of Covid-19, when it was thought that the virus began because of people in China eating contaminated bats. The thought of these exotic animals carrying gross diseases that would be passed onto people who ate them was not far from a reality. Yesterday's *parashah* tells us that we are not allowed to eat *sheratzim,* creepy-crawlers.

Even though we, as Hashem's servants, do not really know the reasons for mitzvos, it seems quite easy for us to not consume the creepy-crawlers that were listed in the *parashah*: insects, rodents, reptiles, etc. In *Bava Metzia* (61b), the Gemara quotes Ravina's response to Rav Chanina of Sura who gives over a Baraisa of R' Yishmael's Academy that Hashem would have happily redeemed *Bnei Yisrael* from Mitzrayim for them to observe only one mitzvah – not to become impure by eating *sheratzim.* Even though other mitzvos have bigger rewards, refraining from this act was enough on its own to redeem the *Yidden.*

The *Ksav Sofer* asks a question: Eating *sheratzim* is naturally repulsive and does not require much self-sacrifice. So what was the great merit that justified freeing our ancestors from slavery? He answers that Hashem would have redeemed the Jewish people for not contaminating themselves by eating these. It is not the icky nature of the creatures or the concern about stomach aches, but rather the damaging effects on the holy *neshamos* of those who eat them. Therefore, Hashem commanded us not to eat them because of the spiritual harm. In other words, were *Bnei Yisrael* to have observed

[1] My Bar Mitzvah *pshetel.*

this mitzvah because of its dangerous spiritual consequences and not because it was naturally gross to them, Hashem would have happily redeemed them. To perform what comes naturally, but to do so for a higher purpose is real dedication!

Until now, my parents, my Rebbeim, and my community have helped me to keep mitzvos as *chinuch* and practice so that now that I am Bar Mitzvah I can keep the Torah as a natural, daily part of life. I pray for Hashem's help towards keeping these for the sake of observing them, since that is what He wants.

*B'ezras Hashem,* may we all strive to serve Hashem for the sake of doing His will.

# HaGaon HaRav Dovid Soloveitchik, *z"l*

## R' Shmuel Strauss [1]

HaGaon HaRav R' Meshulam Dovid Soloveitchik, *z"l,* was born in the famous city of Brisk in 1921. He was the son of the Brisker Rav, grandson of Rav Chaim, and the great-grandson of the Bais Halevi. He was brought up in a home of tremendous *ahavas hatorah* and *dikduk hamitzvos.* During WWII Rav Dovid fled to Vilna where he was a refugee with students from many other yeshivos. He told us in Chumash *shiur* about those years and how the *Tatte's shiurim* were the best during that *tekufah.*[2] He said how there was not enough room where his father was staying in Vilna, so he slept on the floor of Rav Leizer Yudel Finkel's house. I heard him say that he was very *nispael* how the Mirrer Rosh Yeshivah woke up between two and three in the morning and learned the rest of the night.

Rav Dovid came to Yerushalayim, where he continued learning at his father's yeshivah, and eventually started his own yeshivah. Even though Rav Dovid moved from Brisk, in spirit he never really left. At his *levayah* all of his children said how he kept very firm in his beliefs all the years, and how he never gave in or compromised for the *emes* and the Torah. When I was *menachem avel* Rav Velvel, he told me that his father was extremely consistent and always served Hashem with the same *geshmak* as if it was his first time.

His Chumash *shiurim* were incredible! He started with *divrei Torah* on the *parashah* and eventually made his way into *hashkafah* and *mussar.* He always spoke about Torah and *yiras Shamayim.* It was amazing to hear his perspective of the war years and the stories of how they got matzos and *daled minim* (his focus was always how to

---

[1] R' Shmuel was *zocheh* to learn in Rav Dovid's *yeshivah* for two years.

[2] He also told us that they learned *Perek Shlosheh Minin* in *Nazir* there.

do mitzvos properly). He also famously spoke very strongly about the Zionists and how the Zionistic ideology destroyed and continues to destroy *Klal Yisrael* and the ways of the Torah.

I believe that many of the *hanhagos* of Rav Dovid came from his *midas haemes. At* Rav Dovid's *levaya*h, his son-in-law, Rav Nechemia Caplan *shlit"a,* explained how Rav Dovid never left Brisk. That is, he never gave in to the modern ideology of "just getting with the times." Rather, he kept his *she'ifos* and aspirations with the standards he was brought up with by his father, the Brisker Rav. He kept these standards with the running of his yeshivah and the expectations of his *talmidim.*

I remember once in Chumash *shiur* when he told the story of how a wealthy man was turned off by the fact that a collector for Rav Chaim Volozhiner's yeshivah was riding a very fancy horse. The wealthy man complained to Rav Chaim that the money he donated should be going to a horse!? Rav Chaim famously told the *gevir* that if you are someone that uses your money for fancy things and don't really care about Torah, your money will go to the horse; but if you really care about the Torah and are giving it for the right reasons, then your money will go to the actual *lomdei Torah.* Rav Dovid gave us Mussar and said that nowadays the *bochurim* in the Yeshivah are like the horse. They need nice *dirahs* and air conditioning, etc. He really expected high levels of *mesiras nefesh* for learning from his *talmidim.*

Rav Dovid also really believed in and cared about his *talmidim* and made an effort to remember them. When I came back married, my wife and I went to visit Rav Dovid and his Rebbetzin (Rebbetzin Judy – Rav Moshe Shternbuch's sister and Rav Asher's "auntee" – she's English). Rav Dovid greeted us very warmly and asked me if I was planning on going back to the Mir (apparently, he remembered I came from the Mir). I told him yes, I was planning to return to the

Mir, but I wanted to continue learning *Kodashim*. Surprisingly, he allowed me to continue going to his *shiur* even though I was learning *Kodashim* in the Mir.

Rav Dovid also spoke about and encouraged coming on time to *seder* in yeshivah and to learning in the yeshivah on Friday and Shabbos. He never used to come to yeshivah, as he gave *shiur* in his house (or in Malachi 40), but he came every Friday to be *mechazeik* learning Friday in yeshivah. Occasionally, he would come randomly during the week towards the beginning of *seder* and would stand by the door and give *mussar* to the *bochurim* arriving late. One day, it was 9:30 and I and only a few others were in the Beis Medrash and Rav David came in and called me over. He turned around and looked up at the clock and asked me, "*Vus is the zeiger*" (what time is it)? I told him 9:30. He told me jokingly "*Mestama deh zeiger is gebrecht*" (the clock is probably broken). Jokingly I told him in a very *temimisdik* tone of voice, "*Mestama, mestama*" (that the Rosh Yeshivah is probably right, and it's broken.) He thought it was a very funny response, and he laughed. (Rav Dovid also had a sense of humor).

Rav Dovid's *midas ha'emes* also came out in his *shiur*. He would ask questions very clearly and to the point. He also demanded that from his *talmidim*. It was known that if you asked a question in *shiur* and he did not agree he would "give it to you." One time I asked a question in *shiur*, and he didn't understand the question. He asked me in front of everyone "what's your name" so I told him "Strauss." He asked me "How long have you been learning in the yeshivah" so I told him, "Two years." He said, "You have been by me two years and you asked such a question?" It didn't matter to him to "give it to you" because Torah is *emes* and if you ask a question in *shiur* it better be *emes*, or else![3]

There is another way the *midas ha'emes* of Rav Dovid came out in *shiur*. I remember one time he asked a simple question on the Gemara and left it *shver*. He opened up a *Rambam* who quoted the Gemara and asked the same exact question. His *shiur* wasn't always eye opening *chidushim*. Many times, it was just saying over the Gemara and the *Rambam* and asking to the point, *emesdik* questions, and not feeling the necessity to say over major *chidushim,* but rather sticking to the *Toras emes*.

I also want to share the differences I observed in the *derech halimud* between Mir and Brisk. I want to start by saying that they aren't as different as people think, but there are still some significant differences.

In my opinion there are three main differences. First of all, the style of *shiur*. I mean to say that in Mir the style of *shiur* is to clarify the general *sugya* with the *shitos* of the *Rishonim*. In Brisk, it is mainly to say over the questions of the Brisker Rav and discuss his in-depth analysis, not necessarily focusing on the main parts of the *sugya* being learned.[4]

Secondly, in Brisk they are *meshubad* to *Acharonim*, mainly the Brisker Rav and Rav Chaim; and if *Rashi* isn't *mashma* like the Brisker Rav, it is left as a *shver Rashi.* In the Mir, they are *meshubad* only to the *Rishonim*, and if an *Acharon* isn't *mashma* like a *Rishon* it is left *shver* (or is said to only have been meant for *daas*

[3] *Baruch Hashem,* I remembered a *Tosafos* that proved my point and showed it to him, and he agreed it was a good question, so I saved myself from embarrassment. But it didn't always end happily ever after.

[4] They say in Brisk, "*Shelo bemikomo is kemikomo*" applying the Gemara in *Zevachim* 26b.

*HaRambam*). The Mir doesn't really focus on *Acharonim* at all, and just quotes them to help explain a difficult *Rishon*; but the focus is to get your own *kinyan* and *pshat* in the *Rishon*.[5]

The third and most significant difference between Brisk and Mir is a bit more subtle. The Mir believes *diyuk* outweighs *sevara,* as opposed to Brisk where they believe *sevara* outweighs *diyuk*. To bring out the point, Rav Tzvi Cheshen told me that there was a *bochur* from Ponevezh who came to learn by Rav Nachum. He said the difference in the *derech halimud* between Ponevezh and Mir was that "Rav Shmuel Rozovsky opened my brain and Rav Nachum opened my eyes." Meaning that the Mir's focus is on *diyuk*. For example, if a *Rishon* is *mashma* one way and *sevara* says otherwise, in the Mir they say *viezt ois* the *Rishon* holds like this, even though it isn't a simply understood *sevara*. In Brisk, if a *Rishon* is *mashma* not like the *pashtus,* they will usually leave it *shver* as a *tzarich iyun*. Put another way, both Mir and Brisk will be extremely *medakdek* and ask the question directly to the point; Rav Dovid was incredible with asking straight to the point questions. However, in Brisk they'll usually leave the question with a *tzarich iyun,* and the Mir will often build *chidushim* from it.

May we be *zocheh* to continue Rav Dovid's legacy and to become *emesdike bnei* Torah and *yarei Shamayim.*

*Yehi Zichro Baruch.*

---

[5] Rav Asher rarely mentions Rav Nachum in *shiur* by name because he wants you to understand the *Rishon* from the *Rishon* himself, and better not to know that Rav Nachum also said it.

# The Founder of Adath Bnai Israel: Rochel Chiena Mechanic

## Rabbi Abba Zvi Naiman

Two years ago, I wrote an article, "From Yosef Moshe to Yosef Moshe," which included a quote from the *Jewish Observer* about my grandfather, Yosef Moshe (Morris) Siegel, *a"h.* The article stated: "Mr. Siegel was one of a small group of young people, who, in 1918 formed Adath Bnai Yisroel, a group that was committed to *shemiras Shabbos*, quite uncommon in those days amongst young people... Young Mordechai Gifter was also influenced by his participation in these gatherings, and he and Mr. Siegel remained friends throughout his life." See there for the story of my grandfather's role in this organization that helped inspire many other American young men to become *talmidei chachamim* (including HaRav Avigdor Miller, *z"l,* and later להבחל"ח, the Rosh HaYeshivah, HaRav Aharon Feldman, *shlit"a,*) and to make Baltimore into the Torah city that it is.

Since then, I discovered another member of this small group who formed the Adath. It was a young woman named Rae Mechanic. An article in the *Where What When* (7/9/21), "Morris Siegel, Shabbos Yid – Recollections" by my cousin Rabbi Elchonon Oberstein states:

> While it is well documented in the annals of Baltimore history that Morris Mechanic built a theater, it is not as well known that his sister Rae actually started the Adas in 1918 and was its first president. (She would later marry the principal of Yeshiva Torah V'Daas, a Rabbi Dr. Stern.)

I looked around a little and could not find anything more said about this "sister Rae." I was curious to learn more about her; if she was the one who had actually started the Adas, all the *zechuyos* of the organization's accomplishments could be attributed to her.

With the help of my cousin Eli Weinreb, I discovered that the "Rabbi Dr. Stern" mentioned in the WWW article was HaRav Dovid Zussman Stern, *z"l,* who was the Rav of the Young Israel of Manhattan and later became the founding rabbi of the whole YI Movement. During the first few years, when many branches did not yet have a Rav, Rav Dovid would write up a *derashah* that was distributed to all those branches and a layperson would read it to the congregation on Shabbos. Some of these *derashos* are found in a book, *Rabbi Dr. David S. Stern Speaks,* compiled by his daughter, Rebbetzin Channa Leah Gross.[1] It was from this book that I was able to learn much about this couple.[2]

Rae's full name was Rochel Chiena. She was born in 1890 to Yisrael Shimon (1871-1919) and Vitel (Yoffe) (1873-1938) Mechanic [presumably from מחנך] in Kovarsk, Lithuania, who had married in 1889. The family emigrated from Kovarsk to Baltimore in 1905-1906. This was just in time because at the end of July 1915, during World War I, Kovarsk Jews were exiled to Russia by the retreating Russian army, which burned down more than half the town. Retreating Cossack battalions carried out a pogrom against them as they robbed, tortured, and murdered.[3]

[1] Rebbetzin Gross's mother-in-law was Tillie Lauer, sister of Jack Lauer, grandfather of Eli Weinreb.

[2] Much of information from this book can be found in an article in *Hamodia,* at https://hamodia.com/frominyan/surprise-beginnings-shining-star/. In addition to these sources, which center on R' Dovid Zussman, I received information about Rochel Chiena from her grandchildren, R' Shlomo Abba Stern, Rebbetzin Vitel (named after Rochel Chiena's mother) Kalmanowitz, and Mrs. Hindy Hillman.

The Mechanics lived on 131 Lloyd Street, just down the block from the Bnai Israel Congregation, the Russishe Shul, on 27 Lloyd which in 1895 had moved into the large building of Chizuk Amuno when Chizuk Amuno moved out of East Baltimore.

Rabbi Abba Chaim Levinson (1852-1912) was the Rabbi of the shul

at the time. He was married to Shayna Rivka (Jennie), daughter of Rabbi Shlomo Abramson, the "Maharsha" of Shavel.[4] He served until his *petirah.* At that point there was no official Rav, but many *talmidei chachamim* gave *shiurim* in the shul.

Later, Rabbi Shmuel Pliskin (1913-1978) became the Rabbi from

1939 until his *petirah.* [Of course, HaRav Michoel Eliezer Forshlager a *talmid* of the *Avnei Neizer,* led study groups for many years at B'nai Israel. I mention Rabbi Pliskin here because we learn a lot of information about the Mechanic family from his letter after Rochel Chiena's *petirah* in 1969 to her daughter, Rebbetzin Chana Leah Gross.[5]] Although Rabbi Pliskin arrived in Baltimore long after Rochel Chiena had moved to New

[3] The birth years are based on Vitel's Petition for Citizenship in New York in 1930, which was filled out by her two oldest children, Rochel Chiena and Zipporah Chaya. The birthplace of the children is based on a Petition for Citizenship in Baltimore in 1927. Vitel herself was born in Kupishok.From arrival records, we learn that Rochel Chiena came to Baltimore first to an "uncle Joffe" in 1905. She apparently had sufficient prodigious talents even as a teenager to work out the details for her family's later arrival. Her parents and siblings followed in 1906 to "brother-in-law N. Joffe." This is presumably Vitel's brother, since her maiden name was Yoffe.

[4] Another daughter, Fruma Bryna (Florence), married Dov Ber (Bernard) Davis. Their descendants include the Rock, Lapidus, and Skaist families of Baltimore. We hope to have an article about this family in a future edition of our *kuntress.*

[5] Printed at the end of this article.

York, she would often visit Baltimore, and he was once in their home in New York. In Rabbi Pliskin's words, R' Yisrael Shimon, *zt"l,* was a *shochet,* a *yarei* and a *chareid,* who gave *shiurim* and was a respected member of the shul. Rochel Chiena's mother Vitel dedicated a Sefer Torah to the shul. She was special in her own right, drawing her *ruach hakodesh* and *chochmah* from her father, Avraham Abba. HaRav Asher Zelig Margalios, *z"l,* called Vitel *"the chasidah,* a woman who fears Hashem, the *tzadeikas."*

R' Yisrael Shimon was *niftar* on 18 Shevat, 5679 (1919), and is buried in Baltimore. Vitel was *niftera* in Baltimore on 18 Teves 5698 (1937), and her *kevurah* was in Eretz Yisrael.[6]

Again, in Rabbi Pliskin's words, during the year of her father's *petirah,*[7] Rochel Chiena, with her good *seichal* and *binah yeseirah,* gathered together several youngsters[8] in the Bnai Israel shul, and organized the Adas Bnei Israel Organization [presumably named after the shul], similar to the Young Israel Movement that R' Dovid Zussman led. [He doesn't mention it, but R' Dovid had become Rav of the Young Israel of Manhattan that very year.] Rabbi Pliskin goes on to praise Rochel Chiena's tremendous accomplishments.

---

[6] Rochel Chiena and her husband asked HaRav Asher Zelig Margaliyos how to spell Vitel on the *matzeivah,* and he wrote back on 27 Nissan, 5698, to spell it ווייטל. An interesting sidelight of her *kevurah* is that when her son was visiting the *kever* on Har HaZeisim, he asked if he could purchase a plot there. He was told that it was only for *Shomrei Shabbos,* so he left dejected. A few days later he came back and said that he had become a *Shomer Shabbos.* So Zeev Gavriel Chaim ben R' Yisrael Shimon is also buried on Har HaZeizim.

[7] It's not clear if she began only after the *petirah* as a *zechus,* or before. Articles about the Adas state that she founded it in 1918, which could still be 5679, but before her father's *petirah.* If it began after the *petirah,* the starting date would be 1919. Either way, we are safe in saying that the Adas began in 5679.

[8] One of them was certainly my grandfather, Yosef Moshe Siegel, who is mentioned in the early records of the Adas.

To have an idea of what the neighborhood was like at that time, here are a few excerpts from *On Middle Ground,* by Goldstein and Weiner:

> The sense of alienation from tradition was most apparent among young Jews, whose daily experiences were most at odds with the priorities of the Orthodox world. While the Talmud Torah enjoyed a measure of success in influencing its pupils, it served only a small fraction of East Baltimore's Jewish youth. The majority who were taught by tutors or attended private chadarim, had a less affirming experience with Hebrew education. Congregations were similarly obtuse about the needs of children. On Sabbaths at Shomrei Mishmeres (which was the *nusach Sephard* shul next door to Bnai Israel), for example, it became customary for the boys of the congregation to gather on Lloyd Street to play softball during the reading of the Torah (158).

It was in this environment that Rochel Chiena gathered together five earnest workers to begin the Adas Organization.

Looking at the minutes from a meeting on Rosh Chodesh Shevat, 1920, (see image below) we read:

> *The regular meeting of the Adath Bnei Israel was called to order at 9 P.M. by the president Miss Rae Mechanic. The meeting began with the reading of Tehillim, kapitle 104, by the secretary. Miss Mechanic, chairman of the Lecture Committee reported who the speakers would be for the next four weeks. Mr. Caplan, chairman of the Library Committee, reported the purchase of four more books for $1.75. Miss Anna Seigel, chairman of the Entertainment Committee reported about the upcoming program on Tu BeShvat. Mr. Morris Seigel read the "Laws of Sabbath." Miss Sara Levi was added to the*

*Educational Committee. A report was given by the Social Clubs Committee regarding a store on Lombard Street that keeps open on Shabbos.*

Rochel Chiena had galvanized these young men and women to become active in improving the Jewish life of the community.

Rochel Chiena married Rabbi Dr.[9] Dovid Zussman Stern on 13 Sivan, 1921.[10] We don't know how they met, but it is certainly possible that someone had heard about the strikingly similar goals of these young adults and suggested the *shidduch.*[11]

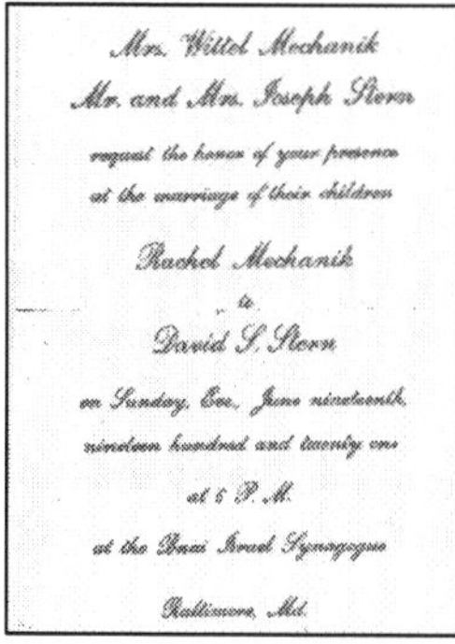
Mrs. Wittel Mechanik
Mr. and Mrs. Joseph Stern
request the honor of your presence
at the marriage of their children
Rachel Mechanik
to
David S. Stern
on Sunday, Eve., June nineteenth,
nineteen hundred and twenty one
at 6 P. M.
at the Bnai Israel Synagogue
Baltimore, Md.

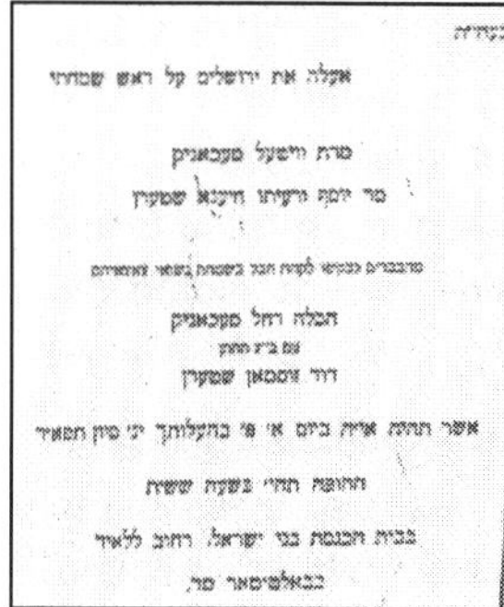
בעזה"י
אעלה את ירושלים על ראש שמחתי
מרת ויטעל מעכאניק
מר יוסף ורעיתו חיענא שטערן
[illegible]
הכלה רחל מעכאניק
עם ב"ג החתן
דוד זוסמאן שטערן
אשר תהיה אי"ה ביום א' פ' בהעלותך י"ג סיון תרפ"א
והחופה תהיה בשעה ששית
בבית הכנסת בני ישראל רחוב לויד
בבאלטימאר מד.

[9] According to his children, R' Dovid enrolled in Columbia University where he earned a doctorate in mathematics, in order to be more successful in reaching the American youths of his day. In a letter written the year before his *petirah,* R' Dovid wrote that during those years he would never miss davening with a *minyan.* He would wake up at 5:00, so he could be in class by 8:00 some years and 9:00 other years. The IRT took an hour to get to school.

[10] Rav Dovid's brother, Yom Tov Lipman, married Chaya Esther Herman, oldest daughter of Yaakov Yosef Herman. One of their children was HaRav Moshe Aharon Stern, *z"l,* who would visit my grandfather, Yosef Moshe when he came to Baltimore in the summers. Perhaps the connection when back to the days of his Aunt Rochel Chiena.

See http://www.chareidi.org/archives5781/voera/fstern1vrh81.htm for a beautiful article about him.

[11] Although Rochel Chiena now lived in New York, she was still in contact with her Baltimore family and her Adath friends. It is interesting to note that when the Adath purchased its first building in 1925 on 4 N. Broadway, the Mechanics were living on 2 N. Broadway during the 1920 census.

On the day they married, they both accepted upon themselves to fast every Monday and Thursday. When Rochel was expecting her first child and feeling weak, R' Dovid wanted her to be *matir neder* and stop fasting to protect their unborn child, but she refused. The *Dvar Avraham* was visiting America in 1924 to raise money, so they went to him with their disagreement. The *Dvar Avraham* said she had to eat, and he promised her that the child would grow to become an *ehrliche Yid.*

After the marriage, Rochel Chiena worked alongside her husband, inspiring and educating women in the observance of mitzvos, and raising funds for the less fortunate. Their opposite dispositions complemented each other. R' Dovid was soft-spoken, gentle, and humble; he appealed to people's intellect. Rochel Chiena, on the other hand, had a vigorous, fiery personality, which she utilized to arouse people's emotions and inspire them to grow in their *Avodas Hashem.*

Her granddaughter recalls spending Shabbos at the Stern home. If the young girl spilled something on the floor, it did not cause Bubby Rochel Chiena to become agitated. But, if she failed to answer *amein* to a *berachah,* it upset Bubby deeply. Her *yiras shamayim* burned in her like a fire.

Interestingly, before Rebbetzin Vichna Kaplan arrived on these shores and opened the first Bais Yaakov, Rebbetzin Rochel Chiena opened a school in Williamsburg called Bais Rochel. When Rochel Chiena heard that a *talmidah* of Sara Schneirer was opening a Bais Yaakov, she closed her own school because she felt the new school would be better. But even though she closed her school, she did not stop serving the *Klal.* She was an expert in *hilchos niddah,* giving *kallah* classes with the approval of the biggest Rabbanim. For a wedding gift, she gave each *kallah* a *negel vasser shise*l and cup so that she could wash *negel vasser* at her bed.

As she and members of the Adath had done in Baltimore, Rochel Chiena continued her fights for *shemiras Shabbos* in New York. Whenever she would go into a Jewish-owned store, she would try to convince the owner to close on Shabbos. This came to the point that her daughter would ask her when they went shopping together not to get into fights with the storekeeper.

In 1927, R' Dovid was invited by HaRav Shraga Feivel Mendlowitz to become the *menahel* of the newly-founded Yeshivah Torah Vodaas, where he served for thirty-five years. Harav Yaakov Kamenetzky, *zt"l*, once told Rabbi Shlomo Abba Gross, Rabbi Stern's grandson, "You don't know who your grandfather was; your mother doesn't know who her father was; and his best quality was that he didn't know himself who he was!"

*L-R: R' Dovid Bender, R' Yaakov Kamenetzky, R' Stern*

Even when they had moved to Williamsburg, R' Dovid Zussman would walk across the Williamsburg Bridge each Shabbos to the Young Israel. He had a *sefer Torah* in his house, and after eating his *seudas* Shabbos, he arranged an early minyan for Minchah so that he would have time to walk to the Lower East Side to give his shiurim at the Young Israel. Since there were conflicting opinions over whether crossing the Williamsburg Bridge was considered going outside the *techum*

*Shabbos*, R' Dovid would place an *eiruvei techumin* on the bridge each Friday to allow him to cross on Shabbos according to all opinions.

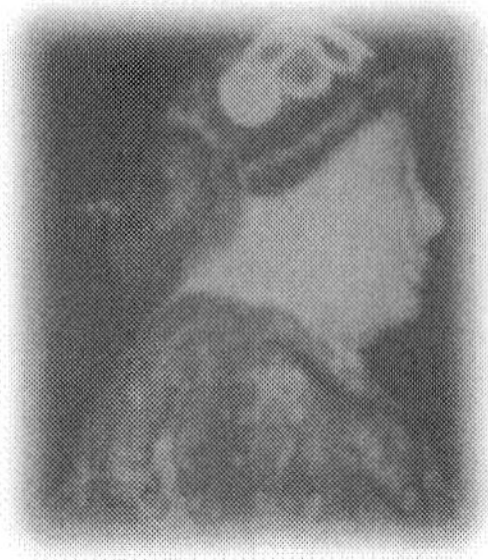

*Rochel Chiyena at a chasunah in Williamsburg*

R' Dovid Zussman and Rochel Chiena moved to Eretz Yisrael in 1962[12] and lived next door to HaRav Shlomo Zalman Auerbach, *z"l*, with whom R' Dovid spent many hours learning.[13] Rav Shlomo Zalman told Harav Yechiel Michel Stern, *shlit"a*, a nephew of Rabbi Stern, "We cannot fathom what a *lamed-vav tzaddik* is, but according to our limited understanding, he was one of them."

In addition, Rav Shlomo Zalman would come every Erev Yom Kippur to receive Rav Dovid's *berachah* until Rabbi Dr. Dovid Zussman was *niftar* on 10 Menachem Av, 5769/1969. Rochel Chiena was *niftera* 29 Menachem-Av 5731/1971. They are buried on Har HaZeisim.

[12] They had travelled to Morocco for their son's *chasunah.* Rochel Chiena said that if they visit Eretz Yisrael, she'll never leave. And that's what happened. R' Dovid went back himself to America to pack up the house.

[13] Another Baltimore connection should be noted. The Sterns were close with Rabbi Chaim Lauer and his family, who lived in the neighborhood. It was R' Chaim's mother, Miss Anna Siegel (later married to Yaakov Lauer), who was the chairman of the Entertainment Committee at Rae Mechanic's Adath meeting mentioned above. Besides this connection, recall that Yaakov Lauer's sister Tillie was a *machateneste* with Rochel Chiena, since Tillie's son R' Avrohom Gross had married Rochel Chiena's daughter Channah Leah.

פ"נ צדיק תמים גדול בתורה וביראה האציל מרוחו הטהורה על אלפי תלמידיו עושה חסד כל ימיו ורבים השיב מעוון הרה"ג ר דוד זוסמן בן הרה"צ ר יוסף שטרן זצ"ל נלב"ע י' מנחם אב תשכ"ט תנצב"ה

פ"נ האשה המהוללה ביראת שמים ובפרי [ידיה] אשת חיל עטרת בעלה ותפארת בניה פעלה חסד וצדק לעני ולאביון פרשה כפיה לבה מלא חכמה ואהבה להדריך במסורת אוהביה זכרה לא ישכח מלב מכיריה וצאצאיה הרבנית הצ' מרת רחל חיענה ע"ה בת ר' ישראל שמעון ז"ל אלמנת הגה"צ ר' דוד זוסמן שטרן זצ"ל נלב"ע כ"ט אב תשל"א תנצב"ה

Letter from Rav Shmuel Pliskin to Rebbetzin Gross upon the petirah of her mother, describing her family.

PHONE. ORLEANS 5-8372

שמואל פליסקין
רב לעדת „בני ישראל", באלטימאר

**Rabbi Samuel Pliskin**
B'NAI ISRAEL CONGREGATION
BALTIMORE, MARYLAND

RESIDENCE:
2204 E. FAIRMOUNT AVE.
BALTIMORE, MD. 21231

בע"ה

יום ב' לסדר: "אנכי (קודשא בריך הוא מדבר מתוך גרונו של ישעי' נביאנו)
אנכי הוא מנחמכם"... ה'תשל"א

חנה לאה תחי',
רבנית כבודה:

גדול הכאב ורב הצער, בשמענו שאת, בקונת "שבעה דנחמתא", נתבשרת בבשורה: —

"עניה סוערה, לא נחמה"!...

ברם, חיי אמך-מורתך היא שרשרת ארוכה, בל נותקה, של מעשים כבירים באירגון צעירי (וצעירות) בני(ות) ישראל לקרבן למקום.

להוי ידוע לך, עוד בשנת עטר"ת, ביום שכבה נרו וחוסרה ע ט ר ת ראש המשפחה (אבית הירא וחרד, מרביץ תורה ונכבד בקהלתנו, רבי ישראל שמעון זצ"ל — שנפטר ביום ח"י לחודש שבט, בשנה ההיא), בתו הצעירה, המחוננת בשכל טוב ובינה יתירה ר ח ל ח י נ א.) אספה צעירים אחדים, לבית מדרשנו (בית הכנסת "בני ישראל", שאני הצעיר באלפי יהודא נקראתי לעמוד ולשרת לפני בני ישראל משנת תרפ"ט) ו... ארגנה את החברא "עדת בני ישראל" — דוגמת "ישראל הצעיר" שאביכם ורבן של אלפי ישראל הגאון וצדיק רד"ז זצ"ל יסד ונהג יותר מיובל בשנים!

זכיתי להתארח בבית הורין, ביחד עם ראש ישיבת ראדין הגאון רמ"מ זאקס שליט"א; כמו כן, זכיתי שאמך-מורתך ביקרה את ביתנו, בעידן ביקורי' המבודיים שלה בבית החיים דקהילתנו. ומה נאמר, ומה נדבר? הרי אשה חכמה ובת-דעת בתורת השם, ובחכמה, במידות הרוממות, ובמעשים ענקיים הופיעה בכל ספסל הדרה בכל מבטה והגה קולה.

יחידה במינה היתה היא — ולא רק מטעם "אשת חבר", ובת גדולים וטובים (הרי בת אמה, הסבתא שלך, מרת אביטל ב"ר אברהם אבא זצ"ל, שמנוחתה-כבוד בארץ ישראל; והיא גם הקדישה ספר-תורה לבית הכנסת שלנו, כפי הידוע לך כל זאת), אלא, אמך היא "ביהוסת" גם ביחוס עצמה — שבאמת קיבלה פי-כמה וכמה מרוח הוריה ומוריה-מאוריה, לרבות גם אבא, שממנו שאבה רוח הקודש וחכמה.

ואני עומד וקורא: הסבא והסבתא, אבא, הדוד מר אברהם אבא, הדודה, צפורה חיה ז"ל — כולם חרותים על כותלי בית מדרשנו, אך על מעילו של ספר התורה — כולם להיים הר... בחיי עולם הבא, שאין לנו שום מושג וידיעה על הזיו והזוהר שהמה מתענגים, הרי ... זכרה לברכה נתקבלה בתוך מעגל-מעונם בעולם החיים הנצחיים!

כן, תתנחמי, את, בתה היחידה; ביחד עם בעלך ידידי וידיד מאות-מאות רבנים בישראל, שהוא מכהן במטארה בתור מנהיגם, הרב ר' אברהם שליט"א, ואחיך, האדיב ויקר ישראל שמעון נ"י, ביחד עם הדוד זאב גבריאל חיים יחי', במיאמי, פלא. — כולכם הזכו לנחמה, בתוך כל בית ישראל, ויקויים בכם, ובנו-כולנו: — (ספה ...הפטרת השבוע)

"כי ניחם השם עמו, גאל ישראל"!

המוהב בצ... ... תנחמה, ובידידות,
שמואל פלי... באלטימאר

נ. ב. הכתיבה הנכונה היא: "ח י נ א" — לשון חן, או חנה — בארמית. אמי, ז"ל, יכתי', תחי', נקראו בשם זה.
(עיין בספרו של הפוסק המקובל, ...
על "משמרת שלום", —מי האיש החפץ חיים, אוהב ימים לראות טוב?
אבן העזר, שמות נשים נצור לשונך מרע, ושפתיך מדבר מרמה; סור מרע ועשה טוב, בקש שלום ורדפהו!
(תהלים ל"ד)

*This letter to his daughter and to his son-in-law, Reb Avrohom Gross, was written on November 9, 1968, less than one year before his passing. He is confined to a wheelchair and has been deprived of his physical independence, yet he remains the same content, cheerful, uncomplaining individual he always was.*

בס"ד מוצש"ק וירא תשכ"ט, ירושלים

Dearest Chana Leah תחי' with all your Dears יחי',

Yesterday, Friday, we got two letters from you, one from ב' נח and one from ב' וירא. The ב' נח letter must have been mislaid somewhere before it came here, so no comment on ancient history. The ב' וירא letter seemed to tell us, unintentionally, that you had a sort of a cold. I hope I am mistaken in my conclusions, and you are well by this time, if you had a cold.

I am also concerned about your worry about the morning minyan in your shul. That AM minyan problems is ever-present in all Y.I. shuls, where the majority is made up of youngsters. Down in NY East Side my old Y.I. always had trouble with the AM minyan. Young boys sleep well, have no worries, so have difficulty to get up early. Again, young married men tend to be awakened at night by babies crying, so they make it up in the morning. Only middle-aged and older people come to morning minyanim. So it was in Y.I. of College Avenue in the Bronx.

In order to make young people come, you have to give them inspiration, and even then, *yeracheim Hashem*. I have no sefarim from which to select *ma'amarim* of inspiration for *tefillah b'tzibur*. I am sure R' Avrohom has such *ma'amarim* from *sefarim* and probably has used them already with limited

**Reprinted from "Rabbi Stern Speaks"**

success. I'll just jot down some *ma'amarim* from memory, and if you or R' Avrohom can make use of them, you are welcome. Maybe they will serve as a *zchus* for me, who cannot go to shul to daven *b'tzibur*.

In *Brachos:* בזמן שהקב"ה בא לביהכ"נ ולא מצא בה עשרה מיד הוא כועס
שנא' מדוע באתי ואין איש

Also there: אין הקב"ה מואס בתפלתן של רבים שנא' הן קל כביר ולא ימיר
In Pirkei Avos: אל תפרוש מן הציבור
In *Avodah Zara*: צבור נפיש זכותי

I heard from Mr. Philip Block ע"ה a nice story; whether true or not, I don't know, but the *mussar* is a good one. Once, at a chasunah, it was noticed how Rabbi Akiva Eiger zt"l was watching the band play their music. After he went away, one of his *talmidim* asked him, "Rebbi, what were you watching?" The Rabbi answered, "Here I have seen a *mussar* of the importance of *tefillah b'tzibur*. I saw how now and then the violin player removed his baton from the violin. That means that his playing temporarily ceased. Yet, the music played on, and no one could feel the lack of the violinist's music. But, had he been playing singly, the moment he'd have paused everyone would have noticed and felt it. The same is true in tefillah. Tefillah b'tzibur is like a Divine orchestra; our minds are the instruments and our thought (kavanah) is the baton. It is almost impossible to have perfect kavanah, but when one person misses kavanah in one bracha, it is quite possible that the rest of the tzibur is having kavanah and the "Divine music" goes up to *Hashem Yisborach* and it is considered as a perfect *tefillah* even for the one who missed kavanah.

Your R' Avrohom 'יחי, who is a real *darshan*, can surely

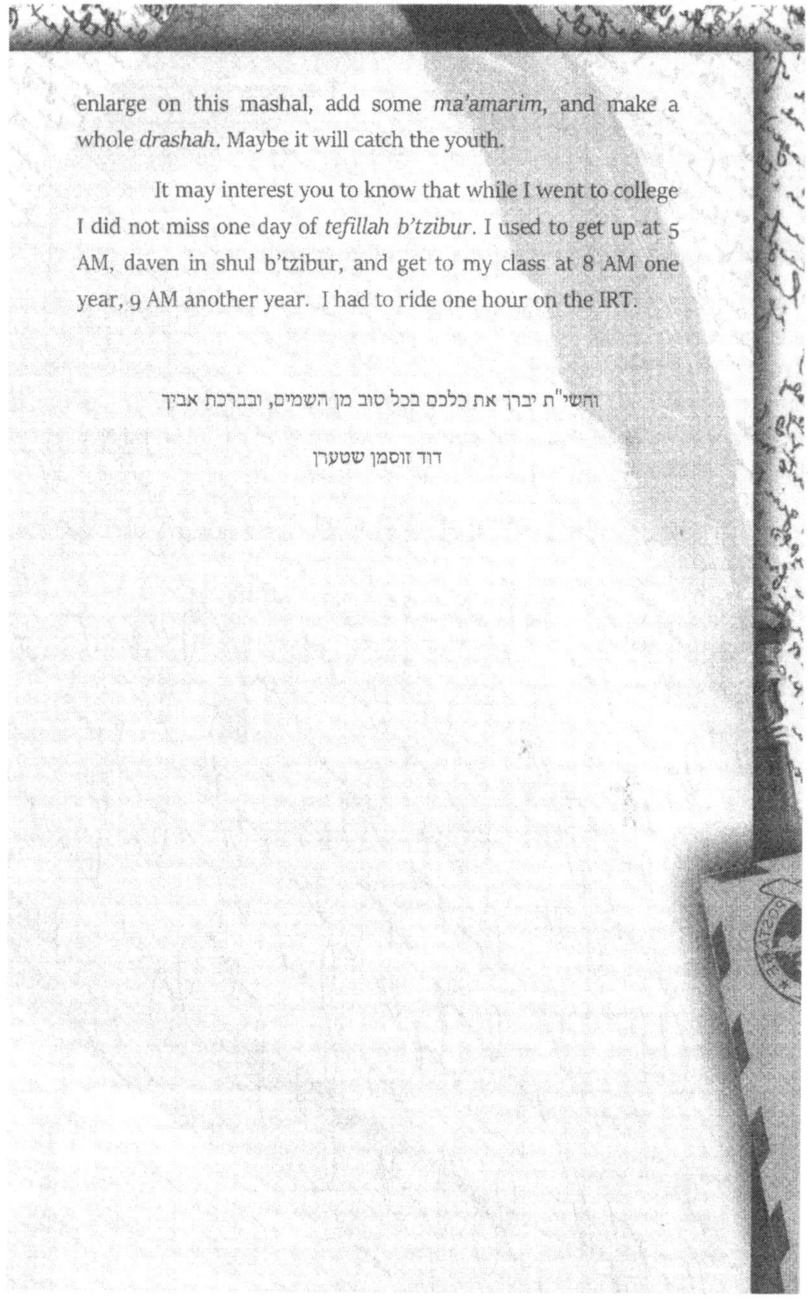

enlarge on this mashal, add some *ma'amarim*, and make a whole *drashah*. Maybe it will catch the youth.

It may interest you to know that while I went to college I did not miss one day of *tefillah b'tzibur*. I used to get up at 5 AM, daven in shul b'tzibur, and get to my class at 8 AM one year, 9 AM another year. I had to ride one hour on the IRT.

והשי"ת יברך את כלכם בכל טוב מן השמים, ובברכת אביך

דוד זוסמן שטערן

1

January 21, 1920. Rosh Chodesh Shevat

The regular meeting of the Adath Bnei Israel was called to order at 9 P.M. by the president Miss Rae Mechanic.
The 104th Psalm of David of was read by the Secretary. The minutes of the previous meeting were read and approved.

Miss Mechanic, chairman of the Lecture committee reported the following speakers for the next four weeks:-

January 23: Rabbi Rabinowich
" 30: " Rirkin
February 6: Mr. Abromowitz
" 13: " Altking

A motion was made and seconded that the report of the Lecture's committee be accepted minus Rabbi Rirkin unless he consents to deliver his lecture at the Parochial School instead of the Eden Street Synagogue. The motion was carried.

Mr. Caplan, chairman of the Library Committee reported that four (4) more books were bought for $1.75.

Miss Anna Seigel chairman of the entertainment committee reported

Adas Minutes, Rosh Chodesh Shevat, 1920

# The Early Adath Bnei Israel: A Postscript

After completing the previous memoriam, I received an email from the Jewish Museum of Maryland containing images of the Adath minutes book from 1920. I had already seen the first three pages, and I had requested the next few pages several months earlier. The museum kindly sent images of the first 58 pages (!), from which we can learn much about the Adath's activities in its first years of creation. These pages cover meetings from January 21/Rosh Chodesh Shevat, 1920 through the Yomim Noraim that year.

First, a general overview of the organization at that time, which can be culled from the minutes. I will center on the Mechanic family and the role of my grandfather Morris (Yosef Moshe) Siegel with three of his sisters, and my grandmother Miriam Friedberg (see next memoriam about the Friedbergs) with one of her cousins; but there is much, much more activity recorded in these pages. These meetings were not merely sporadic formalities. They were held every single week on Wednesday evenings, for about two hours. There were meetings on Wednesday three days before Pesach, Wednesday Chol HaMoed Pesach, and the Wednesday after Pesach. The meetings were an opportunity for these idealistic young men and women to share *Divrei Torah* and discuss topics of Jewish content, in addition to making plans to further Jewish observance in the community.

Here are highlights from several meetings in the first few months:

> ***1/21, Rosh Chodesh Shevat:*** *Read above, p. 206. (Just to note that Miss Anna Seigel was Morris Siegel's sister, the future Mrs. Ann Lauer. Miss Sara Levi was first cousin of Miriam Friedberg, also the recording secretary of these minutes.)*
> ***2/3, 15 Shevat:*** *Called to order by Miss Rae Mechanic in the chair. Chapter VIII Deuteronomy was read by Miss Anna Seigel as part of the Entertainment Committee's programme. A brief explanation of Chamisha Asar B'Shevat was given by Miss Rae Mechanic.*

***2/18, 29 Shevat:*** *Called to order by Miss Rae Mechanic in the chair. The president read a Psalm of David. Miss Lena Seigel moved that the Library Committee be instructed to buy a library which can be purchased for $75. (Miss Lena Seigel was a sister of Morris Seigel, the future Mrs. Lena Sugarman.)*

***2/25, 8 Adar:*** *Called to order by the president Miss Rochel Chiene Mechanic. The "Thirteen Principles of Faith" was read by the secretary (Miss Anna Seigel). The Education committed reported that three (3) junior clubs had been organized; one for girls and two for boys. The committee is planning a Purim party for the three clubs to take place at the home of Miss Mechanic. Miss Rachael Chiene Mechanic read a clipping from the Tageblatt entitled "Straight from the Shoulder" by I. L. Brill. The "Laws Concerning Forbidden Food" was read by Miss Miriam Friedberg.*

***3/10, 20 Adar:*** *Called to order by the president Miss Rochel Chiene Mechanic. Miss Anna Seigel, chairman of the Entertainment Committee, reported that the Purim entertainment cost approximately $8.00. Mr. Maurice Seigel, chairman of the Laws of Israel Committee, reported that since Passover was approaching, the laws concerning that holiday will be read at the next few meetings.*

***3/17, 27 Adar:*** *Called to order by Vice President Mr. Leon Rivkin in the chair and eight (8) members present. Miss Celia Mechanic (Rochel Chiene's sister) read a paper entitled "The Book of the Prophets."*

***3/24, 5 Nissan:*** *Miss Anna Seigel reported that $50.00 was sent to the American Jewish Relief. Miss Lena Seigel read a paper on the "Sanhedrin." The Laws Concerning the Preparation of the Seder was read by S. Levi. Nominations for officers were opened, including Vice President: Miss Anna Seigel; Executive Committee: Misses Miriam Friedberg, Celia Mechanic, and Sara Levi.*

***4/7, 19 Nissan:*** *Nomination of Rose Seigel (the future Mrs. Rose Scherr) as corresponding secretary.*

This gives us a sense of the activities of these young men and women. I would just like to one last citation. In the June 2 meeting, "a motion was made, seconded, and passed that a bouquet of flowers be sent to Miss Friedberg's commencement." Yes, my future grandmother Miriam Siegel was just graduating high school.

# Possville to Baltimore: Abba Zvi Friedberg

## Rabbi Abba Zvi Naiman [1]

We live in our own private *daled amos.* By this I mean that we see what stands before us: our immediate families and our current home. But truth be told, this is but a footstep in a long trail of footsteps leading from wherever we live, across the ocean to one of many trails of footsteps in Europe or India or South America or Africa back to home, Eretz Yisrael before the Churban where the trail of our journey in *galus* began. We often cannot trace these footsteps all the way back to Eretz Yisrael, but with a little time, patience, research, and *hashgachah pratis,* we can discover the details of several steps in the trail – the shoe style, size, and its color, so to speak.

One such trail was that of R' Chaim Nissin ben Elchanan Luria and his wife Braina bas R' Zvi from Possville (Pasvalys), Lithuania. This couple's daughter born in 1847 was named Sarah Menucha, and it is this Sarah Menucha who married our trailblazer Kasriel Friedberg, born around 1847 to R' Moshe ben R' Avraham Abba and Pesha bas R' Shlomo.

Chaim Nissim Luria

Sarah Menucha Friedberg

[1] With many thanks to the Rebbetzin for her editing.

Now Kasriel was quite learned; his Machzorim show his notations to conform with *Minhag HaGra.* He loved to sign his signature in his *sefarim,* even writing it several times in his Orach Chaim.

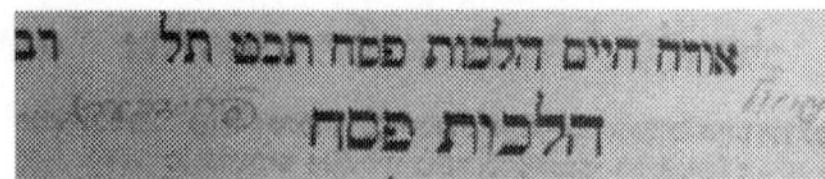


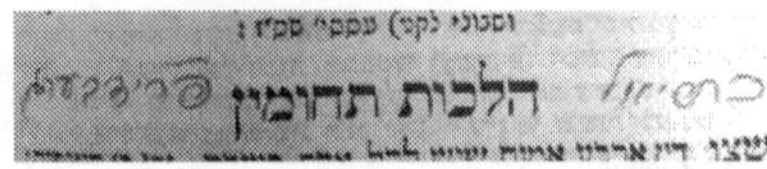


Kasriel and Sarah Menucha married in 1867 and sadly, but not uncommonly back then, they had a large family of which only three children survived – Shlomo, my namesake Abba Zvi,[2] and Moshe. And even sadder and also not uncommon then – Kasriel passed away from appendicitis when his son Abba Zvi was only five years old. But this couple had a third surviving child, Moshe! In other words, Sarah Menucha was pregnant with Moshe when her husband Kasriel died. She was left a widow with at least two children and one on the way; this is why Moshe's full name was Kasriel Moshe. Pause and ponder: how did Sarah Menucha manage? Presumably her parents, Chaim Nissin and Braina Luria helped, Sarah Menucha persevere.

The trail takes a sharp turn westward. The ship manifest shows that on 27 Elul, 5651 (9/30/1891), Abba Zvi and Moshe Friedberg arrived in Baltimore via traveling from their home in Possville to Bremen, Germany where they boarded the S.S. Stuttgart. Abba Zvi was 19 years old; Moshe was 13. The steerage quarters they paid for provided them with little more than the conditions for shipping cattle

across the ocean: hundreds of passengers in one large room, almost no privacy, poor food, inadequate sanitary conditions. This particular passage held 762 passengers in steerage alone.

[2] It is interesting note that the Lithuanian birth records call him Abelle Hirsch (Hirsch being Yiddish for *Zvi,* deer). HaRav Rottenberg, *shlit"a,* would also call me "Abba Hirsch" at times.

Abba Zvi and Moshe arrived in Baltimore a few days before Rosh Hashanah with all their belongings in one suitcase, having left their family and a town where more than half the residents were Jews, a Torah-true town boasting scholars such as R' Abele Possviller, who was the Rav from 1802 until 1832 when he left to become the Rav of Vilna.[3] But why did Abba Zvi and Moshe leave?

Perhaps they left for a reason we can so sadly recognize throughout our history: to flee antisemitism. At that time there were official government policies against Jews that intensified after the assassination of Tsar Alexander II on March 13, 1881. Again, hauntingly familiar, the Tsar's assassination was blamed on the Jews. Pogroms were rampant from April 27, 1881 until 1884. Abba Zvi and Moshe may have been two of the thousands of Jews fleeing these pogroms, many emigrating to the USA or South Africa.

And now the trail surprisingly strengthens. Devoid of their home community and immediate family, Abba Zvi and Moshe meet up with their mother's brother, Uncle Koppel Luria, who had arrived two years earlier at an even younger age than that of Abba Zvi. By 1894, Abba Zvi had earned enough money to pay for the passage of his mother, Sarah Menucha and her father, Chaim Nissim, to join the family in Baltimore. [Braina had already passed away in 1887.]

How was he able to earn this money? Shabbos observance was one of the greatest challenges for the immigrants at that time. There was no five-day week or flex-hours like nowadays. Many men had to find a new job every Monday after being fired for not showing on Shabbos. In order to be able properly observe Shabbos, Abba Zvi became a manufacturer of lounges and upholstery in his furniture factory so he could choose his own hours and days to work.

[3] Family tradition tells us that Abba Zvi was named after R' Abbele, but we have not yet confirmed the exact relationship. This is a subject for further research.

Abba Zvi marries Pessa (Bessie) Goldberg in 1900. She had arrived

in Baltimore in 1888 with her family from Upyna, Lithuania by way of Cyprus, Turkey, Egypt, France, and England.[4] Abba Zvi and Pessa begin their married life in Fells Point where most East-European Jews lived at that time. And by 1901 Abba Zvi, Moshe, and their Uncle Koppel have joined together to create the Friedberg Bros and Lewis company, manufacturing upholstery.

Shabbos observance has been preserved in this family. But the challenges are far from over.

On the third of Shevat, 1908, Abba Zvi's grandfather Chaim Nissin perished in a fire in his home. Just two years later on the twenty-first of Adar-I of 1910, Abba Zvi and his wife Pessa lost their oldest son Shlomo Kasriel to scarlet fever when the boy was only nine years old. His playmate and cousin Rivka Goldberg died soon after from the same illness. Abba Zvi was a different man now. Losing his first-born son changed him, causing his livelihood to suffer.

Abba Zvi Friedberg will live to see his daughter Miriam marry Yosef Moshe Siegel in 1926. Yosef Moshe Siegel will become the father of three children and save countless children from missionaries by helping to form the Adas; later, he will be instrumental in inspiring a generation of American young men in Torah study, including HaRav Mordechai Gifter, *z"l,* HaRav Avigdor Miller, *z"l,* and later להבחל"ח, the Rosh HaYeshivah, HaRav Aharon Feldman, *shlit"a.*[5]

---

[4] This family's arrival deserves a story of its own.

[5] See previous article about the early days of the Adath. Miriam, too, had joined the organization close to its start (see Adath Postcript above).

Abba Zvi will live to see his son Moshe Leib marry Simma Kirshenblatt, but they will be childless. Abba Zvi will also live to see his daughter Nessa marry Ber Leib (Ben) Pernikoff, who will have three daughters. Abba Zvi will see the beginnings of many *Torahdik* homes in America.

Before Abba Zvi's *petirah* on the third of Shevat, 5710/1950, the same day as that of his grandfather Chaim Nissin's *petirah,* he will lose his wife Pessa in 1936 when she was in her early 60's; and a few months later, his mother Sarah Menucha on the 27th of Teves. He will move into his daughter Miriam's home until he passes away in 1950 – 14 years a widower. The last years of his life are a testament to his *chashivus* because he continued to walk in his path as a Torah Jew.

So much *hisorerus* we gain by tracing our family's footsteps! We are supposed to look to our forefathers for strength and direction in life. R' Kasriel's family, and the descendant we have followed in Abba Zvi Friedberg, blazed a trail of commitment to Torah that continued to burn no matter the challenges sent their way. The *mesiras nefesh* of R' Chaim Nissin, Sarah Menucha, R' Kasriel, Abba Zvi Friedberg should be a *zechus* for all of their descendants.

**Addendum: Shuls Near Abba Zvi Friedberg's Homes**

This is an opportunity to learn about some of the shuls that were in Baltimore a century ago, where Abba Zvi *davened.*

**Mikro Kodesh Congregation**

There were Jews in Baltimore who arrived from Pokroy (today, Pakruojis), Lithuania. Rabbi Shmuel Eliezer Horowitz was one of the founders in 1886. He had arrived from Yaniskel (Joniškėlis), Lithuania, which was less than 10 miles away from Possville, so it is likely that Abba Zvi would be comfortable in his shul. The congregation dedicated a remodeled residence at 19 South High Street on 9/2/1888. In 1892, they signed a contract to erect a new building there for $21,016, plus $500 additional "for not working on Saturdays." Mayor Charles Latrobe assisted in the dedication of Mikro Kodesh's new, ornate synagogue in March 1893 and performed the ceremony of opening its doors.

**Anshe Emunah Congregation, Tavriger Shul**

The shul was chartered in 1887 by immigrants from Tauragė, Lithuania, with services held over a Chinese laundry at 313 South Hanover. It moved to 513 Hanover Street in 1893.

Rabbi Zev Volf Samuelson was the Rabbi 1898-1899. He was from Kovno Province and he served as a rabbi in various Russian cities and in Baltimore. R' Samuelsohn was the father-in-law of Rabbi Zvi Hirsch Berman of the Adath Yeshurun Shadover shul on Exeter and Pratt among other shuls in Baltimore. R' Jacob Even Frommer Halevi was another son-in-law, a Rabbi in New Haven. This is the *shaar blatt* of Rabbi Samuelson's *sefer* on *Shir HaShirim*:

שיר השירים

חבצלת השרון

Rabbi Reuven Rivkin arrived in Baltimore in 1914, and was Rabbi of the Tavriger shul until 1919. He was known as a *masmid* and an *illuy* in the Kovno Yeshiva. As a young Rov in Kovno, he was sent throughout Europe and The United States to raise funds for the Kovno Yeshiva. He was a contributor to the *Sefer Otzar Yisrael*, authoring articles on *mayim acharonim, milvos,* and *shuluach hakan.* After leaving Anshe Emunah he became Rabbi of Aitz Chaim Congregation (see below for further details).

R' Yechiel Shoham was the Rabbi in 1929. He had learned in the Slobodka Yeshiva. He was married to the daughter of Rabbi Yosef Marcus of the Mishkan Israel Congregation, and took over his position in 1932 when his father-in-law, R' Marcus, died while laying tefillin as he was visiting relatives in N.J.

R' Noach Kahn, a *musmach* of Rav Boruch Ber Leibovitz, became Rabbi in 1935. His father-in-law, R' Dovid Mordechai Yudovsky, was the main Rabbi in Drohicyn, Poland. R' Noach replaced his father-in-law after his death, until 1929, when he and his family moved to the United States. This picture is his wife Esther at her father's *matzeivah* in Drohicyn. (R' Noach was father-in-law of Rabbi Simchah Shafran of Adath Yeshurun.)

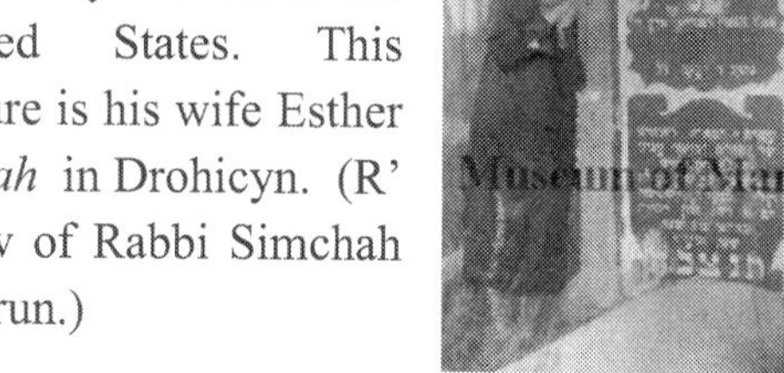

Rabbi Yehoshua Leib Schenker was the Rabbi there in 1943, when he became a Rebbi at Ner Yisrael. His mother, Lea Genendel, was the daughter of R' Yosef Chaim Sonnenfeld. He was learning in the Chevron Yeshiva and was miraculously saved from the pogrom there in 1929. One of his daughters was Chana Caplan/Gelernter, my kindergarten teacher at Yeshivas Chofetz Chaim/ Talmudical Academy. Another daughter, Rachel, married Steven Hill in 1967, and they would visit Rabbi Schenker on Jonquil Avenue.

In 1955, Anshe Emunah was merged with Liberty Jewish Center, forming Anshe Emunah, Liberty Jewish Center. This was then merged in June 1961 with Aitz Chaim Congregation (see below) to form Anshe Emunah-Aitz Chaim, Liberty Jewish Center.

**Aitz Chaim, the Eden Street Shul**

The Aitz Chaim Congregation was founded in 1887. They began davening at 16-18 North Exeter Street, the former home of Chizuk Amuno Congregation, until 1902. In 1902, they moved 50 15-21 South Eden Street, which was the former home of the Oheb Israel Congregation since 1848. Rabbi Reuven Rivkin was Rabbi from 1919 after he left the Tavriger shul until his *petirah* in 1950.

In June, 1961, Aitz Chaim merged with Anshe Emunah, Liberty Jewish Center, as stated above.

**Aitz Chaim Rabbi's Funeral Being Held**

Funeral services are being held late today for Reuben Rivkin, 79, rabbi emeritus of Aitz Chaim Synagogue, who died at Sinai Hospital yesterday after a three-months illness.

The services are being held from the synagogue, in the first block South Eden street, which the rabbi had served from 1919 until his death. Burial was to be in the synagogue cemetery at Lansdowne, Maryland.

Rabbi Rivkin, who was the dean of the orthodox rabbis here, immigrated to this country from Kovno, Lithuania, in 1906 and was naturalized a citizen ten years later.

He came to Baltimore in 1914 to serve the Anshe Amuno congregation on South Hanover street and later transferred to Aitz Chaim.

He is survived by his wife, Mrs. Lena Rivkin; six sons and ten grandchildren. Rabbi Rivkin lived at 1809 East Baltimore street.

**Ohr Knesseth Israel Congregation, Franklin Street Shul**

About 1908, the Knesseth Israel Congregation was listed at Franklin and Abel Streets. About 1929, its name had become Ohr Knesseth Israel.

Rabbi Moshe Marcus was the Rabbi from 1925 until 1930, when he died on the day of his nephew's wedding, the son of his brother Rabbi Yosef Marcus (see above).

**Rabbi Morris Marcus Dies Just Before Nephew's Wedding**

Leading Talmudical Scholar's Demise Not Announced Until After Ceremony Uniting Namesake And Miss Ida Hudies Takes Place

Rabbi Yosef Feldman, father of the Rosh HaYeshiva, Rav Aharon Feldman, *shlit"a,* was Rabbi 1939-1946. He had moved from Manchester, New Hampshire so his sons could attend a Hebrew day school. He knew Rabbi Chaim Samson of the Hebrew Parochial School (later called Talmudical Academy) from Lomza.

On November 19, 1950, Ohr Knesseth merged with Anshe Sphard Congregation (1887) to form the Ohr Knesseth Israel-Anshe Sphard Congregation, Rogers Avenue Synagogue.

Abba Zvi Friedberg later in life

# *Nega Tzaraas*

## Rabbi Yitzchak Friedman [1]

During the discussion of the sacrificial order, the Torah introduces us to the world of *tzaraas* (commonly translated as leprosy). What is the Torah trying to teach us with this apparently random continuum? Also, what is the nature of *tzaraas* that a metaphysical intervention is prescribed and not a medical one?

The *Nesivos Shalom* (*Tazria,* בענין הנגעים) explains the nature of *tzaraas,* via the definition of the *Targum Onkelos*. *Onkelos* translates נגע צרעת as מכתש סגירו, a disease of being confined. What exactly is meant by being confined? The *Nesivos Shalom* explains that the sin of *lashon hara,* the cause of *tzaraas,* imprisons one's spiritual self. Spiritual light and metaphysical goodness become inaccessible. One's heart becomes closed to spiritual messages. It becomes hard to be inspired by the presence of Hashem. So much so that the leper must be brought to the Kohen as he is impervious to his own spiritual shortcomings. This state is referred to by *David HaMelech* when he prays הוציאה ממסגר נפשי.

How does this work? If I come bright and early to shul, with the intention to learn and then *daven*, how does slandering a friend over the pre-learning latte impugn the power of my Torah and *tefillah*? Admittedly, the slandering of my friend does not find favor in Hashem's eyes, but logically we would apply the dictum of the *Yerushalmi,* אין עבירה מכבה מצוה! Though the *lashon hara* one speaks is abhorrent, how does it detract from the fact that the *davening* might have been inspirational and uplifting?

The *Nesivos Shalom* gives an analogy to a superficial skin infection, whose cure is the application of topical creams and the use of

[1] לע"נ א"מ ר' צבי בר' יוסף משה זצ"ל

antibiotics. However, if the infection goes septic, these superficial cures won't help. The Kohen must be brought in to assess and decide the nature of the affliction. If it is skin-deep, routine dermatological care is in order. However, the infection might have penetrated עמוק מעור הבשר, got into the bloodstream and caused the patient to become toxic. At that point, says the *Zohar HaKadosh,* the only antidote is developing a relationship with the Kohen. To attach oneself as closely as the poles were attached to the Holy Ark. The Kohen can save the sinner from the clutches of his personal evil and reconnect him to Hashem. This is the way for the Divine light to reach the afflicted individual. Much like being hooked up to a dialysis machine, the Kohen can cleanse the most toxic of bloods.

Fully understanding the *Zohar* that is quoted by the *Nesivos Shalom* is above my pay grade. However, its comparison of the Kohen to the *Aron* (which houses the *luchos*) might indicate that the Kohen, functioning in his role as teacher of Torah, is what opens the heart of the slanderer! *Shevet Levi* is tasked by Moshe, יורו משפטך ליעקב ותורתך לישראל. Learning Torah with a Kohen cleanses and frees the soul to pursue its higher ideals. This is what the slanderer needs to embrace, serious *limud HaTorah*! But how does *limud HaTorah* free the soul from its state of confinement?

The *Nesivos Shalom* explains that the soul of the slanderer is so perverted that it wants to destroy people's reputations.[2] Hence, any independent Torah that he learns becomes a vessel to be used to destroy others. One's soul must escape the clutches of this evil to

---

[2]The simple understanding is that the Kohen's attribute to pursue interpersonal harmony will influence the slanderer to not rip society apart with his talebearing.

Rav Leib Gurewitz, the Rosh Yeshiva of Gateshead Yeshiva, asked a question on the verse, אין יתרון לבעל הלשון. Is there no gratification derived from slandering others? He answered that there is nothing positively added through slander, just reputations destroyed. In other words, there is no happiness from accomplishment through tearing someone else down, just dancing on the grave of your friend's good name.

have his mitzvos accomplish positive results, as opposed to further the cause of evil. Why does that change if the sinner becomes attached to the Kohen?

The Torah is about building. The Kohen is the ultimate person of *chesed;* Aharon was the ultimate אוהב את הבריאות, builder of people, not a destroyer. עולם חסד יבנה. The Gemara (*Berachos* 64a) states that Torah scholars are builders. It is the positive, benevolent, and constructive aspects of Torah that the Kohen imparts to the *metzora.* If he is willing to cleave to the Kohen, he will be able to change his destructiveness into building, nurturing and supporting other people.

I should add that the *Chasam Sofer* (*Derashos* 407:4) says that the Kohen, following his majestic and critical *avodas Yom HaKippurim*, removes his priestly garments. The *pasuk* tells us that he left them in a holy place and proceeded to sacrifice his fire offering and that of the people. The *Chasam Sofer* explains homiletically, that even after the *avodah* he needed to go to the *makom kadosh,* the Bais HaMedrash. It is there where he ultimately raises the level of the Jewish people through the Torah that he teaches עולתו ואת עולת העם. The *Navi* tells us that it is not the Kohen's main job to bring sacrifices but rather כי שפתי כהן ישמרו דעת, תורה יבקש מפיהו.

My father, Dr. Erwin Friedman, was a psychologist in both Lakewood, NJ, Silver Spring, MD and Kew Gardens, NY. In Lakewood, he was friendly with Rav Aharon Kotler *zt"l* who referred *bachurim* to his private practice. Rebbetzin Rischel Kotler *z"l* once told me that her father-in-law loved my father despite his being a psychologist. It was because he was a "*klugeh mentsch,"* a sharp person. Perhaps Rav Aharon was referring to his unwavering belief in people and his ability to guide them in becoming productive and successful people, spouses, parents and children.

*Yehi Zichro Baruch.*

# Once a *Yid,* Always a *Yid*

## Moshe Arie Michelsohn

My father, Eliyahu ben Moshe Leib, *z"l,* liked to tell the following joke —my personal favorite, as it is really a very deep joke.

There was a *Yid* who was once approached by a *galach* who came knocking at the *Yid's* door demanding that he either convert to Christianity or face death. The *Yid* asked what was involved in converting. The *galach* explained that he would come to the *Yid's* house to give him lessons for several weeks and once he understood the lessons he would then be converted. The *Yid* figured he could at least stay alive for the lessons, so he agreed.

The *galach* came the next week for the first lesson. He said to the *Yid,* remember: on Fridays, you only eat fish, no meat. Remember: only fish, no meat. The *Yid* said fine, Fridays only fish, no meat. The next week the *galach* came again and reviewed the lesson: Remember, on Fridays, only fish, no meat. This went on for several more weeks, at which point, the *galach* was satisfied that the *Yid* had learned his lessons and it was time to convert. The *galach* asked the *Yid* if he was ready, upon which the *Yid* said, yes, I remember, on Fridays, only fish, no meat.

The *galach* said, so now you can become a Christian: First you were a Jew, now you are a Christian! First you were a Jew, now you are a Christian! First you were a Jew, now you are a Christian!

The next week, the *galach* came to the *Yid's* house on Friday night to check to make sure the *Yid* was being a good Christian. The *Yid* opened the door, and the *galach* saw that the *Yid* had Shabbos candles lit on the dining table, and at the center of the table there was a big roast beef. The *galach*, astonished, said to the *Yid*, how could you do this! It is Friday –did I not teach you that on Fridays, only fish, no meat? How could you have a roast beef on the table?

The *Yid* said to the *galach*: It's not a roast beef, it's a fish!

The *galach* said to the *Yid*: What, are you crazy? It's a roast beef!

The *Yid* answered: No, it's a fish: I said, first you were a roast beef, now you're a fish! First you were a roast beef, now you're a fish! First you were a roast beef, now you're a fish! 🕯

# CONSOLIDATED TABLE OF CONTENTS 5772-5781

**Compiled by Yehoshua Dixler**

# Consolidated Table of Contents

## PREPARING FOR PESACH

## THE *AVOS* AND *GALUS MITZRAYIM*

Made in the USA
Middletown, DE
12 March 2022

62440900R00222

In Loving Memory of our Dear Grandparents

***Yitzchak ben Mordechai Yehudah***
Mr. Herb Prager

***Avraham Chanoch ben Tuvyah Elazar***
Mr. Avraham Krakauer

***Rachel Leah bas Tzvi Dovid***
Mrs. Rita B. Shames

***Ozer ben Yisrael***
Mr. Oscar Shames

by **Eliezer and Bracha Shames**

---

לעילוי נשמת

**ר' נפתלי בן נחום גרשון הכהן** ז"ל

**שרה רבקה בת יהודה אריה ליב** ע"ה

by

**the Raczkowski Family**

לעילוי נשמת

**אהרן ישראל בן אריה ליב** ע"ה

**הרב חיים אריה בן יצחק אליעזר** ז"ל

**מלכה בת קהת הלוי** ע"ה

**נפתלי מאיר בן הרב חיים אריה** ע"ה

by

**Eli and Janice Friedman**

and Family

---

לעילוי נשמת

**הרב יעקב יצחק בן שמואל יהודה** ז"ל

**הענא רחל בת בנימין חיים** ע"ה

מאת

**משפחת ריינר**

# לזכר נשמתם

לזכר נשמת

**יעקב בן דוד הלוי**, ע"ה

**Wiesel**

תנצב"ה

לעילוי נשמת

**ר' חיים דוד הירש ב"ר גדליה יוסף** ז"ל

**סילברמן**

מאת

משפחת מענשעל

In Memory of

**Shlomo (Manfried) Strauss**

**שלמה בן שמואל** ע"ה

תנצב"ה

With Gratitude to Hashem for bringing me back to my family, and gratitude to all those that davened for me

**Yitzchak Yochanan ben Sarah**

In Honor of
Rabbi and Rebbetzin Naiman

by

**Dani and Ora Zuckerbrod**

---

Best wishes to
Rabbi Yitzchak Friedman
for many years of good health

by

**the Raczkowski Family**

In Honor and Appreciation of
Rabbi and Rebbetzin Naiman
for all they do for the Bais Medrash
and the entire kehillah

by

**Eli and Janice Friedman**
and Family

---

In Honor of our esteemed Gabbai,
Shamash, Treasurer, and Secretary
Eli Friedman

by

**Anonymous**

# In Appreciation of the Rav and the Rebbetzin

by

**the Solomons**

In Honor of
the Rav & Rebbetzin

by

**the Singmans**

With Gratitude

to

Rabbi and Rebbetzin Naiman

and the

Bais Medrash of Ranchleigh

by

**Moshe Arie Michelsohn**

In Honor of the

Rav, Gabba'im,

and Kiddush Committee

for their tireless efforts

at BMR

by

**the Sugars**

In honor of
the Rav and the Rebbetzin

by

**Mr. and Mrs. Ari Weiss**

In Appreciation of
Rabbi and Rebbetzin Naiman
for welcoming us so warmly to
the community

by

**Bonnie and Yitz Szyf**
**and family**

In Honor of the

Zichron Yaakov Eliyahu

Kollel

by

**the Kimelfelds**

In Gratitude

to

Hashem Yisborach

by

**the Silverbergs**

In Honor of our Dear Mother,

**Deborah Naiman**

Thank you for all that you have done and continue to do for us.

Love,

**Irvin and Family**

# לעילוי נשמת

## **יעקב אליהו** בן דוד ע״ה **ניימאן**

**י** ליד באלטימאר מעורב עם הבריה
**ע** וד בנערותו שימש גדולים בתורה
**ק** יים מצות בשדה מלחמה
**ב** אשת נעוריו שמח נ״א שנה

**א** ח נאמן עד דשבק חיים
**ל** אחר שנעשה ע״ז בשנים
**י** סורים סבל בסבר פנים
**ה** ניח אחריו בנים ובני בנים
**ו** כולם עוסקים בתורה וחסדים

נפטר בשם טוב ח׳ שבט תשס״ה לפ״ק

ת. נ. צ. ב. ה.

# *Dedications*

→

# מדור

# לשון הקודש

←

# תוכן הענינים

# ביאור עמוק ב"הא לחמא עניא"

## הגאון הרב נחום מאיר הלוי לנסקי [א]

כתב הגר"א ז"ל בביאור הא לחמא עניא:

פי' כי הה"א הוא מצה (והיינו כי ההבדל שבין מלת מצה למלת חמץ הוא ה"א) ועכשיו הוא עניא, כי כאשר חסר ממנה הוי"ו נעשית דל"ת והיא עניא. ולמה נקרא העני דלי"ת הוא לפי שד' מיני עניות יש. א' הוא מי שאין לו לאכול כמ"ש (דברים ח, ג) "ויענך וירעיבך". והב' הוא שיש לו לאכול אך אין לו כל צרכו וזהו נקרא אביון. כמ"ש (תהלים פו, א) "כי עני ואביון אני" כו'. והג' הוא עינוי דרך כמ"ש (שם קב, כד) "ענה בדרך כחי". והד' הוא עינוי שעבוד וכמ"ש (בראשית טו, ו) "ותענה שרה ותברח מפניה". וזהו מה שאמר כל הד' הנ"ל, דהיינו כל דכפין היינו עינוי רעבון, ייתי ויכול, כל דצריך הוא עינוי ב', שאין לו כל צרכו, ייתי ויטול צרכי פסח. הג' הוא עינוי הדרך, אמר השתא הכא, כלומר שכולנו עכשיו בדרך. ונגד הד' אמר השתא עבדי.

והענין שד' צריכין להודות, יורדי הים, והולכי מדברות, וחולה שנתרפא, ויוצא מבית האסורין. והן נגד הד' עינויים הנ"ל. עינוי רעבון נגד חולה ונתרפא כמ"ש (תהלים קז, יח) "כל אוכל תתעב נפשם" כו', (עינוי שעבוד נגד יוצא מבית האסורין) [עינוי דרך נגד יוצא לשיירא במדבר], עינוי אביון התאב ואינו משיג כל צרכו הוא נגד יורדי הים, שכל נחותי ימא לא מיתבא דעתייהו עד דנחתי ליבשתא, וענין לא מיתבא דעתייהו הוא כאדם התאב לדבר ואינו משיגו. ועינוי שעבוד הוא נגד יוצא מבית האסורין, והיא "בכור השפחה אשר אחר הרחיים" (שמות יא, ה), "בכור השבי אשר בבית

---

[א] שנת תש"פ. נכתב ע"י הרב אליהו מאיר ליפסקי.

> הבור" (שם יב, כט), והכל אחד. וכאשר היינו עבדים במצרים היינו בכל העינויים הנ"ל. וכאשר יצאנו משם יצאנו מכל אלו העינויים... אמר כאן הא לחמא עניא מחמת די אכלו אבהתנא בארעא דמצרים, ששם היו כל העינויים. ומפרש הד' עינויים שגאלנו השם מהם, וצריכים אנחנו להודות עליהם.

בפי' הא לחמא עניא כתב הגר"א ז"ל אריכות דברים, ולכאורה ר"ל שהוא בגדר הקדמה, שזהו שורש של ההגדה. וגם סוף של קידוש, ואז מוזגין לו כוס שני וכאן הבן שואל. נמצא שהוא האמצעי בין קידוש ומגיד. וכתב שהוא רמז לד' מיני עינויים וכו' וזה כנגד הד' צריכים להודות וכו', שבגלות מצרים היו בכל עינויים האלו, וכיון שיצאנו משם צריכים להודות. ולכאורה יש להעיר שבהא לחמא עניא לא אומרים אותו בדרך הודאה רק כל דצריך וכו' מזמינים העניים אבל לא בדרך הודאה שיש לנו הכל. אף שהגר"א ז"ל מפרש שאומרים ד' דברים כנגד הד' צריכים להודות, אבל לא מודים בפירוש לקב"ה. כשאומרים כל דכפין ייתי ויכול אין זה להגיד הודאה שלנו אלא אומרים זה בעבור אחר להזמינו לסעודתינו, ולמה זו הנקודה של ד' צריכים להודות. ונחזור לזה לקמן.

וכתב הגר"א ז"ל עוד:

> ...והיינו כמו שכתוב בהגדה לקמן, שאלו לא יצאנו הרי אנו ובנינו משועבדים היינו לפרעה במצרים, אבל עכשיו הגם שבב' דברים אנחנו שווין להם גם כן, שאנו בגולה בדרך, גם אנחנו עבדים, אבל עתה אנחנו מעותדים בכל עת להגאל, אשר מחכים אנחנו בכל יום. וזהו השתא הכא לשנה הבאה כו' השתא עבדי לשנה הבאה כו' אשר לא כן היה כאשר היינו במצרים, שאם לא היו נגאלים אבותינו ברגע זו, הרי אנו ובנינו משועבדים כו'.

ביצ״מ היה היציאה מכל מיני הד׳ עינויים, ואז צריכים להודות, שהיה הגאולה מזה באופן שכלל ישראל לא שייכים עוד בכלל לדברים אלו. ולכן אומרים לשנה הבאה וכו׳ ר״ל שביצ״מ נשרש זה ואומרים בבטחון גמור שנבא לירושלים. שעכשיו לא שייך לנו להגיע להיות נשאר בגלות אחרי שניתן לנו יצ״מ. אברהם אבינו שאל במה אדע כי אירשנה, הוא רצה לידע, בדעת, שהוא גילוי ברור שיהיה ירושת הארץ, והתשובה לזה היא ידוע תדע כי גר יהיה זרעך וכו׳ שיהי׳ יצ״מ ובזה הם מובטחים בירושת הארץ.

בחדש הראשון של ניסן מתחיל סיבוב השנה. פסח, שבועות, סוכות, שמ״ע, ואח״כ י״ז בתמוז וט׳ באב. עי׳ בדברי טור הידועים (סי׳ תכה) שסימן לקביעות המועדים א״ת ב״ש וכו׳, פירוש ביום א׳ של פסח יהיה לעולם ט׳ באב וסימן על מצות ומרורים יאכלוהו. נמצא שיש קשר בין פסח וט׳ באב. תיקון השנה הוא יצ״מ. הפגם ששייך לבא מיצ״מ נעשה בט׳ באב במרגלים וחורבן בית, והתיקון לזה הוא פסח. בפ׳ ציצית אומרים לא תתורו וכו׳ והוא כנגד המרגלים שהלכו לתור הארץ. במעשה המרגלים היה החורבן של דור יוצאי מצרים, וזאת היתה בט׳ באב. ואח״כ נאמר שם זכר ליצ״מ. התיקון הוא בזכירת יצ״מ, אף שהדור דיעה שיצאו ממצרים נגזר עליהם כל זה בעבור אי אמונה ובטחון שהיה להם, אעפ״כ התיקון לזה הוא הזכר ליצ״מ, ובפסח זוכים לאמונה ובטחון שצריכים.

הגר״א ז״ל ממשיך:

> ויש עוד עינוי ה׳ שהוא כלל כל הד׳ והוא עינוי הדעת [עי׳ נדרים אין עני אלא בדעת, סנהדרין ע׳ עץ שאכל אדה״ר חטה היה, תדע כו׳] וזהו עינוי נעלם. וזהו שאמר הא לחמא עניא, פי׳ שבה״א דברים הוא עניא, ואמר לחמא פי׳ לחם א׳, שעל ידי הא׳ הוא עניא. כי כאשר חסר מן הלחם א׳ אז היא חסרון דעה, אבל כאשר יהיה נשלם הא׳ יהיה מלאה הארץ דעה.

ידוע שגלות מצרים הוא גלות הדעת וגלות הדיבור. יש לאדם כח להודיע בהבריאה ידיעת ה׳, ודבר זה נתמעט בירידת מצרים. וביצ״מ היה גילוי של בחי׳ הדעת.

איתא בספר יצירה שהעולם נברא בג׳ ספרים, ספר ספר וסיפור. ופי׳ הגר״א ז״ל שהבריאה הוא בחי׳ ספר וסיפור, שהוא דיבור ע״י אותיות התורה. כמ״ש (דברים ח, ג) ״כי על כל מוצא פי ה׳ ״ וכו׳. משל לאדם, כשיש רצון הוא רק במוחו ואינו בגלוי, ויש ב׳ מיני אופנים לגלות מחשבתו, או שיכתוב בספר או שידבר. בכתיבת הספר שלב הראשון הוא שכותב האותיות, וזה בחי׳ חכמה, כח מ״ה. כ״ח, אותיות א״ב עם מנצפ״ך וא׳ שחוזר לראש. וזה כ״ח מ״ה. והוא גילוי הראשון שרבש״ע גילה בהבריאה, בחי׳ שהקב״ה א״ס. וזה גילוי שיש. והבנה של זה, לגלות עוד, צריך פירוט וציורים. בינה היא שלב השני, ספר שמצייר הדבר לפרטים מבין דבר מתוך דבר. זהו מ״ה ומ״י. מ״ה הוא מה שהוא, ומ״י הוא מפרט הדבר יותר, מי הוא. בחכמה, הכל אחד, אין האותיות ניכרים לעצמם. רק כשנעשה בפרטיות יש להבין הענין, ע״י שמפרט אותו לבחי׳ הגבול. וכן בהשגת האדם, לפעמים עוסק בדבר עד הגבולים של שכלו, ואז מבטל עצמו להאין, חכמה מאין. שאז אין השגה מצד עצמו, ויש לו גילוי מבחי׳ האין. יגעת ומצאת, אחרי היגיעה זוכה למצוא אותו אבל ניתן לו כמו מציאה. ואחר שמשיג התי׳ מבין דבר מתוך דבר ובא לדעת ומוציאו לפועל. והג׳ הוא דעת, ע״י הדעת מדבר לחוץ ממש. זה בחי׳ הדעת כשיש סיפור ויכול להיות סיפור של מחשבה ורצון בלא מדרגת כתיבת ספר. רק בחיבור ישיר למחשבתו שמדבר ומוציא מחשבתו. וכן היה ג׳ דברים אלו במתן תורה, בשני לוחות ועשרת הדברות ובזה היה כולל כל התורה כולה, גילוי של רצונו ומחשבתו לכלל ישראל.

וכותב שבבריאת העולם היה הבריאה ע״י ספר וספר. וזה גילוי של אות ב׳ של בראשית. איתא בחז״ל שכל האותיות באו לפני הקב״ה ואמר שיברא בו את העולם, ר״ל שכל אות הוא כלי לגלות הקב״ה, כלי שמגלה אור של קב״ה,

וכל אות רצה להיות תחילת הגילוי. והב׳ נבחר שהוא בחי׳ ברכה, וכולל בתוכו כל הבריאה. ואח״כ בא האות א׳ והקב״ה אמר להאות א׳ שלא יהי׳ יחודי אלא בך, ור״ל שיפתח מתן תורה באות א׳ של אנכי. שבאות א׳ הוא בחי׳ היחוד. דהיינו, בבריאת העולם, אף שמגלה חכמתו ובינתו כביכול בהבריאה, עדיין הוא שנים, ואע״פ שבב׳ יש ברכה, זוג, פרו ורבו, אבל הגילוי של פנימיות רצון ה׳ זהו בחי׳ א׳ של אנכי ורק בזה יש גילוי רצונו ומחשבתו. למשל כמו ג׳ שותפין יש באדם, שאף שיש אב ואם לא שייך שיחיה האדם עם נשמה בלי שיבא מא״ס. בלא שותף הג׳, שהוא בחי׳ היחוד, אין פרי׳ ורבי׳ ואין התחדשות וברכה. בכלל ישראל ההולדה רק עי״ז. באוה״ע הפו״ר הוא באופן טבעי, הם רק לבחי׳ ״לשבת יצרה״ (ישעיה מה, יח), למען ישוב העולם. אבל פו״ר של כלל ישראל, הוא ריבוי השכינה. אין בן דוד בא עד שיכלה כל הנשמות שבתוך הגוף (נדה יג:). זה ענין גילוי הקב״ה בהבריאה ע״י בנים של כלל ישראל.

וזה בחי׳ הדעת, שמגיע לגילוי רצון ה׳. והוא גילוי אחר שנתגלה חכמה ובינה, אבל שרשו לקשר הבריאה לאחד ממש. שהבריאה הוא ריבוי. איש ואשה, רוח ונפש, לא מגלה האחד שרצונו להטיב, רצונו שהוא בחי׳ היחוד, שיש שליטה על הכל, רצונו להטיב שמחזיר כל רע לטוב, אף מה שנראה חוץ מרצונו ית׳ באמת הכל היה ברצונו, מהפך הרע לטוב. שבשרשו של הרע הוא להיות מנוצח. וזה היה שליחות הנחש, וזה תכליתו, להיות מנוצח, ואילו עמדו בנסיון הנחש היה נעשה מלאך של קדושה. וכמו שהאריך הרמח״ל בכל ענינים האלו.

ענין הדעת הוא הכרה של הקב״ה, ״בכל דרכך דעהו״ (משלי ג, ו). בכל דבר יש בחי׳ הדעת שהוא מאת הקב״ה שהוא מטיב, וכשיש דעת מכירים את זה, שגם זה לטוב. וכן יהי׳ לעת״ל שרק מברכים הטוב והמטיב (עי׳ פסחים נ.). אז באים לידיעה שלימה שהיתה הטבה גמור. ״אודך ה׳ כי אנפת בי״ (ישעיה יב, א).

בחטא אדה"ר באכילת עה"ד הפריד בין הגוף והרוח, נפש ורוח. מקודם הנפש היה כל כולו טועם הטבת הקב"ה. "מכל עץ הגן תאכל" (בראשית ב, טז). אכילת האדם שהוא בחי' בהמיות של אדם, בחי' נפש, היה במדרגת אדם. שכל אכילותיו ודברים גשמיים שעשה, לעבדה ולשמרה, היו בחי' רוחניות. "לעבדה ולשמרה" (שם ב, טו), זו מ"ע ומל"ת (זוה"ק ח"א כז.). ונפש בהמיות היה טועם טעם של קדושה בעבודת הגשמיות ומתענג בו. ולמשל כמו כל המענג את השבת כו', שיש ענין עונג שבת שבא מנשמה יתירה. והנחש פיתה את חוה והטיל בה זוהמא והיה אכילת עה"ד טו"ר, ואז היה אי הכרה ואי דעת שהקב"ה כל כולו הטבה. וזה גופא החילוק בין לשמה ולא לשמה. איזהו חסיד המתחסד עם קונו (זוה"ק ח"ב, קיד:), עושה לרבש"ע משום שהוא רוצה להטיב לנו. ע"י עבודה כזו אדם מכיר התכלית של רצון הרבש"ע, שרצונו להטיב בחסד גמור. ותורה ומצות לשמה מתחסד עם קונו מה הוא אף אתה, נעשה כביכול דומה לרבש"ע. ונחש הביא ענין שלא לשמה, עשה ספק, שאמר שאין התכלית משום הטבה אלא משום עצמו שזה אומנתו. וע"י ספק זה בא אכילת עה"ד ונעשה שלא לשמה תוך האדם. שאף בדברים של קדושה, שייך הרגש של שלא לשמה שעושה לעצמו. אינו מרגיש הטבת ה' בהבריאה ורק עושה שלא לשמה. והשכינה עלה לרקיע הז', ולא נתגלה למטה בעוה"ז. ורק יש "בזיעת אפיך תאכל לחם" (בראשית ג, יט). עניני עבודה, אינו לעבדה בבחי' רוחניות, אלא בבחי' מרירות וגשמיות.

ולעתיד לבא נזכה ל"מה רב טובך אשר צפנת" (תהלים לא, כ) וכו'. מה שהיה מכוסה מקודם, ונעשה הטבה שרואה שאין דבר שלא היה להטבה. וזהו עומק ההשגה. וזה שכר עוה"ב, גילוי היחוד הזה. הנה יש שני מדרגות, נהנים מזיו השכינה וניזונים מזיו השכינה. נהנים הוא שיש הנאה, וניזונים ר"ל שעצם חיים שלו ניזון מהשגה זו כאילו אוכל ממש. השגת אלו נעשו חלק מפנימיותו. וכמו שאכילה עדיף יותר מהנאה, שבאכילה הוא שמרגיש עצם החיות. וזה ענין סעודת לויתן, ושלחן עורך מדרגת סעודה זו, תחיית המתים, שגם הגוף מרגיש דבר זה. והגדה מסובב על השלחן, מצה קרבן פסח ומרור, עניני

אכילה. ובשבת, האכילה השגת עוה״ב, טועם טעם עוה״ב, וכן בפסח טועמים ענין הטבת הקב״ה, ונעשה שאין פירוד בין גוף ונפש.

מבאר הגר״א ז״ל כאן שבגלות מצרים היה כולל כל עניני הד׳ עינויים, אבל היה עוד עינוי ה׳ שכולל כל הד׳ וזה עינוי הדעת והוא עינוי נעלם [ומש״כ שהוא נעלם ר״ל שזה עינוי פנימיות, כמו שדעת הוא ענין פנימי שלא רואים אותו]. במצרים היה שעבוד של הגוף ומלאכה אבל גם היה עינוי בפנימיות שהוא עינוי הדעת שכולל כולם. שבמצרים היה גלות הדעת, וזה העינוי הגדול ביותר. במצרים היה הכיסוי הגדול ביותר של תכלית הבריאה, והיה חשך של גילוי רצונו ומחשבתו ע״י כח של מצרים. וכמו שאמרנו לעיל בחילוק בין א״י וארץ מצרים. שהיה יציאה ממלך פרעה, אבל גם היה יציאה מארץ מצרים. שהארץ עצמה היה הכיסוי הגדול ביותר של גילוי רצונו בתכלית הבריאה. א״י הוא בחי׳ עיני ה׳ וכו׳ השגחה פרטית, ובשלימותה כשיש ביהמ״ק היו רואים על כל פרט ופרט ההשגחה פרטית, שאם מקיימים תורה ומצות יש גילוי שפע ואם ח״ו לא יש הסתר פנים. והיפך זה במצרים, המים עולים מהנילוס, שהכל בא מלמטה. ובחיצינות נראה אין צורך כביכול של השגחת ה׳. אבל עיקר עבודת האדם הוא בהכרה זו, כמ״ש ואדם אין לעבוד את האדמה, זהו עבודת האדם להתפלל להגשמים. שהם באים מהשגחת ה׳. וארץ מצרים היא כיסוי לדבר זה.

והמצריים פעלו דבר זה ע״י השעבוד של כלל ישראל שעשאם לעבדים. שיש חילוק בין בן ועבד. מצינו בכנען שע״י החטא שראה בערות אביו נעשה מבחי׳ בן לעבד. שלא שייך להיות בן להקב״ה אבל שם ויפת עדיין הם בנים. וכלל ישראל נקראו ״בני בכורי ישראל״ (שמות ד, כב). אבל רצון המצריים היה לעשות כלל ישראל לעבדים, ובזה לנתק הקשר שיש בין כלל ישראל והקב״ה. ושעבדו את ישראל באופן שיהיו כמו בהמות שלהם, כשור וחמור. וכל תכליתם רק להאדון שלהם, שהוא פרעה. ואין להם תכלית אחר כלל. באד״א כתב שעבודת פרך היא העבודה הקשה ביותר שהיה במצרים, וזהו עבודה

ללא תכלית. וזה בחי׳ ריק, שפחה בישא. שהמצריים רצה בעבודה זו לעשות שאין תכלית לכלל ישראל בהבריאה, ואף למצריים שעובדים אין להם תכלית בעבודה זו. שלא יהי׳ להם תכלית לעצמם רק בטלים למצרים בנ׳ שערי טומאה, מנותק מהקב״ה.

והגאולה ממצרים הוא גאולת הדעת. כתוב (שמות ג, ו) ״ושמי הוי״ה לא נדעתי להם״. ששהקב״ה גילה למשה רבינו שהיציאה יהי׳ משם הוי״ה. ולא היה להאבות בחי׳ ידיעה זו, דעת זו, בירור זה. אברהם אבינו אמר במה אדע. והתשובה היא ידוע תדע וכו׳ ירידת מצרים מברר דבר זה. לא היה בפועל ידיעה של דבר זה, להאבות היה להם רק באמונה. וזהו הא לחמא עניא, שהיינו חסרים בחי׳ הדעת.

גילוי הדעת הוא בשם הוי״ה. כתב הגר״א ז״ל שאף שיש שמות שהם למעלה כמו שם אקי״ק, אבל תכלית השם, גילוי העצם ע״י שם הוי״ה, ולכן הוא נקרא שם העצם. ושאר השמות יותר מכוסים. והשם שמגלה היותר שייך לנבראים הוא בשם הזה ובזה יש גילוי על הא״ס, והוא גילוי היחוד. שאין גבולים להטבתו. ואמונת ישראל בא״ס, שרצונו להטיב.

בסיפור ההגדה מתחילים מראשית השעבוד עד סוף השעבוד. מארמי אובד אבי וכו׳, שבאמת היה טמון בכל סיבוב הדברים רצון ה׳ להטיב בכל דבר. וזהו ״מה רב טובך אשר צפנת״ וכו׳. השכר של לעת״ל יבא ממידת צפון שהוא מידת הדין, שזה השכר היותר גדול. בחציוניות הדין קשה, אבל יש לנו האמונה של ״מה רב טובך אשר צפנת״. שיש עומק בהדין עצמו המדרגה הגבוה ביותר של הטבתו. לעת״ל נאמר ״אודך ה׳ כי אנפת בי״ כמ״ש הרמח״ל. וזהו גילוי היחוד ה׳. שבכל דבר בהבריאה אין דבר עומד נגד רצונו ית׳ שיכול למנוע אותו חסד. אף שמהלך הבריאה ע״י בחירה, אין דבר מונע. כל מהלך הבריאה בא מבחירה, חטא אדה״ר, מכירת יוסף וכו׳ ירידת וגלות מצרים. אבל ע״פ סדר היחוד זהו רק התלייה. בפנימיות זה היה מתחילת

העולם. כבר נגזר בברית בין הבתרים, "ידוע תדע". קודם כל מהלך הגלו כבר היה מקודם הכל עומד לכך. ומזה ישתלשל שיהי' שייכות לרבש"ע בא"י, כמ"ש "במה אדע כי אירשנה "וכו' "ידוע תדע" וכו', זה גילוי בתחילתו קודם ירידת מצרים. וזה מהלך היחוד. "אנכי וכו' אשר הצאתיך מא"מ", אין זה בדיעבד. בפינמיות הכל מצד סדר הידיעה. ומצד בחירה, סדר המשפט. אבל הסיבה לבא לגילוי היחוד היא סדר המשפט. ומתחיל עשרת הדברות בא', שהכל אחד. כל הדין ועינויים במצרים הכל מאת אחד, אחד שרצונו להטיב.

ביציאה מחשך זה של מצרים היה גילוי זה, שכולו הטבה ורצונו להטיב, ויש תכלית והמשך לכלל ישראל. עבודת פרך היא מלאכה שאינה צריכה, אין תכלית, בחי' "הבור ריק," היפך באר שהוא גילוי שהקב"ה א"ס. וכנגד זה, פרו ורבו. אין חייס לעבדים, אבל לבן יש יחוס, וכשאינו עבד יש המשך של האומה ע"י פו"ר. וזה באוה"ע, אבל בכלל ישראל הוא יותר מהמשך האומה, אלא שפו"ר שלהם הוא לתכלית גילוי ה' בהבריאה. כשיש יותר התפשטות של כלל ישראל יש יותר גילוי של השכינה בהבריאה. ולעומת הבור ריק, שפחה בישא יש אשה של קדושה, מילוי הארץ ע"י בנים של כלל ישראל. ובזה יש דעת בארץ, שהוא תכלית הבריאה של פו"ר. באברהם אבינו יש ברית מילה, רק פו"ר של כלל ישראל מבחי' הברית. וזה גילוי רצונו בהבריאה. פו"ר כדי להתחסד. באוה"ע הוא רק לקיום המין, אבל בכלל ישראל הוא גילוי ה' בבחי' ברכה. הקב"ה בירך את האדם "פרו ורבו ומלאו את הארץ". ואחרי החטא שנקנסה עליו מיתה תשובתו היתה שעמד בנהר ופירש מאשתו לק"ל שנה, ומזה יצא בחי' שפחה בישא, ליל', אם הערב רב, מצרים, שאור שבעיסה, בור ריק, לריק. והתיקון של דבר זה היה במצרים, שם נתגלה שפו"ר אינו לריק אלא כל כולו לתכלית.

איתא בהגדה כנגד ד' בנים דברה תורה. ובלשון המשנה "כאן הבן שואל". הסיפור יצ"מ נתקיים בתשובת שאלת הבן. בחי' בן הוא בחי' פו"ר ובכלל ישראל הוא גילוי הקב"ה בהבריאה.

והדור שיצאו הם הדור דיעה, ושייכים למשה רבינו שהוא בחי׳ הדעת של כלל ישראל. הקב״ה אמר למשה רבינו שידבר לפרעה אבל משה רבינו אמר ״כי כבד פה״ וכו׳, ור״ל שלא שייך שדיבור שלי יגלה הקב״ה בהבריאה. ואה״נ ודאי ידע שאם המהלך יהי׳ ע״י הקב״ה בעצמו כביכול אין ספק כלל באמונה שלו שיכול הדבר ליעשות, רק מאחר שהרבש״ע בחר באופן שיהי׳ ע״י בשר ודם, בשליחות משה, משה אמר שאין ביכלתו לגלות הקב״ה בהבריאה לפרעה, שהוא שורש הרע, שמגיע למדרגה הגבוה ביותר של הרע. פרעה נקרא תנין ביאור (ע״פ יחזקאל כט, ג), לעומת משה שג״כ נקרא תנין. וגם זה מדרגת נחש. וכתב הגר״א ז״ל שלכן אות הראשון לפרעה הוא במה שהמטה נהפך לנחש ואח״כ למטה. שזה כח פרעה מצד הרע, נחש הקדמוני שגרם החטא עה״ד. ולכן נתן אות זה ואחז בזנבו, וע״י מעשה זו החליש כח פרעה. היה כח של נחש שאחוז זנבו בראשו, וזה אחיזת פרעה, בעורף, שהוא כנגד מקום הדעת שהוא הפנים של האדם. במקום דעת הוא מקום הדיבור בהגרון. וכן בנחש שעומד נגד זה יש בו כח הדיבור ופיתוי. ומשה עומד כנגדו, ע״י המטה וגילוי דיבור קב״ה.

ובחי׳ דעת באה מהאות א׳. ובמצרים היה חסר א׳, חסר בחי׳ הדעת ואין פו״ר. ובליל פסח יש גדלות הדעת. וכתב הגר״א ז״ל כאשר יהיה נשלם הא׳ יהיה מלאה הארץ דעה. ר״ל שהארץ תמלא דעה. תכלית הדעת, בארץ דוקא. לדעת בארץ דרכך. ״בכל דרכך דעהו״, אפי׳ עניני רשות. אפי בעולם זה שהוא ארץ וגשמיות, מדרגת הארץ היתה תהו ובהו, בחי׳ חורבן. ונשרש זה שעבודת האדם לתקן הארץ שהיא ארעא באתלטיא. וע״י הדעת שייך לתקן דבר זה. יצ״מ היתה כדי לבא למתן תורה בשבועות, גילוי שאל הא׳ של אנכי, ובפסח היה גילוי הא׳, גילוי שרצונו להטיב.

הגר״א ז״ל ממשיך:

> וכנגדן אמרו בגמרא (פסחים קטו:) לחם עוני שעונין עליו דברים הרבה, לחם עוני מה דרכו של עני בפרוסה. לחם עוני, מה דרכו של

עני הוא אופה ואשתו לשה. לחם עוני פרט לנילושה ביין שמן ודבש. והענין שבכל דבר יש פועל צורה חומר ותכלית. ובכולן יש חילוק בין עני לעשיר. למשל אם צריכין לעשות שלחן, העשיר יעשה החומר מכסף או מעץ טוב, אבל העני מעץ הדיוט. וכן בפועל, העשיר יבקש חרש טוב או צורף, והעני אינו כן אלא עושה בעצמו, בשביל שלא להוציא מעט ממון שיש לו. וכן הצורה, שהעשיר מצייר שולחנו בסממנים, והעני אינו כן אלא עושה אותו ונשאר כמו שהיה. והתכלית, שהעשיר אוכל עליו תענוגים ומעדנים, והעני שהלחם הוא בכל הנ״ל עני, החומר שאין רשאי לעשות משמן ודבש, והצורה היא פרוסה, כמו דרך העני. והפועל הוא אופה ואשתו לשה. והתכלית, שעונין עליו דברים הרבה דהיינו צרותינו, וזהו עבדים היינו כו׳...

די אכלו אבהתנא. מה שאמר די אכלו אבהתנא בארעא דמצרים, והלא כתבו על שלא הספיק בצקם של אבותינו. והענין שבאמת אכלו אבותינו לחם כזה במצרים, כמו שכתבו הראשונים שדרכם של מצרים היה להאכיל לעבדים להם עוני כזה. וגם כשהוציא ה׳ אותנו ממצרים היה בחפזון עד שלא הספיק כו׳. ומה שצוה לעשות חג המצות ונקרא על שם הלחם הזה, אינו על אכילתן במצרים, רק על יציאתן לחירות. אך מחמת הלחם אשר אכלו מחמת חפזון איננו שייך לקרא לחם עוני, מחמת שהיה ברצון טוב ובשמחה, אמר כאן הא לחמא עניא מחמת די אכלו אבהתנא בארעא דמצרים, ששם היו כל העינויים. ומפרש הד׳ עינויים שגאלנו השם מהם, וצריכים אנחנו להודות עליהם.

הגר״א ז״ל כתב שמש״כ די אכלא אבהתנא בארעא דמצרים ר״ל כשהיו עבדים כך היה מאכלם, שהיה לוקח זמן הרבה להעיכול והיו שבעים ליותר זמן, וגם שלא צריך להחמיץ ויכול למהר לחזור לעבודתם. פרעה אמר ״נרפים אתם״, שרצה שלא יהי׳ להם מחשבה או רוח, מקוצר רוח, ולא יתובי דעתי׳, לא ישוב הדעת. שאדם נעשה ממש לבחי׳ בהמה, וכך הוא עצת יצה״ר, עצת פרעה. הוא רצה להוריד כל מציאותם לגשמיות, הא לחמא עניא, כך אכלנו. אבל

במצת מצוה, על שם כך נקרא חג המצות. וזהו שמחה. ואף שמקודם היה מצת עני, אבל במצת מצוה יש שמחה.

וממשיך לבאר ד׳ דברים שיש במצה שיש בו הד׳ עניני עניות עי״ש. וזהו עונין עליו דברים הרבה, כשהעני מתוך דחקותו מדבר על צרותיו. וזהו הסמיכה לעבדים היינו וכו׳. בעשיר, כל כולו הוא בשלימות ואינו חסר כלום, ואין מקום להרגיש צער. אבל העני מרגיש צער בחסרונו ומדבר בצרותיו. ולכן ההמשך להא לחמא עניא הוא עבדים היינו, מדבר על צרותיו. נמצא שלחם עוני הוא המצה שקודם למצת מצוה. וכענין שכתב הרמח״ל שהחילוק בין מצה ומצוה הוא האות ו׳. בחי׳ מצה הוא לחם עוני, בלא ו׳ של מצוה. לית לה מגרמא כלום. הוא בחי׳ דל״ת, דלות, בחי׳ עני כמ״ש הגר״א ז״ל שכולל ד׳ מיני עניות. וזה כנגד מלכות דלית לה מגרמא כלום. אבל כשנעשה מצוה, מתייחד באור השפעה של הזכר, האות ו׳, ונעשה חלק מהמצה עצמה. לא שהאות ו׳ מבחוץ אלא בתוכו ממש, שמצה נעשה למצוה. וזה בליל פסח. מצת מצוה חג המצות. אין זה הלחם עוני, אלא התיקון הוא שמצה נעשה למצוה. [והנה מה שאמרו שעונין עליו דברים הרבה זהו על המצה שאוכלים בליל פסח לצאת בו מצות אכילת, והייתי אומר שבמצת המצוה היתה גאולת הדעת ועונין הוא בחי׳ דיבור ודעת, ודעת חל על המצת מצוה. אבל מדברי הגר״א ז״ל מבואר שזה נאמר על הא לחמא עניא, צ״ל שיש גם במצה זו בחי׳ של לחם עוני, ורק שנעשה אח״כ של מצוה.]

ואומרים כל דכפין, שבליל פסח נעשים מלא דעת, שהקב״ה נתן לנו גדלות שני קודם גדלות ראשון. ושלימות הדעת הוא כשיכול להשפיע לאחרים. דעת הוא כשגלוי וידוע בהבריאה, שברא עולם כדי לאשתמודע, כדי לגלות כביכול לנבראים מציאותו שהוא אין סוף, ותכלית של זה כדי להיטיב. ובחי׳ הדעת של הבריאה הוא כשהבריאה מגלה הרבש״ע. וממילא אם יודעים שחיות שלנו מרבש״ע זה לא שלימות הדעת, רק כשמגלה לאחרים.

בעניות הדעת במצרים הוא עניות בכל דבר, והיו רחוקים ביותר מבחי׳ זו שיכול להשפיע. ובלידת כלל ישראל ביצ״מ באו לשלימות הדעת. שכל קלקול העולם בא מחסרון הדעת, ובליל פסח הוא לידת הדעת.

ולכן ענין שלימות הדעת הוא ליתן לעני, לנפש האדם, שהוא בחי׳ עני. צדיק גומל נפש בהמתו. שזה שפע הדעת. להודיע, לאשתמודע. ושפע זה משיגים בליל פסח. ואומרים כל דכפין וכו׳ להשפיע לעניים, ליתן להם נקודה זו של אכילת מצה ופסח שהוא עצם החיים כמו שאמרנו לעיל, שבפסח נתגלה עצם החיים ע״י מוצא פי ה׳ שרואים בליל פסח. ולכן אומרים כל דכפין וכו׳ כדי שיתן לבחי׳ עני שבעצמנו ובחוץ. בעוה״ז, קדש עצמך. קדושה, הוא ענין חכמה. גילוי חסד הדעת. כדי להודיע לעניים בין בגשמיות בין ברוחניות. וזה נקודת אכילה בפסח.

# ליל שימרים

## הרב רפאל שעפטיל הלוי נויברגר

שני עניינים ב'ליל שימורים'

א. שאין מפחדין מן המזיקין, ב. שבו עתידין ליגאל

איתא בגמרא (ראש השנה י, ב – יא, ב), תניא רבי אליעזר אומר, בתשרי נברא העולם וכו׳ בתשרי עתידין ליגאל. רבי יהושע אומר, בניסן נברא העולם וכו׳ בניסן עתידין ליגאל, ע״כ. ובגמרא שם מפרש פלוגתתם, בתשרי עתידין ליגאל, אתיא שופר שופר כתיב הכא תקעו בחדש שופר וכתיב התם ביום ההוא יתקע בשופר גדול. רבי יהושע אומר בניסן נגאלו בניסן עתידין ליגאל מנלן, אמר קרא ״ליל שימורים״, ליל המשומר ובא משֵשת ימי בראשית. ואידך, לילה המשומר ובא מן המזיקין, ע״כ.

וכתבו בתוס׳ שם וז״ל, לילה המשומר ובא מן המזיקין – ורבי יהושע תרתי שמעת מינה, דכולהו מודו דמשומר מן המזיקין כדמוכח בערבי פסחים (פסחים קט:) דתקון ארבע כוסות ולא חייש אזוגות, עכ״ל. ומבואר מזה, דלפי רבי אליעזר בתשרי עתידין ליגאל, וא״כ הא דדרשינן מליל שימורים דהלילה הזה משומר היינו רק דהוא משומר מן המזיקין. ולפי רבי יהושע על כרחך יש ב׳ עניינים בהך שמירה, חדא, דהלילה הזה משומר מן המזיקין כדהוכיחו התוס׳ מארבע כוסות דלא חיישינן לזוגות, וגם דרשינן מהך קרא דלעתיד לבוא יגאלו ישראל בניסן, דזהו הלילה המשומר לגאולה מימי בראשית.

ודברי התוס׳ צ״ע, דהנה הא דשותין ארבע כוסות בליל הסדר ולא חיישינן לזוגות, באמת נחלקו בזה האמוראים, דהכי איתא בגמרא (פסחים שם), ולא יפחתו לו מארבעה – היכי מתקני רבנן מידי דאתי בה לידי סכנה, והתניא לא יאכל אדם תרי ולא ישתה תרי וכו׳. אמר רב נחמן, אמר קרא ״ליל שימורים״ ליל המשומר ובא מן המזיקין. רבא אמר, כוס של ברכה מצטרף לטובה ואינו

מצטרף לרעה. רבינא אמר, ארבעה כסי תקינו רבנן דרך חירות, כל חד וחד מצוה באפי נפשה הוא, ע״כ.

הרי מבואר בגמרא שנחלקו האמוראים בטעם הדבר דלא חיישינן לזוגות בארבע כוסות דליל הסדר, וא״כ צריך ביאור מה הכריחם לבעלי התוס׳ לומר דאף רבי יהושע מודה דדרשינן הך קרא ד״ליל שימורים״ לומר דהוא משומר מן המזיקין, דלכאורה בפשיטות י״ל דסבירא ליה לרבי יהושע כשאר האמוראים דלא דרשו פסוק זה לגבי ליל הסדר, ועיקר הך קרא ד״ליל שימורים״ מיירי רק לגבי הגאולה העתידה לבוא ולא לגבי השמירה מן המזיקין בליל הסדר, והא דשותים ארבע כוסות ואין חוששין לזוגות, היינו טעמא או משום דכוס של ברכה אינו מצטרף לרעה, או משום דכל כוס וכוס הוי מצוה בפני עצמה. ושוב מצאתי שכבר עמד בזה הערוך לנר (על התוס׳ שם), עיי״ש מה שתירץ.

וכמו כן יש להקשות גם בדברי הרמ״א (אורח חיים תפא, ב) שכתב וז״ל, נוהגים שלא לקרות על מטתו רק פרשת שמע, ולא שאר דברים שקורין בשאר לילות כדי להגן, כי ליל שימורים הוא מן המזיקין, עכ״ל. ומבואר שהרמ״א פסק לדינא דמהך קרא ד״ליל שימורים״ דרשינן שיש שמירה מיוחדת בלילה הזה מן המזיקין, ולפיכך נוהגין בקריאת שמע שעל המטה שאין קוראים את כל הפסוקים שעניינם לשמור מן המזיקין.

אולם עוד כתב שם הרמ״א (תפ, א) וז״ל, יש אומרים שיש לומר ״שפוך חמתך״ (תהלים עט, ו) וכו׳ קודם לא לנו, ולפתוח הפתח כדי לזכור שהוא ליל שימורים, ובזכות אמונה זו יבא משיח וישפוך חמתו על המכחשים בה׳, עכ״ל. ומבואר בזה, דהפסוק ד״ליל שימורים״ דרשינן ליה גם לגבי הענין השני שהוזכר בדברי התוס׳, דלא רק דיש שמירה מיוחדת בלילה הזה מן המזיקין, אלא גם עוד יש בפסוק זה דרשא לגבי העתיד לבוא שאנו עתידין ליגאל בניסן, ומשום

זה פותחין את הדלת לאליהו הנביא בזמן אמירת "שפוך חמתך" כדי להראות את האמונה שאנו מאמינים שיבוא אליהו לבשר לנו את הגאולה.

ואמנם המשנה ברורה (שם ס"ק י) ביאר גם מנהג זה של פתיחת הדלת דזהו כדי להראות שאין מפחדין מן המזיקין, וא"כ נמצא שהמנהג לפתוח הדלת ב"שפוך חמתך" אינו משום עצם האמונה שאליהו הנביא יבוא לבשר את הגאולה, אלא עיקר הענין הוא כדי להראות שאין מפחדין מן המזיקין, ורק דהרמ"א כתב שבזכות אמונה זו יבוא אליהו הנביא לבשר את הגאולה. וכ"כ בשולחן ערוך הרב (שם סעיף ד). אבל מפשטות דברי הרמ"א נראה דעיקר ענין פתיחת הדלת הוא כדי להראות על ביאת הגאולה, ואינו שייך כלל לענין הראשון שהוא להראות שאין מפחדין מן המזיקין.

ובאמת הדבר מפורש בארחות חיים ובדרכי משה, דהנה הדרכי משה (שם) כתב שמקור מנהג זה שפותחין הדלת בזמן אמירת "שפוך חמתך", הוא במה שכתבו הראשונים שבליל הסדר נוהגין שלא לנעול הדלתות כלל במשך כל הלילה. ומנהג זה מקורו בדברי הארחות חיים (חלק א סדר ליל הפסח אות לז) שכתב וז"ל, מנהג בכמה מקומות שאין נועלין שם החדרים שישנים שם בלילי הפסח, כי בניסן נגאלו ובניסן עתידין ליגאל, דכתיב "ליל שימורים הוא לה'" לילה המשומר ובא מששת ימי בראשית, ואם יבוא אליהו ימצא הפתח פתוח ויצא לקראתו מהר וכו', עכ"ל. הרי להדיא בדברי הרמ"א והארחות חיים שמנהג זה לפתוח את הדלת בזמן אמירת "שפוך חמתך" אינו שייך כלל להבטחה שיש בלילה הזה שאין המזיקים יכולים להזיק, אלא דכיון שזהו הלילה המשומר לגאולה לכן אין נועלין את הדלתות כדי שיבוא אליהו ולא ימצא את הפתח נעול, ומכח זה נהגו גם לפתוח את הדלת בזמן "שפוך חמתך".

ולאחר כל זה שוב צ"ע מה דהוקשה לעיל בדברי התוס', דכיון שמבואר בדברי הרמ"א והארחות חיים דיש ב' עניינים בהך קרא ד"ליל שימורים", חדא עצם

הדבר שאין מפחדין מן המזיקין, וכמו שכתב הרמ״א דזהו הטעם להא דאין קוראין את כל הפסוקים בקריאת שמע, ועוד יש ענין אחר שהלילה הזה הוא הלילה המשומר לגאולה העתידה לבוא, א״כ צריך ביאור האיך דרשינן ב׳ עניינים אלו מפסוק אחד, דמפשטות דברי הגמרא בפסחים משמע שנחלקו האמוראים האיך דרשינן פסוק זה, ומהיכא תיתי דיש שני עניינים בהך קרא ד׳ליל שימורים׳, וכנ״ל.

הצעת סוגיית הגמרא בהא דאין מברכין ברכת המזון על כוס שני, וקושיית הראשונים בסתירת הסוגיות לגבי חשש זוגות בכוס של ברכה

וכדי לבאר כל זה, נראה להקדים מה דאיתא בגמרא (ברכות נא:), אמר רב אסי אין מברכין [- ברכת המזון] על כוס של פורענות, מאי כוס של פורענות, אמר רב נחמן בר יצחק כוס שני, ע״כ. ופירש רש״י שם וז״ל, כוס שני – שהוא של זוגות, והעומד על שולחנו ושתי זוגות ניזוק על ידי שדים, עכ״ל. אולם תלמידי רבינו יונה כתבו שם (לח. מדפי הרי״ף ד״ה מאי) וז״ל, נראה למורי הרב נר״ו לפרש, דכוס שני ר״ל שכבר שתה בתוך הסעודה שתי פעמים, ור״ל שכיון ששתה זוגות שהמזיקין שולטין בהם ובא פורענות לאדם על ידם, אין מברכין עליהם בכוס אחר, עכ״ל.

ונמצא דלפי רש״י הגמרא איירי במי ששתה כוס אחד בלבד בתוך סעודתו, ועל זה אמרו דלא יברך על כוס שני כיון שע״י זה ישלטו הזוגות. אולם לפי רבינו יונה הגמרא מיירי במי שכבר שתה שני כוסות בתוך הסעודה, ועל זה איתא בגמרא דלא יברך על כוס שלישי כיון שכבר שלטו הזוגות ע״י שתייתו הראשונה.

ועל עיקר דברי הגמרא דלא יברך על כוס שני משום המזיקין, הקשו הראשונים שם, דהרי מבואר בגמרא בפסחים (קט:) דליכא חשש היזק של זוגות בליל הסדר, וביאר שם רבא דהיינו טעמא משום דכוס של ברכה מצטרף לטובה ואינו מצטרף לרעה. וביאור הדברים, שהכוס השלישי מצטרף לטובה לשני

הכוסות הראשונים דלא יהיו חשובים כזוג בפני עצמן, ונמצא דעכשיו שתה שלושה כוסות, ולאידך גיסא, אע״פ שלבסוף שותה ארבע כוסות מ״מ הכוס השלישי אינו מצטרף לרעה כיון דהוי כוס של ברכה, ונמצא דעכשיו חשבינן ליה כאילו שתה רק שלושה כוסות. ולפי זה הקשו הראשונים מאי טעמא בכוס של ברכת המזון דעלמא חששו חז״ל להיזק זה של זוגות, והא כוס של ברכה מצטרף לטובה ולא לרעה.

ותמיהה זו קיימת בין לפירושו של רש״י ובין לפירושו של רבינו יונה, דלפי רש״י דהגמרא איירי במי ששתה כוס אחד בתוך סעודתו, יקשה מאי טעמא לא יברך על הכוס השני, והרי כוס של ברכת המזון אינו מצטרף לרעה. ולאידך גיסא יקשה על שיטת רבינו יונה, דאם הגמרא איירי במי שכבר שתה שני כוסות בתוך סעודתו, א״כ מאי טעמא לא יברך על הכוס השלישי, והרי כוס של ברכה מצטרף לטובה, ונמצא דלבסוף שתה שלושה כוסות ולית ליה חשש היזק של זוגות.

### דוקא כוס של חובה מצטרף לטובה ולא לרעה, משא"כ כוס של ברכת המזון דעלמא שהוא רשות – דברי רבינו יונה ליישב את הסתירה הנ"ל, וכמה הערות בדבריו

וביישוב הקושיא כתב רבינו יונה שם וז״ל, וא״ת ולמה אינו מברך בזה הכוס השלישי, דהא אמרינן בפסחים (קט): כוס של ברכה מצטרף לטובה, וכיון שזה הכוס מצטרף עם השנים נמצא דלא הוו זוגות, וליכא חשש מזיקין, ולא הוי כוס של פורענות. יש לומר, שלא אמרו כוס של ברכה מצטרף לטובה אלא בכוסות של פסח שהם תקנת חכמים וחייב בהם אפילו העני כדתנן (פסחים צט:) ולא יפחתו לו מארבע כוסות של יין, וכיון שחייב בהם ועכ״פ יש לו לשתותו אמרו שמצטרף עם השנים לטובה כדי שלא יהיו זוגות, אבל הכא שאינו מחוייב בזה אלא כשיש לו יין לא אמרינן שמצטרף עם השנים הראשונים, עכ״ל.

ודברי רבינו יונה צ"ע מכמה אנפי. ראשית כל, עצם החילוק בין כוס של חובה לכוס רשות צריך ביאור טובא, דהא מאחר דמבואר בגמרא בפסחים שהכוס השלישי מצטרף לשני הכוסות הראשונים דלא יהא חשש של זוגות, א"כ מאי נפקא מינה אם כוס זה הוי מצוה גמורה שהיא חובה או דהוי מצוה של רשות, והא סוף סוף מאחר ששותה כוס שלישי דהוי כוס של ברכה מאי טעמא לא יצטרף כוס זה דלא יהא ניזוק ע"י שני הכוסות הראשונים.

ועוד יש להקשות בזה, דאין הכי נמי דכך היא שיטת רבינו יונה שכוס של זימון הוא רשות, אבל באמת הרבה ראשונים סבירא להו דהוי חובה גמורה, דכך היא מסקנת התוס' במסכת פסחים (קה: ד"ה שמע מינה) דברכת המזון טעונה כוס אפילו ביחיד, וכן הסיק הרא"ש (פסחים פרק י סימן יד), וגם השולחן ערוך (אורח חיים קפב, א) לא הכריע בפלוגתתא זו אלא הביא את כל השיטות בענין זה. ועיין במשנה ברורה (ס"ק ד) שדעת כמה מהאחרונים להלכה דברכת המזון טעונה כוס אפילו ביחיד, וזה הוי חובה גמורה, עיי"ש. וממילא שוב צריך ביאור מה יתרצו הני ראשונים לקושיית רבינו יונה, דכיון דס"ל להני ראשונים דכוס של ברכת המזון הוי חובה, א"כ מאי שנא דלגבי כוס שלישי בליל הסדר אין חשש היזק של זוגות כיון דכוס של מצוה מצטרף לטובה, ואילו לגבי כוס של ברכת המזון דעלמא מבואר בגמרא דאינו מצטרף לטובה לענין זה, והא שניהם חובה.

ועוד יש לעיין לפי דרכו של רש"י בהך סוגיא במסכת ברכות דאין מברכין ברכת המזון על כוס שני. דהנה כבר נתבאר בדעת רש"י דהגמרא שם איירי במי ששתה כוס אחד בתוך הסעודה, ועל זה אמרו דלא יברך על הכוס השני משום היזק של זוגות. ואכן עיקר קושיית הראשונים בסתירת הסוגיות א"ש גם לפי דרכו של רש"י, וכמו שכתב רבינו יונה בשיטת עצמו, דיש לומר דהא דמבואר בגמרא בפסחים דכוס של ברכה אינו מצטרף לרעה לכוס הראשון או השלישי, זהו דוקא בכוס דהוי חובה כמו ד' כוסות, אבל כוס של ברכת המזון דעלמא דהוי רשות אין הכי נמי דמצטרף הוא לרעה, ומשום הכי אין מברכין

על הכוס השני. ונמצא, דכמו שביאר רבינו יונה הך סברא לגבי הכלל דכוס של ברכה מצטרף לטובה, כן יש לומר גם לגבי הכלל דאינו מצטרף לרעה, וכנ״ל.

אבל אכתי אין זה מיישב לגמרי את סתירת הסוגיות בענין זה, דהרי כבר הובאה לעיל סוגיית הגמרא בפסחים, ושם מבואר ג׳ טעמים מאי טעמא ליכא חשש של זוגות בארבע כוסות שבליל הסדר, דרב נחמן אמר דזהו משום דליל הסדר הוי לילה המשומר מן המזיקין, ורבא אמר דזהו משום שכוס של ברכה מצטרף לטובה ואינו מצטרף לרעה, ורבינא אמר דכל כוס וכוס הוי מצוה בפני עצמה, ומשום הכי אין מצטרפין כלל לזוגות.

ולפי״ז יקשה טובא האיך תתיישב סתירת הסוגיות אליבא דרש״י, דבשלמא בדעת רבא שפיר חילק רבינו יונה שדוקא בכוס דהוי חובה אמרינן הך סברא דמצטרף לטובה ולא לרעה, ומשא״כ בכוס של זימון דהוי רשות. וכמו כן בדעת רב נחמן לא קשיא מידי, שדוקא בליל הסדר לא חששו חכמים להיזק של זוגות כיון שלילה זה משומר מן המזיקין. אבל אכתי תיקשי לדעת רבינא, דאם הסברא שלא חששו חז״ל להיזק זוגות בליל הסדר היינו משום שכל כוס הוי מצוה בפני עצמה ומשום הכי אינן מצטרפין, הרי קל וחומר הוא דבכהאי גוונא ששותה כוס שני לברכת המזון דלא יצטרף כלל להכוס הראשון ששתה בתוך הסעודה, דאם בארבע כוסות שכולם מצוה גמורה אעפ״כ אמרו חז״ל דליכא חשש היזק של זוגות כיון שכל אחד הוי מצוה נפרדת בפני עצמה, כל שכן הוא דאם שתה כוס אחת של רשות בתוך הסעודה וכוס שנית של מצוה לברכת המזון דבזה ודאי לא יצטרפו, ושוב צריך ביאור מאי טעמא אין מברכין על כוס שני לברכת המזון.

ובשלמא לדעת רבינו יונה עצמו לא תיקשי כלל, שהרי לדרכו של רבינו יונה הסוגיא איירי במי ששתה שני כוסות של רשות בתוך הסעודה, ועל זה אמרו דלא ישתה כוס שלישי לברכת המזון משום ההיזק שכבר בא ע״י הזוגות. וא״כ

שפיר אמרו בגמרא דהכוס השלישי אינו מצטרף לשני הכוסות לבטל את ההיזק, דאע״פ דהכוס השלישי של ברכת המזון הוי מצוה של רשות, מ״מ אין זה רשות גמור עד כדי כך שיהא חשוב כמי ששותה ג׳ כוסות בעלמא, דסוף סוף יש כאן ב׳ כוסות שהם רשות גמור וכוס אחר של ברכת המזון דהוי מצוה, ומשום הכי אתי שפיר גם לדעת רבינא מאי טעמא חששו כאן להיזק של זוגות, דהכוס השלישי אינו מצטרף לשנים הראשונים כדי לבטל את הזוגות.

אבל לפי רש״י הרי הקושיא היא בהיפוך, דלפי רש״י הסוגיא איירי בכוס שני והחשש היזק הוא ע״י שיצטרף הכוס השני של ברכת המזון להכוס הראשון ששתה בתוך הסעודה, ואם כן יקשה כנ״ל, דמאחר דמבואר בדברי רבינא שד׳ כוסות אינן מצטרפין זה עם זה כיון שכל אחד הוי מצוה בפני עצמה ומשום הכי ליכא חשש של זוגות כלל, קל וחומר דהך כוס השני של ברכת המזון לא יצטרף לכוס הראשון, דהכוס הראשון הוי רשות גמור ואילו הכוס השני הוי מצוה, ומאי טעמא יש בזה חשש של זוגות.

יישוב כל הקושיות, דבליל הסדר לא חששו חכמים להיזק של זוגות כיון שהוא 'ליל שימורים', ובדבר זה לא נחלקו האמוראים כלל

והנראה מוכרח בזה, דשאר הראשונים נחלקו בזה על רבינו יונה, וסבירא להו לכל הראשונים הנ״ל שמעולם לא נחלקו האמוראים בהך קרא ד׳ליל שימורים׳, דודאי לכולי עלמא זהו עיקר הטעם שלא חששו חז״ל להיזק של זוגות בארבע כוסות דליל הסדר, דכיון שהוא לילה המשומר מן המזיקין לכן אין לחשוש לזוגות. וממילא נמצא שאין כאן סתירה כלל בין הסוגיות, שדוקא בליל הסדר לא חששו חז״ל להיזק של זוגות, ומשא״כ בכוס של ברכת המזון דעלמא [ומה שנחלקו שם רבינא ורבא יתבאר להלן].

וממילא אתי שפיר דברי התוס׳ והרמ״א דיש ב׳ עניינים בהך קרא ד׳ליל שימורים׳, דכיון שמוכרח מסוגיות הגמרא שעיקר הטעם דליכא חשש זוגות בליל הסדר הוא משום הך קרא ד׳ליל שימורים׳ דהלילה הזה משומר מן

המזיקין, ומוכרח נמי דכולי עלמא מודים בזה וכנ״ל, אם כן הא דמבואר בגמרא שרבי יהושע דרש מפסוק זה דזהו הלילה המשומר לגאולה העתידה לבוא, על כרחך אין כוונתו לחלוק על הענין הראשון דהוי לילה המשומר מן המזיקין, אלא כוונתו לומר דתרווייהו ילפינן מיניה, וכיון שדבר זה מוכרח מעצם סוגיות הגמרא משום הכי נקטו כן התוס׳ בפשיטות, וגם הרמ״א הלך בדרכם של התוס׳ בזה.

### אע"פ שמובטח לשליח מצוה שאינו ניזוק, מ"מ צריך לעשות השתדלות שלא יהא ניזוק גם בדרך הטבע – ביאור פלוגתת האמוראים במסכת פסחים

ואולם עדיין יש להבין במה נחלקו האמוראים שם במסכת פסחים, דאם נימא דכולי עלמא מודים לטעם זה דהוי לילה המשומר מן המזיקין ומשום הכי ליכא חשש של זוגות בשתיית ארבע כוסות, א״כ מדוע הוסיפו רבא ורבינא עוד טעמים נוספים דזהו משום דכוס של ברכה אינו מצטרף לרעה או משום דכל כוס הוי מצוה בפני עצמה, והרי גם רבא ורבינא מודים לדברי רב נחמן דהוי לילה המשומר מן המזיקין, וצריך ביאור מה באו רבא ורבינא להוסיף בדבריהם.

והנראה בזה ע״פ מה דמבואר בגמרא (פסחים ח:) דאע״ג דקיימא לן דשלוחי מצוה אינן ניזוקין, מ״מ היכא דשכיח היזקא אין הבטחה זו. ודבר זה ילפינן שם בגמרא מהא דהקב״ה שלח את שמואל למשוח את דוד למלך, ואעפ״כ אמר שמואל להקב״ה שירא משאול שישמע מכך ויהרגנו, והקב״ה השיב לו שיקח עגלת בקר ויאמר לזבוח לה׳ באתי (שמואל-א טז, ב). ולכאורה מאי טעמא לא השיב לו הקב״ה דהוא שליח מצוה שאינו ניזוק, ועל כרחך חזינן דהיכא דשכיח היזקא אין סומכין על הבטחה זו דשלוחי מצוה אינן ניזוקין, עכת״ד הגמרא שם.

ובביאור הענין דאין סומכין על שליחות מצוה שלא יהא ניזוק במקום דשכיח היזקא, כתב המאירי (יומא יא: ד״ה כל) וז״ל, אע״פ שאמרו שלוחי מצוה אין

ניזוקין, היכא דשכיח היזקא שאני, שאין הקדוש ברוך הוא רוצה שיהא מוסר עצמו לסכנה ולסמוך על הנס בשביל קיום מצוה, וכדכתיב ויאמר שמואל איך אלך ושמע שאול והרגני, עכ״ל. וכן כתב הרד״ק (שמואל א שם) וז״ל, מצאנו כי אע״פ שהיה מבטיח הקדוש ברוך הוא הנביא או הצדיק, אעפ״כ הוא נשמר מלכת במקום סכנה. כמו שראינו ביעקב אבינו שהבטיחו הקדוש ברוך הוא בעברו ארם נהרים ואמר לו והשיבותיך אל האדמה הזאת וכו׳, וכאשר שמע כי עשו בא לקראתו ויירא יעקב מאד וייצר לו. וכן דוד שהיה נמשח למלך על פי ה׳ היה בורח מפני שאול וכו׳. וכן ציוה לשמואל הנביא תחבולה אע״פ שהיה הולך במצוותו. והטעם, כי אע״פ שהקדוש ברוך הוא עושה נסים ונפלאות עם יראיו, ברוב הם על מנהג העולם, וכן על מנהג העולם היה לו ליעקב לירא מפני עשו, ולדוד מפני שאול אם היה מושח מלך בחייו, והיה לו לבקש תחבולה איך אלך, וזו היתה שאלתו איך אלך, ואמר לו הקדוש ברוך הוא עגלת בקר תקח בידך, עכ״ל.

הרי מבואר בזה, דאפילו אם יש לצדיק הבטחה גמורה מהקב״ה שילך לשליחות מצוה ולא יהא ניזוק, מ״מ ההנהגה הראויה היא לבקש דרכים לעשות את המצוה באופן שלא יהא ניזוק בדרך הטבע, דכך הוא רצון הקב״ה שהאדם יעשה השתדלות בדרך הטבע, כדי שלא יהיו הניסים שלא בדרך הטבע. ולכן אע״פ שודאי לא יהא ניזוק משום ההבטחה של הקב״ה או משום שהוא שליח מצוה, מ״מ היכא דשכיח היזקא אין סומכין על הבטחה זו, דכך היא חובת ההשתדלות לעשות מעשים באופן שיהא בטוח מן ההיזק גם בדרך הטבע.[א]

[א] והדברים מפורשים גם בזוה״ק (חלק א פרשת ויגש רט, א), דאיתא שם, אוקמוה דצדיקיא לא בעאן לאטרחא למאריהון באתר דנזקא אשתכחת (ליה) לעינא, כגוונא דשמואל דכתיב (שמואל א, טז, ב) איך אלך ושמע שאול והרגני, א״ל עגלת בקר תקח בידך, בגין דצדיקיא לא בעאן לאטרחא למאריהון באתר דנזקא אשתכח, ע״כ.

ולפי״ז מבואר היטב מאי טעמא הוצרכו האמוראים להוסיף טעמים בהא דלא חששו חז״ל להיזק של זוגות בליל הסדר, דודאי כל האמוראים מודים שעיקר הטעם הוא משום דליל הסדר הוי לילה המשומר מן המזיקין, אבל כיון שהאדם צריך לעשות השתדלות שלא יהא ניזוק גם בדרך הטבע, לכן הוסיפו רבא ורבינא עוד טעמים בזה, דאו משום שכוס של ברכה אינו מצטרף לרעה או משום דכל כוס הוי מצוה בפני עצמה, אבל גם הם ס״ל שטעמים אלו אינם מועילים בפני עצמן, אלא עיקר הצלת ההיזק בליל הסדר היינו משום דהוי לילה המשומר מן המזיקין, ורק שהוסיפו דאפילו בדרך הטבע יש כאן השתדלות למה לא יהא ניזוק משום הטעמים הנ״ל.[ב]

וביותר נראה לומר בזה, דאפילו רב נחמן שביאר הטעם דשותין ארבע כוסות ואין חוששין לזוגות דהיינו משום דהוי לילה המשומר מן המזיקין, אין כוונתו לחלוק על רבא ורבינא שאמרו טעמים נוספים לזה, דלכולי עלמא זהו עיקר הטעם כמו שאמר רב נחמן דהוי לילה המשומר מן המזיקין, ורק רבא ורבינא הוסיפו ליישב ענין אחר, דאע״ג דיש הבטחה שלא יהא ניזוק מ״מ הרי צריך להשתדל גם ע״פ דרך הטבע שלא יהא ניזוק, ועל זה הוסיפו את הטעמים הנוספים וכנ״ל, אבל גם רב נחמן מודה להם בזה, ומר אמר חדא ומר אמר חדא ולא פליגי.

ועוד יש לבאר את שיטת רב נחמן באופן אחר, דהנה עיקר סוגיית הגמרא בפסחים דמבואר שם שאסור לשלוחי מצוה לסמוך על נס היכא דשכיח

[ב] ועי״פ זה נראה ליישב עוד קושיא עצומה בהא דמבואר בגמרא (יבמות סה, ב) שיש מצוה לשנות מפני השלום, ולמדו דבר זה מהא דהקב״ה אמר לשמואל לשנות בדבריו ולומר שרק בא לזבוח עגלת בקר, עיי״ש. והקשה שם הערוך לנר, דהא מאחר דהתם היה שכיח ההיזק כמבואר בגמרא בפסחים, א״כ לא היתה לו לשמואל הבטחה שלא יהא ניזוק, וכיון שהיה לו חשש פיקוח נפש ששאול יהרגנו ודאי היה מחוייב מצד הדין לומר שקר, והאיך ילפינן מזה דמצוה לשנות משום השלום, עיי״ש מה שתירץ בזה.

אכן לפי הנ״ל הא לא קשיא כלל, שהרי נתבאר דודאי היה לו לשמואל הבטחה מאת הקב״ה שלא ינזק ע״י שאול, ואע״פ דהיה שכיח שם ההיזק מ״מ כך הובטח לו, וא״כ לא היה לשמואל שום חשש של פיקוח נפש כלל. והא דילפינן מהתם שאין לסמוך על הך דשלוחי מצוה אינן ניזוקין במקום דשכיח היזקא, היינו מהא דשמואל שאל את הקב״ה האיך יעשה תחבולה שיהא ניצול גם ע״פ דרך הטבע, וכנ״ל.

היזקא, התם איירי בהיזק המצוי בדרך הטבע, וא״כ יש לומר דבהיזק של זוגות דהוא משום המזיקין לא נאמר הך כללא. וממילא יתכן שבזה גופא נחלקו האמוראים, דרבא ורבינא ס״ל שגם לגבי היזק של המזיקין צריך להשתדל שלא יהא ניזוק בדרך הטבע, והוי כמו שלוחי מצוה דעלמא. אולם רב נחמן פליג בזה וס״ל שכל ענין ההשתדלות בדרך הטבע היינו דוקא היכא דההיזק עצמו בא גם כן ע״י דרך הטבע, אבל בהיזק כזה דהוא משום המזיקין יכול לסמוך על ההבטחה שלא יהא ניזוק אפילו בלא שום השתדלות.

אכן גם בלאו הכי יש לבאר את שיטת רב נחמן בפשיטות, דיש לחלק בזה בין ליל הסדר לשאר היזק דעלמא. שהרי כל עניינו של ליל הסדר הוא לספר בניסים של יציאת מצרים ובגבורתו של הקב״ה, וכיון שזהו עיקר ענין הלילה להראות את האמונה שיש לנו בהקב״ה, לפיכך אע״פ שלגבי כל המצוות קיימא לן שאין סומכין על הבטחה שלא ינזק היכא דשכיח היזקא, מ״מ בלילה הזה אנו סומכין על ההבטחה הזו בלבד, דזהו עיקר מצות הלילה הזה להראות שאנו בוטחים וסומכים על הקב״ה לבדו, וכנ״ל.

לגבי שב ואל תעשה מותר לסמוך על ההבטחה שלא יהא ניזוק, ואין צריך לעשות השתדלות בקום ועשה

אמנם אחר כל הדברים האלה עדיין יש לעיין בדברי הרמ״א, דהנה הובא לעיל מה שכתב הרמ״א (אורח חיים תפא, ב) שנהגו שלא לקרות בליל הסדר את כל הפסוקים שאומרים כל השנה בקריאת שמע שעל המטה, דכיון שכל ענין אמירתם הוא רק כדי לשמור מן המזיקין לכן בליל הסדר אין אומרים אותם. ולפי האמור זה צ״ע קצת, שהרי נתבאר שאין לסמוך על טעם זה לבדו כדי לשתות ד׳ כוסות, אלא צריך גם טעמים נוספים שיועילו גם מדרכי ההשתדלות בדרך הטבע, וא״כ מאי טעמא הרמ״א פסק כן לדינא דאין קוראים את הפסוקים האלו שהם כדי לשמור מן המזיקין.

אכן ביאור הדברים פשוט הוא, דכל סוגיית הגמרא לדון לגבי שתיית ד׳ כוסות בליל הסדר היינו דוקא משום דהוי בקום ועשה, דבזה דנו האמוראים האם סמכינן על הבטחה שלא יהא ניזוק משום דהוי ליל שמורים או דלא סמכינן על זה בלבד רק בצירוף הטעמים הנוספים, אבל אם יושב ולא עושה מאומה אינו צריך לחשוש שיקום עליו היזק, דכיון דהוי לילה המשומר מן המזיקין ודאי אינו צריך לקום ולעשות מעשה כדי שלא יהא ניזוק. וממילא שפיר נקט הרמ״א דבקריאת שמע שעל המטה אין קוראים בליל הסדר את כל הפסוקים שעניינים לשמור מן המזיקין, דלגבי שב ואל תעשה שפיר סמכינן לכולי עלמא על הבטחה זו שאין ניזוקין בלילה הזה.

# תושב״כ ותושבע״פ

## הרב אליהו מאיר ליפסקי[א]

החילוק בין תושב״כ ותושבע״פ • תושבע״פ ומצות - לימוד לשמה • הארץ מגיע לתיקונה ע״י הלימוד לשמה וקיום המצות • שורש תושבע״פ למעלה מהשמים • למה אחד בכתב ואחד בע״פ • לתושבע״פ צריך להמית עצמו עליה.

### החילוק בין תושב״כ ותושבע״פ

הנה ידוע החילוק שבין תושב״כ ותושבע״פ, שהמצות הם כתובים בתורה בדרך כללות, וע״י דרשות הפסוקים ובמסורה שבעל פה מתפרש כל הלכותיהם. ואף שבודאי הכל רמוז בתושב״כ, אבל בפועל אינו מתגלה לעולם ע״י התושב״כ אלא ע״י התושבע״פ. וכדאיתא במדרש תנחומא (פ׳ נח פרק ג):

> יתברך שמו של ממ״ה הקב״ה שבחר בישראל משבעים אומות כמ״ש ״כי חלק ה׳ עמו יעקב חבל נחלתו״ (דברים ל״ב), ונתן לנו את התורה בכתב ברמז צפונות וסתומות ופרשום בתורה שבע״פ וגלה אותם לישראל ולא עוד אלא שתורה שבכתב כללות ותורה שבע״פ פרטות ותורה שבע״פ הרבה ותורה שבכתב מעט ועל שבע״פ נאמר ״ארוכה מארץ מדה ורחבה מני ים״ (איוב יא, יט).

וצריך לבאר למה באמת לא נכתב הכל, ואם משום שזה לא אפשר אחרי שהתורה ארוכה מארץ מידה ורחבה מיני ים, למה אין הכל בעל פה.

עוד מצינו שאופן הלימוד של תושבע״פ שונה מתושב״כ, שענין חיי צער והמתת עצמו על התורה נאמר בפרט על תושבע״פ, וכדאיתא בתנחומא (פ׳ נח שם):

> וכתיב ״ולא תמצא בארץ החיים״ (איוב כח, יג) ומאי ״לא תמצא בארץ החיים״, וכי בארץ המתים תמצא אלא שלא תמצא תורה שבע״פ אצל

---

[א] פרק מספרו החשוב פתחי אמרים, באלטימאר, תשע״ט.

> מי שיבקש עונג העולם תאוה וכבוד וגדולה בעולם הזה אלא במי שממית עצמו עליה שנאמר "זאת התורה אדם כי ימות באהל" (במדבר י"ט).

וכך דרכה של תורה פת במלח תאכל ומים במשורה תשתה ועל הארץ תישן וחיי צער תחיה ובתורה אתה עמל לפי שלא כרת הקב"ה ברית עם ישראל אלא על התורה שבע"פ שנאמר "כי על פי הדברים האלה כרתי אתך ברית" (שמות ל"ד). ואמרו חז"ל לא כתב הקב"ה בתורה למען הדברים האלה ולא בעבור הדברים האלה ולא בגלל הדברים אלא ע"פ הדברים וזו היא תורה שבע"פ שהיא קשה ללמוד ויש בה צער גדול שהוא משולה לחשך שנאמר "העם ההולכים בחשך ראו אור גדול" (ישעיה ט, א) אלו בעלי התלמוד שראו אור גדול שהקב"ה מאיר עיניהם באיסור והיתר בטמא ובטהור ולעתיד לבא "ואוהביו כצאת השמש בגבורתו" (שופטים ה, לא).

וצ"ב למה צריך להיות צער כ"כ כדי להשיג התורה. משמע שזהו מציאות הלימוד של תושבע"פ שלא יתכן בלא זה. ולמה ניתנה לנו באופן כזה.

### תושבע"פ ומצות - לימוד לשמה

וקודם שנבאר קצת מה שהקשינו, צריך להקדים כמה הקדמות ואח"כ נבוא אל המכוון. הנה כתב הגר"א ז"ל בשיר שירים (א, ג פי' א):

> ושמים הוא כולל כל הבריות אף אומות העולם, כמ"ש "ואתה מחיה את כולם", בין ישראל ובין האומות, אבל מן הארץ הם נפרדים, כי ישראל לבדם נפשותם מן ארץ ישראל והם דבקים בה, אבל האומות העולם אינם מקבלים שפע רק מן השמים בכללות, מפאת רוחם, וישראל לבדן נוטלין גם ביחוד מן הארץ... וכן האומות אין לומדין תורה שבעל פה, כי תורה שבעל פה היא ביחוד לישראל לבדן. ובתורה שבכתב מחמת שהיא גבוה נכללין בזה גם שאר האומות.

ועוד כתב שם (פי' ב) באו"א קצת:

> וידוע גם כן שנפשותינו פחותה מנפשות האומות, כי נפשותינו מהארץ, כמ"ש "תוצא הארץ נפש חיה", ונפש האומות מן השמים וכוכביהם... ומפני שנפשותיהם יותר גבוה שהיא מן השמים, והם על הארץ רחוק משרשם, שמשם אינם יכולים לקבל רק התמצית, שהוא

בבחינת הריח, מה שאין כן אנו בני ישראל הסמוכים לארץ ולשרשינו, ונהנים בבחינת הטעם.

ואל תתמה על זה כי משל הוא, כי עבדי המלך נוטלים אפסמיא שלהם מיד המלך לחם חוקם, מה שאין כן אנו בני המלך, נותן המלך סכום עצום ליד המלכה והיא נותנת טרף לביתה, ואם כן אף שהעבדים מקבלים מיד המלך, מכל מקום הסברא נותנת שהבנים מקבלים יותר מובחר מהעבדים, כי משולחן גבוה קא זכו, ואמם נותנת המובחר לבנים בוודאי, כן הוא הנמשל בין האומות לישראל.

ולכן האומות אין צריכין למצות כי יש להם בלאו הכי פרנסה בריוח, אבל בני ישראל שמקבלים מן הארץ, והארץ לית לה מגרמה כלום רק כשזורעין לתוכה אז נותנת, ולכן אנו צריכים למצות... ונבוא אל הענין שתורה שבכתב ותורה שבעל פה הם שתי בחינות, שמים וארץ כידוע, והם שתי בחינות טעם וריח כנ״ל, ולכן מתורה שבכתב נהנין ממנה העכו״ם מעט בבחינת הריח, אבל מתורה שבעל פה שהיא בחינת טעם כנ״ל, אין יכולין ליהנות לגמרי כי אינם משרשה.

ונשתדל להבין פרט אחד בדבריו, והוא מה שכתב שתושב״כ מיוחד לשמים ותושבע״פ לארץ. אבל גם כתב שמה שאנו צריכים למצות הוא בעבור שנפשותינו מן הארץ והמצות מקושרים להארץ. וצ״ב מה הקשר בין מצות ותושבע״פ בענין זה. ועוד יש להעיר, שבישעיה (א, ב) כתב הגר״א ז״ל:

הענין הוא כי האדם נחלק לשתים, הגוף אשר בארץ יסודו והנפש אשר משמים ממעל, וכנגדם שני חלקי התורה, תורה אשר בשמים והמצות אשר בארץ. האדם בקיימו התורה והמצות מחבר שמים וארץ.

הרי ששם מבואר שתורה בשמים ומצות הם בארץ, ולא הזכיר ענין זה שתושבע״פ ג״כ בארץ. ומשמע שהוא בכלל מש״כ שהמצות הם בארץ וזה צ״ב. והנראה בביאור הענין, כי עיקר ענין לימוד תושבע״פ לשמה הוא לימוד ע״מ לעשות. וכמבואר בדברי הגר״א ז״ל במשלי (לא, ל):

״שקר החן״. כי לא הלימוד עיקר אלא המעשה, שהוא אחר כוונתו, כי רחמנא ליבא בעי, וכמ״ש אחר המרבה ואחד הממעיט ובלבד שיכוון וכו׳. ואמרו חז״ל ״אל תהיו כעבדים המשמשין וכו׳ אלא הוו

וכו׳״. ולכאורה תמוה, דבתחילה אמר לשון אזהרה ״אל תהיו״, ואחר כך אמר לשון עצה ״אלא הוו״. וכפול. והעניין, דשלושה מיני מעשים. אחד, הלומד בשביל פניות, אקרא בכדי שיקראוני וכו׳, והוא מפני כבוד ועושר. שני, שלומד בשביל בוראו, שימצא חן בעיניו ויתן שכר טוב לעולם הבא. והשלישי הוא רק טוב ביראה ה׳ כאשר ציוונו לשמור ולעשות, ולא לשום פנייה כלל. וזה אמר תחילה לשון אזהרה ושלילה ״אל תהיו כו׳״ על פנייה הראשונה, ועל כוונתו השלישית אמר ״אלא הוו וכו׳״ שתשתדלו עצמכם לבוא לידי כך ללמוד בלי פנייה כלל. וזה שאמר ״שקר החן״ שעושה בשביל למצוא חן בעיני אדם, כי לא נתקיימה בידן והמעשה בעצמו הוא שקר. וזהו פירוש כמו שהן מבלין העולם. והבל היופי. שמיפה עצמו נגד הקב״ה, אף שהמעשה בעצמו הוא טוב, כמ״ש חז״ל ״האומר סלע זו לצדקה בשביל וכו׳ הרי זה צדיק גמור״, מכל מקום הוא הבל, וכמ״ש ״ראיתי את כל המעשים שנעשו תחת השמש והנה הכל הבל ורעות רוח״, ״ואין יתרון תחת השמש״. ופירושו כמ״ש בגמ׳ פסחים ״מעל שמים חסדך וכו׳״, ״עד שמים חסדך וכו׳״ כאן בעושין לשמה וכו׳ שלא לשמה וכו׳, כי העושין לשמה הוא דבר שלמעלה מהשמים, לכן על השמים חסדו להם, מה שאין כן אותן העושין שלא לשמה הוא תחת השמים. וזה שאמר ״ואין יתרון תחת השמש״.

וכ״כ בביאורו לתיקונ״ז (ב.):

והענין של לשמה שלומד ע״מ לקיים מצותי׳ של התורה.

ונמצא שגם לימוד התושבע״פ שייך לענין הארץ מאותו הטעם שמצות שייכים להארץ, שהרי עיקר הלימוד ראוי להיות באופן שהוא כדי לבא לקיום המצות.

### הארץ מגיע לתיקונה ע״י הלימוד לשמה וקיום המצות

וע״י לימוד באופן זה, הארץ מקבל תיקון כשהוא מייחד הארץ, השכינה, לקב״ה. וכמ״ש הגר״א ז״ל בתיקונ״ז שם:

דעסקין באורייתא לשמה – ר״ל בשביל השכינה לייחד אותה עם התורה והענין של לשמה שלומד ע״מ לקיים מצותי׳ של התורה

> והמצות הן בשכינה א״כ הוא לשמה... בכל אברין דיליה - שתרי״ג מצות הן נגד איבריו של אדם מ״ע נגד רמ״ח איברים ומל״ת נגד שס״ה גידין וע״י עסק התורה שהוא שם ה׳ לקיים המצות שהוא בשכינה מתיחדים.

והנה עבודה זו של כלל ישראל לתקן הארץ הוא בעבור שנפשותינו מן הארץ. ואנו במדרגה פחותה, אבל הא גופא, בעבור זה ניתנה לנו מדרגה זו כדי להעלותה לשרשה למעלה. וזהו ענין תושבע״פ והמצות שניתן לנו לעשות עבודה זו ע״י הלימוד ע״מ לעשות, לעסוק במצות בעניני הארץ ועי״ז מעלים את הארץ ומחברים אותה למעלה.

## שורש תושבע״פ למעלה מהשמים

ונראה לבאר עוד בהיכולת הזו להעלות הארץ, שהרי אע״פ שאנו מושרשים בארץ ואפילו פחותים מנפשות האומות, אבל מכיון ששורש התושב״פ היא למעלה מזה העולם, יש לנו הכח להעלות הדבר הפחות למעלה ממדרגתה. וכמו שהבאנו לעיל שלימוד לשמה, שהוא ע״מ לעשות, הוא מעל השמים. וביתר ביאור בדבר זה, כתב הגרי״א חבר בשיח יצחק (דרוש לשבת תרומה עמ׳ יב):

> כי התורה הכתובה, כבר כתבנו שציורי אותיותיה הם ממש ציורי הנבראים העליונים ותחתונים והיא כתובה למעלה במרום, ומשה רבינו היה כמעתיק מספר לספר, והיא כתובה בכל עולם כפי ערך כוחות הנבראים שבהם, ולפי ציורם ומעמדם, ורומז על פרטי הרכבת כוחותיהם, ולמטה בארץ נתגלמה בציור הכתובה אשורית, שהם ממש מכוונים לעומת העליונים, והרי התורה הזאת מושגת לכל צבאי מעלה, ולמה״ש כל אחד לפי מדרגתו. אבל תורה שבע״פ מקורה למעלה למעלה מה שלא נתן להשגת מה״ש, ואינם לפי ערכם, והיא נמסרה בע״פ לישראל מצד שורש נשמותיהם החצובה מתחת כסא הכבוד, שהוא למעלה ממדרגת מה״ש, וע״ז בקשו מה״ש (שבת פח:), ואמרו (תהילים ח, ב), ״אשר תנה הודך על השמים״, ונתנה לארץ ולכן אמר הכתוב שבה כרת השי״ת ברית עם ישראל.

וגם יוצא מדבריו הבנה יתירה במש״כ הגר״א ז״ל שתושב״כ שרשה בשמים. אבל תושבע״פ בנוגע לזה העולם, מקומה בהארץ, ששם ניתנה כדי לתקן ולהעלות הארץ.

וכמו כן מצינו במצות, שהגם שמקומם הם בהארץ ותורה היא בשמים וכמ״ש הגר״א ז״ל, אבל שורשם למעלה מתורה, וכמ״ש הגר״א ז״ל במשלי(ו, כ):

> ״נצור מצות אביך״, כבר כתבתי שהמצות אינן אלא בזמנן וכשבא לידו לכן אומר נצור עד הזמן או עד כאשר יבא לידך. ״ואל תטוש תורת אמך״ תמיד אפילו רגע אחד כי תורה צריך ללמוד תמיד בכל עת ובכל שעה. ואמר אצל ״מצות״ ״אביך״, ואצל ״תורת״ ״אמך״ כי או״א הם חו״ב והטיפה באבא הוא בנסתר ונעלם וכשבא לאמא מצטיירת שם כן החכמה נעלמת מעין כל חי שהיא במחשבה ובבינה היא מצטיירת ושם הוא בגלוי יותר. ושורש המצות הן בחכמה והתורה היא בבינה בסוד ״ה׳ בחכמה יסד ארץ כונן שמים בתבונה״ (משלי ג, יט). ולכן כל דבר בארץ הוא בנעלם אבל בשמים הם נגלים יותר וכן אדם הראשון היה יודע בארץ מחמת שהיה יודע שרשן בשמים ומצות הן מן הארץ כמו סוכה ולולב ותורה הוא מן השמים. ולכן אמר ״מצות אביך״ ו״תורת אמך״ ועוד ״נצור מצות אביך״ סבב אותך במצות שהיא אור מקיף ״ואל תטוש תורת אמך״ הוא הוא אור פנימי והיינו שנתן לנו ה׳ ד׳ מצות תפילין וציצית ומזוזה והן סביב האדם.

## למה אחד בכתב ואחד בע״פ

והנה בביאור שאלתנו הראשונה למה לא ניתנו תושב״כ ותושבע״פ שוין, שיש לכתוב שניהם או להיות שניהם בעל פה, למה אחד בכתב ואחד בעל פה, כתב המהר״ל (תפארת ישראל פרק סח):

> דע כי אין ראוי שתהיה התורה שבעל פה בכתיבה מפני שהתורה שבעל פה הם פרטי המצוה ופרושיה ודבר זה אין קץ וסוף כי הפרטים אין להם קץ ולא היה דבר שלם אם היה כותב מקצת בלבד, לכך אין לכתוב כלל התורה שבעל פה חסירה כי הכתיבה מורה על התמימות שיהיה כאן הכל ביחד והרי בתורה שבעל פה אי אפשר כמו שאמרנו. אבל על פה הרי כי ענין הפה כך הוא שאין הכל ביחד

> כי כאשר מדבר דבור ואחר כך השני כבר הלך לו דבור הראשון ולא שייך בדבור תמימות ולפיכך תורה שבעל פה אין לכתוב כלל, והפך זה גם כן שהתורה שבכתב היא שלימה ותמימה מחויב שתהא בכתב ולא בעל פה שאם לא כן כיון שראוי לה הכתיבה אם יאמר אותה בעל פה אין כאן שלימות ותמימות ואפילו אם יאמר כל התורה כולה ביחד מכל מקום הרי בשעה שיאמר החלק האחר כבר אין כאן החלק הראשון ואין תורת ה׳ תמימה ושלימה ולפיכך דברים שבכתב אי אתה רשאי לאומרם בעל פה.

וע״פ מה שנתבאר לעיל יש להבין קצת בעומק כוונתו, כי תושב״כ הוא כולל כל העולם כולו, וכמ״ש אסתכל באורייתא וברא עלמא. וכל התורה כולה ביחד היא צורה שלימה של בריאה זו. ולכן גם למלאכים יש שייכות לתושב״כ, שהם בכלל צורת הבריאה של תושב״כ. אבל תושבע״פ עולה למעלה מזה, שהיא ארוכה מארץ מידה, ואין לומר שיש לה קץ או סוף. וכמו כן בתושב״כ עצמה, מצד מה שרמוז בו ונלמד מתושבע״פ ג״כ אין לה סוף, אבל מצד האופן שהיא כתובה לפי פשוטו הוא דבר שלם ביחד שכלולה בה כל הבריאה כולה.

## לתושבע״פ צריך להמית עצמו עליה

ועכשיו נחזור לבאר למה האופן של לימוד תושבע״פ הוא רק במסירת נפש ויגיעה עצומה. ומתחילה נביא המשך דברי המדרש תנחומא בפ׳ נח שם:

> ולא קבלו ישראל את התורה עד שכפה עליהם הקב״ה את ההר כגיגית שנאמר ״ויתיצבו בתחתית ההר״ (שמות יט, יז), ואמר רב דימי בר חמא א״ל הקב״ה לישראל אם מקבלים אתם את התורה מוטב ואם לאו שם תהא קבורתכם. ואם תאמר על התורה שבכתב כפה עליהם את ההר והלא משעה שאמר להן מקבלין אתם את התורה ענו כלם ואמרו ״נעשה ונשמע״ מפני שאין בה יגיעה וצער והיא מעט. אלא אמר להן על התורה שבע״פ שיש בה דקדוקי מצות קלות וחמורות והיא ״עזה כמות וקשה כשאול קנאתה״ (שיר השירים ח, ו) לפי שאין לומד אותה אלא מי שאוהב הקב״ה בכל לבו ובכל נפשו ובכל מאודו שנא׳ ״ואהבת את ה׳ אלהיך בכל לבבך ובכל נפשך ובכל

> מאודך" (דברים ו, ה) ומנין אתה למד שאין אהבה זו אלא לשון תלמוד ראה מה כתיב אחריו והיו הדברים האלה אשר אנכי מצוך היום על לבבך ואי זה זה תלמוד שהוא על הלב הוי אומר ושננתם לבניך זו תלמוד שצריך שנון ללמדך שפרשה ראשונה שבק"ש אין בה פירוש מתן שכרה בעוה"ז כמ"ש בפרשה שנייה "והיה אם שמוע תשמעו וגו' ונתתי מטר ארצכם" זה מתן שכר עוסקי מצות (ס"א תורה שבכתב) שאין עוסקין בתלמוד ובפ' שנייה כתיב בה "בכל לבבכם ובכל נפשכם" ולא כתב בכל מאדכם ללמדך שכל מי שאוהב עושר ותענוג אינו יכול ללמוד תורה שבע"פ לפי שיש בה צער גדול ונדוד שינה ויש מבלה ומנבל עצמו עליה לפיכך מתן שכרה לעה"ב שנאמר "העם ההולכים בחשך ראו אור גדול", אור גדול אור שנברא ביום ראשון שגנזו הקב"ה לעמלי תורה שבע"פ ביום ובלילה שבזכותן העולם עומד שנאמר (ירמיה לג, כה) "כה אמר ה' אם לא בריתי יומם ולילה חוקות שמים וארץ לא שמתי", אי זה הוא ברית שנוהג ביום ובלילה זו תלמוד, וכן הוא אומר (שם לג, כ-כא) "כה אמר ה' אם תפרו את בריתי היום ואת בריתי הלילה, גם בריתי תפר את דוד עבדי" וגו', ואומר (תהלים א, ב) "כי אם בתורת ה' חפצו ובתורתו יהגה יומם ולילה."

ונראה בביאור הענין, כי כפי חיי עוה"ז אין האדם שייך לתושבע"פ, שהיא ממעל ומעבר לזה העולם. רק ע"י שממית חייו של זה העולם יכול לתפוס התושבע"פ. ולכן הוצרכו לכפיית הר כגגית, שהרי לא יוכלו בגופם לקבל דבר זה אחרי שמתנגד לגופם וחייהם. וכן זה הכוונה שאין שייך שכר מצות בעוה"ז ללימוד תושבע"פ. כי שכר מצות הוא ענין הדביקות כמ"ש השל"ה (תולדות אדם, בית חכמה - תניינא):

> תרי"ג מצות אשר נצטוינו עליהם בעולם המעשה היום לעשותם ולמחר לקבל שכרם, אין השכר והעונש הסכמיי, רק הוא טבעיי רוחניי נמשך בעצם, כהא דתנן (אבות ד, ב) שכר מצוה מצוה שכר עבירה עבירה. כי שכר מצוה גשמיית שפועל זהו בעצמו שכרו, דהיינו רוחניות המצוה הזו, כענין שכתבתי למעלה שכל התוארים והתיבות שנזכרו בתורה שורש ועצמיות אלו התיבות הוא לשון קודש, רצוני לומר שהשם למעלה הוא בקדושה באמת, רק בהשתלשלות נמשך שנקרא כך הגשמיות בהשאלה, כן בפעולת

> המצות אין לך אפילו מצוה קלה שאין לה שורש גדול מלמעלה, וזה השורש הוא בעצמו השכר ששם נדבק נשמתו.

ועיי״ש בכל דבריו שם שהאריך בביאור הענין. ואפשר לומר שזה רק יתכן בשכר מצות מעשיות שעשה בגופו בתוך הארץ, אבל הדביקות שנולדה מלימוד תושבע״פ אינה דביקות ששייכת להשפעה וברכה של עוה״ז, שהרי היא ״גדול מעל שמים חסדך״ (תהלים קח, ה).

# ספר תורה בלשון יוונית בזמן הזה

## יהושע דיקסלער

איתא במשנה (מגילה ח:): אין בין ספרים לתפלין ומזוזות, אלא שהספרים נכתבין בכל לשון, ותפלין ומזוזות אינן נכתבות אלא אשורית. רבן שמעון בן גמליאל אומר, אף בספרים לא התירו שיכתבו אלא יוונית.

בפשטות משנה זו מלמדת שאפשר לכתוב ספר תורה בכל שפה, או לפחות ביוונית לפי רשב״ג. עם זאת, הגמרא מביאה משנה (ידים ד, ה) סותרת האומרת שאין זה נחשב ספר ״עד שיכתבנו בכתב אשורית, על הספר, ובדיו.״

הגמרא (ט.) מתרצת הסתירה בשתי דרכים: (א) תורה יכולה להיות בכל שפה כדברי המשנה במגילה, אבל המשנה במס׳ ידים מדברת רק במגילה שחייבת להיות אשורית כפי שמצוין בביטוי ״ככתבם וכזמנם.״ (ב) ספר תורה יכולה להיות בכל שפה, אבל המשנה בידים מדברת רק בספרי נ״ך אחרים שחייבים להיות אשורית. אבל נראה מגמרא זו שאפשר לכתוב ספר תורה ביוונית לפי כל הדעות.

איתא עוד במשנה (מגילה יז.): הקורא את המגילה למפרע, לא יצא. קראה על פה, קראה תרגום בכל לשון, לא יצא. אבל קורין אותה ללועזות בלעז, והלועז ששמע אשורית, יצא. ע״כ. הגמרא מפרשת את המשנה שאפשר לקרוא את המגילה בכל לשון רק למי שמבין את הלשון, אבל לא למי שאינו מבין אותו הלשון. עם זאת, אשורית (לשון קודש) מקובלת על כולם. רב ושמואל, שפוסקין כמו רשב״ג, סוברים שיוונית היא בדיוק כמו אשורית וניתן להשתמש בה גם לתורה וגם למגילה, גם למי שאינו מבין יוונית. זה מסקנת הגמרא, וגם היא בקנה אחד עם הפסק של ר׳ יוחנן כרשב״ג (מגילה ט:).

עם זאת, הרי״ף אינו מייחס כל מעלה ללשון יוונית, וכותב שהשומע צריך להבין את הלשון הזרה, אפילו יוונית, כדי ליוצא חובתו. הבעל המאור מקשה על הרי״ף שדבריו נראים כסותרים את הגמרא. הרמב״ן והר״ן מתרצים בפשיטות שלדברי הרי״ף מסקנת הגמרא אינו כשיטת רשב״ג.

הרמב״ם פוסק (תפילין ומזוזה א, יט): אין כותבין תפלין ומזוזה אלא בכתב אשורית. והתירו בספרים לכתב אף ביוני בלבד. וכבר נשקע יוני מן העולם ונשתבש ואבד, לפיכך אין כותבין היום שלשתן אלא אשורית. ע״כ. ומפרש הכסף משנה (שם): ומ״ש רבינו וכבר נשתקע יונית, אותו לשון יוני שהיו מדברים בו בימי חכמי משנה כבר נשתקע. ע״כ.

לכאורה בניגוד להרי״ף, הרמב״ם מתיר יוונית מעיקר הדין. עם זאת, הוא אומר שזה כבר אינו נוגע למעשה כי הלשון יוונית שלנו איננו הלשון שהתיר רשב״ג. אמנם הבית יוסף (אורח חיים, סי׳ תר״צ) מסביר שהרי״ף השמיט את היתר הכתיבה בלשון היוונית כי הוא סובר כמו הרמב״ם שזה אינו נוגע למעשה בזמננו כי כבר נשתקע יוניתץ

מעניין לציין שבכסף משנה כתב שרק ״לשון״ יוני אינו אפשרי עכשיו, אבל יש לדייק ש״כתב״ היווני לא נשתקע ואפשר להשתמש בו. הכסף משנה בהלכות מגילה וחנוכה (ב, ג-ד) מדגיש שחשובה רק הלשון, לא האותיות. כשקוראים בתורה כזו שנכתב ביוונית אנשים ישמעו את המילים בלשון קודש, וזה מספיק גם אם הם לא מבינים.

הרמב״ם כותב בפירוש המשנה (מגילה ב:): ומה שנשתנה לשון יוני משאר הלשונות לפי שהיה מובן אצלם. הטעם מפני שהם פרשו התורה בלשון יון לתלמי המלך ונתפרסמה אצלם אותה העתקה עד שהיתה אצלם אותו לשון כמו לשונם וכאלו היתה אשורית.

לפי הרמב"ם הזה, לשון יוונית נחשבה באותה מדרגה של לשון הקודש משום שהיהודים השתמשו עם התרגום שכתבו הרבנים לתלמי. אבל קשה שנראה נגד טעם המובא בגמרא (מגילה ט:) המסבירה שליוונית יש יופי ייחודי המתאים לשימוש על ידי היהודים שהם צאצאי שם בן נח: "יפת אלהים ליפת וישכן באהלי שם."

אפשר לשאול על דין זה מסנהדרין (כא:): אמר מר זוטרא ואיתימא מר עוקבא, בתחלה ניתנה תורה לישראל בכתב עברי ולשון הקודש, חזרה וניתנה להם בימי עזרא בכתב אשורית ולשון ארמי, ביררו להן לישראל כתב אשורית ולשון הקודש. ע"כ.

לפני תקנת עזרא התורה היתה נכתבת בשפות אחרות. א"כ למה חייב עזרא בימיו שתהא נכתבת דוקא בכתב אשורית? הרד"ל (מובא בספר תקנות ישראל) מסביר שזה היה כדי שלא ישתמשו בתורות הכותיים שהיו כותבים בלשון עברית. ויחד עם תקנה לאסור פתם, ימנעו היהודים להתערבב עם הכותיים.

א"כ צריכים לעיין איך יכלו הדורות המאוחרים, להתיר כתיבת ספר תורה בלשון יוונית נגד תקנת עזרא? אלא אפשר לבאר שהם הבינו שעזרא לא גזר שספר תורה צריך ליכתב בכתב אשורית, אלא רק אסר כתב עברית מפני הכותים. וממילא יהיה מותר להשתמש בתרגום אחר שנעשה בלשון מעולה מעברית. הם הצליחו למצוא רמז בתורה שלא רק התיר את לשון יוונית, אלא הרים אותה מעל לשפות אחרות. וכדי לתת חוזק לשנות את תקנת עזרא, נבחרו במיוחד מספר ע' רבנים, שיהיו בכמות של סנהדרין. שני טעמים אלו מספיקים בעת צרה זו תחת שלטון יוונים שבמלכות תלמי היווני.

באופן כללי תקנה לא הופכת לחיובי עד שרוב הציבור מקבלים אותה. זה קרה למעשה לתורה שנכתב ביוונית, כפי שמסביר הרמב"ם במשנה. לאחר מכן, תורה ביוונית הייתה במדרגה של אשורית כמו שהיתה לפני עזרא. התרגום

הזה התבסס עד כדי כך שהנוצרים המוקדמים, שהיו יהודים אפיקורסים, היו משתמשים בתרגום זו לעיקר תורתם, וכינו אותו "ספטואגינט," שמשמעו שבעים.

אבל מכיוון שאנו יודעים שהנוצרים שמרו על תרגום זה עד היום, כיצד יכול הרמב"ם לטעון שהשפה הייתה "נשקע ונשתבש" וכבר אי אפשר להשתמש בה? ואפשר לומר שדחיית היוונית על ידי רמב"ם הייתה באמת דחייה נגד הנוצרים. ברגע שהנוצרים משתמשים ביוונית לעיקר תורתם, הטעם המקורי של עזרא חוזר וניעור להפריד היהודים מהנוצרים ושוב לא הותרו היהודים להשתמש בתרגום יוונית. כך משמעות הפירוש שכתב הרמב"ם "וכבר נשקע יוני מן העולם ונשתבש ואבד." הוא לא כתב שהיוונית נשכחה, מה שלמעשה לא אירע עקב תחזוקת תרגום השבעים בספטואגינט. במקום זאת, הוא כתב "נשקע" כלומר היה "שקוע", ור"ל שכעת הוא שקוע בידי הנוצרים. בנוסף כתב "ונשתבש", שכן הנוצרים שינו את התרגום בכמה מקומות כדי לחזק אמונתם.

אם כן ניתן לחקור אם היינו מוצאים את התרגום המקורי ביוונית שכתבו שבעים הרבנים האם זה היה כשר היום? לכאורה זה יהיה תלוי איך אנחנו מבינים את הרמב"ם. הרמב"ם פירש על במשנה שהצליחו הרבנים לתקן כנגד התקנה של עזרא, בעזרת היהודים שקיבלו את התרגום החדש, ובעזרת התורה הרומזת ליפוי היוונית על שפות אחרות. כיון שהתקנה של חכמי הגמרא כבר נתקנה, אולי היא נשארת עד היום והיוונית תהיה מותרת.

מצד שני, כיון שבתקופת הרמב"ם (המאה ה-יב') הנוצרים כבר חזקו את התרגום היווני, שוב אסור ליהודים להשתמש בה. ייתכן שהצורך החשוב להפריד את היהודים מן הנוצרים, במיוחד בתקופת התחייה הדתית שהביאה למסעות הצלב בתקופה זו, מביא להחזרת התקנה המקורית של עזרא, כפי שרומז הרמב"ם ביד החזקה, ויהיה אסור לקראת ביוונית בזמן הזה.

# קדושת ארץ ישראל בכח ובפועל

## הרב שמואל חיים ניימאן [א]

### מקום העבודה

ארץ ישראל אינה ענין פרטי בתורה, אלא כלל גדול המקיף את רוב התורה. אינו רחוק לסכם שכמעט כל תורת משה, מ"לך לך... אל הארץ אשר אראך" עד "ויראהו ה' את כל הארץ...", הוא הסיפור של בנין האומה כדי שיכנסו לארץ ישראל. עד כדי כך שהרמב"ן (ויקרא יח, כה) כתב ש"עיקר כל המצוות ליושבים בארץ ה'", והטעם שאנו "מצויינים במצוות" בחו"ל הוא כדי שלא יהיו חדשים כשנחזור לארץ, וכידוע.

אולם יש להתבונן למה עם ישראל צריך לארץ המיוחדת שלהם, הנקראת על שמם? הרי הקב"ה נתן לנו את התורה במדבר, ואנחנו לומדים אותה ושומרים את מצוותיה הרבה יותר זמן בגלות בחו"ל מאשר שהיינו בא"י. למה היותנו "ממלכת כהנים וגוי קדוש" מחייב ארץ שהיא קדושה כמונו?

נראה לי ששאלה זו מונחת בטעות בהבנת המושג של עבודה בכלל. מושג זה נמצא בשורש של קבלת התורה כמש"כ "תעבדון את אלקים בהר הזה", וכמ"ש בגמרא "אדם לעמל יולד – לעמל תורה". והנה אם עבודה היתה להמציא מציאות חדשה, 'יש מאין', אה"נ לא היה צריך אליה מקום מסויים ומיוחד. אדרבה, כל המהלך היה יוצא מתוך האדם עצמו, ובכל מקום שהוא עומד יכול הוא לעשות את עבודתו. אבל האמת שאין לאדם שום זיקה ישרה אל 'יש מאין', כי איננו 'אלקים' שברא את השמים והארץ, אלא 'צלם אלקים' שיכול וחייב ליצור את עולמו בדרך של 'יש מיש'. ולכן עבודה פירושה לקחת

---

[א] לפני שנה ערכתי חוברת על הגבולות וקדושות של ארץ ישראל, המבוסס על ספר נפלא בנושא שחיבור הרה"ג הרב אריאל בוקוולד, "אני ה' שוכן בתוכה". מאמר זה העוסק בכלל הענין של א"י מובא מפרק א, והוא הקדמה אל פרטי הסוגיות שנתבארו שם בהרחבה.

איזה מציאות שהיא כבר קיימת בצורה גולמית, ׳בכח׳, ולעמול כדי להוציאה אל הפועל בצורה שלימה יותר. ליתן ׳צורה׳ אל ׳חומר׳.

כך היא המהלך בכל עבודה, בין בגשמיות ובין ברוחניות. האדם אינו ממציא בית מתוך גופו, אלא אוסף חומרי גלם ומסדר אותם בצורה שהם נהפכים לבית מפואר שאפשר לגור בו. וכמו״כ אין האדם ממציא עבודת ה׳ מתוך נשמתו, אלא הוא מעצב את החומר הגשמי של העולם מסביבו בצורה של רצונו ית׳.

ומכאן יש להבין שכל ׳עבודה׳ מחייבת מקום בתוך העולם, מה שבעוה״ז מופיע לנו כ׳ארץ׳. הארץ כוללת בתוכה כל המציאויות החומריות העומדות ומחכות אל האדם שיתן להם צורה שלימה, וכל מקום בתוכה יש לה את הסגולות המיוחדות שנמצאים בו ׳בכח׳ ויכולים לצאת אל הפועל. כך היא תכונת הארץ העשויה מיסוד העפר: מצד עצמה אין בה שום צורה מסוימת, אבל ״הכל יצא מן העפר״ (מ״ר) כי היא החומר גלם שהוליד את כל הצורות המסוימות. ובתוך העולם של ׳ארץ׳, יש ארצות עם אבנים שטובים לבנין, ויש ארצות שטוב לגדל מהם אוכל, ויש ארצות שאפשר להפיק מהם מעלות רוחניות. כל ארץ תובעת את האדם למלאות אותה בצורה הנכונה לו, וכמ״ש הקב״ה לאדה״ר ״מלאו את הארץ וכבשוה״.

בנקודה זו האדם מיוחד מכל שאר בעלי החיים: כל האחרים הם ׳בה-מה׳ ר״ל שמהותם כבר נמצא בפועל בתוכם, משא״כ תפיסת האדם הנק׳ ע״ש ״עפר מן האדמה״ הוא בעצם המציאות ׳בכח׳, להוציאה מהכח אל הפועל בעמלו. לאדם בלבד ניתן ׳חכ-מה׳ – ׳כח מה׳, ר״ל מהות העומדת בכח ושואפת לצאת אל הפועל.

וכשנתבונן בתהליך העבודה, נראה שיש להבחין שתי מדריגות בכל מציאות חומרי ששייך עליה עבודה. מצד אחד, פשוט שכל האפשריות העתידיות לצאת אל הפועל הם כבר מונחים ׳בכח׳ בתוך החומר, דאל״כ הופעתם יהיה

ב׳יש מאין׳ ולא מתוך החומר. אבל גם כשעמלים לממש את היכולות שלו עד שנהפך למציאות שלימה ׳בפועל׳, עדיין החומר קיים כחומר, אלא שאנו אומרים על אותו חומר שקיבל צורה. למשל, כשחומרי בנייה נהפכים לבית אין ה׳בית׳ מפקיע מציאותם של העצים ואבנים שבנו אותו, אלא שאותם חומרים קיבלו צורה שלימה של בית ע״י עבודת הבנין.

ועכ״ז אפשר להבין הצורך של ארץ קדושה בשביל עם קדוש, וגם השורש לשני הגדרים שמצינו לקדושתה. כפי שביארנו, אי אפשר להמציא עבודה בתורה ומצוות מתוך עצמינו, שעבודה אינה אלא לפעול על מציאות קיימת וליתן לה צורה שלימה יותר, שלענייננו הוא לבנות עולם חומרי כפי רצונו ית׳. ולכן אותו רצון של הקב״ה לעם הנבחר שיקיימו את רצונו בעולם ע״כ הוא גם רצון בשביל מציאות חומרית ב׳ארץ׳ שעליה הם יעבדו. התורה והמצוות נאמרו אל החלק של האנושות הנקרא ׳כלל ישראל׳ כדרכים להוציא אל הפועל החלק של העולם החומרי הנקרא ׳ארץ ישראל׳. כשם שאי אפשר לבנות בית מפואר במיוחד מעצים ואבנים פשוטים, כמו״כ לא יתכן לבנות אומה של עובדי השם בלא מקום המיוחד ומסוגל בשבילם.

וכמו שראינו אצל כל תהליך של עבודה, גם בקדושה של ארץ ישראל אפשר להבחין שני ענינים – המעלות של א״י הנמצאים ׳בכח׳ בעצם טבעה, והמצב של הארץ כשהיא עצמה ׳בפועל׳ ושלימה עם כל יושביה הקדושים עליה. ומכיון שקדושת ארץ ישראל אינה אלא כדי לקבל את עבודת כלל ישראל בקיום מצוות התורה, וכל מהותן של המצוות הם המחויבות לרצונו ית׳, מסתבר ששני הענינים האלו יתבטאו במצוות התלויות בארץ. ולהבין קצת בזה, נציע שני הענינים האלו של קדושת א״י בשורשיהם, עם הקבוצות של מצוות התלויות בארץ שלכאורה תלויים בהם.

## קדושת החומר של הארץ

כשהחבר בספר הכוזרי אמר ש״קרני אור אלהי מועילים אצל עמו בארצו״, שאל לו המלך את שאלתנו הנ״ל שהתינח ״אצל עמו״ מובן לו מכל מה שהחבר לימד אותו על מעלת כלל ישראל ממין האנושי, אבל למה דוקא ״בארצו״. והחבר ענה לו שהרי אנו רואים מקומות שמסוגלים לגדל צמחים ובעלי חיים מסויימים יותר מאחרים, וכתוצאה מכך האנשים היושבים בהם מקבלים תכונות נפשיות מסויומות, הכל משום ש״לפי המזג תהחיה שלימת הנפש וחסרונה״.

וכששאל לו הכוזרי שלא שמענו על מעלה מיוחדת לאנשים שיושבים בא״י, ענה לו עם המשל הידוע אל הכרם (ב, יב, בתרגום הרב שילת): כך הרכם זה שאתם אומרים שגדל בו הכרם, אילו לא היו נוטעים בו הגפנים ועובדים העבודה הראויה להם, לא היה עושה ענבים. והתכונה המיוחדת הראשונה היא לעם, אשר הם הסגולה והלב, כמו שהזכרתי, ואח״כ יש לארץ בזה עזר עם המעשים והמצוות הכרוכים בה, אשר הם כעבודה לכרם. אבל לא תצליח הסגולה הזאת לדבוק בענין האלקי בזולת המקום הזה, כמו שיצליח הכרם לגדול בהר הזה.

ויש להבין עומק כוונתו עפ״ד. מעלת א״י אינה דבר שלם הנמצא בפועל מתחילת הבריאה, גלוי וידוע לעין כל. אלא מעלתה היא דוקא בתור ׳ארץ׳, מציאות ׳בכח׳ עם סגולות נפלאות המחכות ורוצות שיבוא כלל ישראל ויוציא אותם אל הפועל בשלימות. ולכן עיקר רצונו ית׳ בבריאה לא היתה הארץ מצד עצמה, אלא לכלל ישראל שישבו עליה ויעבדו אותה ויקיימו את מצוותיה, שהם נותנים הצורת השלימה של הארץ כמו שהכרם היא התכלית של ההר המיוחד לגדל גפנים מעולים. באופן שקיום רצון ה׳ בארץ ישראל היא פעולה מקבילה אל עם עבודת הכרם בארץ המיוחדת לה: עמל ועבודה לעצב חומרי גלם המתאימים לקבל צורה מסוימת.

ונראה שהקדושה הטבעית 'בכח' המבוארת בכוזרי שייכת אל הגבולות של א"י המוזכרים בתורה כהבטחה אל האבות, יותר מהקדושה המגיע מתוך הכיבוש וקידוש בפועל. ולכאו' כך מבואר להדיא מדבריו. שאחרי המשל הנ"ל אל הכרם שאל הכוזרי שמצינו נבואה גם בחו"ל, ואיך תאמר שרק א"י מסוגל לדביקות בענין האלקי. וענה החבר שבאמת "כל מי שהתנבא אמנם התנבא בה או בעבורה", והאריך טובא לתאר איך כל סדר הדורות כבר מאדה"ר סבבו מסביב לנחלת א"י, ובתו"ד תיאר גבולות שהם כוללים גם מדבר סיני ופארן, ובמק"א בספר (ד, ג) הזכיר גם שעיר ומצרים ב"ארץ הנבואה". ולהלן (סוף פרק ב) נרחיב לבאר בשיטת הכוזרי שכבר בזה"ז ארץ ישראל לענין נבואה כולל את הגבולות הרחבות ביותר שיגיעו לה לע"ל, גם במקומות שעכשיו אין שום קדושת א"י בפועל.

ולכאו' עומק הענין מבואר עפ"ד. שהנה השגה דרך נבואה הנק' תמיד "ראייה" ו"חזון" הוא תפיסת כלל המציאות האמיתית שמחוץ לאדם, ועניגה כמו כל ראייה שמשגת את התמונה הכללית, החומר 'בכח', בלא פירוטה לחלקים מסויימים בעלי צורה. ולכן נבואה תלויה על כח הדמיון כמבואר ברמב"ם בהרחבה, כי הדמיון הוא תפיסה של חומר לפני עבודה. (וכל זה לעומת שכל וחכמה שהם תפיסה של פרטים וצורה בפועל.) וזה הטעם שלענין נבואה א"י מוגדרת כפי הרחבתה לע"ל, שלמרות שלענין עבודתנו בפועל בזה"ז מדריגה זו נשגבה מאיתנו, עדיין כל הסגולות הרוחניות הטבעיות שלה נמצאים בה 'בכח', מחכים ומשתוקקים אל ימות המשיח כדי לצאת אל הפועל בעבודה.

**המצוות מחמת קדושת החומר**

אבל גם בגבולות היותר מצומצים של א"י בזה"ז, שפרטיהם נלמד היטב בפנים, יש נפק"מ גדולה לקדושת א"י מצד עצם טבעה. שהעולה מהחזו"א (שביעית ס"ג סק"ב, ערלה ס"א סקי"א [מד"ה ל"ח א' והלאה], שם סקי"ב וי"ד) ע"פ הסוגיות בסופ"ק דקידושין הוא שיש שני סוגים של מצוות התלויות בארץ.

יש מצוות שהתחייבו רק לאחר כיבוש וחילוק, והם תלויים על קדושה ע״פ ב״ד, ולכן הם פטורים מה״ת אחרי שבטלה קדושה ראשונה בגלות בבל (כדלהלן): תרו״מ, שביעית ויובל (וכל המצוות בהל׳ שמיטה ויובל התלויים בהם), לשו״פ פרט ועוללות, וביכורים (ונחזור להם בסמוך). אבל יש מצוות שהתחייבו מיד בכניסתם לארץ, ולכן חיובם יתכן לישאר מה״ת גם לאחר החורבן: ערלה, כלאים, חדש ואיסור קצירה לפני העומר, וחלה. ואף שבזמן שנכנסו לארץ עדיין לא נתקדשה ע״פ ב״ד, אבל ״א״צ לחלה אלא קדושת א״י שהיא ארץ קדושה ומובחרת מאליה״ (ערלה שם סוסקי״א), ו״חלה א״צ לתנאי של קידוש הארץ בכיבוש וקידוש אלא בזה שהארץ ניתנה לאברהם אע״ה סגי״ (שביעית).

ולהלן (פרק ג) נרחיב טובא בשיטת הרמב״ם על גדר קדושה זו של א״י שאינה תלויה על כיבוש בפועל, ונראה שבגללה הקבוצה השנייה של מצוות שייכים בזה״ז בכל גבול עו״מ, ושזה כולל כל עניני חיבת הארץ ואפילו סמיכת חכמים. ואציע עוד שעד גלות בבל היא חייבה במצוות אלו בכל הגבולות שנצטוו עולי מצרים לכבוש, ואפילו במקומות שלעולם לא הגיעו עליהם, עיי״ש. וכעת נבין בשורש הענין שקדושה זו מגיעה מעצם הסגולה הטבעית של הארץ, שמיד כשנכנסו לארץ התגלו מעלותיה כדי לחייב במצוות המגיעים מחמת ׳קדושת הבכח׳ שלה.

וכעת אני מבין רק חלק מארבע המצוות האלו למה הם נובעים מקדושת החומר של א״י. שלגבי ערלה וכלאים מבואר מהרמב״ם (מו״נ ח״ג פל״ז) שיש להם טעם אחרת משאר המצוות התלויות בארץ, וענינם לאפוקי מעבודה זרה וכישוף שנהגו במעשים אלו. ולכאו׳ עומק מש״כ בענין כלאים הוא ע״ד מה שהרחיבו הרמב״ן (ויקרא יט, יט) והחינוך (מצוה סב על כישוף) בטעם המצוה שלא לערב כחות הטבע באופן אחר מאיך שסידר אותם הקב״ה בבריאה, עיי״ש. ועומק מש״כ על ערלה אפשר להבין ממה שהאריך השערי אורה (ש״ה עמ׳ 142-143 במהדו׳ בקר תשע״ט, סוף שער י), עיי״ש. ולכן מצוות אלו אוסרים

לגמרי פעולת ההרכבה, ואסרו את הערלה וכלאי הכרם בהנאה, כי לא באו לקבוע מידות טובות ולסדר החברה שכל אחד יקבל מיבול הארץ את הראוי לו, אלא להפריד החומר הלא-נכון משימוש של קדושה. ומובן היטב איך מצוות אלו מושרשות בעצם החומר של א״י.

וגם איסור חדש וקצירה לפני העומר אולי יש להבין שענינו מצד עצם קדושת החומר של א״י. שמקרבן אחד שמביאים ביום אחד אין כ״כ תועלת מצד תיקון המידות וסידור המדינה, להורות לעם הקדוש איך ליתן צורה שלימה אל הארץ הקדושה (כמו תרו״מ וביכורים שהם שייכים לכל אחד, וכולם חוץ מביכורים בכל השנה). ולכן יש להבין שעיקר טעמו מצד עצם קדושת הארץ, להקריב את ראשית תבואתה אל השם. וצע״ע. (וע״ע בחינוך מצוה שב, שג.)

אך איני יודע למה חלה שייכת לקדושת החומר ׳בכח׳ של א״י שהתחייבו בה מיד בכניסתם, שלכאו׳ ענינה ממש כמו תרו״מ וכו׳. וכך נראה שהניחו הראשונים ז״ל בטעם המצוה, עי׳ ברמב״ם (ח״ג פל״ט) וחינוך (מצוה שפה). וצ״ע. [ויש לשים לב שחלה שונה קצת מערלה וכלאים וחדש, שיש בה תנאי שצריך רוב ישראל עליה, ומטעם זה אינה מה״ת היום למרות שאינו צריך קידוש בפועל, וכדלהלן. ואולי רואים מזה שחלה אינה לגמרי בקבוצה זו.]

### המעלות החומריים של הארץ

ויש להתבונן עוד בטיבם של מעלות הטבעיות של א״י הנמצאים בה ׳בכח׳ כבר לפני שכלל ישראל נכנסו בו (ואפילו לפני שנהיו לעם), שעל ידם התגלה שאיפת הארץ לצאת אל הפועל מיד בכניסתם לארץ כבר לפני כיבוש וחילוק, עד כדי כח שחייבו קבוצה שלימה של מצוות התלויות בארץ. שהרי למרות שמעלות רוחניות הם אמיתיים וטבעיים לא פחות מהגשמיים, בדרך כלל אי אפשר לתפוס אותם באופן ישיר עם החושים גשמיים. אבל מכיון שהסוגיא של ארץ ישראל עוסקת במעלות רוחניות הנמצאות דוקא כתכונות של החומר

ה׳ארצי׳, מסתבר שאפשר להשיג משהו מהם מתוך טבעה הגלויה לעינים. וכעת אני מבין בזה שני דברים, אחד מפורש בפסוקים והשני ברבותינו ז״ל.

כתוב בתורה (דברים יא, י) מיד לפני הפרשה השנייה של ק״ש: כי הארץ אשר אתה בא שמה לרשתה לא כארץ מצרים הוא אשר יצאתם משם אשר תזרע את זרעך והשקית ברגלך כגן הירק. והארץ אשר אתם עברים שמה לרשתה ארץ הרים ובקעת למטר השמים תשתה מים. ארץ אשר ה׳ אלהיך דרש אתה תמיד עיני ה׳ אלהיך בה מרשית השנה ועד אחרית שנה.

ולכאו׳ ביאור הענין עפ״ד. קלקול החומר הוא כשרואה את עצמו שלם ואינו צריך עבודה לצאת אל הפועל, וכמ״ש בגמרא שאם היה יצה״ר בעובר ״היה מבעט באמו ויוצא״ כי לא היה רואה צורך לקבל ולגדול עוד. במצב כזה החומר עצמו הופך להיות צורה לא-נכונה של עצמו. וארץ מצרים הוא הראש של קלקול זו, כי ה׳ארץ׳ שלה השקה את עצמה. כתוצאה מכך, האנשים במצרים היו מכשפים ושטופים בזימה, שהחומר השטחי הפך אצלם להיות כל המציאות. במקום להפעיל את השכל וליתן צורה אל החומר, מצרים הוא ארץ של דמיון וחושים. כל עבודה במקום כזה אינה אלא להוציא את החומר ׳בכח׳ אל עוד יותר ׳בכח׳, לטבוע עמוק יותר בדמיון.

משא״כ ארץ ישראל אין לה מקורות מים מספיקים, והיא נחוצה אל גשמים מהשמים כדי להוציא חיים. וכשהארץ היא חסירה, שואפת ותועבת מילוי מהשמים, אז היא חומר שרוצה (׳ארץ׳ מלשון ׳רצון׳) לקבל צורה, לצאת מהכח אל הפועל בעבודה עליה. כאן המצב הנכון של הארץ, כשכל פעולתה היא בנכונות לקבל שלימות מחוצה לה. ולכן עצם טבעה של ארץ ישראל מסוגלת לעבודה אמיתית, ליתן צורה שלימה ונכונה אל החומר שלה. זהו החומר הראוי לכלל ישראל, שתפיסת מקבלי התורה אל החומר הוא כדבר חסר שצריך להשלים כפי רצונו ית׳.

וראיתי תכונה נוספת של א"י בכוזרי (א, צה): **ושם סגולת נח, לפי שהוא יורש האקלימים הממוזגים אשר אמצעיתם וחמדתם ארץ ישראל, ארץ הנבואה, ויצא יפת אל הצפון וחם אל הדרום.**[ב]

המיקום של א"י באמצע העולם מורה על מיזוגו. אינו קר כמו ארצות יפת לצפון, ולא חם כמו ארצות חם לדרום, אלא ממוזג בין החום לקור. [וכמדומה כך ראיתי בספרי הטבע שבא"י נמצאים ביחד הצמחים ובעלי חיים של אירופה, אסיא, ואפריקה.] והסוגיא הזו של מיזוג ודרך האמצעי הוא עיקר גדול בתורה, וכמש"כ הרמב"ם (הקדמה לאבות פ"ד) שרוב מצוות התורה ניתנו ללמד דרכי החסידות כדי שלא יטה לאחד מהקצוות, עיי"ש. ולכאו' ענין זה שייך דוקא אל החומר, ששם נמצאים המידות וכחות הנפש שיכולים לנטות לקצוות ולהתקלקל (כמבואר היטב בשערי קדושה). בצורת האדם, הלכות דעות באו לפני הלכות ת"ת מכיון ש"דרך ארץ שקדמה לתורה", ובמקביל לזה בעולם קדושת החומר 'בכח' של א"י קודמת לישיבת כלל ישראל עליה המוציא את סגולותיה הממוצעות אל הפועל. ואכמ"ל.

## הארץ של כלל ישראל

אולם הרמב"ם קבע להלכה גדר אחרת של ארץ ישראל, שכתב (הל' תרומות פ"א ה"ב) "ארץ ישראל האמורה בכל מקום היא הארצות שכובש אותן מלך ישראל או שופט או נביא מדעת רוב ישראל, וזה הוא הנקרא כיבוש רבים...". והמשיך שאם יחידים כבשו מקום לעצמם "אפילו מן הארץ שניתנה לאברהם – אינו נקרא א"י כדי שינהגו בו כל המצוות", ולכן יהושע ובית דינו חילקו כל הארץ לשבטים כדי שכשיכבשו אח"כ לא יהא כיבוש יחיד. ופסק עוד (שם ה"ג, הל' מלכים פ"ה ה"ו) שאם כבש המלך ע"פ ב"ד כל מקום בעולם אחרי

---

[ב] וכ"כ הרמב"ן בקיצור (ויקרא יח, כה): "...א"י אמצעות הישוב היא נחלת ה' מיוחדת לשמו...". וע"ע ברמב"ם (פרקי משה מאמר כה, הו"ד ב'בין הכוזרי לרמב"ם' עמ' קעב-ג) שמהאקלימים הממוצעים נוצרים שפות ברורים ונאים, וכלל בזה כל איזור מזרח התיכון ("היוונים, הערבים, העברי, והסורים והפרסים").

כיבוש כל א״י האמורה בתורה הרי זה נהפך להיות א״י, ואפילו אפשר להתיר ע״ז לישב במצרים – כי ע״י הכיבוש יהפך להיות א״י (הל׳ מלכים שם ה״ח).

ומבואר מהרמב״ם שעיקר הסוגיא של א״י לענין מצוות הוא מהיותה המקום שבה יושבים כלל ישראל, שזה הופכת אותה להיות קדושה כמותם[ג]. אבל לכאו׳ פשוט שאין כוונתו לאפוקי מכל הנ״ל ע״פ הכוזרי בקדושת החומר הטבעית של הארץ, ושלדעתו כל קדושתה מגיע משום שכלל ישראל נמצאים בתוכה. שא״כ הדרא קושיא הנ״ל לדוכתא, איזה מעלה וקדושה יש למקום המסוים הזה עד כדי כך שרוב מהלך התורה הוא מסביב לה? למה לא כל מקום שעם הנבחר ירצה לשבת בתוכו יהפך להיות קדוש משום שהוא משרת את ייעודם בקיום מצוות התורה – אפילו לפני שכבשו כל ארץ כנען שמשום מה הובטחה לאברהם? ובכלל יהיה קשה להבין הקדושה הרוחנית והחיבה הגדולה של הארץ, וכמו שהרחיב הרמב״ם עצמו לתאר (הל׳ מלכים פ״ה ה״ט-יב) שלכן אסור לצאת ממנה, וגדולי החכמים היו מנשקין אותה כשהגיע לתחומיה, והישיבה וקבורה בתוכה מכפר על העוונות, ועוד, שהרי אינה יותר מהמקום שנמצאים כלל ישראל לקיים את התורה. (ובשלמא המצוות התלויות בארץ היה אפשר לפרש כולם מצד תיקון האומה שבמקרה יושבים בארץ זו.)

אלא ברור שכל דברי הרמב״ם נאמרו לגבי הארץ כשהיא יוצאת אל הפועל בעבודת כלל ישראל עליה, שלענין זה עיקר קדושתה מגיע מהצורה השלימה שכלל ישראל נותנים לה כשמקיימים את מצוותיה. ולענין זה כתב שהשם ׳ארץ ישראל׳ נקבע ע״י כיבוש בפועל ׳על דעת רוב ישראל׳, שזה הופכת את הארץ מחומר עם תכונות מיוחדות ׳בכח׳ להיות כל המימוש במציאות של

[ג] למדתי לראשונה הבחנה זו בגדר קדושת א״י מספר הנפלא ״בין הכוזרי לרמב״ם״ (סוגיא ח), עיי״ש איך שהעמיד הענין לפי דרכו בטו״ט. ולענ״ד יש מקום לדון בחלק מראיותיו מהרמב״ם אם הם מוכרחות, וצ״ע למה לא הביא הדברים המפורשים האלו בהלכותיו, ובפרט שהדגיש הרמב״ם ״מדעת רוב ישראל״ שהוא חידוש גדול שאינו ידוע מקורו (וכמו שהעיר החזו״א שביעית ס״ג סקט״ז ד״ה שבועות), ודין זה הוא השורש לפירושו על חלוקת יהושע לשבטים (וכמש״כ הדרך אמונה ליישב הערת המהר״י קורקוס).

עבודת כלל ישראל. הכוזרי הגדיר את ה"הר" הראוי לגדל את כרם ישראל, והרמב"ם מגדיר את הגפנים בעצמם.[ד]

ומענין זה של ארץ ישראל יצא הקבוצה הראשונה הנ"ל של מצוות התלויות בארץ, שכולם באו למען סדר החברה והמדינה של כלל ישראל ולתיקון מידותיהם. וכך מבאר הרמב"ם (מו"נ ח"ג פל"ט, וע"ע הקדמה לאבות פ"ד) בהרחבה איך מצוות אלו באו לחזק מידות טובות אצל הנותן כמו נדיבות ורחמנות, ולתמוך בעניים ובאלו שמיוחדים לעבודת ה' וידיעת תורתו, עיי"ש. וכך מבאר החינוך (שצה, שצו, תקז) בטעם תרו"מ, עיי"ש. ועפ"ד גם מצוות אלו שייכים דוקא לארץ ישראל מחמת קדושתה, ואינם רק מאותו ענין של הרבה מצוות אחרות שיש להם טעמים האלו והם חייבים מה"ת גם בחו"ל (כמו צדקה והשבת אבידה וכו'), אלא מצוות אלו דוקא מבטאים איך החומר של הארץ בעצמה מקבלת צורה שלימה כשיושבים בה ומקיימים את מצוותיה.[ה]

ויש לציין עוד בקצרה שלכאו' מצינו ב' דרכים בעבודת הארץ המוציא את קדושתה אל הפועל בצורה שלימה. שכל השבטים חוץ מלוי עובדים את

[ד] וגם ב'בין הכוזרי לרמב"ם' השוה בין דרכיהם, כי ההבדל ביניהם הוא באיזה ענין להדגיש, עיי"ש בסוף הפרק. וע"ע במהר"י קורקוס (על הרמב"ם שם) בשם הכפו"פ שדייק ככה ממש"כ "אינו נק' א"י **כדי שינהגו בו כל המצות**", שדוקא לענין המצוות אינה קדושה, אבל כל שאר הדינים של קדושה כמו לענין דירה יש בה. ולכאו' יש לדייק ככה אפילו לגבי מצוות, שכתב רק שלא "כל המצוות" נוהגין בה, אבל הקבוצה הראשונה הנ"ל שייכים בה (לפחות עד גלות בבל, וכדלהלן). ויש ללמוד כזה עוד ממה שיבואר בהרחבה (פרק ג) שלדעת הרמב"ם קדושת מהות א"י נשארת לעולם בכל גבולי עו"מ, והקבוצה של מצוות השייכים לזה הם מה"ת שם בזה"ז, וכל זה מובן היטב ע"פ יסוד הכוזרי, וכפי שיתבאר.

[ה] וילה"ע ששמיטה יש לה ענין מצד קדושת הטבע שמורה על בריאת העולם בששת ימים כמש"כ רש"י והרמב"ן (ויקרא כה א) והחינוך (מצוה פה) ע"פ מש"כ (ויקרא שם) "ושבתה הארץ שבת לה'", והיה אפשר להבין מזה ששייך לקבוצה של קדושת החומר הטבעית (אף שלכאו' אי"ז מוכח). אלא שעוד יותר מפורש בפסוקים ענין מידות החמלה והנדיבות והבטחון אצל שמיטה כמש"כ (שמות כג, יא) "ואכלו אביוני עמך ויתרם תאכל חית השדה", וכמבואר היטב ברמב"ם (מו"נ ח"ג פל"ט) ובחינוך (שם), ופשוט שטעם שמיטת כספים ושחרור עבדים ועוד בשמיטה ויובל הוא ענין של תיקון המידות והחברה הקדושה (עי' דברים טו).

האדמה כפשוטה, והם מקיימים רצונו ית׳ כשמפרישים תרו״מ ונותנים ללוי ולכהן, ושובתים מעבודת האדמה בשמיטה, ומחזירים הנחלות ביובל, ועוד.

אולם שבט לוי אין להם רוב מצוות אלו, כי אין להם נחלה לעבוד, ואדרבה הם **מקבלים** את התרו״מ חלף עבודתם במקדש. ובפרט ביובל אין להם נחלה להחזיר, ועי׳ היטב בסוף הל׳ שמיטה ויובל שלכן קבע שם הרמב״ם עניני הנחלה של שבט לוי לאפוקי ממהלך הרגיל של יובל אצל שאר השבטים. אבל אין הכוונה ח״ו שאין להם עבודה, ואפילו לא שעבודתם אינה שייך לקדושת החומר של ארץ ישראל (של״מ שום שינוי אצלם בקבוצה הנ״ל של מצוות השייכים לזה). אלא הענין כמו שהרמב״ם מבאר היטב ששבט לוי (וגם כל ״באי עולם אשר נדבר רוחו אותו...״) לא קיבלו נחלה בא״י כי הובדלו ״לעבוד את ה׳ ולשרתו ולהורות דרכיו הישרים ומשפטיו הצדיקים לישראל״, ולכן הקב״ה בעצמו הוא נחלתם כמש״כ ״אני חלקך ונחלתך״, עיי״ש. הרי שיש דרך לעבודת את הקב״ה מתוך החומר של עוה״ז ע״י שעובדים במקדש ומלמדים תורה לכלל ישראל. ואולי הענין שהם מוציאים לפועל קדושת החומר של מקום המקדש, ששם השראת השכינה ועצם נחלת ה׳, ו״מציון תצא תורה״. (וזש״כ על כל מי ״שנדבה לבו...״ ש״נתקדש קודש קדשים״, וממזר ת״ח קודם לכה״ג ע״ה.) ואכמ״ל.

### קדושת הארץ בכל העולם

ויש לשים לב להבדל נוסף בין שתי הקבוצות של מצוות התלויות בארץ, מלבד אם הם יכולים להיות מה״ת גם כשאין קדושת א״י מדין כיבוש או חזקה. שלמרות ששתי הקבוצות לא נתחייבו עד שנכנסו לארץ, אבל אחד מהם אח״כ התרחב חיובם לכלול גם חו״ל בדרגא או לפי שיטה מסוימת. שתרו״מ ושביעית וביכורים ולשו״פ הם מצוות בא״י בלבד, ואינם חייבים כלל בחו״ל. [ורק מצינו תרו״מ מד״ס בארצות הסמוכים לא״י. ולשו״פ אינו ברור כעת אם חייבים מדרבנן בחו״ל, עי׳ הל׳ מתנו״ע פ״א הי״ד.] אבל ערלה חייבת בחו״ל מהלמ״מ, וחדש לרוב הפוסקים קיי״ל כהתנאים הסוברים שהוא מה״ת

בחו״ל, וחלה חייבת בחו״ל מדינא דמשנה (״שלש ארצות לחלה״), וכלאי הכרם הם בחו״ל מד״ס. [רק כלאי זרעים יצאו מכלל זה שהם מותרים לגמרי בחו״ל.] וכבר מצינו במשנה (סוף ערלה, קידושין פ״א מ״ט) שמנה ערלה וכלאים וחדש כשונים משאר מצוות התלויות בארץ שהם נוגעים בחו״ל.

ולכאו׳ ברור שהטעם שמצוות אלו חייבים בחו״ל אינו משום שהם פחות ״תלויים בארץ״, שהרי החזו״א (שם) מבאר שגם הם לא נתחייבו עד שעברו את הירדן. וגם בלא״ה כולם בדרגא פחותה בחו״ל מבא״י, או בחומר החיוב או ששנויה במחלוקת. ולכן נל״פ הענין משום שכשכלל ישראל נכנסו לארץ כל העולם קיבל דרגא מסוימת של ארץ שראויה לעבודת תורה ומצוות, למרות שאינו באותו דרגא של א״י. אלא שאי״ז אלא מצד החומר ה׳בכח׳ של העולם, אבל עצם העבודה של כלל ישראל תמיד הוא בא״י, ולכן המצוות התלויות בעבודה בפועל אינם אלא בא״י ממש. ולכאו׳ יש שורש בהלכה לקדושת א״י בכל העולם במש״כ הרמב״ם הנ״ל שאפשר להפוך כל העולם לא״י ע״י כיבוש אחרי שיכבשו עיקר א״י. (ויש שורש מקביל בקדושת ישראל ׳בכח׳ באו״ה המאפשרת גירות.)

[ולא נכנסתי כאן לבאר הטעם שדוקא ארץ קטנה אחת קיבלה החומר הראוי לקבל הצורה בפועל של עבודת השם, ולמה כל העולם לא יכולה להיות שוה בזה, ששאלה זו נופלת על ישראל בכלל: למה דוקא עם נבחר אחד קיבל את התורה. ולכאו׳ כל הענין נעוץ בחטא אדה״ר כידוע (עי׳ למשל בדרך ה׳), שכשם שנפגם האנושות כמו״כ נפגם החומר שעליה הם צריכים לעבוד, שבזה היתה עיקר החטא: לראות את החומר כמטרה בפנ״ע, ולא להוציאו אל הפועל ב״לעבדה ולשמרה״. ואכן מבואר הרבה בפסוקים על קללת האדמה מחמת החטא. וכתב הרמח״ל בפירוש (קה״צ עמ׳ קכט) שכל העולם נטמא בחטא אדה״ר חוץ מא״י. ועכ״פ לכאו׳ גם כאן נמצא השורש הפנימי של קדושת א״י ׳בכח׳ בכל העולם, שלפני החטא כל העולם היה ראוי להיות ׳ארץ ישראל׳ כמו שכל בני האדם היו ׳כלל ישראל׳.]

## משפחות בני כנען

להשלמת הענין של שורש קדושת ארץ ישראל, נעיין במצבה המקורי של הארץ לפני שהגיעו אל כלל ישראל.

בסוף פרשת נח התורה מפרטת התולדות של שם חם ויפת שמהם יצאו אומות העולם. מובא אחד עשרה בני כנען (י, טו-יח): צידון, חת, היבוסי, האמורי, הגרגשי, החוי, הערקי, הסיני, הארודי, הצמרי, והחמתי. מתוך הבנים האלו "אחר נפוצו משפחות הכנעני", וישבו "בגבול הכנעני".

והרמב"ן (שם) מבאר שבנים אלו הם הם העשר אומות שנבטחו לאברהם, "כי כל זרע כנען נמכר לעבד עולם". אלא שעד ימי אברהם חלקם נתחלפו שמותם, אולי כי נקראו ע"ש ארצותם שישבו בהם. אולם כאן מצינו י"א בנים, ובהבטחה לאברהם נאמר עשר אומות. ובאמת מצינו סה"כ י"ב, שאצל אברהם נאמר האב "כנעני" כאומה בפנ"ע. ולכן מפרש הרמב"ן שכנראה אחד מהאומות לא התגבר לאומה כאחיו, ולכן הוא הצטרף עם עוד אחד להיות שניהם ביחד נקראים ע"ש אביהם "כנען". והציע שיתכן שהבכור צידון הוא זה שנקרא "כנעני" עם עוד מישהו. ומבואר מתו"ד שאיננו יודעים איך התחלפו השמות, איזה מהבנים נהפך לאיזה מהאומות, והביא "על דרך משל" שאולי הערקי והסיני הם הקיני והקניזי. ונמצא מהרמב"ן שיש הקבלה מליאה בין הבנים של נח אל העשר אומות.

והרמב"ן העיר מארץ הפלישתים שהוא נכלל בגבולות ארץ כנען "באכה גררה עד עזה", וגם צידון הוא של הפלישתים כמש"כ כמ"פ בנביאים (יהושע יג, ו; יואל ד, ד), והרי הפלישתים יצאו ממצרים שהיה אחיו של כנען (בראשית י, יד). ותירץ שהפלישתים כבשו וישבו בחלקים אלו של ארץ כנען. ולכאו' מבואר מדבריו שהמקום הידוע לנו כ"צידון" אינו למעשה מקום ה"צידונים" מבני כנען, כי עכשיו הוא של הפלישתים, אלא ה"צידונים" הם אחד משאר האומות של ארץ כנען ממש, ולפי הצעת הרמב"ן יתכן שהם ה"כנעני".

אמנם מבואר מהגר״א (אדרת אליהו בלק תליתאה כב, ה) דרך אחרת בהקבלת המשפחות של כנען בפרשת נח עם העשרה אומות שהובטחו לאברהם. שיסד כלל שהאומות (ובמקביל להם כלל ישראל, עיי״ש) הם שבעים שמתחלקים לששים ועשר, כי ״מן ע׳ אומות ששים סובבים לארץ ישראל ועשרה יושבים בארץ ישראל״ כמבואר מההבטחה לאברהם. והוסיף עוד ששנים מתוך הששים הם סובבים את א״י, כי הי״ב של פרשת נח (עם משפחת האב, ״כנעני״) הם י״ב ממש. ומבאר מי הם השנים הנוספים על העשר שבתוך א״י: ״הם סיני וצידן, סיני יושב על גבול דרום וצידן על גבול צפון, והן נכללין בתוך ארץ ישראל ולעתיד יתוספו אלו הב׳ אומות על נחלת ארץ ישראל. וסיני הוא יושב בדרום כמו שנאמר (ישעיה מט, יב) ׳אלה יבואו מארץ סינים׳ כו׳[ו], וכן כתוב ביחזקאל (מז, יז-יט) שיתוסף לדרומה ולצפונה״. אבל השנים האלו לא הוזכרו בברית בין הבתרים ״לפי שהם היו חוץ לא״י״. והולך ומפרט איך העשרה מקבילים זל״ז, שהארודי וצמרי וחמתי הם הקיני וקניזי וקדמוני, החוי הוא הרפאים כמ״ש בשבת (פה.), והערקי הוא הפרזי.

והגר״א גם מיישב מה שילה״ע איך הקיני וקניזי וקדמוני נמצאים בבני כנען, הרי הם אדום עמון ומואב שכולם מבני שם[ז]. ומפרש הגר״א שאדום עמון ומואב לקחו ארצות הקיני וקניזי וקדמוני מהם ולכן נקראו על שמם. ולכאו׳

---

[ו] ובהכתב והקבלה (בראשית טו, יט) בשם הגר״א הוסיף שבתרגום שם ״מארעא דרומא״, ושצידון הוא בצפון כמש״כ אצל גבול נפתלי. (ואיני יודע אם כוונתו לפרש הגר״א כאן או שהיה לו מקור אחר.) וילה״ע במש״כ שצידון בגבול נפתלי שא״כ איך הוא בחו״ל. וצ״ל שרק חלק ממקומם הוא בחו״ל, ואינו ברור איפה הגבול בזה. ועי׳ מש״כ להלן עפ״ז במיקום הר ההר. וצע״ע.

[ז] נחלקו התנאים (עי׳ ב״ב נו., ירושלמי שביעית פ״ו ה״א מג.) בזהות השלש אומות, וברש״י נקט בכל מקום כשיטה זו. וכ״כ הגר״א (כאן, וגם בדבריו להלן סוף פרק ב מאד״א דברים), וכך מבואר מחסד לאברהם (עי׳ בסמוך בהערה) שכתב שסיחון ועוג טיהור מהג׳ אומות. ולדרך זה כל אזהרות התורה לא לכבוש ארצות עמון ומואב ואדום מובנים משום שהם במקום של הג׳ אומות האלו (למרות שאינם האומות עצמם, וכנ״ל מהגר״א). אבל הרא״ב שליט״א העיר לי על שיטה זו מפסוקים מפורשים (דברים ב,י-יא כ) שעמון ומואב ירשו את ארצם מה״רפאים״, והרי הרפאים הם אחד מהשבעה אומות בברית בין הבתרים (החוי או האמורי, עי׳ בסמוך). והציע שמסתבר מאד כהתנא שהזכיר אותם ב״אספמיא״ ו״אסיא״, עיי״ש, שיש להבין שזהו ארץ חמת ודמשק שלע״ל יכנס לא״י כמבואר בפסוקים ביחזקאל (כדלהלן).

בלא"ה מוכח שהקיני וקניזי וקדמוני אינם עמון ומואב ואדום ממש, כי כל העשרה אומות נזכרו בהבטחה לאברהם לפני שנולדו עמון ומואב ואדום. (ומסתמא זה נכון גם לרמב"ן.)

ועכ"פ משמע מהגר"א שצידון וסיני הם המקומות הידועים לנו בשמות אלו, צידון וסיני בצפון ובדרום של א"י. ואף שגם הם מבני כנען, היום אינם בתוך גבולות הארץ כי אינם מהעשר אומות שהובטחו לאברהם, אבל לע"ל יתרחב הארץ לכלול גם אותם. וכ"ז דלא כהרמב"ן שהבין ששני אומות אלו הם מהעשר אומות ממש, ולדרכו לא מצינו אומות נוספות מבני כנען חוץ מהעשר.

ויוצא מהגר"א יסוד וחידוש גדול, שיש שתי דרגות של האומות שיתוספו לע"ל. שהרי גם שלש מתוך העשר אומות אינם חלק מא"י בזה"ז למרות שהובטחו לאברהם. אבל אעפ"כ יש לנו איזה תפיסה בהם כא"י בזה שנתגלו כחלק מהארץ בברית בין הבתרים. משא"כ השנים האחרים לא נזכרו בפירוש בתושב"כ שהם חלק מא"י, ורק שאפשר להבין ככה כשלומדים הפסוקים של בני כנען בפ' נח עם נבואת יחזקאל.

ובהמשך נחזור לעיין במה שיש ללמוד מהרמב"ן והגר"א לגבי גבולות א"י בצפון ובדרום (עי' בענין נהר פרת בצפון, הר ההר בצפון, בביאור הגבול עד י"ס בדרום, בסיכום בסוף גבולות התורה [כל זה פרק ב], ובענין צידון בקדושת עו"מ מעכו ולצפון [פרק ג]).

# איתן [א]

## הרב שמואל חיים ניימאן

איתא בגמרא (ר"ה יא.): רבי אליעזר אומר מנין שבתשרי נולדו אבות, שנאמר "ויקהלו אל המלך שלמה כל איש ישראל בירח האיתנים בחג" (מלכים-א ח, ב), ירח שנולדו בו איתני עולם. מאי משמע דהאי איתן לישנא דתקיפי הוא? כדכתיב "איתן מושבך" (במדבר כד, כא), ואומר "שמעו הרים את ריב ה' והאיתנים מוסדי ארץ" (מיכה ו, ב), ואומר "קול דודי הנה זה בא מדלג על ההרים מקפץ על הגבעות" (שיר השירים ב, ח), "מדלג על ההרים" בזכות אבות "מקפץ על הגבעות" בזכות אמהות.

**א] האבות נק' 'איתנים' ע"ש לידתם, ואברהם נק' 'איתן' לפני שהגיע לאמונה**
מהפסוק "איתן מושבך" דרשו ש'איתן' מורה על חוזק של ישיבה, ומ"שמעו הרים..." שענינו הר כמו שנקראו האבות (עי' רש"י). וכנראה הכוונה לחוזק של יציבות, שדבר 'איתן' הוא מיושב במקומו ודרכו ואי אפשר להזיז אותו ממנו. 'איתן' אינו הגבורה של העוקר הרים אלא היציבות של ההר בעצמו. ועד"ז כתוב (בראשית מט, כד) "ותשב באיתן קשתו", הרי ששנים מתוך הכמה מקומות ששורש זה מופיע בתורת משה מדברים על חוזק של ישיבה במקומו. וכך יש להבין מש"כ אחרי קרי"ס (שמות יד, כז) "וישב הים לאיתנו", ר"ל העוצמה של מים הקבועים במקומם בים. [ולהלן נראה עוד עד"ז בסוגיא של 'נחל איתן'.]

והנה המהרש"א מבאר שהאבות נקראו 'איתנים' ע"ש שהעולם עומד בזכותם, ולכן העולם נברא באותו חודש שהם נולדו. ומבואר שהשם 'איתן' שלהם הגיע משעת לידתם, ולדעת ר"א זהו אותו חודש שנברא ו'נולד' העולם הקיים עליהם. וצ"ב איך איתנותם של האבות שייך לזמן לידתם דוקא, ולא לחודש

[א] דברי תורה לכבוד הברית של בנינו איתן, כח אלול תשפ"א.

שעשו עיקר עבודתם להקב״ה, אולי עקידת יצחק או קבלת יעקב לברכות וכדו׳?

גם אצל אברהם אבינו הנק׳ ׳איתן׳ מצינו ששם זה הופיע דוקא בתחילת דרכו, לפני שגילה את שמו ית׳ אל באי העולם. שדרשו (ב״ב טו.) שהפרק ״משכיל לאיתן האזרחי״ (תהלים פט, א) נאמר ע״י אברהם מהפסוק ״מי העיר ממזרח צדק״ (ישעיה מא, ב), ר״ל אברהם שהגיע מעובדי ע״ז של ארץ ארם במזרחו של א״י (עי׳ רד״ק). גם באופן כללי הצד מזרח מורה על התחלה ושורש הענין, כמו השמש העולה ממזרח. וכנראה הצורתא דשמעתתא הוא ששם זה נאמר עליו לפני הופעתו בתושב״כ ב׳לך לך׳ ביציאתו בדרך אל ארץ ישראל, ושייך לחיפושו לאמונה שקבלנו בתושב״פ. אבל צ״ב למה מענין זה קיבל שם בפנ״ע?

וכך עוד יותר מפורש בדברי הרמב״ם (הל׳ ע״ז פ״א). שמתאר מצב העולם שהיה מתגלגל והולך בע״ז ״עד שנולד עמודו של עולם שהוא א״א, כיון שנגמל **איתן** זה התחיל לשוטט בדעתו והוא קטן ולחושב ביום ובלילה, והיה תמיה היאך אפשר שיהיה הגלגל הזה נוהג תמיד... ואביו ואמו וכל עע״ז והוא היה עובד עמהן, ולבו משוטט ומבין עד שהשיג דרך האמת... ובן מ׳ שנה הכיר אברהם את בוראו...״. עיי״ש היטב שמתאר דרכו לאמונה, ואח״כ ממשיך עם עוד שלש ׳כיון...׳ לתאר קריאתו בשם ה׳ אל כל הברואים. ומבואר להדיא שאיתנותו של אברהם הגיע דוקא בתחילת דרכו כשהיה נער עובד ע״ז שהתחיל לחפש ולבדוק, מה שהיום נקרא ׳ילד מבולבל׳. כבר מלידתו (״עד שנולד״) השתנה העולם, ותחילת התנוצצות דעתו (״כיון שנגמל״) היה מספיק להגדירו כ׳איתן׳. והדברים מושרשים עם הנ״ל מחז״ל ששם זה נאמר דוקא על ילדותו בארצות של עע״ז, ש׳איתן׳ הוא מתואר כ׳אזרחי׳.

וכל זה צ״ב טובא, איזה איתנות וישיבה בחוזק היה לאברהם דוקא לפני שהכיר את בוראו, אדרבה לכאו׳ מה ש״מתחילה עובדי עבודה זרה היו

עבודתנו" מורה על חולשה, בפשטות כדי ללמד ענוה כי כל מעלתנו משום ש"עכשיו קרבנו **המקום** לעבודתו"? ולכאו' המהלך של שוטטתו וחיפושו הוא ההיפך הגמור מהיציבות של 'איתן'!

**ב] טעות עבודה זרה – הורדת הרצון של השכל**

ונל"פ ע"פ ענין ע"ז כמבואר ברמב"ם בתחילת הפרק. בדור אנוש "טעו בנ"א טעות גדולה" כשאמרו שראוי לשבח ולכבד את הכוכבים וגלגלים המשמשים את הקב"ה, "וזהו רצון האל ב"ה לגדל ולכבד מי שגדלו וכבדו, כמו שהמלך רוצה לכבד עבדיו והעומדים לפניו". מחמת סברא זו התחילו לבנות היכלות ולהקריב קרבנות וכו' לכוכבים "כדי להשיג רצון הבורא בדעתם הרעה, וזהו עיקר ע"ז". וצ"ב מה טעותם הגדולה, הרי גם אנחנו מכבדים ת"ח ומלכים משום שחלק מחכמתו וכבודו לבשר ודם, ולמה לא לכבד גם הכוכבים מחמת זה? ואפילו אם נחלק בין בעלי בחירה למוכרחים, איזה "דעת רעה" יש בשיטתם, הרי לכל היותר טעו בהבנת רצונו ית'? איך יתכן שכל התורה כולה (עי' המשך הפרק ופי"ב) מיוסדת לאפוקי מטעות תמימה בסברא? ועד"ז יש לשאול במעלת אברהם ש"הבין קו הצדק מדעתו הנכונה", איזה בחירה לטובה עשה כשהצליח בשכלו החריף להגיע למסקנא הפילוסופית הנכונה שע"כ מישהו ברא ומסובב את הגלגלים?

ונראה בכוונת הרמב"ם שטעותם היתה בעצם הנסיון להבין רצונו ית' בדרכי השכל. יתכן שהסברא היתה טובה, אבל עדיין פתחו המסלול המרכזי של רע בעולם כשהעיזו להשתמש בשכלם כדי לתפוס את הרצון שבאמת נמצא למעלה מהשכל. כאן נמצאת הפרשת דרכים בין טו"ר: האם אני כאדם בעל שכל יכול להחזיק את כל המציאות בתוכי, עד כדי כך שגם רצונו של הסיבה הראשונה ח"ו אינו אלא עוד סברא שאפשר וצריך להבין ולהגדיר. או שמציאותו של כל נברא מושרשת ברצון הפשוט של הבורא שהוא יתקיים במציאות, ברצון טהור שאי אפשר לפרש ולהבין את הכרחו בדרכי השכל. רצון אמיתי כזה אינו תוצאה של סיבה קודמת המכריחה אותו, שא"כ אינו

רצון אלא התולדה המוכרחת של סיבתו. אלא הרצון בעצמו הוא המקור אל היוצא ממנו, בלא שאף סיבה אחרת יכריח אותו לפעול. וזש״כ בעלי הרמז ש׳רצון׳ עולה במנין ׳מקור׳, וגם ׳שמו׳ ר״ל הרצון להתגלות ולצאת החוצה אל הקוראים בשם.

עובדי ע״ז הראשונים התחילו מהלך של מחיקת רצונו ית׳ מהבריאה ח״ו, וכפי שמבאר הרמב״ם בהמשך ״נשתקע **השם** הנכבד והנורא מפי כל היקום ומדעתם ולא הכירוהו... **צור העולמים** לא היה שם מכירו ולא יודעו...״. במו״נ (ח״א פט״ז) מבאר ׳צור׳ שהוא הר או אבן קשה, וגם המקור שממנו חוצבים האבנים. ומוסיף ש״אח״כ הושאל... לשורש כל דבר והתחלתו, ולזה אמר אחר אמרו הביטו אל צור חוצבתם, הביטו אל אברהם אביכם וכו׳, כאילו באר שהצור שחוצבתם ממנו הוא אברהם אביכם, ע״כ לכו בדרכיו והאמינו בתורתו והתנהגו במידותיו, כי טבע המקור ראוי שיהיה נמצא במה שיחצב ממנו״. ומכאן גם הקב״ה נק׳ ׳צור׳ ״כי הוא ההתחלה והסיבה הפועלת לכל אשר זולתו״. הטעות של דור אנוש היתה לראות הבו״ע כסיבה הראשונה בתוך המערכת של סיבה ומסובב, לא כ׳צור׳ העומד למעלה מכל הנבראים שנחצבו ממנו. [וע״ע במו״נ יסוד גדול ששורש ע״ז באמונת הקדמות, וכך יש לראות מסדר העיקרים ד-ה, ואכמ״ל.]

**ג] חידושו הראשון של אברהם – חוזק הבריאה הוא במקורו**

אברהם אבינו נולד לתוך עולם מנותק מ׳צור׳, שבו כל דבר קיים כמסובב של הסיבה שקדמה לו, ומוכרח להיות סיבה אל דבר הבא אחריו. אין ׳מקור׳ שממנו הכל נחצב, אין ׳רצון׳ של בורא שבו קיומו של כל נברא מושרש. אבל הוא לא הסכים לקבל שכל המציאות נתפס ונמצא בשכל האדם, אלא ״התחיל לשוטט בדעתו״ היתכן שאין משהו יותר נעלה שהוא המקור היחיד המסובב את כל הגלגלים מרצונו בלבד? לא היה סתם ילד מבולבל, אלא יצא ו׳שטט׳ בשכלו אל מחוץ למערכת הנתפסת בשכל, הלך לחפש את המקור של חכמת הבריאה הנמצא מעבר לה. חיפוש זה לא היה פרי המסקנא של שכל מבוגר

שהוכיח שצריך להיות כך וכך, אלא התחיל כבר בהיותו ילד קטן עם ראשית התנוצצות הדעת ("כיון שנגמל איתן זה", לכאו' ר"ל כשטעם טעם דגן...), והמשיך עד גיל ארבעים כשהכיר את בוראו, ר"ל שהגיע אל המקור שממנו נחצב כל הבריאה.

כך היה חידושו הראשון של אברהם: יש 'צור' לעולם הנראה כמנותק מהמקור. ומכיון שהוא גילה את המקור בתוך עולם של העדר מקור, קנה בזה משהו מהמקור עד שלומדים ממנו מידת ה'צור' כמש"כ הרמב"ם מהפסוק. אח"כ המשיך להכניס רעיון זה לתוך העולם, ולהציע לאנשים דרך של חיים היוצאים מהמקור ואינם מוגבלים למערכות הטבע.

ועכ"ז מובן היטב מה שנק' אברהם בשם 'איתן' דוקא ע"ש דרכו להשיג האמונה, כבר לפני שהגיע למסקנותיו ולימדם לכל העולם. איתנותו היתה בזה שחיפש חוזקו מה'מקור' שלו ושל כל העולם, ולא הספיק בלסדר את הכוחות השונים של הכוכבים לפי דעתו ורצונו. ולכן, כפי שראינו מחז"ל, המילה 'איתן' מורה על החוזק של ישיבה ביציבות, ונאמר בפסוקים על הרים ואבנים – בדיוק הפירושים שכתב הרמב"ם על המילה 'צור' שהביאו את המילה ההיא להורות על לענין 'מקור'. להיות 'איתן' אינו ר"ל להיות גבור היכול להגן על עצמו ולכבוש אויביו, אלא להיות מושרש במקור ורצון שמעבר לו עד כדי כך ששאר הנמצאים בדרגתו לא יכולים להזיז אותו ממקומו.

עצם מסקנתו של אברהם לא היתה נקודת 'איתן' שלו, שהשכל האנושי אינו יכול להגיע לסוף המציאות. אלא הוא נק' 'איתן' ע"ש שיצא בשכלו לחפש את המקור של השכל ומסקנותיו, ומקור זה ע"כ הוא למעלה מהשכל. וכשם שעובדי ע"ז טעו לרע כשחשבו שהמציאות נמצאת בשכלם, אברהם אבינו זכה בטוב כש"התחיל לשוטט בדעתו" כדי לחפש את מקורו. ולכן מצינו בחז"ל וברמב"ם שאברהם נק' 'איתן האזרחי' משום שיצא מעובדי ע"ז שבמזרח אל האמונה ברצונו ית' שאי אפשר להשיג בשכל.

ועפ״ד נבין עוד מה שהדגיש ר׳ אליעזר האיתנות של האבות על חודש לידתם בתשרי דוקא, החודש שלדעתו נברא העולם. שכשם שהעולם מיושב בחוזק ע״י יציאתו ממקור הנעלם בחודש תשרי, כמו״כ האבות הם ׳איתנים׳ משום שתפסו את עצמם כנולדים ממקור שלמעלה מהם. איתנות אמיתית אינו מתוך האדם עצמו, אלא משרשיו בבורא ית׳ המקיימו. (וע״ע היטב במו״נ שהמשל הדוחה טענת הקדמות הוא מלידת האדם המראה שאי אפשר ללמוד על מקור הדבר מאיך שהוא נראה אחר היותו במציאות.) וגם זה יש להבין במש״כ הרמב״ם כאן שבשעת לידת אברהם נגמר תקופת שליטת ע״ז, שאחרי ש״איתן זה״ נגמל והתחיל לשוטט וכו׳ הוא גילה למפרע שלידתו היתה גילוי חדש של חיים ממקור החיים, ולא עוד סיבוב מוכרח של הגלגלים. ואולי זהו עומק הדרשה ״בהבראם – באברהם״, ר״ל אברהם לימד על ההיבראות של הנבראים.

**ד] ׳נחל איתן׳**

יש להתבונן עוד בענין בסוגיא של ׳נחל איתן׳. עיקר פירוש המילה כ׳קשה׳ כנ״ל כבר מובא במשנה (סוטה מה:): ״איתן כמשמעו, קשה״. ובגמרא (מו.-מו:) דרשו את זה מאותם פסוקים הנ״ל. דרך רש״י בסוגיא ש׳נחל איתן׳ הוא אדמה קשה של סלע, וזהו גם ענין ההר כי ״כל הר של אבנים הוא״. אולם הרמב״ם (הל׳ רוצח וכעי״ז בפיה״מ) מפרש שהוא ״נחל שוטף בחזקה״, ואפילו הוסיף להדגיש ״וזהו איתן הכתוב בתורה״. רבותינו זצ״ל (המהרי״ק, תוס׳ יו״ט, שו״ת חכם צבי, ועוד; הובא בהכתב והקבלה) הרחיבו להביא ראיות לשני השיטות, עיי״ש. בספר ׳במסילה העולה׳ (מהרב שילת שליט״א) מציע שמדובר בוואדי שרוב השנה הוא יבש וקשה, אבל בשעת הגשמים מגיעים פתאום מים בחזקה. ויתכן שעולה מהראיות ששני הדרכים מושרשים בחז״ל. ואולי הענין ש׳נחל׳ מורה על זרימת מים בחוזק כמש״כ הרמב״ם, אבל משמע מהפסוקים המובאים בגמרא ש׳איתן׳ הוא מקום קשה כאבן והר.

ועכ"פ לכאו' גם להרמב"ם המילה 'איתן' פי' מיושב בחוזק כנ"ל, אלא שלדעתו יש ענין נוסף שעצם הישיבה בחוזק יכול להתבטא כפעולה אקטיבית, כמו נחל של מים הזורם חזק באופן שכל הנמצא בתוכו נסחף אחרי זרימתו שאי אפשר להפסיק ולבטל. ואולי הלך לשיטתו כשכתב שאיתנותו של אברהם היה בשוטטו וחיפושו ביום ובלילה, שההליכה אל השגת המקור הקבוע שלא שייך בו הליכה הוא בהליכה אקטיבית, ביציאה ממסגרת המוכרחת אל הרצון והמקור, כנ"ל. באופן שלדעת הרמב"ם היציבות של 'איתן' אינו דוקא ב'צור' ומקור בעצמו שלא שייך בהם תנועה, אלא גם התנועה עצמה יכול לקבל פנים של 'איתן' בהיותו חזק ומושרש במקור המניע אותו.

# בענין הבא לפרוע מנכסי יתומים

## הרב יוסף משהניימאן

בגמ׳ צ״ו. איתא בעי ר׳ יוחנן יתומים אומרים נתננו והיא אומרת לא נטלתי על מי להביא ראיה, נכסי בחזקת יתמי קיימי ועל האלמנה להביא ראיה, או נכסי בחזקת אלמנה קיימי ועל היתומים להביא ראיה וכו׳. ועיין ברמב״ם (אישות י״ח כ״ז) ״אלמנה שתבעה וכו׳ כל זמן שלא נישאת על היתומים להביא ראיה או נשבע היסת ותטול״, והיינו שהרמב״ם פסק כמ״ד שבחזקת אלמנה קיימי ומש״ה אינה נשבעת שבועת הנוטלין אלא שבועת הנפטרים שהרי הנכסים בחזקתה ואינה נחשבת נוטלת. ולכאורה קשה שהרי במשנה (פז.) איתא שאלמנה שגובה מנכסי יתומים אינה נפרעת אלא בשבועה והיינו שבועת המשנה שהוא שבועת הנוטלין, והרמב״ם קבע בהלכה י״ט שגם במזונות צריך שבועת הנוטלין. ושני ההלכות סותרות אהדדי שכאן פסק הרמב״ם שנשבע רק שבועת הנפטרים.

אמנם נראה דלק״מ, שהרמב״ם בהלכה י״ט מיירי כשבאה מתחילה לב״ד לתבוע מזונות ואז משביעין אותה שבועת הנוטלין קודם שיפסקו לה מזונות, אבל הרמב״ם בהלכה כז מיירי כשכבר פסקו לה מזונות אלא דהיתומים טוענים שכבר נתנו, ובזה אמרינן שנשבעת רק שבועת הנפטרים.

ועצם חילוק זה שהמשנה של שבועת הנוטלין מיירי כשבאה מתחילה לפסוק לה מזונות ובסוגיין מיירי אחר שפסקו לה מזונות והיתומים טוענין שנתנו, מוכח בעצם הגמ׳. שהרי למ״ד נכסי בחזקת יתמי קיימי, איתא ברש״י ש״כל זמן שלא הביא עדים לא תגבה״, וקשה שבמשנה הנ״ל איתא שנאמן האשה לגבות בשבועה ולמה צריך עדים. ומוכח כנ״ל שהמשנה מיירי כשבאה מתחילה לתבוע שאז נשבעת שבועת הנוטלין וב״ד פוסקין לה מזונות על פיה. והגמ׳ מיירי כשאח״כ היתומים אומרים שנתנו ואז הדין הוא שצריך עדים לגבות למ״ד שבחזקת יתמי קיימי.

אמנם יש לעיין קצת במה שביארנו בשיטת הרמב״ם שכשבאה מתחילה לב״ד שמשביעין אותה שבועת הנוטלין, דלמה לא אמרינן שמכיון שבחזקת אלמנה קיימי לא נחשב נוטל, וכמו שאמרינן כשהיתומים אומרים שנתנו. ובפשטות י״ל דמבואר מזה שמה שהוה בחזקת אלמנה, זהו רק לאחר שנפסק ונתברר החיוב בב״ד שאז הוא שנחשב בחזקתה, אבל בלי זה אינם בחזקתה.

ב] עיין בשו״ת הרא״ש (כלל פ״ה סי׳ ז) וז״ל מלוה שירד מעצמו לנכסי יתומים קודם שתבעם לדין גזלן הוא דאין נפרעים מנכסי יתומים אלא בשבועה וקודם שנשבע אין לו שום זכות בנכסי יתומים שמי יימר דמשתבע, ובעוד שלא נשבע נכסי בחזקת יתמי קיימי כדאמר ר״ע ינתנו ליורשים שכולם צריכים שבועה וכל פירות שאכל מנכין לו בחובו והמותר מגבין לו ב״ד מנכסי יתומים״.

והנה כאן קבע הרא״ש שמי שגבה בלי לישבע שבועת היתומים שאין גבייתו כלום וגזלן הוא, אבל בשאר שבועות הנוטלין איתא בראשונים וכן ברא״ש עצמו (בפרק הכותב סי׳ כה) שאם תפס קודם שנשבע שבועה דרבנן לא נחתינן לנכסי. ומבואר להיפך דכשתפס נפטרה משבועתו. והצ״ל לכאורה שדברי הרא״ש כאן שהגובה בלי שבועה אין גבייתו כלום הוא חומרא בשבועת היתומים אבל בשאר שבועות לא אמרינן הכי. (ועיין אבנ״מ סי׳ צ״ג ס״ק כ״ב שהביא שמצינו חומרא לשבועת יתומים יותר משאר שבועות, וכתב ג״כ שחלוק לגבי דינא של ר״ע שהוא מקור של הרא״ש, ודוקא בשבועת היתומים הוא).

ויש לציין במה שביארנו בדברי הרא״ש שיש חילוק בין דין שבועת יתומים לשאר שבועות הנוטלין, שמדברי התוס׳ בשבועות יוצא ששבועת יתומים הוא ביסודה שבועה אחרת. דהנה רש״י בכתובות דף פז ד״ה ״בנכסים משועבדים״ ביאר שיסוד השבועה של הבא לפרוע מנכסים משועבדים הוא משום שבועת רב פפא דאיתא בגמ׳ שבועות מא. שהבא לפרוע מחבירו וטען אישתבע לי, שחייב לישבע שבועת הנוטלין, וטענינן ללקוחות וחייב לישבע שבועת ר״פ.

והוסיף רש״י ״ומנכסי יתומים ושלא בפניו משום האי טעמא הוא״. ומבואר שרש״י למד ששבועת היתומים הוא שבועת ר׳ פפא שטענינן ליתמי. אמנם תוס׳ בשבועות מא. ד״ה וכו׳ הקשו דלמה לא הקשה הגמ׳ על ר׳ פפא מה בין זה להבא ליפרע מנכסי יתומים, שגם שבועת היתומים מדין טענינן הוא ומשום שבועת ר״פ. ותי׳ ״שלא משום הכי הוא דאפי׳ לא מצי אבוהון טעין טענינן ליתמי דבפרק הכותב אמרינן כתב לאשתו נקי נדר נקי שבועה לא תפרע מן היתומים אלא בשבועה אלמא עביד רבנן תקנתא ליתמי אפי׳ במקום שאין האב יכול להשביע״. ומבואר בתוס׳ שחולקים על רש״י וסוברים שביתומים גם היכא דליכא טענינן יש שבועת יתומים, ואין היסוד של שבועת יתומים משום דטענינן ומשום שבועת ר׳ פפא, וחלוק משאר שבועת הנוטלין שמשום טענינן הוא. ויוצא לכאורה מדברי תוס׳ ששבועת יתומים חלוק ביסודו משאר שבועת הנוטלין. ולדברי התוס׳ א״ש מה שהבאנו לחלק שבשבועת יתומים אמר הרא״ש שאינה גביה בלי שבועה ובשאר שבועת לא אמרינן הכי, שלדברי התוס׳ יוצא ששבועה אחרת הוא.

ג] והנה עיין ברמב״ם (אישות פ״ו הי״ח) שאע״פ שכשמת האלמנה אמרינן שיורשי כתובתה [היינו יורשיה] חייבין בקבורתה, אבל אם לא נשבע בחייה שבועת אלמנה וא״כ אין יורשיה יכולים לגבות, אמרינן שיורשי הבעל חייבין בקבורה. עיי״ש. וכתב הראב״ד ״דעתא קלישא חזינן כאן שמפני שלא נשבעה קרא ליורשי הבעל יורשי כתובתה והלא הם אומרים שכבר נפרעה מכתובתה ונטלה צררי והורישנה.״ עיי״ש״

ובפשטות קושייתו הוא שזה שיורשי הבעל פטורים היינו משום שהם נאמנים לאמר דכבר נפרעה, וא״כ האיך נחשבו מש״ז שהם ירשו הכתובה, שאדרבה הרי אמרינן שכבר נתנו ולא ירשו הכתובה. אמנם נראה פשוט דאי״ז קושייתו שוודאי גם כשהלוה עצמו טוען פרעתי ומשביעין המלוה משום שבועת ר׳ פפא, אין הפשט שנאמן שפרע שהרי יש כאן שטר ושטרך בידי מאי בעי, אלא

שמשום הטענה משביענן לי׳ ודין שבועה בעלמא הוא. וכמו״כ ביתומים וודאי אין להם נאמנות לאמר שפרעו אלא שמשום טענינן משבעינן לי׳.

אלא נראה שקושייתו הוא דהאיך אמרינן שמשום שלא נשבע האלמנה קרינן ליורשי הבעל יורשי הכתובה, שהרי זה וודאי שיורשי כתובתה פירושו מי שדינו הוא לירש הכתובה ותלוי בהדין של הכתובה, ולכן הקשה הראב״ד שכאן כל הפטור שלהם היא רק מחמת טענתם שטוענין שפרעו, ודין הכתובה הוא שחייבים אלא שמחמת טענתם לא מגבינן לה בלי שבועה, וא״כ האיך נחשב מש״ז יורשי הכתובה. (ועיין בה״ג אע״ה סי׳ פט אות כ׳ שכתב בשיטת הראב״ד ״כיון שדינם לירש כתובתה״.) וצ״ע באמת בדברי הרמב״ם דאטו נימא שהרמב״ם סובר שכיון שלמעשה אין יורשי הבעל חייבים משום זה גופא נחשבו יורשי כתובתה וצ״ע.

ואולי יש לפרש דעת הרמב״ם ע״פ הנ״ל, שהרי הבאנו מהרא״ש שאע״פ דבעלמא אין השבועה מעכבת הגביה ואע״פ שלא נשבע הוה גבייתו גביה אבל ביתומים לא אמרינן הכי אלא עד שלא נשבע אין לו שום זכות. וא״כ י״ל שהרמב״ם סובר שבאלמנה שלא נשבע, נמצא שאין היורשים פטורים משום טענת פרעון בלבד, ושחייבת לישבע קודם שגובין מהן, אלא כיון שלא נשבעה א״כ אין כאן חיוב כלל והדין הוא שפטור, שבלי שבועה אין תביעתה תביעה כלל, ומש״ה נחשבו יורשי כתובתה, שהדין הוא שפטורים מלשלם.

והנה עיין בתוס׳ דף צה: ד״ה ״ואין״ שלמד בהמשנה דאם ליכא ליתומים קרקע להגבות ממנה כתובתה ונמצא שהיורשים פטורים דס״ד לומר שאז יורשי הבעל נחשבים יורשי כתובתה וקמ״ל המשנה שלא אמרינן הכי אלא שיורשיה נחשבים יורשי כתובתה. ועיין בריטב״א שכתב שלפ״ז יש להסתפק בהיכ״ת של הרמב״ם שהאלמנה לא נשבעה האם ג״כ אמרינן הכי. ולהנ״ל יש להסביר ספיקו, שבאם ליכא קרקע הרי יש כאן תביעה אלא שאין כאן מקום גביה, אבל לפי מה שהבאנו מהרא״ש שבלי נשבעה אין לה שום זכות א״כ אין

כאן תביעה כלל ומש״ה י״ל שיורשי הבעל נחשבו יורשי כתובתה (ועיין רש״ש בתוס׳ הנ״ל שכתב להיפך מהריטב״א).

ד] והנה הבאנו לעיל שמדברי הרמב״ם יוצא שרק אחר השבועה אמרינן שבחזקת אלמנה קיימי. וביארנו שי״ל שהוא סברא בדין של בחזקת אלמנה שרק כשנתברר ונפסק החיוב בב״ד הוה בחזקתה, ול״ד משום שבועה אלא גם אם מטעם אחר לא נפסק בב״ד. אמנם לפי מה שביארנו שבשבועת יתומים אמרינן שאין תביעתה תביעה עד שנשבע, א״כ י״ל בדרך אחר, דודאי מכיון שיש לה תביעה מיד נעשית מוחזק גם אם לא נפסק בב״ד אלא שבלי שבועה לא הוה תביעתה תביעה ומש״ה לא הוחזקה, שעד שנשבעה אין לה זכות כלל.

אלא שיש לפקפק בכ״ז שהרי עיקר דין של הרא״ש בתשובה שאם לא נשבע המלוה אין גבייתו כלום, משמע ברמב״ם שאינו סובר כן, שהרי כתב בהלכות אישות (פי״ז הי״ד) ״אלמנה שמכרה קרקע בכתובתה בינו לבין עצמה אם מכרה שוה בשוה מכרה קיים ונשבעת שבועת אלמנה אחר שמכרה״. ולכאורה מבואר שלא כהרא״ש, דחזינן שמכירתה הוה מכירה אע״פ שעדיין לא נשבע. אמנם יש להסתפק שאולי הרמב״ם מודה ליסודו של הרא״ש, ובמלוה הדין הוא שאין גבייתו כלום, שהרי לא קבע הרמב״ם לגבי מלוה שיכול לישבע אח״כ, וי״ל שדוקא בגביית אלמנה כשגובה בינו לבין עצמה אמרינן הכי שקולא הקילו באלמנה שגבייתה הוה גבייה בלי ב״ד וגם בלי שבועה. ומש״ה קבע הרמב״ם הלכה זו דוקא בגביית אלמנה בינה לבין עצמה. וצ״ע.

# בענין העונש של אחשורוש משום כלי המקדש

בנימין נתן ורגפטמאן

איתא בגמ׳ (מגילה יא:): כיון דחזו דמלו שבעין ולא איפרוק אמר השתא ודאי תו לא מיפרקי, אפיק מאני דבי מקדשא ואשתמש בהו, בא שטן וריקד ביניהן והרג את ושתי. עכ״ל. וצ״ב למה אחשורוש לא נהרג כשהשתמש בכלי המקדש אבל נהרג בלשצר מטעם זה.

ונקדים בדברי הבן יהוידע (שם). היה קשיא לו למה בלשצר נהרג הוא עצמו אבל גבי אחשורוש נהרגה אשתו. הוא תירץ שאחשורוש חטא משום שראה שבלשצר עשה חשבון להע׳ שנה והלך אחריו והשתמש בכלי המקדש וכו׳ והוא גם עשה אותו דבר. נמצא שבלשצר היה שותף עם אחשורוש באותו חטא. וז״ל: ולכך בחטא אחשורוש נעשה העונש בשותפות שניהם שנהרגה ושתי שהיא בתו יחידתו של בלשצר, וכלה זרעו בה והגיע עונש זה לבלשצר וגם הגיע העונש לאחשורוש, כי היתה ושתי אשתו שהיא כגופו, והיה אוהב אותה יותר מנפשו. עכ״ל. נמצא מדבריו דעל ידי זה הכל נכון והעונשים עשויים כדין.

וקשה לי, למה היה צריך ה׳ להשאיר אחשורוש חי. נהי דיש לומר כהבן יהוידע אבל מה היה הצורך לכל זה.

וי״ל, הנה ראיתי בהארטסקרול מגילת אסתר (אנגלית א:ז) בפירושם שם אומרים שכשאחשורוש הוציא כלי המקדש היה ראוי לו למות אלא רצה ה׳ שדריוש יצא ממנו כדי שהוא יתן רשות לבנות הבית המקדש בעתיד.

ולפ״ז הכל מתיישב, למה ה׳ הזמין את מעשים כאשר קרו. היה צורך שאחשורוש ילד את דריוש, ואיך יתקיים זו אם השתמש בכלי המקדש וחייב מיתה. לפיכך נהרגה ושתי והוי כאילו הוא עצמו מת, אבל באמת הוא חי.

# מדור
# לשון הקודש

# English Sections

←

## מדור לשון הקדש

## ADDENDUM: THE CORONA *MAGEIFAH*

## OTHER TOPICS:

## IN MEMORIAM

## BAR MITZVAH *DIVREI TORAH*

## OTHER *GEULOS*



## SEFIRAH AND SHAVUOS

## TEFILLAH ON PESACH AND BEYOND

## YOM TOV, CHOL HAMOED AND THE LAST DAY

## THE HAGADAH

## THE SEDER

## *GEULAS MITZRAYIM AND THE MIDBAR*